Wakefield Press

Sex and Savagery in the Good Colony

Julie Marcus is an anthropologist and writer. Her doctoral research investigated the relationship between Islam and women's lives in urban Turkey; later work focused on how race, gender and sexuality appeared in public discussions of social life in Australia. She is the author of *The Indomitable Miss Pink: A life in anthropology*, a family memoir, *The Flavour of Her Years: Culinary memories of Mother and domestic life in the 1950s*, plus several edited volumes.

Sex and Savagery in the Good Colony

SOUTH AUSTRALIA 1836–1901

Julie Marcus

Wakefield Press

Wakefield Press
16 Rose Street
Mile End
South Australia 5031
www.wakefieldpress.com.au

First published 2025

Copyright © Julie Marcus, 2025

All rights reserved. This book is copyright. Apart from any fair dealing for the purposes of private study, research, criticism or review, as permitted under the Copyright Act, no part may be reproduced without written permission. Enquiries should be addressed to the publisher.

Typeset by Michael Deves

ISBN 978 1 92304 228 5

 A catalogue record for this book is available from the National Library of Australia

 Wakefield Press thanks Coriole Vineyards for continued support

DEDICATION

Rita Huggins 1921–1996
and
Jackie Huggins, AM

I dedicate this book to the memory of Rita Huggins, to her tireless campaigning and the warmth, gentleness and humour she brought to her work and life. She was a great woman in every sense of the word. She drew people together in order to better address the circumstances that her people and her family had been forced to live through. Hers was a personal politics of enabling and attention to the detail of daily life. She was sharply aware of the ways politicians and others slipped and slid around anything to do with advancing Indigenous rights, as well as of the benefits that could flow from co-operation between opposing forces. Her skills live on in her daughter, Jackie Huggins – scholar, writer, social critic and activist. She, too, has devoted her life to constant political activism and service. Many of us have drawn on their strength, making the time I spent with Rita in Albury a pleasure as well as gently enlightening. In the account of Rita's remarkable life, published as *Auntie Rita* in 1994, Jackie wrote: 'My mother does not want to talk even to me about the kinds of bitter treatment she experienced ... These events should be exposed ...'

I hope that the histories gathered up, drawn together here and dedicated to her memory will serve to make clear how and why so much of what is written about the value and impact of the colonisation of Australia on its First Peoples, the kind of events that even to the end of her life Rita Huggins could not speak about, need to be exposed. And stopped.

Contents

Acknowledgements		ix
Preface		xii
Prologue		1

Part One – Coming into Being

Chapter One	Utopian Dreams and a *Good* Colony	9
Chapter Two	The Pre-Colony	17
Chapter Three	The Righteousness of Colonisation	23
Chapter Four	Empty Lands	34
Chapter Five	Land into Landscape	46
Chapter Six	The Kaurna See the Colonists	57
Chapter Seven	Locke's Blessing	67
Chapter Eight	The First Degree of Separation	75
Chapter Nine	Intimations of Unrest	84
Chapter Ten	The Coming of Colonial Law	90

Part Two – Governor Gawler Arrives

Chapter Eleven	Governor Gawler's Time in the Colony Begins	101
Chapter Twelve	The Massacre of the Survivors of the Wreck of the *Maria* 1840	108
Chapter Thirteen	The First Missionaries – The Dresden Lutherans	121
Chapter Fourteen	Eyre's Children	133
Chapter Fifteen	Becoming a Man	143
Chapter Sixteen	Heroes & Myths	151

Part Three – Trouble on the Murray

Chapter Seventeen	Fear Rising	163
Chapter Eighteen	Lake Victoria and the Rufus River – Prelude	171
Chapter Nineteen	Massacre on the Rufus	176
Chapter Twenty	After the Rufus	181

Part Four – Toward the South-East

Chapter Twenty-One	Wellington	197
Chapter Twenty-Two	1842, Murder of George McGrath	200
Chapter Twenty-Three	Cannibals at the Margins of Society	205

Part Five – The North and Eyre Peninsula

Chapter Twenty-Four	Port Lincoln	219
Chapter Twenty-Five	'Dead or Alive Without Discrimination'	225
Chapter Twenty-Six	Poonindie	234
Chapter Twenty-Seven	In and Around the Flinders	247
Chapter Twenty-Eight	Hayward and McKinlay	254
Chapter Twenty-Nine	Women and Children	265

Part Six – The North-East

Chapter Thirty	Into the Dry Lands	275
Chapter Thirty-One	War in the North-East	288

Part Seven – The Overland Telegraph Line

Chapter Thirty-Two	The Silence of the Lands, 1870	299
Chapter Thirty-Three	Building the Line	305
Chapter Thirty-Four	After the Line – Central Australia	313
Chapter Thirty-Five	On Arrernte Country	325
Chapter Thirty-Six	The 'Top End' of the Territory	336
Chapter Thirty-Seven	Willshire, Pornography and a Man's World	349

Part Eight – Zones of Exclusion

Chapter Thirty-Eight	Zones of Exclusion	365
Chapter Thirty-Nine	The Pastoral Zone	368
Chapter Forty	A Zone of Indigenous Policing	376
Chapter Forty-One	The Mission Zone	387

Part Nine – At the End of the Century

Chapter Forty-Two	Adelaide, 1880s–90s	399
Chapter Forty-Three	Colonial Holocaust	415
Chapter Forty-Four	1901 – The Birth of a Racial State	421
Chapter Forty-Five	The Mission Zone in the 'Post-Colony'	426
Notes		438
References		470

Acknowledgements

I was fortunate in beginning my studies just as access to tertiary education in Australia was being opened up. It was the short-lived Labor government of Gough Whitlam that opened university doors for women like me when they abolished the fees that had maintained Australian universities as bastions of male privilege. At Macquarie University in Sydney in 1971 I found a faculty that included many strongly intellectual women, a degree structure that was open and flexible, and the teaching that made me an anthropologist. I was fortunate, too, in finding there the distinguished anthropologist Professor Chandra Jayawardena, and when he died unexpectedly, fortunate again in having Dr Ian Bedford take over the supervision of my doctoral research. I learned a great deal from Ian as his meticulous and detailed commentary on my writing helped in opening up paths that I had thought closed. I must also thank Professor Annette Hamilton who succeeded Chandra to the Chair of Anthropology at Macquarie University for her remarkable ability to deal calmly with the crises that beset the later stages of my doctoral candidacy and her ability to keep things on track. It was with her assistance that I went to work on a project aiming to document Arrernte women's sacred sites within the town of Alice Springs in central Australia. There I met a number of extraordinary Arrernte women and men. Chief among them was Rosie Ferber, her parents, Hilda and Walter Rice, the Stuart family, and their dense networks of kin and political and cultural collaborators. Life in Alice Springs was an experience that provoked a shift of research focus away from the religious practices of Turkish women to the powerful forces and impacts of racial discrimination in Australia that have shaped my writing ever since.

While teaching at the University of Adelaide and preparing a series of essays on patterns of race in Australian culture as well as on the struggles of women wanting to do anthropological field work, I was again fortunate in my colleagues. Among them were Thomas Ernst, Andrew Lattas, Barry Morris and Susan Bagot-Barham, all of whom had benefited from the stimulating collegiality of Professor Bruce Kapferer and who, in turn, provided the same intellectual stimulus for me. At the National Museum of Australia where I applied for a position as Senior Curator in Anthropology only to find myself appointed as an historian, a subject of which I was largely ignorant and certainly untrained, I found myself among a group of enthusiastic and varied curatorial staff, almost all of whom were committed to rewriting the rule book for museums and exhibitions. Alas, a heavy governmental and bureaucratic hand fell upon us so that a limiting dullness descended upon an innovative and creative team of curators. I learned a great deal from them, particularly from Dr Betty Meehan, Brenda Factor, Catriona Vignando, Fiona Hooten, Ruth Lane, Richard Baker and Luke Taylor. While in Canberra, the encouragement and guidance of two outstanding scholars, the incomparable anthropologist, Sally White, and cultural archaeologist Professor Isabel McBryde, was invaluable.

Of my colleagues at Charles Sturt University, Marion Tulloch was a steady and helpful presence, John Tulloch a great supporter, while Thomas Ernst was there again, a sociable, collegial and generous benefactor to all; it was there also that Catherine Rogers introduced me to the pleasures of the photograph and of drawing, where Dr Eva Mackey brought all the benefits of a Canadian perspective to the familiar tropes of Australian anthropology and where Katrina Schlunke created a vibrant intellectual environment among her students and colleagues. And it was there that I first met the distinguished anthropologist and photographer Roslyn Poignant, who was probably unaware of how much she has enriched my thinking and ways of looking. And most importantly, it was there that I came to know Dr Jackie Huggins, to see how she worked at research and writing and to watch how she drew people together, in even the most conflicted of circumstances.

ACKNOWLEDGEMENTS

I must also thank Shirley Ardener for providing a haven of intellectual comfort at the Women's Studies Research Centre in Oxford. There I found congenial colleagues: Helen Callaway, Barbara Harrell-Bond, Irene Szylowicz, Judith Okely. There also the impeccable scholarship and humour of Renée Hirschon offered particularly productive insights into my own projects. I had also the good fortune to meet Susan Wright whose disciplined thought and friendship over so many years since has been a privilege.

For those who have helped with the preparation for the writing of this book I thank Anne Morphett who will be surprised to learn that her comments on the waters of Moolooloo Station have helped to shape the discussions of water used in this book; Anneke Hoffman for her careful art work; Catherine Rogers for help with advice as well as for her many years of thought-provoking curiosity; Brenda Factor for her friendship over many years and help with organising the mechanics of this book; Vicki Crowley whose creative imagination, intellectual provocations and conversation have provided both a theoretical as well as empirical grounding; and Julie Finlayson and David Martin for much thoughtful and amusing conversation. In Alice Springs Sue O'Connor of Tangentyere Aboriginal Art Centre helped with the processes of getting permission to publish Arrernte art works. And importantly I thank those who read early drafts to offer comment and encouragement: David Marcus, Stephen Marcus, Lisa Watts, Lindsay Dent and Joanne Dent.

But most of all I thank Andrea Malone for thirty-seven years of rewarding intellectual stimulation and support that can only be described as saintly.

My path through the now troubled world of the university has been invigorating. There have been the pleasures of teaching, of wonderful colleagues and a sense of being valued by those committed to the intellectual, educational and political ideals that drew me there at the beginning and remain still. Now retired and working at the edges of the academic world I have found a certain freedom. It has been worth reaching for. It is a comfortable and peaceful place to live and write within.

Preface

Those of us who write in order to understand what we see and what we think about it, do so not just to describe objects, events or lives observed, but to find a way towards a destination that is as yet unimagined, invisible even. The ink flowing from pen to paper creates the surprise and freshness of unexpected thought that must guide the writer. So I began this book to answer a question posed only in shadowy form and without knowing where the path to any answer might start, let alone finish. That question was: what would the story of the colonisation of Australia look like if the violence that so many have sought to obliterate from it was made more visible? The answer that emerged from the writing was that in recognising and writing-in the violence of colonial men, Indigenous and colonial women alike moved from the margins of the story to its centre. These are major shifts that shape a very different story of Australia's colonisation. That new story is a melancholy one but it is important, particularly now, as a new government works rapidly toward facilitating the constitutional change and truth-telling sought by First Australians encapsulated in the Uluru Statement and the concept of The Voice – a voice into the Australian parliament. This new story of colonisation is, I believe, worth the telling.

This book, therefore, has been written about the elements of colonisation that I consider important to that task: the incidents, actions and individuals that have been central to understanding why colonisation casts such long shadows, not just in South Australia (site of my case study) but over Australia as a whole. I have taken this path as a South Australian born and bred, as one reared within a kind of post-war, middle class society that is both the same and characteristically different from other regions of Australia. To some extent, I write for those who will come after me as well as for those of today who sometimes wonder why things are the way they are. I have looked back in time in order to get a feel for how grand plans for building a new world in a new place were realised in myriad small acts and decisions by individuals as well as in the ways in which colonial policies, laws and good intentions work out in reality. And to do this, I have had to remember that the colony established as the Province of South Australia once included the Northern Territory, a region so coveted by investors, miners and pastoralists that for a time it was governed from Adelaide.

The full colony of South Australia and its Northern Territory provides a geographical slice right through the middle of the continent. Following those colonists as they spread out from the south to the north illustrates how the benign complacency of Adelaide's early colonists rested upon terrible violence, particularly in the far north but also closer to Adelaide and the more southerly districts. My choice to focus on just one of the Australian colonies provides a case study that can be generalised more widely. I have omitted much that others consider important – I focus on much that is already published and known but ignored or misrepresented. I ask different questions of it and make different forms of connection. In the act of writing I have found the possibility of a story that contrasts strongly with well-known pioneer legends, one impossible to ignore, in which fantasies and myths of race, sex and violence are given the prominence I think each demands.

On the other hand, there is not much here by way of political science, of monarchs, prime ministers, or the games that governments play on a global stage. Instead there is material about the effects of religious beliefs and their place in the shaping of a secular social and political world, the social and cultural preoccupations of the nineteenth century, a little about art and its power to transform ideas, the relationship of accusations of cannibalism and infanticide to displacement and conscience, and a good deal about the ways in which the Victorian-era cult of heroes and heroism papers over both stupidity and brutality. But my look at historical writings is driven in part by a fascination with them – with how history is made and what can be found out by looking back – and with how its assumptions circulate to produce a kind of theatre in the mind that provides a stage on which much history and memory can take place. So I have relied on historians as well as on secondary sources from aligned disciplines like archaeology and art history, even though I have thought about their research writings as an anthropologist would – as a story told about pasts that often slip loose from scholarly constraints. I have kept in mind the way in which the accumulation of facts can blur or obscure as much as reveal. So as with any work of synthesis, this is a book about what is already known (or could be) rather than what is not; a lot of that *is* history, at least of a kind. I have relied on the creative spirit of the pen itself to find a focused path through an ever-expanding sea of historical facts. I have wanted to find the stories that people tell themselves about their pasts, the stories about what they believe to be true that direct attention to what they want to believe or wish were true.

As mine is a book not written to the prescriptions of a publisher or beliefs about whether there is a market for this or that sort of book, it has not been constrained by market forces, concerns about word length, print runs, or indeed, publishers' profits. It has been written, I hope, to be intelligible to a more general reading public than that usually faced by academic anthropologists and historians – more in the tradition of Margaret Mead than the works of some of those who came after her. It reflects my own interests and the kind of information that I have found illuminating or thought-provoking. The book reflects, therefore, writing strategies and interests that have informed my work throughout my academic life, interests that were shaped long before I entered the university and the world of analytical thought. I have

PREFACE

found the absence of academic and commercial constraints to offer a great freedom – in this book I have attempted to seize it. I am indebted to all those whose works I have drawn upon as well as to those whose teaching and encouragement made possible a rewarding career of research and writing. I am indebted, too, to the support of the Art Galley of South Australia, the State Library of New South Wales, and to Mandy Paul of the History Trust of South Australia.

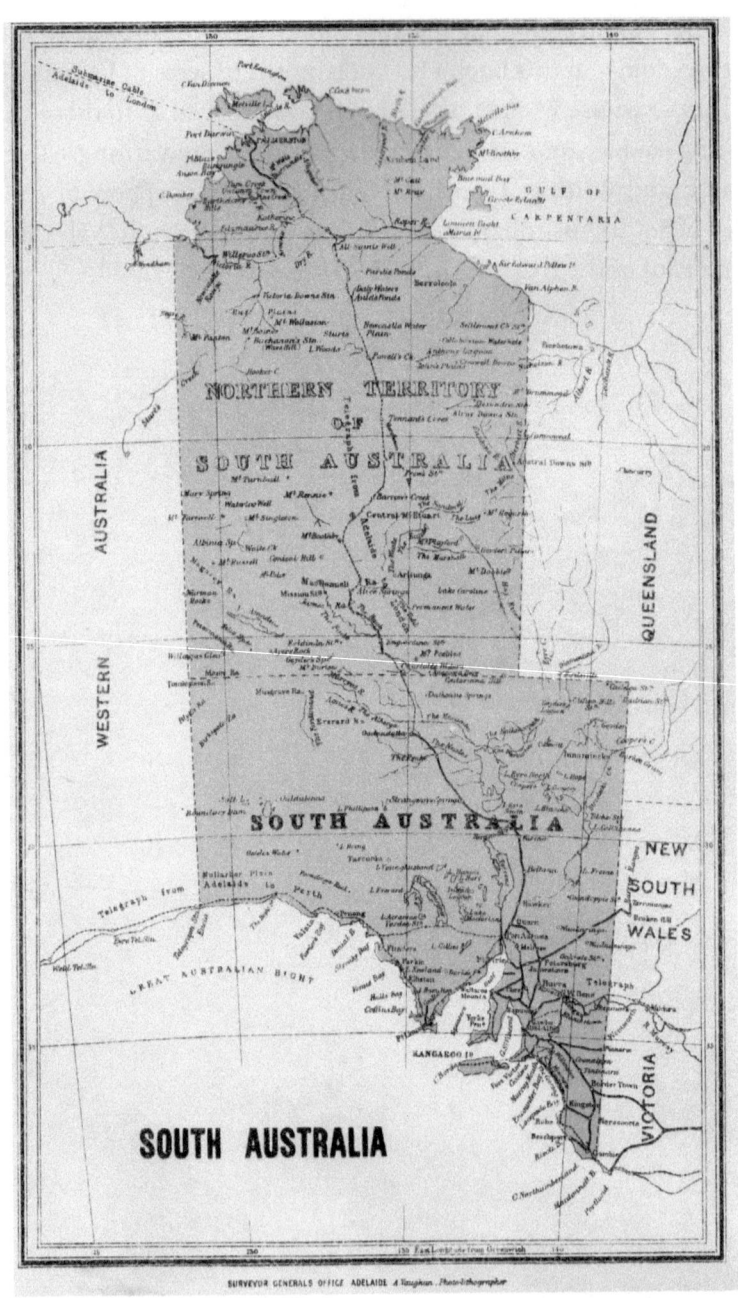

The colony of South Australia with its Northern Territory. Prepared for David J. Gordon, *Handbook of South Australia, Progress and Resources*, Adelaide.

Prologue

Sometime around September 1848 the pastoralist James Brown and his hut-keeper, 'Yorky' Eastwood, shot at least nine Tatiara people living on their Country south of Adelaide, the seat of government of the British colony of South Australia.[1] Among the nine dead were three adult women, two teenaged girls and three younger female children; one of the dead men was old and blind. The murders came to light because they were witnessed by a woman known as Leandermin and the colonist with whom she was travelling, a Mr Parker. Both had heard the shots, seen the bodies and the shooters. Unusually, they reported them. When Protector of Aborigines Matthew Moorhouse rode out from Adelaide to see what had happened he was shown 'graves'. In the meantime the bodies had been removed and burnt, the bones scattered. Using the language of the time, Moorhouse referred to the killings as 'an instance of collision'.[2] But collision it was not. The dead had been unarmed, seated peaceably around a small fire, undefended, unable to escape and quite unable to retaliate. *Massacre*, perhaps, is the best description of the slaughter, or perhaps *mass murder*. Following Protector Moorhouse's investigation there was to be a trial of James Brown, the colonist involved, for from its first day the colony of South Australia was intended to be a peaceable and lawful place. It was one of the few established with a judge at the head of a Supreme Court, right from the start. The prosecution of James Brown for the murders was resisted by the colonists who would come to be described as 'the practical men' of the colony rather than those wedded to the doctrines of peace and equality on which the colony was founded. When Brown was eventually charged, witnesses revoked their evidence: Leandermin, the woman travelling with Mr Parker, 'disappeared', never to be seen again; Brown's offsider, 'Yorky', got away on board a departing ship. Eventually the repeatedly delayed trial seems to have dropped off the court listings.

The James Brown murders were neither the first nor the last. Nor were they secret. But in the great colonial narratives of Australia's foundation and history, the murders and brutalisation of the colony's First Peoples tend to be marginalised at best, rewritten or ignored if possible.[3] They remain prominent, however, in the histories and memories of Indigenous Australians, many of which have now been recorded: 'If I had any intention of shooting anybody', Maurie Ryan has said,

> it would have been the stockmen that worked on Wave Hill Station. Because they used to shoot – after getting drunk on OP rum – into the [our] camp. One of my mothers has a bullet hole in the side of her stomach, old Kitty (Mintawurr). They were a law unto themselves, and they could do what they want, rape the women, physically harm the men.[4]

Mary Anderson's testimony in 'Unfortunately I wasn't one of those', refers to the sexual relations that went along with the violence characteristic of the colonial period:

> I don't really know who my father is, but I think my father is the station manager. You know, in those days they used our mothers for their pleasures and didn't acknowledge us as their children ... I was grown up by an old man, Pitjantjatjara man who comes from Pipalyatjara in South Australia. He married my mum when I was very young, when I was about maybe four, and raised me as his own daughter. [When I tried to contact my father] he said, I've got no black daughter, if she's saying that I'm her father she'll have to prove it in court.[5]

PROLOGUE

Then there is Jimmy Manngayarri's eye-witness account of his uncle's death at the hands of Jack Cusack and Jack Carpenter, a record created in 1975:

Cusack and Carpenter meikim im cartim jangilany. 'Alrait yu cartim wud.' Wal imin gedim wud na. Imin gedim wud, stackimap. 'Rait yu stand up deya. Stand up longsaid langa faya.' Jutim deya binij on top of the wood. Gedim kerosin an barnimap rait deya top of the wud jukim kerosine barnim. Puka kartiya brobli. Dat ai bin siim acting langa mairoun eye ai bin siim wen ai was piccininny.

Translation: Cusack and Carpenter made my uncle get some firewood. 'Alright, you cart some wood,' they told him. Well, he got some wood then and stacked it up. 'Right you stand up there,' they said. 'Stand lengthways to the pile of firewood.' Then they shot him so he fell on top of the wood. They got some kerosene and burnt him right there. Those whitefellas were rotten to the core. I saw them do these things with my own eyes when I was a child.[6]

Such events were neither isolated nor uncommon. Nor are they limited to a distant colonial-era past. In the hot September of 1955, for example, five Aboriginal people living then on Eva Downs Station (about 300 kilometres north-east of Tennant Creek on the Barkley Tableland) fled in fear of their lives. Dolly Ross had told the station manager that she felt too ill to cook for the men working in the stock camp. The manager replied that he would 'liven her up'. When he went to get his gun, Dolly, her husband Jim, and her young brother also known as Jim, picked up their swags and ran towards the distant police station at Anthony Lagoon. When overtaken by the manager and his men who were travelling on horseback, stockwhips were used to drive them back to the homestead. Aboriginal men attempting to intervene were also whipped; shots were fired. 'When they saw a large hole being dug some days later, the five Aboriginal people assumed that they were going to be shot.'[7] So fearful were the twelve Aboriginal people still living on Eva Downs that all slipped away under darkness, only to find that Dolly's husband Jim was too badly injured to travel. Dolly was also injured, as was Isaac Walayunkum.

In a strange turn of events, floggings and beatings that would commonly pass unreported came to light when the station manager's false charges of theft against the group set in train a police search for the culprits. It took Constable R.F. Corbin four days to find them but when he did, he was shocked. His report detailed the extraordinary level of cruelty meted out as punishment for Dolly Ross's refusal to carry out an instruction to cook, whether she felt up to it or not. The constable reported that 'Jim Ross became so crippled as a result of the flogging that he could not continue'. Tony Roberts, who has documented the ferocity deployed across the north-eastern segment of the Territory, went on to say 'When he [Constable Corbin] counted and photographed the unhealed and suppurating wounds of the victims, [he] found that Jim Ross had 47, Dolly 21, and Isaac Walayunkum 19.' Two other young men had fewer.

The remarkable aspects of this case were first, that the police constable decided to bring charges against a pastoralist and second, that when Martin Kriewaldt, then sole judge of the Northern Territory's Supreme Court, heard evidence against the pastoralists, he found them guilty. 'The two principal offenders were each sentenced to six months' gaol with hard labour and fined £400.' Another of the stockmen was fined £50 as an accomplice.

Tony Roberts saw their sentencing as 'serving notice to station managers and stockmen that the old days, the days of guns, hobble chains and whips – the days of frontier justice – were finally over.' By Tony Robert's reckoning, the Northern Territory's 'killing times' and the gross violence and sexual predation that characterised them had lasted about eighty-five years. Unfortunately this would not be the last incident in which pastoralists or stock workers felt free to apply violence to Australia's First people. But coming so many years after the initial occupation of the 'Top End' of South Australia's Northern Territory, this 1955 example is a reminder of the persistence of old established pastoral privileges and of the sustained violence and predatory sexual relations of colonisation. They are episodes that speak directly to themes that are central to this book, themes that are important because of their often unrecognised continuity.

*****

So what precisely was it that had caused colonial forms of social structure to persist from 1836 at least up until 1955 and as the following chapters make clear, much later? This is a particularly poignant question because the colony of South Australia was intended to be a good colony and a peaceful colony, one in which the protections of the laws of England, civil rights and freedoms of British citizenship were to apply to *all* those living in the new colony, regardless of whether they were British-born or the Australian-born First Peoples of the colony, and regardless of religious beliefs. As it developed, the colony of South Australia-Northern Territory saw itself as socially progressive, humane and philanthropic. And often it was.

It was a colony that came into existence as a province of Britain, not only with a British Governor, a set of officials of the Crown and a Supreme Court judge but shortly had a rudimentary police force, a Protector of Aborigines with instructions that good country was to be reserved for them to allow them to live according to their own customs. Massacres, murders and rapes of Aboriginal South Australians, however much lamented, nevertheless gained at least a degree of acceptance. Within the first decade of its formal proclamation, the freedoms granted by charter and law to the colony's Indigenous members were systematically truncated, the country that should have remained available to them simply usurped. Instead, by mid-century violence and predatory sex had become to some degree normalised until in the colony's northern districts it developed a hideous, sadistic element so excessive as to lose any connection with either cause or effect. The 'good colony' of South Australia–Northern Territory had unleashed, and often turned a blind eye to, practices that from the 1870s created what Deborah Bird Rose labelled a 'deathscape'. In the familiar Australian myths of heroic pioneering and settlement, the violence of colonisation appears as generated by 'wild Aborigines', to whom sporadic separate, small 'collisions' taught a lesson or two. Most often the scale and reach of violence is overlooked or denied and minimised. What is almost entirely lost sight of is that the deathscape was also a 'sexscape' in which colonial men sought and achieved total access to Indigenous women. They could do with them whatever they wished with or without the consent of their families.

The heroism of First Nations women as their bodies were abused and used to save the lives of their families often goes unrecognised and unmentionable. Rarely described and often matters of shame, the great sacrifices made by First Nations women challenge male narratives of righteous pioneering, and male-oriented, colonial heroism.

The questions to be addressed, therefore, are first: how did the good, lawful colony of peaceful, largely Protestant settlers come to preside over the holocaust years of the 1880s? And second: how did colonial South Australia morph into a fully racial state in which colonial wars and methods of colonisation deriving from its first days continued? How should we understand why so many Indigenous Australians are imprisoned today, *especially* children and women, and especially in the Northern Territory? Why do police violence, shootings and killings still go unpunished? Why are so many Indigenous children still removed from their families to live in church-run homes and foster families that are notorious for their sexual violence and abuse? What is meant today when Australians and their politicians speak of 'equality' and 'a fair go' as characteristics of a distinctive 'Australian way' of life? And finally, what would those mythic narratives describing how brave and hardy British pioneers brought civilisation and Christianity to the Australian 'barbarians' look like if the violence and sexual abuses were brought in from the shadowy margins of that story to its centre? We need to understand and come to terms with how and why the 'good colony of South Australia and its Northern Territory' went so dreadfully wrong.

As we moved (in 2023) towards a national referendum, the truth-telling and the Voice proposed by the First Nations peoples of Australia in the *Uluru Statement* of 2017, these questions became more important than ever.

Part One

Coming into Being

Chapter One

Utopian Dreams and a *Good* Colony

Early in the nineteenth-century Britain's very profitable slave empire (London had 147 registered slave dealers in 1755, with more in port cities like Bristol) was under moral challenge. At the same time, increasing social disruption caused by unregulated, rapid industrialisation, the terrible working conditions in factories, quarries and mines, as well as the wars and revolutions across Europe that followed the French Revolution, were profoundly unsettling both to workers and the established order: rule by an entrenched landed aristocracy and a theocratic Church of England. A rising middling class was wanting parliamentary representation. Workers, too, were looking for the right to be heard in the parliament. They were resisted. The 1819 massacre of men, women and children on St Peter's Field near Manchester had demonstrated just how far the government in London was prepared to go to make sure their sources of labour stayed quietly in their place in what was a strongly hierarchical society of concentrated wealth. By 1830 agricultural labourers in the south of England were masked and out at night, burning farmers' haystacks under the rubric of 'Captain Swing'; by 1832 factory workers in the industrial north took up the name to attack and threaten wealthy factory owners. In these early nineteenth-century years radical economic, political and religious ferment went hand in hand. Indeed, England was covered by a dense cloud of religious ferment, with the Bible's account of history itself under challenge.

Dissenters from the established Church of England (several forms of Wesleyan Methodism, Presbyterians, Baptists, Congregationalists), the Quaker and Unitarian congregations sometimes regarded as heretical, the wandering independent preachers, as well as Roman Catholics, were practising individual and sometimes ecstatic forms of personal belief and preaching, intent on the restoration or reform of their civil rights. Radical public preachers like the Reverend Robert Taylor (1784-1844) known as the 'Infidel Preacher', drew congregations of thousands that were often dispersed by police.

As people were pushed off the land and common lands enclosed by landowners, as machines replaced human labour, cities and unemployment expanded. London's population grew to about 1.2 million in very short order. Not everyone could find well paid work, so children were drafted into the workforce as soon as they could become useful, sometimes as young as four. They worked excruciatingly long hours for pitiful wages, often in very unsafe conditions. Many looked to the margins of society for some kind of living, to crime, one of which was of course prostitution, and the related crimes of abortion and infanticide.

Those specifically women's crimes are a reminder that women's rights were also at issue, that the powers of men and their laws controlling women's bodies and fortunes were being questioned but not changed until 1870. Mary Wollstonecraft's *Vindication of the Rights of Women*, for instance, had been published in 1790, her unconventional life a challenge to doctrines of the Church of England that was not ignored. Mrs Gaskell's 1848 novel *Mary Barton* gives an account of the fraught lives of Manchester's working men in the 1830s, men with an interest in trade unions. Many British hearts and minds turned toward trying to imagine a less conflicted society, and a safer and more secure future. Reform was in the air. Social reformers like Robert Owen, who established a model settlement and cotton mill at New Lanark outside Glasgow, looked not just to reforming the relations between labour and capital but to reshaping the moral community and improving the education and health of workers.

Robert Owen was one of a group known as 'utopian socialists'. Utopias could be of many kinds, depending on how their proponents diagnosed the causes of the wrongs they wished to right. While dreams of building new worlds or of making *this* world into a better place are very common, they are particularly prominent in Christianity and the partially secularised societies in which it still flourishes. Such hopes and dreams, whether grounded in theological dogma or secular doctrines, are often dismissed as utopian fantasies, as foolish impossibilities that are purely fictitious. Utopias are often thought of as sites having no real place in the world, as being entirely imaginary fantasies that 'present society itself in a perfected form or as a society in which the social order of everyday life was turned entirely upside down, so that the Biblical promise of the meek inheriting the earth could be realised'.[1] Yet as Robert Owen's New Lanark cotton mills and workers' village illustrates, in England and America a number of those inculcated with the reformist principles of enlightenment philosophies of rational planning, education and human improvement set out to bring their imagined utopias into reality. The riots, protests, bombs and widespread unrest that characterised England early in the nineteenth century fuelled just such longings for a better world.[2]

The colonisation of South Australia in the first part of the nineteenth century was overlaid by just such dreams, although the radical rethinking of sexual and family relations found in many European and American utopian experiments (communal living and polygamous families, for example) seems almost entirely absent. Perhaps the staunch Dissenting voice in South Australia that placed the patriarchal family firmly at the centre of society, along with the rapid emergence of the sexual freedoms for men created by the progress of colonisation, made radical utopian criticisms of family and sexual relations less relevant. Looking back at the colony as it was in 1839, the feminist, writer, and political activist Catherine Helen Spence saw some of those early utopian ideals surviving at least into the colony's first years. In them, she wrote, 'we see something of that Utopia where man learns the usefulness, the dignity, and the blessedness of labour, where work is paid for according to its hardness and its disagreeableness, and not after the standard of overcrowded countries where bread is dear and human life and strength cheap'.[3] While South Australia was a utopia to be built on labour and religious reforms rather than those of gender it is a reminder that in British eyes, colonisation was a profoundly *moral* activity intended to benefit those brought under their control. Inevitably, however, beneath utopian dreams of improvement and perfection there runs a dark undercurrent that, as in twentieth-century fascist and terrorist doctrines, can have lethal consequences. For how can a new world come into being if an old one, often described as impure and corrupt, is standing in its way? And how can a new social world – or even a 'new man' – come into being if the old one knows not where true virtue lies?

The best known of the early English Utopianists, Thomas More, offered an answer to this question by imagining his Utopia as built upon an island, quite cut off from the world to be left behind. A distant place, remote from the evils of the old world, is a good place for starting again from the ground up, for installing a new world without the moral decay, injustices and laws of the old one. Such a colony could offer a new start, the possibility of living in new ways without the corroding corruptions of the old world. Among many of the entrepreneurial backers of South Australia such dreams framed the way they thought about both the righteousness of their purpose in founding a colony that could produce the profits that canny speculators were seeking, as well as their thinking about the nature of the world they wanted to create. When South Australia was founded in 1836 it was placed upon what was seen as the largest island in the world known to Europeans, one almost at the bottom of their globe – beyond it lay only ice and snow, howling gales and nothingness.

Many of those who fought long and hard to justify its establishment intended South Australia to be a good colony, indeed a model colony. Unlike the earlier colonial settlements on Australia's eastern coast, South Australia was not to be a penal colony filled with Britain's unwanted criminals, the despised Irish paupers from the workhouses, and the indigent. All these were to be left behind. What was wanted was a colony of free, enterprising men who would build their homes and work the land with paid workers rather than indentured labourers, convicts or slaves. The colony's planners favoured a better kind of emigrant – family men, God-fearing men free to follow the religious beliefs of their choice. Although it was to be a colony of the largely Protestant, often non-conforming, middling classes rather than the haunt of the then unpopular Irish Catholics, nevertheless, Catholic Christians were also to enjoy the religious and civil freedoms of all other colonists; and as the wealthy Sephardi Jewish financier Jacob Montefiore was a member of the South Australian Colonization Commission in London, Jews too would be welcomed as equal citizens. Furthermore, the numerous dissenting Protestants held staunchly to the view that religious toleration could only be guaranteed by the absolute separation of church and state. The Archbishop of Canterbury was not to be entwined in the practices of the government of the land as well as of the spirit. There were to be no religious taxes or tithes; each congregation would guarantee its freedom of thought by supporting itself.

In backing the colony, merchant-banker George French Angas looked to the much earlier model of colonisation provided by William Penn's plan for Pennsylvania, one of the founding colonies of the United States of America. Penn had joined the Society of Friends, the Quakers, setting up his colony in order to provide them with a place of freedom and political participation, one in which he would buy the land he was taking over from its Native American owners. Angas looked to Penn's plan for a practical example of how a good colony could be established peacefully. While there were slaves in Penn's colony, in Angas's vision for South Australia, there were to be none. Where he diverged further from Penn's model, and this was crucial, was in the funding for his colony. Instead of paying First Australians for the colony's land as Penn had done in America, South Australia's land was simply usurped then sold on to colonists and investors. Angas was more or less using Edward Gibbon Wakefield's colonisation plan, written while he was in

Newgate prison as a result of abducting a fifteen-year-old heiress. His time of reflection there led to an interest in emigration and eventually to his view that squatting on free land and using convict labour as had been the case in colonial New South Wales was to be avoided if colonies were to succeed in establishing a decent social order. In his eyes, the colonists of South Australia should pay in order become landowners so that the money raised from land sales could be used to help bring out the free labour force they needed.

This difference between the planning of Penn's colony and that of South Australia made Indigenous Australians into immediate landless paupers and shut them out of the new colonial economy. To understand how a good Protestant colony founded on utopian dreams of building a better world could deteriorate into the sex and savagery that blighted their enterprise almost from the start, the dark side of utopian dreams of perfection and new worlds has to be remembered. How will that longed-for new world be born? The desire for an improved society, a new man, or a perfected race that can be found in so much Christian evangelism, the longing for a new and empty land on which to start again and the powerful Biblical images of the terrible destruction and punishments that make possible the entrance of Believers into the heavenly world-to-come, cloaked the enterprise of colonisation with what Deborah Bird Rose has called its 'whiff of redemption'. Such are the beliefs that can lead to, excuse, or even sanctify acts that in ordinary daily life would be considered ruthless, criminal or inhumane.[4] And certainly far from the gentleness so commonly associated with the teachings of Jesus.

In South Australia, colonisation was underpinned by ways of thinking that accepted both the need for profits and the necessity of the destruction of what immediately became *the Indigenous past* in order to install a superior, modern civilisation that was properly Christian. For all its faults and disappointments, utopian thought seems never to die. It flows along, a current of hope, always there to be drawn upon when political and social alternatives are being sought, when existing power structures are being criticised, when the future needs to be born anew. It is part of human life, just like the violence so often associated with it. In this strong and eddying Biblical current an almost common-sense understanding that an inevitable and *better* future arrives only with the destruction of the present is a view that could only affect the First Australians very badly.

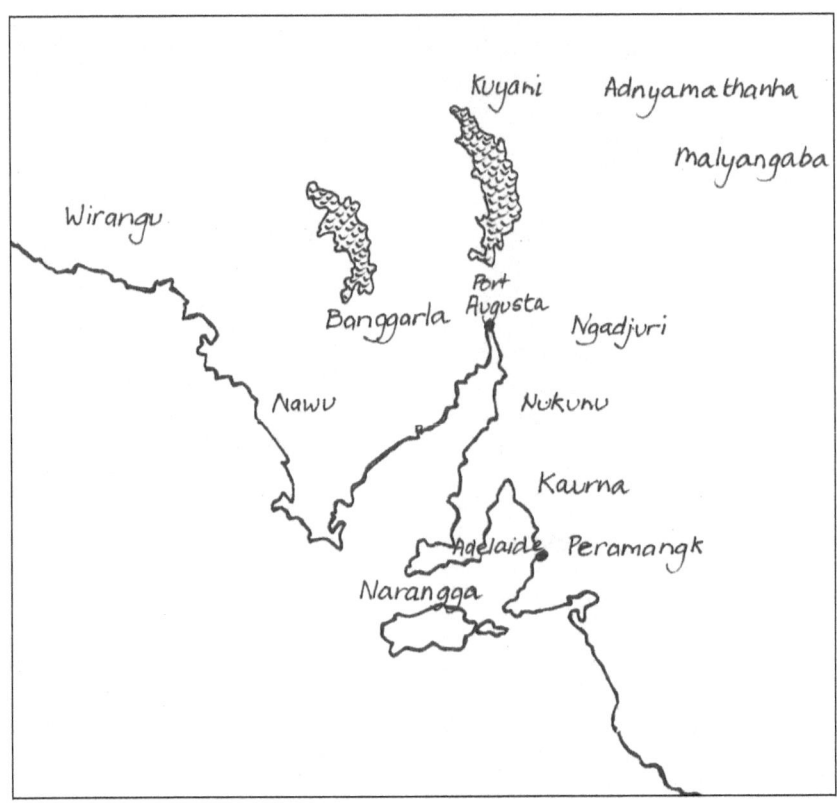

The Pre-Colony at the time of English Invasion, 1936

Chapter Two

The Pre-Colony

Well before the first South Australian colonists dropped anchor in Holdfast Bay in December of 1836, the lives of the coastal peoples of Australia had been touched by the trade and military imperatives of the new economic axis emerging across the northern hemisphere. Along the continent's northern coasts there had long been the trade with Makassan seafarers from Sulawesi whose visits are recorded in the rock paintings of the Australia's northern peoples; there may also have been visits from the Chinese, and one wonders about the great sailors of the Pacific who often sailed at night in order to see the stars more clearly, people like the Tikopia. From the early eighteen hundreds the French had taken an interest in Australia. The memory of Matthew Flinders' visit to the south-western tip of the continent while charting its coasts lived on for over a century in the *Koorannup* dance that incorporated the steps of Flinders' farewell drill parade, the smart moves as guns were shouldered, the stamping feet as they marched first one way then the other, bodies painted with the red of the soldiers' jackets and the white of their bandoliers.[1] From the work of Matthew Flinders and others, by 1803 it was known that Australia was an island rather than being attached to a larger land-form, most of its coasts had been charted by the British, some of the rivers had been identified; and it was known that Van Diemen's Land (now Tasmania) was not a peninsula but an island separated from the mainland by seas that could be very rough indeed.

Since 1788 the east coast of Australia had been home to a garrison town and its outposts on Van Diemen's Land. Set up to deal with convicts shipped out from overflowing prisons and hulks, with increasing numbers of free settlers and government officials, all had an interest in pushing out from Sydney Town to grab the best land they could find. But inland from the coast was another matter. Very little was known of it and in the absence of knowledge, fantasy tended to fill the gaps. Belief in the existence of an inland sea was widespread. It was not until 1830 that exploration of the River Murray by Captain Charles Sturt brought the country surrounding the river into colonial view, opening up the possibility of the colonisation of what would become, in 1836, the new colony of South Australia.

At the time, those most familiar with the coast of South Australia were whalers, sealers and mutton-bird hunters. The rewards of the trade were sufficient to tempt small sailing ships carrying determined crews recruited from ports right across the globe into the dangerous southern oceans.[2] These pre-colonisation crews had ranged around the southern coasts of Australia for many years, putting into shore for supplies of food and water, for repairs, for workers and for women.

Although by 1836 profits were declining, the whaling trade meant that the people living along the coasts of South Australia had been subjected to seafarer raids, seasonal foreign settlements and to years of killings, rapes and abductions. The place of such incidents in Aboriginal oral records is a reminder of the horror their actions provoked. Little wonder that even in the 1940s, the anthropologists Catherine and Ronald Berndt, who spent much time with the elderly Albert Karloan and Pinkie Mack of the Ngarrindjeri people living south of Adelaide, recorded among them resentments and a continuing hatred of Europeans that had been generated by the actions of those men a century earlier.[3]

The Buandig people living around Willijam (Rivoli Bay) also spoke of such encounters. Their oral narratives dating from about 1822 or 1823 were recorded by the Scottish missionary Christina Smith who worked among them. Some of them thought [the first boat they saw] was a drifting island, she wrote, *and all who saw it became alarmed, and began to think of a hiding-place. Mothers with their children secured themselves in some safe retreat, while others courageously watched the movements of this strange visitor. One morning some of the women went along the beach for shellfish, and returning were surprised by two white men. In running away one of the women dropped her child, and, on stopping to pick it up, was captured and taken away to the ship. About three months after, the ship put into Guichen Bay, and the woman took opportunity to escape, taking with her some clothing. She reached the Narrow Neck, and came across a 'posse' of her countrywomen lamenting her loss.*

As Christina Smith put it, 'She did not give a very favourable account of the treatment she received from the crew'.[4]

This incident might be the first one recorded from colonial South Australia in which the memories of women and their experiences come through so clearly. And it brings out how significant had been the treatment of women by seafarers. Although the impact of traders and colonisation on women does not figure largely in the written annals of South Australia, the Buandig incident was not an isolated one. Albert Karloan described another in which a Ramindjeri woman from Yaltung on the upper Inman River was abducted, forced to leave her child behind, and taken to Kingscote on Kangaroo Island where she was 'passed around the camp of Europeans'.[5] Other women were kidnapped from Tasmania, dumped on remote coastal islands to capture mutton birds or other animals, and left there until their captors could return at the end of the season. The ruthlessness and cruelties of the later eighteenth and early nineteenth centuries were widespread across the southern coasts. The determined hostility faced by later colonists attempting to settle on the Eyre Peninsula of South Australia is thought to have been fuelled by those earlier experiences.

For a very long time the rape of Indigenous women by colonising men was justified in public by claiming that as those women had no sense of sexual morality, their sexual violation could not be either a sin or a crime.[6] That argument, too, has had a long life in Australia. In Buandig narratives, it is made plain that in the 1820s, then as now, women distinguished clearly between rape and various forms of consensual sex, no matter what European rapists might wish to believe. Indeed, in the early years of the nineteenth century issues of sexual consent were only slowly being worked through in English moral and legal codes. The age of consent and the right of women to refuse sex to their husbands were to become particularly difficult within the sexual politics of empire and colonisation and remain so today. Regardless of the efforts of philanthropic charities to protect Indigenous women from unscrupulous colonists and no matter how godly the intentions of the colony's founders, when it came to sexual relations South Australia was to prove little different from colonies elsewhere. With the sealers and whalers had come their diseases. Gonorrhoea and syphilis arrived, diseases that afflicted children as well as adults and lowered rates of fertility. The Lutheran missionary who arrived in Adelaide in 1838, Clamor Schürmann, believed that, as the Encounter Bay people had an Indigenous name for such 'loathsome diseases', the diseases themselves pre-dated colonisation.[7]

The question of whether syphilis was an indigenous disease or the gift of colonisation has been fiercely argued over ever since, but with venereal diseases common among ships' crews and their predilection for sexual relations with Australian women it seems unlikely that infection could have been avoided. In addition, the logic behind the assumption that the existence of a Ramindjeri word for syphilis indicates an indigenous Ramindjeri disease is faulty – not all introduced phenomena carry their original names with them. But as well as venereal diseases came tuberculosis and the other pulmonary and contagious afflictions of ships' crews, and there was smallpox.

There had been a smallpox epidemic in South Australia in about 1789;[8] another travelled from the east coast, along the Murray River in about 1829–30, decimating those people it passed through, the survivors bearing the tell-tale marks on their skin.[9] Survivors of that first wave of engagement with the disease could be, of course, relatively healthy later, a fact South Australia's colonists would remark upon, but they were relatively few. And the visiting sailors left other traces of themselves. In 1836 the newly arriving colonists remarked that Kangaroo Island was over-run by ships' rats. Rats and fleas would trouble them again as they camped at Holdfast Bay awaiting a decision on where to build their new town, Adelaide. *Pindi-kudlo*, the Kaurna called the fleas that arrived with the Europeans.[10]

In addition to the intermittent presence of Europeans along the southern coasts, the earlier eastern colonies also had an impact that preceded the establishment of South Australia. It is easy to overlook the ways in which the permanent taking of the eastern lands and the increasing numbers of free settlers there, all hoping for land and riches, had consequences to the west of the limits of actual settlement. By about 1828 the Wiradjuri and the Kamilaroi were facing the effects of a massive expansion of pastoralism onto their lands, the central lands of colonial New South Wales.[11] The consequences of mounting pressure from such disruption flowing inland from the east could not help but ripple westwards toward the people who would eventually find themselves enclosed within the colonial boundaries of South Australia. The introduction of pastoralism, agriculture and land-clearing in the east forced many of the displaced steadily outwards, sometimes toward Country not their own, regardless of whether earlier ties with neighbouring people had been of friendly exchanges or intermittent hostility. Pressure on basic food and water resources could lead to increasing conflict among First Nations peoples as well as between them and the colonists. Struggle as people might to stay on their own Countries, at the very least some were pushed into new political and social alignments with each other as well as having to learn how to deal with the easterly colonists. When South Australia was colonised, such pressures had been under way for the best part of fifty years. The colonial opinion that Indigenous Australians were a people living locked in a timeless kind of unchanging stasis was far from the truth.

Just as the coastal peoples had had to deal directly with sealers, whalers and eventually escaped convicts, as more land was taken for settlement the river peoples came under pressure from the extensive flocks and herds moving westwards from the east coast. Rivers are crucially important in Australia because of its climate, its size and the fragility of many water sources. The River Murray is South Australia's largest and most reliable waterway. As those living along it felt the pressure from the east, they became interested in what was happening as the first colonists arrived on Kaurna country. They were not always welcome on the plain on which Adelaide would be built. Those from further up-river began encroaching on Kaurna Country in ways that were new. By 1836, they were regarded already as aggressive.[12]

Pressed from the sea and pressed from the east, by the time of formal colonisation the Kaurna of the Adelaide plain and their immediate neighbours, the Peramangk living around Mt Barker, the Ramindjeri, Ngarrindjeri and the peoples living around the lower Murray lakes had been living within a world that for well over thirty years had been uncertain, unsettled and often dangerous. The people that the colonists saw as unchanging, as well as entirely uncivilised, had had to respond to dramatic and shifting political and economic pressures, waves of disease and population depletion. Far from static, the societies on the mainland were in ferment, flexing and responding in turn to pressures from without as well as to those pressing upon them from within – their trading practices, food and water sources, demographic shifts and most importantly, the political alliances and kinship connections between neighbouring groups all had to be reconsidered. Given their first-hand experience of Europeans and their ways, the 'unreasoning terror' that Ronald Berndt and Catherine Berndt (1951) described as typical of the first reactions of Australians to Europeans should be taken as a slight misreading of the history of engagement between the parties. The damaging effects of the violence and cruelty of many of the earlier encounters have to be taken into account.[13] There were many sources for those early terrors; they were far from unreasoned and well known to critics of colonisation and the British government alike.

Chapter Three

The Righteousness of Colonisation

In the England of the early years of the nineteenth century, the setting up of new colonies was contentious. Governments were finding colonies could be expensive, unruly, demanding, and likely to lead to unexpected wars. If the first colonists and their financial backers saw the creation of a new English province in a land untrammelled by civilisation's ills, as providing an opportunity to continue with the great march of progress through continuous improvement, even perhaps as joining in the works of a benign providence, not everyone thought the same.

In the 1820s Lord Castlereagh's plans to settle London's paupers in Southern Africa, for instance, had sparked an upsurge of political controversy over colonisation schemes, and there was uncertainty over the value of New Zealand to British colonists. Even earlier, in his *Emancipate Your Colonies!* written originally to the Comte de Mirabeau in the wake of the French Revolution of 1789, Jeremy Bentham had urged his view that beneath its rhetoric, imperial glory was merely another name for personal plunder, that American greatness rested in part upon its absence of colonies, and furthermore, that an empire provided an expanded battle-ground for party warfare among politicians, just one further removed from home.[1] Despite their desire to bring foreign souls to Christ, evangelical opinion was divided on the righteousness of the colonial cause.[2] Indeed, looking at the steady rush to colonise Africa and the lands of the southern hemisphere, the influential Wesleyan preacher and writer John Beecham (1787–1856) was quite against them.[3]

While firm in his understanding of Christianity as essential to the civilising process, Beecham was equally clear that if the history of British colonisation showed one single thing, it was that all colonies to the date of his writing (1838) had been founded on 'unrighteousness', an unrighteousness that was a consequence of English legislation intended to bring each new English colony into a lawful existence. While the notion of a civilising process so characteristic of nineteenth-century England was not theirs alone, a belief in the universal value and superiority of their own civilisation was useful to those who would colonise. It turned colonisation into a good deed. The unavoidable moral questions raised by colonisation – of whether immoral means could ever be justified by their intended ends, or of how to take land legally – were as evident to Beecham as they were to those who were losing their lands and independence. While many among the British found the consequences of colonisation easy to push aside, others found the unavoidable, fundamental, foundational conundrums created by colonisation troubling. In its starkest terms colonisation raised questions about the real nature of humanity and of who, in a colony, was the true possessor of a superior civilisation? For if the founding of a colony required actions otherwise regarded as immoral (murder, plunder, kidnapping, extortion, rape, torture), how many such acts could be committed without the civilisers losing not only their claim to rectitude but their claim to be a superior people, the bearers of a superior society? Who then would be the savage, who the barbarian?

When moral critics like Beecham pointed to the *South Australian Act* mentioned in the 'Report of the Parliamentary Select Committee on Aborigines', his main focus was directly upon the land and the processes and legality of taking it from its original owners. The legislation by 'which an immense tract of country is disposed of as "waste lands"', he wrote,

> *on which a single habitation of man was not to be found, and whose soil was not imprinted with a human footstep; while the [South Australian] Company themselves, in whose favour the Act was framed, state that 'great numbers of natives' have been seen along that part of the coast where they are commencing operations. Is this capable of vindication? or even of apology? What right have we to sit and coolly dispose of distant countries, inhabited by Aboriginal people, who have as valid a claim to the lands which they occupy as we have to our native soil? What excuse can be offered for the insult which, in some cases, at least, we add to this wrong, by legislatively pronouncing those countries to be mere 'waste lands', thus practically denying to the inhabitants their claims to humanity, and classing them with the wild beasts of the forest? ... what can be offered as an apology for us, who in the spirit of boasting, are so apt to place ourselves at the head of the most enlightened, and even philanthropic, nations of the earth?*[4]

Beecham's attack on colonisation rested upon his view that it had known, visible, harmful effects on Aboriginal peoples. In his view and with unrelenting faith and logic he saw the failure to provide any religious instruction for colonised peoples as a key issue:

> *the fact is, that barbarous nations require to be enlightened and elevated, before they can be brought to recognize and act according to the rules by which civilized communities live ... it is indispensably necessary to adopt means for enlightening and improving the character of the natives, in order that they may be taught properly to exercise their own rights, and duly to respect the rights of others.*[5]

Not simply true to his faith, but because he marshalled evidence to show that the passing of laws alone cannot bring about the necessary beneficial result, Beecham saw the Christian Gospel as the only means of achieving the improvement they needed and deserved.

Where he differed from others, however, was in his persistent pursuit of a state of enlightenment that would qualify colonised peoples to exercise the rights that the Christian Gospel and enlightenment principles combined could bring to them. His vision of the place of Indigenous peoples within a colony was one based on their fully recognised humanity, each with the full range of human and civil rights that go with such a state. But because of each colony's foundation on unrighteousness and the consequent dismal effects on those brought unwillingly under an unrighteous regime of law, it was his opinion that colonisation was to be opposed in principle. It followed from his argument that he was against the proposed establishment of New Zealand as a new colony (the matter he discussed) and that he saw the proposal to base it upon the 'old but wrong principle of obtaining possession of the lands of the natives at a price little more than nominal' as no advance in righteousness at all.

Given his views, it comes as no surprise to find Beecham's final words predicting a godly chastisement upon Britain as a result of its evil actions in founding colonies. He had no doubt that all would be taken away, 'leaving Britain dwelling alone – a melancholy instance of a nation whom God has signally chastised for persisting to do wrong, in neglect of the clearest light, and regardless of the most solemn admonitions'. That was his final word. Although Britain may have done wrong in founding colonies in New Holland, New Zealand and elsewhere, Beecham's God has not yet taken quite all away from them (although he may well be doing so now). But in his diagnosis and his facts, Beecham was right. The land to be taken for the colony was neither 'waste' in the English legal sense of the term, nor empty. Nor could taking it from its owners be righteous. It is the first loss of righteousness that continues to fuel a desire for its restoration and makes the moral criticisms of people deemed to be living somewhere between backwardness and the 'stone age' so important. Already fully elaborated in British criticisms of polygamous Muslim societies and the seclusion of women in an imaginary and seductive 'orient', the family and women's place in Indigenous societies have been the focus of Christian colonial criticism over many generations. Women and the monogamous Christian family operate as a key and highly charged marker of social and moral differences that have produced a constant swirl of claims that other people's women need to be liberated from their masters, and that the British are the ones to do it.

But if it were the members of the Colonization Commission who secured the British government's approval for the colonisation of South Australia, it was the industrious and deeply religious George Fife Angas who threw his heart and soul into it as well as his money. For what Angas wanted was a colony that would become a model to the world. Born in Newcastle in 1789 into a family of Particular Baptists (those following the teachings of Calvin rather than Luther), his family's experience of the mahogany trade with British Honduras shaped his attitude to colonisation and slavery, along with a lifelong concern for the moral welfare of seafarers.[6] Although an active emancipist, Angas was one of those who benefited greatly from the 1835 compensation fund set up for those whose slaves were freed in the wake of British laws intended to stamp out the slave trade. He received £6942 for emancipating his 121 slaves.[7] Angas was a hard businessman, patriarchal in the full sense of the term; he was also a man for whom the colony offered a place for realising a particular moral vision, a place in which the labour of those building it would be rewarded. The peace that a successful colony needed would come only, he believed, through justice:

> *If I can get pious people sent out to that land the ground will be blessed for their sake and if justice be done to the aborigines as was done by William Penn then we shall have peace in all our borders for I reckon that the principles of God's Government will apply to South Australia as elsewhere.*[8]

In his major history of the colony, Douglas Pike wrote that he thought that Angas's biographer (Edwin Hodder) had rather over-stated the significance of Angas to the colony's foundation. But if Robert Gouger can be described as the colony's most devoted promoter in London, Angas was a long-term powerhouse. Such was the intimate inter-twining of mercantile endeavour and strict Calvinist moralism within Angas's thought, prayer and practice, that it is easy to underplay the driving role of his vision of a new moral order and the building of a better world upon a new and untainted land.[9] From his days in British Honduras, Angas knew that slaves cut and processed the great mahogany trees exported into Britain, knew about the Mayan troubles in central America that had followed colonisation by Spain, and knew also of the attitudes and behaviour of British timber traders and plantation owners in many colonial outposts. He knew that if godliness were to reign, justice to the Indigenous peoples of a colony would need to be done before peace could prevail. It was he who sought out the pious colonists who would build his new world, he who attempted to regulate the unruly conduct of ships' crews and emigrants while sailing to the colony, he who brought out dissenting German Lutherans and he who intended to evangelise the people being displaced and had the energy and the money that was needed to do it. It was he who held to the moral vision. Despite the failures of implementation so characteristic of many utopian dreams, the ideas embedded within the mix of enlightenment improvement ideals and evangelical hopes for a better world had effects on how the colonists thought about the project of colonisation and how they would respond with acts that were far from kindness, light and peace. The political need to accept ways of dealing with the Indigenous peoples of the colony that would not create anew the bloodiness of the east coast colonies, the widespread piety and the strong current of utopian new world theologies were all the work of George Fife Angas.

*****

Angas had the strong moral vision that intended the colonists to be not only of good character and pious but preferably, *family men*. He envisioned a colony built on the families those first colonists would bring with them, a family headed by a patriarch. Among the various Protestants sought out for the first contingents of emigrants he was far from alone in his views. His letter to his daughter Sarah, living then at Evandale near Angaston and newly married to Henry Evans, gives the flavour of the patriarchal family as it lived within the minds of the more austere and religious of the colonists. In setting out the requirements of a successful marriage his voice can be heard, loud and clear. Written from England in May of 1838, he said:

> ... *Take pains to please your husband, and think nothing a trouble which will smooth his passage through the harassing and vexatious cares of business. Should he at any time appear cold, or evince the semblance of neglect, attribute it to the depressing influence of such things, and redouble your efforts to please on such occasions. The smiles and sympathy of a wife at such times have a more powerful influence in reviving the spirits and restoring the elasticity of the mind than any other restorative on earth. But woe to that man, when bowed down with the pressure of his accumulated exertions to provide support and comforts for his wife and family, if on his return for repose to his own roof his exhaustion of body and mind should be yet further increased by the cold look, icy sympathy, or callous indifference, if not, still worse by the irritating droppings of contention. I have seen much of the world and of the goings on in private families, and as the result of it all you may take my present advice to you, my dear, as the best proof of my affection for you, because I am sure, if you act upon it, it will preserve for you a happy home and a peaceful conscience.*
>
> *From what I have seen, such advice does indeed appear unnecessary for you, but should it ever be needed henceforth, which I pray God may never be, it will not be without its benefit.*[10]

Edwin Hodder, who knew Angas personally, described his concept of family: 'The head was to be', Hodder wrote, 'as in patriarchal days, prophet, priest, and king of the household.' Angas might not have called himself a patriarch but he insisted on the unquestioning obedience that he believed was due under the laws of God as well as laws of man that submerged the person of a married woman into that of her husband. He believed that God had put him at the head of his family and that therefore no-one could do other than let him be first. He liked to say, 'Honour thy parents as the word of God.' From this position,

Hodder says, his children could never displace him. He was, in short, a patriarchalist in the fullest sense of the term. In his own eyes at least, he and his God were as one. His was a model of masculinity, manhood and family that has never lost its allure.

While there were many like him, such opinions had been under challenge for some time, in the fierce, analytical writings of Mary Wollstonecraft for example. Her criticisms of the way in which women were forced to live without rights under male power were expressed in *Vindication of the Rights of Women*, published in 1792. Coming from a Dissenting family, her demand that women be given their right to education and to the pleasures of their bodies did not sit well with either religious or secular legal codes. Men like George Fife Angas, born in 1789, came of the next generation when the readership of Mary's book had been diminished by revelations that she had lived unmarried with the American Gilbert Imlay. Nevertheless, marriage and English-women's lot were under challenge. If Angas's strict Calvinism justified his concepts of family and patriarchal control of women, other Dissenters – Quakers and Unitarians notable among them – were more open to reforming the practices that disadvantaged women so greatly. Their views would become important when women began to demand the right to vote.

*****

In the colony, however, as they observed what they took to be the practices of family life among the Indigenous peoples beside whom they were living, it was the Aboriginal man who appeared as an absolute patriarch, the man who could exercise his powers against his wife without restraint and did so. Popular ideas about the nature of Aboriginal marriages and the way men treated women circulated in newspapers, letters home, and in publications. W.H. Leigh's widely read account of his journey to South Australia is one example. In a fit of pure fantasy he wrote, 'Their manner of courtship is one which would not be popular among English ladies. If a chief, or any other individual, be smitten by a female of a different tribe, he endeavours to way-lay her; and if she be surprised in any quiet place, the ambushed lover rushes upon her, beats her about the head with his waddie till she becomes senseless, when she is dragged in triumph to his hut, and thenceforth is his lawful bride.'[11]

Aboriginal men were quickly dubbed 'the lords of creation', an expression harking back to the popular seventeenth-century hymn, 'Praise to the Lord, the Almighty, the King of Creation'. And even though they observed that the wives of the Kaurna men living around Adelaide often seemed remarkably happy, they judged those families as savage and barbaric nevertheless, as one more example of their desperate need for Christian reformation. The British focus on the family came about because of the way in which their own concepts of family were so intricately woven into the moral exhortations and laws of Christianity that the reshaping of Indigenous families came to be seen as fundamental and necessary. That initial colonial diagnosis and calls for family 'reform' has never ceased. In its earliest stages, as illustrated particularly clearly at Poonindie mission, the task of breaking un-Christian marriage practices was undertaken by Protestant missions. In later years, governments, patrol officers, police and welfare officials would have more to say and do about it. The need to understand the role of the family as a political tool of oppression was illustrated again in 2007 when an imagined moral 'collapse' of the Indigenous family was used by the conservative government to stage its race-based political 'intervention' in the Northern Territory to remove civil rights and establish a new regime of controls and surveillance over Indigenous Australians. For many of the families caught up in it, it has been disastrous.

Patriarchal theologies become particularly attractive whenever women's roles seem to be changing in ways that give them more autonomy, especially of the kind demanded by Mary Wollstonecraft. They also flourished during those times when family life came to be seen as occupying a private domain quite separate from that of the public life of men outside it. The creation of a separate private domain for women acted as a constraint on their opportunities and participation in the world beyond it. It also created an often separate male domain of action and autonomy and superiority. For missionaries, the government and a good many of the colonists, conversion to Christianity required not simply an acceptance of the Bible and Jesus as the son of God, but a radically different way of living. That new way pivoted upon a form of family that placed power over women firmly in the hands of men. Despite the commonly expressed opinion of the colonists that First Nations women were subjected by their husbands to violence and horrors unmentionable, the small monogamous Christian family took away powers from Indigenous Australian women, restricted their use of violence against men, created difficulties among groups as customary patterns of food distributions were disrupted, and cut off women from that practical support that kin relations would have offered them. If family structures were to be the foundation upon which a Christian life was to rest, they were also the basis of the Aboriginal societies whose lands were being taken. Yet the two groups of men, the colonisers and the colonised, both held powers over women although they did so in rather different ways.

The assessment and judgement of Kaurna ways by the first generations of colonists was distorted for a number of reasons, but first among them was the way in which they compared the two quite different forms of family life. The middle-class Christian family of nineteenth-century Britain that gave men legal control of the women who were their wives was idealised to a degree that any transgressions or unfortunate incidents of violence within it were seen as exceptions to a general practice of family harmony and happiness. The sometimes hidden physical chastisement of British women by their husbands was generally regarded as an unremarkable part of family life. By contrast, the Indigenous family was seen as ineradicably savage in its nature. Moments of harmony, co-operation and happiness were construed as exceptional as well as puzzling. And if it were plain that for much of the time the women living within polygamous and often extended families did not seem particularly unhappy or discontented and appeared to enjoy a measure of independence quite foreign to their colonial sisters, the colonial diagnosis of the Indigenous family's failings remained intact because it had an important political function. The pre-supposed barbarism of the Indigenous family served to reinforce the superior design of the Christian model being introduced by the colonists. For them, despite the polygamy and chastisements characterising the Biblical patriarchs, it was Christian monogamy that had become essential to the social practices and moral sensibilities of the rising middling classes, essential to their sense of themselves. Both the canon law of the churches and the laws of the land insisted upon it. To them, the family and women's subjugation to men was a clear point of social difference, one that reinforced their own moral superiority, their own Christian righteousness and thus, the righteousness of colonisation. It was also one that ignored the brothels and male philandering.

Chapter Four

Empty Lands

That sense of colonial righteousness and male entitlement was reinforced by imagining their new lands as 'waste', as boundless and empty. This way of thinking tapped into long-established British ways of defining lands that were beyond their reach but about to be put under their control. Beecham was right when he spoke against the proposition that Indigenous lands were 'waste' either in the established legal sense of the term or in the practices of daily life. Beecham also denied that those supposed waste lands were empty apart from a few 'wanderers'. Not only were they not empty, they were known and mapped in detail by their inhabitants, the entire continent of Australia was crossed by major trade and ceremonial routes that traversed the known boundaries of those holding rights to particular places, those routes and places spoken of today as making up a particular *Country*. So persistent were the notions of wasteland, emptiness and the absence of boundaries that when in 1918 the South Australian Museum's anthropologist, Norman Tindale, mapped the boundaries of the Groote Eylandt and Roper River peoples, his editors removed them from his report. As wanderers, he was told, Aborigines had no fixed attachment to land and thus no boundaries.[1] In this context the word 'wanderer' comes with an English history of its own, having emerged as way of describing the men and women who were displaced by the land clearances and enclosures of the eighteenth century, many of whom emigrated to America and Australia. As well as men with no land and no work, British wanderers were men who had no master to control them. It was the absence of a master that seems to have provoked so many of the moves against the unemployed, the displaced poor, and the rise of the greatly feared 'workhouses' that stood in place of the absent masters of the dispossessed. This is the meaning of the word 'wanderer' attached so often to First Nations Australians. It was a negative word that did not refer to the images of the wanderer strolling through the primaeval forest glades of English versions of the ancient myths of the Greeks, nor did it refer to those of the twentieth-century European popular song who 'loved to go a-wandering, along a mountain track …' singing as they went, a knapsack on their back.²

*****

Indeed, the early colonists of South Australia needed to rely on romanticised images of a place of unbounded emptiness to justify their enterprise. But the emptiness of the colony's 'new' lands was a fantasy. Albert Karloan's fascinating work shows that it was most certainly mapped.

Albert Karloan, Murray Bridge, 1949.
Courtesy Berndt Museum, University of Western Australia.

Born in 1864 on Lake Albert, one of the lakes guarding the mouth of the Murray, the only major river in the colony, Albert Karloan was a man fully educated in the Law of his country. His map of what is now known as the Fleurieu Peninsula shows the main Kaurna and Ramindjeri walking tracks as he had known them in the 1860s.[3] As the routes Karloan walked in the 1860s had been used by his father in the 1830s and earlier, his mapping gives a glimpse of the country around Adelaide, its named places, the disposition of peoples and their languages much as it was known when the colonists sailed up the gulf in search of a site for the capital of South Australia. Karloan's map shows that far from being empty or unmapped, the rich lands of the coastal regions around Adelaide were traversed by well-known local pathways used by numerous people speaking different languages and living on different Countries.[4] The people of the Adelaide plain did not live in isolation. Their pathways joined them to neighbours living far to the north as well as to the great trading routes of the continent's interior. To the south, Kaurna tracks traversed Ngarrindjeri country, linking them to those living along the Murray River and to those living eastwards in what is now the state of Victoria.

The scale and reach of some of the major routes becomes evident in Ronald and Catherine Berndts' composite map of the whole continent of Australia, published in *The World of the First Australians* in 1964.[5] Based largely on the records of early European observers and far from comprehensive, it gives an idea of how people appearing to colonial eyes as living in supposedly remote or isolated pockets of country were in fact linked into major networks along which people, ceremonies, information and trade goods flowed right across the country.

Across such routes travelled supplies of pigment, weaponry, pituri (a form of tobacco), the special stone used for axes, the different stone used for grinding grains, iridescent pearl shells from the north coast, songs and dances, news of the effects of colonisation and, unavoidably, disease.

The pituri so enjoyed by the Kaurna people around Adelaide, for example, was carried down from Queensland through the trading centres of Dieri country in the north-east of the colony; from there onwards to the renowned ochre centre at Parachilna in the northern

Karloan's Map

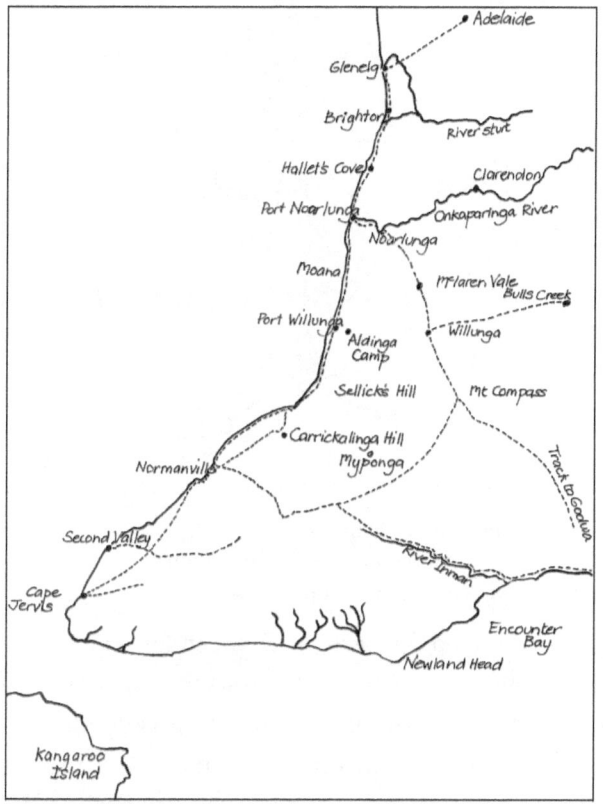

A simplified version of Albert Karloan's Fleurieu Peninsula–Kaurna & Ramindjeri lands and main routes, c. 1860s. Reconstructed through Ronald Berndt's conversations with Albert Karloan and Pinkie Mack. Redrawn and simplified with permission. Original map from: R. and C. Berndt (1993: pp. 330), titled: Map 10 'Kukabrak clan lands. From Newland Head to Glenelg'.

Flinders Range, and onwards again, traded by the Ngadjuri to the Kaurna.[6] Although there are ochre deposits on Kaurna country at Moana just south of Adelaide, for the important ceremonial transition of a boy into adulthood, the powerful, shimmering ochre from near Parachilna was the more highly prized.[7] From Parachilna, great quantities of ochre were traded northwards on the ochre expeditions that took place in the good years when waterholes, creeks and soakages allowed for long-distance travel; from Kaurna country, too, both types

Transcontinental Trade Routes Traversing the 'empty lands'
of the Colonial Imagination.
Berndt and Berndt, 1964, p. 19

of ochre could be traded onwards, exchanged for scarce goods coming the other way. Isabel McBryde's meticulous records of the distribution of axes fabricated in greenstone quarries at Mt William and Mt Camel in western Victoria shows them entering south-eastern South Australia via Millicent and Mt Schank. From the Ngaiawung people living higher up the Murray around Moorundie, the Ngarrindjeri at the river's mouth received the kangaroo skins and warm possum pelts used to make cloaks and rugs, as well as kangaroo sinews and bones.[8] Far from wandering aimlessly across the countryside, the First Australians encountered by the early colonists were great traders as well as great travellers so that, as one might expect, the relationships with those living along their pathways were formalised through kin, ceremonial and political agreements. Even so, in some Countries relationships could be fraught. Ooldea, another of the important nineteenth-century trading centres of South Australia, now joined to Adelaide and Perth by rail and road, is still regarded as remote and isolated. But for Indigenous Australians it was not so.

The Ooldea Trade and Ceremonial Centre

The large waterhole in the sandhills of Ooldea lies just inland from the top of the Great Australian Bight and its dramatic cliffs. Surrounded by the dry plains of the Nullarbor, Ooldea supported a major trading and ceremonial centre at which hundreds of people from many different and distant locations might gather for months at a time. One overland route came down from the north, several from the west and another from the east.[9] To travel there safely required detailed cartographic knowledge of a very special and specific kind.[10] Indigenous knowledge of country was not written or drawn according to European conventions but lived in the mind and memory, instilled with great care.

When Mutdubinga, for example, described the routes into Ooldea used by Antakirinja people as they carried trade goods southwards over the five or six hundred kilometres from Kamena in the Everard Range, he could name the twenty-seven waterholes leading into Palinga and how to reach each of them. The journey, he said, took about thirty-five days in all. As they travelled they carried the highly valued form of pituri, *Nicotiana suaveolans*, produced around Kamena. At Ooldea the Antakirinja could trade their pituri for wombat fur and the red, white and yellow ochres so crucial for painting; and they could carry out the rites needed to bring young males to maturity, as well as exchange news and ceremonies. They might also find there Mirning people from the coastal country south of Ooldea who traded in high quality flint, mined from the immense cliffs near Eucla. Others would have walked in from the region known today as the Western Desert, yet it too could be traversed in good years by those who carried the knowledge of its waters in the mind and in the body. The transcontinental nature of the trade routes can be seen in the way that the highly valued pearl shells from as far away as the northern coasts also arrived at Ooldea.[11]

Maps like those based on Karloan's knowledge and those prepared by non-Indigenous researchers are not of a kind that any Indigenous Australian would have made for their own use. They are translations of Indigenous linguistic, musical and visual information re-expressed for colonial eyes into European spatial and pictorial conventions.

Indigenous Australian concepts of mapping depict and describe country as seen and experienced from a very different starting point, one in which a 'place' is understood through the relationships of specific groups of people to it and through the relationships of individuals with the creative beings whose acts and bodies are living, embedded within a country. *Country*, in Aboriginal English, can refer to the seas and skies as well as to land; each Country has its people and their responsibilities to it, its origin stories, and its Law. These together make up its life that must be nurtured by the people who have arisen from it. This is why for English-speakers the term *autochthonous* (arising from the earth) is a more appropriate general name for the First Peoples of Australia than *Aboriginal* or *Indigenous*, although it is more difficult for English-speakers to grapple with. As will become apparent, an Aboriginal Country cannot be equated with the European concept of a landscape; nor can Aboriginal maps be equated with the maps and charts used by seafarers and colonists as they sailed south from England on the long journey to Australia.[12] Sky-maps were, of course, used by both.

There are many ways of creating a map other than preparing an outline of coastlines or a land mass, or of naming rivers as a totality rather than as a series of places along it. Maps can be expressed as lists (as in the Old Testament) or, as the Romans did, show only significant markers along the way; or they can be carved in three dimensions (like the wooden maps of Indigenous Greenlanders). Examples of carved maps from Australia are less common but a Pintupi map engraved upon a spear-thrower from the western desert region shows thirty-six named waterholes (the loops and circles), all lying along the tracks of the ancestral snake, Liru, a path that can still be followed provided that the traveller understands the narrative and its imagery. Other visual forms of Indigenous Country can be found in paintings on bark and later, on canvas. But as with the Pintupi spear-thrower they cannot be read directly from the image without additional detailed knowledge. Using such a map needs ritual knowledge, memory, narrative and song.

It is within song and ceremony that travelling routes across

Country come alive. They are the 'land maps' carried in the head that Catherine Berndt described at Ooldea during the 1940s and that the distinguished musicologist Catherine Ellis and anthropologist Linda Barwick described for the desert cultures of central Australia.[13] For the Antakirinja women of the north of South Australia, for example, each song is made up of a number of short verses, each verse relating an element of the activities of an Ancestral figure either at a particular place or during a period of moving across the country. 'The performance of the correct sequence of small songs', Ellis and Barwick noted, 'constitutes a map of the ancestor's journey ...'.[14] This distinctive mode of knowing the country, relying as it does on evoking the real presence of the era of Creation in the present, extends far beyond south and central Australia. For example, in a presentation given by Mussolini Harvey, a Yanyuwa man from the Gulf of Carpentaria in the far north who worked with Deborah Bird Rose, Harvey describes the significance of song and its line in a way that he intended to be intelligible to a non-Indigenous audience:

> *The Dreamings named all of the country and the sea as they travelled, they named everything they saw. The Dreamings gave us our songs. The songs are sacred and we call them kujika. These songs tell the story of the Dreaming as they travelled over the country, everything the Dreaming did is in the songs, the country is in the songs, the names of people are in the songs. These songs that we sing in the ceremony are very long, they can take many days of all night singing to finish them. These songs are like maps, they tell us about our country, they are maps which we carry in our heads.*[15]

As well as taking the form of song, the maps that Harvey is describing are embedded within stories, dance, and related ritual performances so that they are indeed within the mind, the voice and probably within the body and its gestures and movements. As such, they are not abstractions of an outer reality but a lived, embodied experience of them. They have been called *performative maps*.[16] Performances of them rely on the complexity, precision and the 'amazing perfection of intonation' that characterises Aboriginal music.[17]

In performative maps, complex rhythms specific to each song's line can provide mnemonic devices for performers that allow songs to cross language boundaries. Rhythms identify the songline to which an alien song belongs so that the meaning of the text can be understood.[18] Children's songs heard in Ooldea also relied on rhythm for meaning – it was the rhythm that even child singers had to locate, rather than the words – for while words can become distorted in transmission, the rhythm must hold fast.[19]

These fundamental musical structures and voicing of the songlines help to explain the underpinnings of the transcontinental mapping practices of Indigenous Australians. Music (song and dance) embeds the route in the body so that it overcomes some of the barriers of language, it allows for transmission over long distances and it transcends regional differences of musical practice. The people of the south of the colony had, Ellis noted, 'an unaccompanied melodic line with a range greater than an octave; it had important higher notes, many ornamental notes and free rhythm. None of this made their reception of northerly music and dance impractical'. Indeed, Ellis wrote that, 'Given that these songlines may map vast tracts of territory ... the informational importance of specific rhythms may be greater than anything we have known from Western music'.[20] As Mussolini Harvey's explanation (mentioned above) shows, very much care and time went into teaching it.

The performative mapping encountered by the colonists in Australia differs greatly from the pictorial conventions of the detailed British ordnance surveys of the nineteenth century that were to form the basis of the charts and maps that the colonists would prepare as they entered onto Kaurna Country. As the maps drawn by Albert Karloan, the Antakirinja women, Mussolini Harvey and other Indigenous transmitters show, Indigenous narratives and geographical information expressed in song, narrative and music can be translated in part into the linear or pictorial forms characteristic of European mapping conventions. But musicological research has shown how and why performative maps cannot be 'read' easily by Europeans and often could not be recognised as maps. The design engraved onto the Pintupi spear-thrower mentioned earlier can only be read by having the details of the movements of the Great Snake Liru from waterhole to waterhole engraved within the mind. And that engraving takes place through music and song and performance. Nevertheless, as the engraving on wood shows, the track from and through named places can be used to navigate a route, it can be understood as a map as well as a history or mnemonic device and as a mythological narrative of creation.

Two Maps
With colonisation, two forms of mapping, two distinctive sets of ideas about knowing the land, traversing it and using it came into play. The practical instrument of the colonists, their instrument of ownership, was the land survey – its chainmen, tripods, lines of sight, and the series of triangulations of the kind used to make the nineteenth-century Ordinance Survey maps of Ireland and Britain. The surveyors marked out the plan of Adelaide ready for sale. As they moved beyond the first point of settlement, they marked-in the geographical features that they considered important: the creeks, the hills, the valleys, pastures suitable as fodder, and any signs of useful minerals. They used a sense of direction that placed north always at the top of the page; they plotted their townships and settlements and marked in their own tracks across the land. If they inquired as to the name of a place, the answers were not always understood, marking down a word for 'creek' rather than which specific creek or more likely, which part of the creek it was. Rather than a general name for a long river like the Murray or the Onkaparinga there could be a series of names, each relating to segments of a creation narrative, to events that took place there and to the relations of that segment to places and people identified in narrative rather than by geographical propinquity.

The first colonists had difficulty in seeing the pathways and tracks of the people they were displacing. They were easily lost in the bush, they did not understand how to find the easier paths through dense scrub and the apparent absence of pathways was frightening. In 1852 when the young artist William Cawthorne walked from Port Elliot to Goolwa for example, he was constantly lost and disoriented despite the existence of the important Dreaming track of Ngurunderi marked on Karloan's maps that would have been visible to him had he know where to look and how to read what he saw.[21]

Some routes were much more visible to the colonists, cleared of rocks or trees to make a broader way like those seen by the colonists Imlay and Hill in January of 1838 when they reached the Murray River at a point near 'the elbow', the point at which its course turns sharply eastward. Even far to the north on the ephemeral Cooper Creek, Charles Sturt was able to follow its course in 1845 by travelling along 'paths as wide as an ordinary gravel walk', just as in 1857 the surveyor A.C. Gregory would also find himself travelling along 'a 'well-beaten path' near Cooper Creek where, he said, 'the aborigines have taken the trouble to remove natural obstacles from their paths.'[22] Routes along the much larger and permanent Murray River were said to be wide enough to get a cart along.[23] Many of today's roads follow those earlier paths with bridges built at what were well established Aboriginal crossing points.

That first generation of colonists, though, had to rely on being guided and shown the easier way, shown too where the watering points were and where game suitable for eating might be found. Yet even when the British relied on local people for directions they tended to ascribe that knowledge either to an almost animal nature (they could read the signs of the animal and natural world to which supposedly they had remained so close) or to superhuman, magical or spiritual powers, all of which denied their guides the full human agency and rationality without which it was impossible for humans to live efficiently, effectively, and indeed comfortably, across Australia. Although the great cycles of the ancestral narratives of the First Australians covered the land 'with an intricate network of mythic paths (or "tracks" as many now say) which draw on incalculable geographic detail', in the eyes of many colonists, (i.e. to a British eye) the land remained empty, a place where 'no roads went by'.[24]

*****

The colonists' belief in the un-mapped nature of an empty land was too important to give up easily despite the insights gained by the more interested of observers. It was their own map that was a visible marker of their sovereignty, one that allowed them to think of their map as the ground plan on which they would build their new, more equal and peaceful world. In making that new land visible to themselves in their own terms they could think about themselves not as unscrupulous invaders but as explorers or pioneers, the new men who were *first*, their own ancestral heroes who walked and rode across an unmapped and empty new land, who survived great hardship and privations in order to fill in the blank spaces of their own map. The survey made visible their imprint on the land; it showed their ownership of what they thought of as theirs and theirs alone. As they spread out into the colony, their new map grew. They wanted to take control, to bring some order into being there. For the first South Australian colonists camped around the Glenelg sandhills and the river Karrawirra Parri–Torrens there would be an urgent need to map what they saw as emptiness, a process that would help to fill the awful void with the new world they were creating.

Chapter Five

Land into Landscape

William Light (1786–1839), 'View at Yankalillah, South Australia', Lithograph published 1838. nla.pic-an7830519. Courtesy National Library of Australia

The diaries and letters of the first colonists make it plain that as they sailed along the coast of South Australia toward their new lives, they were relieved to find that what they saw was not just a strange new land but a recognisable *landscape*. Although the words *land* and *landscape* are commonly used as interchangeable, they are not precisely the same. A *landscape* is the result of looking at land in a particular way, a way that makes sense of what is being looked at by composing its component parts to shape a view or scene that is peculiarly European in origin.[1] Not everyone looks at land or pictures it in that way and certainly the colony's Indigenous peoples did not. By understanding land as a landscape, the land itself is drawn into this specifically European way-of-looking that disengages a landscape from the land itself by organising its natural features according to well-established aesthetic conventions. Making a picture of land requires an act of transformation, not only of exact copying. In other words, painting a landscape is an expression of a specific way of thinking and looking as much as it is of replicating what is actually seen by the eye. Like the transformations of reality played out in theatrical performances and religious rituals, the transformations involved in making a picture hold the power to alter perceptions of where reality lies. To make a picture is therefore a powerful act indeed, one that has helped to establish how the histories of the colony are seen and understood by the colonists and their descendants.[2] The colonists' way of looking at their new land is known as *the picturesque*.

The picturesque style of painting was a specific way of thinking about and looking at the land, as well as a way of composing its features. For the first of the colonists, the aesthetic conventions of the English picturesque movement shaped their view of what they were seeing. By 1836 those conventions were so accepted as to seem not only normal but natural. Neither was the case. Developing in England in the eighteenth century and flourishing in the nineteenth, the picturesque style of painting landscapes has never really gone away. The colonists' habit of seeing and thinking about their new land through the prism of the picturesque form of landscape painting helped to make a new place seem more familiar. Its familiarity bolstered their sense that they were the builders of a new province of old England. Only better.

William Light, the colony's surveyor, was a competent painter. His picture of the camp of his survey party at Yankalilla just south of Adelaide (above) is a good example of land pictured as a landscape when described through the conventions of the picturesque. Light's landscape shows the carefully framed, tripartite composition characteristic of the picturesque: the darkened, detailed foreground, the strongly lit middle ground against the hazy skies of the background and an S-shaped river snaking off into the distance that helps give depth and perspective. Although Light included the men of his party within the scene, a landscape is not a picture of rural life (as are S.T. Gill's well-known paintings of the agricultural seasons of the year), but a picture referring to the nature of the land and the feelings it evokes in the person looking at it. Within those conventions any human presence within a painted landscape is typically reduced to tiny figures, a convention that influenced the way in which the early colonists figured the people they were displacing.

In his picture of the camp at Yankalilla William Light shows all the people there as tiny, the colonists busy and active, an Aboriginal family present but standing motionless, looking on from the margins.[3] His is a powerful image of the realities of the colony just as the land was being taken, one often replicated by the early Adelaide painters. In those days before photography, Adelaide was lucky to have had a number of competent painters on the very first ships – some amateurs, some trained in the military and occasionally a professional. They provide a glimpse of how the first colonists saw their new land and of how it changed. The painting of a 'Pine Forest 1838' by John Michael Skipper who trained within the Norwich School of landscape painters in England, for example, shows how Aboriginal people most commonly entered the early colonial landscapes as tiny figures, often very still, usually at the margins.[4] Their marginalisation and stillness was far from the reality at the time.

Seeing the Colony through the Picturesque

The first shipload of colonists arrived at Holdfast Bay on the *Africaine* on 10 November 1836. The painters among them, like John Michael Skipper, were keen to document the new world they were seeing and building. Mary Thomas pictured the land they were taking in words. 'The country as far as we could see,' she wrote, 'resembled an English park with long grass in abundance and fine trees scattered about'.[5] The land around Rapid Bay, too, she had heard, 'everywhere resembled a gentleman's park – grass growing in the greatest luxuriance, the most beautiful flowers in abundance, and the birds of splendid plumage'.[6] Mary Thomas spoke and wrote in pictures just as others would paint them. And before Colonel William Light began to survey the land around Yankalilla he also was taken with his first views of the coast. He likened the land around Rapid Bay to a paradise; in an extraordinary comparison, he wrote that the country around Yankalilla reminded him of Devon's apple orchards.[7] When Theresa Chauncy arrived early in the new year of 1837, her artist's eye also delighted in all that she saw. She recorded her first sight of Glenelg as having 'the appearance of an English Park, the trees being interspersed at a moderate distance from each other. They consist chiefly of the Shea Oak, tea tree, gum trees, also many others which we had never seen before.' In an unexpected comparison she wrote of how the Adelaide plain resembled Windsor Forest 'more than any place I ever saw only the foliage is of a brighter green and the trees have a fresher aspect'.[8] It is not clear whether Chauncy's mention of Windsor Forest refers to the spaciousness of some of its areas or to Alexander Pope's much earlier poem of that name. Owned by the monarch, in lines 7–10 of 'Windsor-Forest' Pope is said to have been offering 'Windsor (and England itself) as a new Eden or paradise'.[9] So perhaps that is what Chauncy had in mind.

A year later, even sharp-eyed critics of the realities of life in a new colony, like W.H. Leigh, could not fault the picturesque nature of the landscape around Adelaide in 1837. After pulling up the river in a cutter, wading through the mud of river flats in order to reach dry land, he and his companions walked three-quarters of an hour across the level plain to reach the town. 'The view which the country presented defies description,' he wrote,

> *another extensive and beautiful plain, and another belt of trees succeeded, giving a park-like appearance to the scene, while before us sprang up birds like the sky or wood lark, with a similar note. I was just in a delightful reverie, wishing to make myself believe*

that those were the Malvern hills, when lo! A flock of white and black cockatoos flew screaming from a gum-tree, and the charm was broken – I was still in Australia.[10]

Nevertheless, after a cooling swim in the river, the Karrawirra Pari (redgum forest river) now known as the Torrens, Leigh remarked again, that 'The situation of Adelaide is very picturesque, it being upon a gradual descent to the River Torrens, and studded with very large gum-trees, which afford an agreeable shade'.

The town itself was another matter, its largely invisible streets and squares and its miserable huts breaking firmly through the bounds of picturesqueness to enter into the realities of daily life were not necessarily close to those of art. Mary Hindmarsh's drawing of Adelaide at its inception shows it as firmly embedded within the park-like landscape of the picturesque, no matter the quality of the roadways, the screeches of the cockatoos or the rudimentary state of its facilities.[11]

The normalcy of picturesque ways of refining land into an aesthetically pleasing landscape were sustained through a small number of pictorial conventions. The first of these can be seen in the use of careful framing. The framing of the scene to be painted cuts out unwanted or unsightly features – it limits the scope of what will be seen as the eye travels into the painting. The form of perspective found in the picturesque landscape is equally characteristic. Most typically it assumes a single viewing point as if the viewer is looking through a window. That kind of perspective and framing structures William Light's picture of his survey boat (below) sailing along the Onkaparinga River, framed left and right by the trees, with the river leading the eye inwards toward the horizon. His picture of the survey boat on the river shows how to create a picturesque scene from what might otherwise have been shown as a rather desolate series of scrubby swamps, mud flats and marshes.

Looking now at the placid picture of the surveying boat sailing quietly up the Onkaparinga River it is striking that although the image offers no real sense of place it seems somehow familiar. The reason

LAND INTO LANDSCAPE

'The surveying boat sailing up the creek, Onkaparinga River [?], South Australia, 30 September 1836.' Part of Frances Amelia Thomas' scrapbook of artworks, poems and music, 1835–1840. This is William Light's surveying boat; it appears on his map, very nicely worked up. Courtesy State Library of South Australia

that Light's small picture seems so familiar, so European in feel and subject, is not because the artist could not yet understand Australian light or draw Australian plants and rivers, but because the scene has been constructed according to familiar, natural, conventions that are entirely English. It shows an Australian land that has been drawn into a European mind to be framed by a European eye, composed through a single point of view to create a picture with well-defined sections, drawn and coloured to create the illusion of distance.[12] Absorbed into English ways of looking at and into the land, the actual location of the scene that the artist has observed has become ambivalent. Light's way of looking at the land and then of picturing what he sees derives from the way in which the English countryside long ago became a series of landscapes. So powerful is this way of seeing and picturing it, that it would be many generations before the new Australian-born painters could challenge it.

It is difficult to over-estimate the significance of the picturesque aesthetic to the new world to be built in the colony. A complex and radical re-visioning of land, a philosophical exploration of nature, culture and the proper relationship of people to the natural world, its effects were significant and far-reaching. As well as being the prevailing form of landscape painting in England, its concern with the improvement of the natural world could not help but be of particular importance in a colony. But its greater significance comes from the ways in which its particular form of visuality – its particular way of looking and knowing – transformed a new land into an imagined landscape that was specifically English and blinded them to the nature and beauty of First Nations art.

That they should do so should not surprise. Their colony was intended to be a new *province* of England and the transformation of colonial lands into replicas of Englishness was well established. When the first colonists wrote that their new land resembled the parks of the landed gentry, they had in mind estates like Attingham Park or Stourhead, one of the earliest of the English picturesque landscaped gardens.[13] Many of the great English parks and estates now visited by tourists were built up by consolidating much smaller parcels of land and often, with the profits of slavery. Being early improvers of agricultural production methods (methods that were to fuel the industrial wealth and the rise of a new bourgeoisie whose wealth lay not in land but in manufacturing and commerce), English land-owners cleared their lands of small tenant farmers. They removed villages if necessary, and enclosed what had been the common lands open to small rural residents to produce the larger fields required for more efficient methods of grain and sheep farming, to improve the breeding of grouse and pheasants for shooting and also the moors they required for breeding, as well as to create the large park-like gardens for which Britain remains famous.[14] This aspect of the improving process was recognised under the name of 'emparkation'.[15] The same processes were set in motion by English colonists in Ireland, which led to the introduction of rhododendrons that have become pests; and also during the Highland Clearances of Scotland in the eighteenth and nineteenth centuries which created great distress to those dispossessed. Even that great apostle of agricultural improvement and efficiency, Jeremy

Bentham, seemed taken aback by the scale and longevity of the poverty such improvements produced, processes that fuelled emigration and helped to create the dispossessed urban poor.[16] The landscaped houses and gardens of the great English estates were therefore built not only with the profits of trade in slaves and their labour but on ruthless dispossession and privatising of common lands in England, Scotland and Ireland. At the same time many of the dispossessed were criminalised through increasingly harsh laws against poaching, vagrancy, petty theft and protest.

Embarkation, clearances and the profits of slavery and new industries created spaces in which the cultural differences in Britain between the wealthy and the poor could be played out, as well as spaces of control in which aristocratic superiority could be expressed safely secluded from the chaos caused by their creation. Inside the walls bounding those spaces, nature could appear as it should be, a living picture of how the natural world ought to be as well as how it was being looked at. The picturesque movement therefore consisted of a reverberating aesthetic, a moral vision and a political trajectory in which imagined landscapes, landscaped land, and private parks reflected back and forth upon each other as the wealthy and educated tried to get closer to a form of nature that looked 'natural' but was actually constrained, contrived and well under control.

Figures in a Landscape

The small size of any humans within a picturesque landscape has already been mentioned. People are so subordinated to the landscape that they appear as tiny even when they are an important part of the subject being portrayed. Their role is to emphasise the grandeur of the land and their subordination to the natural world. This effect can be seen in one of the most park-like of the paintings of Kaurna Country on which the colonists were building. The land itself was Nga:no Country, the place of the ancestral Giant Red Kangaroo, the hills in the background being associated with a phase in his narrative in which, after a battle, he lay down to die, his body forming the edge of the plain (renamed as the Mount Lofty Ranges). Nga:no's two ears, Yurridla, are visible on the horizon, split apart to be named by the colonists as Mount Lofty and Mount Bonython.[17]

Martha Berkeley's painting of Mount Lofty, made in about 1840 when the new settlement of Adelaide was well under way is one of those images that holds the viewer captive. Its power to fascinate comes at least in part from the many different ideas it draws upon and pictures. At the time of her painting much of the land around Adelaide had been surveyed and sold and already the consequences of colonisation for the local people were clear. Berkeley's painting is a saddened one. In this she was typical of her generation, those early arrivals who had seen something of how life had been before the people were fully displaced, those who wanted to do no harm but who came to see that they had. Bill Gammage has pointed to the way in which the Mt Lofty painting shows how the failure of the regular burning cycles that produced the greatly admired park-like grasslands was, after just four years of colonisation, leading to their demise. Berkeley has shown the small stands of young saplings that if left unburnt will produce a choking scrub rather than graceful open park lands. The lower reaches of the hills will soon go the same way, as we know from historical images of the bareness of the now tree-covered Green Hill, for example, at the top of what is now Greenhill Road.[18]

As well as offering an image that speaks to current misunderstandings of the pre-colonial Australian landscape as being natural and untouched, Berkeley's painting also provides a comment on the social life of the colony in 1840. Art historian Jane Hylton has pointed to the way Berkeley deals with the impact of colonisation by showing how 'a small Aboriginal family wanders in a landscape that has become scarred by the intrusion of another race with an entirely different set of values. A settler walks beside his bullock dray against the background of the hills surrounding Adelaide, with trees dotted through the park-like landscape.'[19] In a reference to the destruction of nature in order to improve it, Berkeley shows the tree knocked down beside the track, perhaps by the road-makers, perhaps by a passing bullock dray. She emphasises the destructive aspect of colonisation. While the composition and framing of the scene – the hills, the trees and the way in which the painting is organised around an almost serpentine line reflect conventions of landscape painting, the central point of the image is that the Aboriginal people are shown as, one way or another, walking out of the picture. A good many of the colonists would have shared both Berkeley's sadness at their exit and her sense of its inevitability.

The Veil of Colonisation

The framing, single viewing-point and perspective utilised by the first of the English colonists in South Australia helped to veil the violence of colonial occupation from colonial minds, and does so still today. The habits of looking at landscape through the conventions of the picturesque style applied also to the ways the colonists looked at Aboriginal society. It framed what they saw, limiting what they saw beyond the frame, limiting the picture's content (verbal or painted or imagined) of the Aboriginal societies that were being observed and distancing them from it. As with paintings, Aboriginal society was abstracted from the whole, a way of looking that would later be incorporated into anthropology. It covered over the new colonial regime of land ownership and its plan to remake the land in its own likeness.

These early colonial paintings are loved today for the glimpses they offer of life at the beginning of colonisation, the land as it was before colonial time began and for the images of early buildings and the people living in them. They are loved too for their glimpses of First Nations peoples living in a world closed off to them, the world of 'before', before their way of life was, as the colonists believed, gone forever, before the disasters of progress struck them. The colonists' picturing of the land took place in a moral environment in which righteous and peacefully obtained ownership was the central plank of the justification of South Australia's colonisation. Inevitably, the picturesque landscapes with their tiny figures of quiet marginalised Indigenous peoples, pictured something that did not exist – a peaceful, conflict-free, taking of the land.

These and many like them were pictures that veiled the violence and the consequences of colonisation from the eyes of those who were involved in it, those who benefitted from it, and those who could not afford to see through the melancholy images of the paintings. To describe the effect of colonial paintings as a 'veil' is useful because a veil does not blot out sight but operates as a permeable screen. It can always be lifted, moved aside; it can always be seen through, although doing so may require some effort. If paintings and drawings are looked at as being like words rather than as offering some mystical experience, as John Berger claimed in his popular television series (BBC 1972) *Ways of Seeing*, then the picture painted or drawn onto paper or canvas has more in common with the written word than is sometimes realised. But we need to enter into that conversation between the two if we want to hear more clearly from the images being set before us.

Picturesque or not, the land itself was more than just scenery. It was the foundation on which the colonists' future rested. No matter how it was looked at, colonised *land* had to be transformed into *property* owned by the colonists and available for sale, re-sale and profit. Among the first wave of colonists were many who, in order to finance South Australia, had bought rights to land while living still in London. As investors, they would have first choice of the new blocks – the most likely-looking agricultural land, well-watered riverside property, the blocks on which the new town would grow. But they could not have that choice until the land was surveyed and legal title established under British law. Picturesque as the land might look, through the survey it would be transformed from Country to landscape and then into private property.[20]

Chapter Six

The Kaurna See the Colonists

As they came off the ships moored on the marine roadways just out from Holdfast Bay's shallow waters to camp among the dunes while waiting for the survey of the town lands to be completed, the colonists were poised between two lives, living in a space that was at once menacing, filled with hope, and relatively free of constraint. Out of their old lives, they waited for the new one to begin – waited to begin to build their new world on the 'wastelands' before them, waited for their surveyor, waited to speak to the Kaurna, waited to reassure them, to present their trade goods, to enter into the peaceable relations with them that their instructions required. Even so, the cases holding the twenty-four muskets were unpacked immediately, a watch was set to guard the camp, and many of the men went armed.

The wary Kaurna watched as makeshift dwellings went up on the sandhills and beside the river's lagoons, 'frail, tents predominating', said Edwin Hodder the historian, 'but interspersed with huts constructed of reeds, bark, and branches of trees'.[1] As the men spread out to shoot or trap the black swans, ducks, possums, parrots and kangaroos that were so welcome after rancid shipboard meals, the Kaurna had to decide how to respond.[2] Unseen, the Kaurna people living on their rich country, *Mikawomma*, watched the colonists closely.[3]

Even if this new batch of foreigners were to differ from their predecessors on Kangaroo Island and at the Encounter Bay whaling camp, the presence of the two thousand colonists who had arrived by

1837 could not help but have an immediate impact on Kaurna Country. With the colonists busily foraging for edible plants, timber for building huts and fuel for cooking fires, with their indiscriminate hunting and gathering of wildlife, and their ever-increasing presence in and around the bay, they presented problems that earlier incursions had not.[4] Rather than having to confront a small party of seamen or whalers of uncertain temper who would eventually disappear, now there were great numbers of people – women and children among them – and more coming. They showed little sign of moving on. The pressure on food and water supplies and the constant felling of the trees that can be seen in early landscape paintings disrupted the spiritual and social linkages holding people, land, and its productivity together. The unregulated over-use of the green and pleasant park-like land so carefully tended into productivity by the Kaurna led to food shortages.[5]

*****

It would be several weeks before the first Kaurna entered the colonists' camps.[6] The first to do so, an adult man and a boy, clearly knew what the guns of Mr Williams and his hunting party could do. On meeting them, they placed their spears on the ground to indicate friendly intentions, and after some form of negotiation consented to travel back to Holdfast Bay with the newcomers. Indeed, in placing their weapons on the ground, the Kaurna man was engaging with the strangers in what he would have regarded as the proper way. Although the gesture of laying down arms was intelligible to the English as one of peaceful intention if not of goodwill, such a gesture was only a small element of the complex protocols governing local interactions between individuals or groups meeting as strangers. Had the strangers been neighbours of the Kaurna, the encounter would have taken a more formal path in which a proper distance and proper timing allowed the intentions of strangers to be assessed – time in which kin or trading relationships could be worked out so that a decision on whether a formal welcome preceded by a ritual settling of old scores or bad feeling would be appropriate.[7] The sudden, unannounced arrival of strangers who seemed to blunder hastily onto lands not theirs without any of the necessary forewarning, preliminary meetings, and declarations of intent, meant that from the start the colonists appeared as unpredictable and untrustworthy as well as much less than civilised. They had no manners.

The important formal ritual aspect of encounters between social groups was quite apparent to the young William Cawthorne when he arrived in Adelaide in 1841. A notable educator and a careful artist, the young Cawthorne recognised, despite all the preconceptions of his time, some of the important elements of Kaurna social practices that went unnoticed by others. In his notes on the manners and customs of the people he knew, he describes how visitors to the Country around Adelaide would paint and decorate themselves before approaching too closely. Although he does not say so, signals or messengers would have forewarned their hosts of their approach so as to allow for a proper reception. Then, he says:

> *When within sight of the opposite tribe, who are ready to receive, all sitting down with arms beside them, they take a run, shouting and going through their war gestures till within a few yards, huddle up together, stamp very loudly, clatter their shields, raise them above their heads, hold up their spears, and shout. This is performed several times before separation. If there are any strangers amongst the opposite tribe they undergo a formal introduction, their lineage and country are described by the older men, and in the evenings different plays are performed alternately.*[8]

Such practices were designed to avert fighting, create pathways between the two parties concerned and to establish and maintain the 'roads' or 'tracks' between two groups of strangers who were wanting to co-operate. By 'plays' Cawthorne means the musical theatre and ritual performances so central to Kaurna life, the dancing and singing of narratives that came to be known to the colonists as corroborees. Such performances could act as a prelude to fighting, should the initial encounter have led to an agreement to settle grievances by doing so. The propriety of announcing one's presence openly, keeping at a correct distance, and the negotiated formal settling of grievances was rarely understood by the colonists.⁹

But by the time of the first encounters between the British colonists and Kaurna people, some of the Kaurna had more of a sense of how the strangers were likely to behave. Relations might have been helped, too, by having a woman known as Princess Con (or Sally) at Glenelg, the woman who had so impressed Mary Thomas on Kangaroo Island by being able to speak both excellent English and Kaurna; or perhaps by the time of this first encounter they were ready to seek out further information, ready to try to establish whether it were possible to enter into decently human relations with the colonists.¹⁰

Once at the Holdfast Bay camp the man and boy brought there by Mr Williams were given food. Mary Thomas showed them her telescope and matches, and later there were clothes, brought out from England for just this purpose. In reciprocation, the two visitors showed Mary how to light a fire properly, how to keep summer's grass fires away from her tent and later, women brought gifts of food and showed her how they made their cloaks and the intricate stitching used in weaving baskets and mats.¹¹

In the meantime, although keeping a certain distance, more of the Kaurna returned to the plain. One of them was Ityamaitpinna. His daughter Ivaritji spoke of how

> her father [was] captured by the white people on some mud islands at Port Adelaide. ... They dressed him in ... sailors' clothes and set him at liberty. He made his way back to the tribe, who were not far off, but when they saw him coming towards them they ran as fast as they could up to Adelaide, and he ran after them.'¹²

In 1927 when she told a journalist of this incident, Ivaritji was very old but not quite old enough to offer a first-hand account of the incident. The historian Tom Gara believes it more likely that Ityamaitpinna's sister (who became known as Maria Welch) was the actual observer of the incident and had passed on the story to her niece. The colonial governor's secretary, George Stevenson, recorded an early incident that Gara suggests might be another account of the one that Ivaritji referred to. In Stevenson's narrative, early in 1837 he met 'a fine-looking manly fellow, near Glenelg and walked with him to the settlement.' This man was given trousers and a military jacket.[13] If this was indeed Ityamaitpinna, then it is not surprising that his appearance in soldier's garb caused his kin to flee.[14] He was, said Stevenson, 'about twenty-five years old, five feet ten inches in height, strong, well-built, narrow chest, with a very good-humoured face and a mouthful of the finest teeth I ever saw'. ... Stevenson went on to say that, 'There was a degree of archness' (by which Stevenson meant consciously playful or teasing behaviour) 'and quickness which places this race many degrees above the savage'. He was taken to a ship in the bay, given meat and pudding, listened to the piano being played, and then rowed back to shore.[15] A brave man indeed.

Quite quickly, the numbers of local people living beside the colonists built up, many of them intent on assessing and interacting with the strangers. By the middle of January 1837 Captain Berkeley found about forty people in all, he thought – seven or eight unarmed men, some women and children – all living close to the tent of the Emigration Agent John Brown, his wife, and sister.[16] Born in 1801, Brown had been educated at the newly established school set up by Non-Conformist ministers and merchants, Mill Hill.[17] He was a very good artist, Robert Gouger copying Brown's painting of a flying fish that had landed on the deck of the *Africaine* as they passed through tropical waters.

By the time of his arrival in the colony Brown had become 'an out-and-out political radical, notorious in his own circle for violent criticism of the traditional order. His mastery of ridicule made him a man to be feared,' wrote Douglas Pike, adding, with rather Anglican disdain, that he had 'all the unpredictable sense of inferiority of a third generation Dissenter.'[18] Dissenters were those who asserted their right to rational dissent from the Church of England's Westminster Confession of Faith, a claim robustly opposed by the Archbishop of Canterbury, his bishops and the English aristocracy, who were much more committed to telling congregations how to think, what to do and how to tax them. The Browns believed that the monies paid by colonists in London for the lands on which they were living now – the 12/- per acre of the preliminary land orders – should be transferred to the Kaurna, a view for which there was very little support in either London or Adelaide.[19] But unpredictable and socially inferior or not, Brown and his wife quickly established good relations with the local people and their willingness to have them settle around their hut was exemplary.

Those whom Captain Berkeley and then the Chauncy sisters saw living around the Browns' hut were probably some of the first people encountered by Brown and his servant James Cronk.[20] Cronk was unusual in that from the first he had made an effort to learn Kaurna. He acted as an interpreter, and was pivotal to establishing reasonable relations between the first colonists and the first wave of local people to return to the plain. Disturbed by the absence of the Indigenous people whom the colonists had been instructed to protect, it was he and John Brown who had gone out to try to find them. When they met four Kaurna men they were able to persuade them to walk with them to their tents. There they presented biscuit and sugar. A few days later, Cronk noted that he was about eighteen miles from town searching for more of the Kaurna when he came across a group of about thirty-five people. Although the women and children were alarmed by his presence, he was recognised by some of the men and friendly relations established. Cronk spent the night with this group, sharing out the six pounds of sugar and fourteen pounds of the hard, re-baked ship's biscuit he was carrying as a sign of goodwill. Following a day spent hunting with the men and enjoying the 'sumptuous feast' of birds and possums that resulted from their efforts, Cronk was able to persuade them to walk with him toward the rudimentary township of Adelaide and to visit the Browns' tents. There they received more food. On this first major Kaurna foray, the people stayed just one night. But, said Cronk in the letter to his mother, they returned about a fortnight later.[21] Mrs Brown found the people friendly and obliging, telling the newly-arrived Captain Berkeley that there had been no stealing, always an issue for the colonists who often failed to reciprocate and share according to Kaurna expectations.[22]

Living close to the Brown's hut was intelligible to the Kaurna as proper behaviour, just as Cawthorne described it. 'When friendly tribes visit,' he said, 'their huts are built as close together as convenient, but each tribe locating in the direction from whence they came.'[23] This is what had happened. Cronk and the Browns had sufficiently accommodated Kaurna protocols for dealing with strangers for the Kaurna to reciprocate by settling close by them, most likely choosing the side of the block that matched the direction in which their own Country lay.

When the Chauncy party was finally able to land and put up their own tent, a party of eight or nine Kaurna men together with an unspecified number of local women and children settled near them too. On one occasion a tall young man entered their tent and took coffee with them. It was among these close-living Kaurna that Theresa Chauncy first saw glass being worked up for use on spear tips, while from her tent she could see and hear 'almost every night by the side of the river dancing and singing'. A further group settled down close to the camp of the South Australian Company's store-keeper and clerk, Daniel Henry Schreivogel, on Montefiore Hill.[24] In mentioning this group, Clamor Schürmann is not clear on whether Schreivogel built his hut close to Kaurna dwellings or whether his store-house and his practice of offering a good return for any work carried out for him drew the people toward him.

By no means all the local people chose to engage with the colonists immediately. A little later in that first year, Stephen Hack came across about one hundred and fifty people living on country on the far side of Mt Lofty. 'The Chief came forward and addressed him in a long oration of which he could not understand a word, but supposed it to imply that he was on his hunting grounds and must consequently retire.'[25] In this case, the absence of a courteous declaration of intent in response to the senior Kaurna man addressing them did not prevent Hack's clothing being examined in some detail. Everyone then walked with him, as was proper, toward his camp. There, the presence of horses seems to have alarmed them sufficiently for them to leave. Nevertheless, the numbers of people returning to the plain quietly and steadily increased. Walking one day from the rudimentary township of Adelaide to North Adelaide on the other side of the river, Mary Thomas was surprised to come across about a hundred people – women, men and children – comfortably settled along her way, their presence there quite unknown to the colonists. Children were playing games, men and women relaxed among the waterproof huts built of bark and boughs, and it is likely that at least some of those there had built the earth ovens that cooked meat so well.[26]

Among those first tentative groups of Kaurna to enter the busy world being built on their country were three 'outstanding [and] clever' men who would be at the forefront of the initial engagement with the colonists.[27] They were Mullawirraburka (1811–1845), Kadlitpinna and Ityamaitpinna.[28] The three men can be seen standing together in 1838, as tiny but central figures in Martha Berkeley's (née Chauncy) painting of the first dinner given for the local people by the governor of the colony.

Mullawirraburka was born near Willunga in about 1811. By 1836 he was already a powerful and respected figure with four wives: Koa Warrarto (Maria), Yerrarto (Jane), Kertanya and Kauwadla. Strongly built, articulate and intelligent, he learned English quickly and spent considerable time teaching Kaurna to those wishing to learn it. Mullawirraburka survived only nine years of colonisation. His biographer, Tom Gara, believes that he was probably carried off by tuberculosis, an introduced disease with no cure that rampaged unchecked within the colony.[29] Mullawirraburka sat for Theresa Chauncy; she modelled a portrait of him in wax in about 1840, showing him in European dress.[30] She also modelled a portrait of a woman whom she named as Mocatta or Pretty Mary, thought to be one of Mullawirraburka's wives.

Ityamaitpinna's own Country lay around the Onkaparinga River to the south of Adelaide, the site of Light's painting of his survey boat. If, as Gara suggests, Ityamaitpinna was about 22 years old when he was taken aboard the ship in Holdfast Bay, he would have been born in about 1814. He died at a Kaurna place near today's Morphett Vale. His sister, the aunt of Ivaritj, was born in about 1825. She lived with Phillip Welch from Western Australia at the Poonindie mission settlement near Port Lincoln until the 1890s, also sometimes at the mission settlements at Point McLeay and Point Pearce on the Yorke Peninsula, dying in December of 1909. Like Mullawirraburka, Ityamaitpinna was taken through the proper Kaurna death rites, his body painted with red ochre before being carefully tied into a seated position, smoked slowly over a fire, and dried.[31]

One of the men Kadlitpinna befriended was young John Adams who had arrived on the *Buffalo* at the end of 1836. On his first visit to town, Adams said he had helped to dress Kadlitpinna with clothes provided by Thomas Gilbert, the South Australia Company's storekeeper, giving him a mirror to look into.[32] Reflecting the significance of such an important exchange, thereafter Kadlitpinna referred to Adams as 'brother'. 'Years after', Adams said, 'if Kadlitpinna was camping near where we lived, he would come or send one of his lubras for his accustomed quantity of sugar and tobacco, etc., that I was in the habit of giving him.'[33]

Kadlitpinna was drawn by George French Angas in 1844. Wearing a warrior's panoply, Kadlitpinna was taken to visit Angas by the young Cawthorne, who in the course of learning Kaurna had come to know him well.

> *'I am going to take Capt. Jack (one of the aborigines so called) up to Mr Angas, full dressed as a warrior oiled, painted, decorated, etc., precisely as they dress themselves when a fight takes place, to be drawn. I wish I could draw him ...'*

Angas did not acknowledge Captain Jack by name as the sitter for his lithograph, Plate XXII, in *South Australia Illustrated*. Nor did he give the modest Cawthorne any credit for making his portrait possible.[34] Angas shows Kadlitpinna painted with red and white ochre. His 'headband is of possum fur, the feathers are from the tail of a black cockatoo; head and face are painted with red and white ochre. He is armed with a wooden shield, spears, throwing stick and wirries.'[35]

Although neither of these three men spoke English at this time, they were not ignorant of English ways. They knew much of what was at stake. What they could not know was that the nature of their country was about to change dramatically. The dense network of personal and spiritual relations through which Kaurna Country was known, protected and nurtured was to the colonists simply 'land'. As such it was there to be exploited as a commodity owned by individual colonists lacking any recognition of a social sensibility differing from their own. Kaurna Country was about to become 'land' that could then become private 'property'.

Chapter Seven

Locke's Blessing

There were good reasons why the philosopher John Locke should have turned his mind to the ownership of property, the problem raised by converting the common lands granted by God to all people to the private ownership and benefit of the few. Good reasons, too, for the persistence of Locke's views through the centuries and therefore, good reasons for attending to them in seeking to understand the realities of colonisation and its consequences. For it was Locke who addressed directly the troubling moral dilemma colonisation posed. How, he asked, could a good Christian justify taking land away from its owners to turn it into private property? Particularly as the Bible teaching was clear – God had given the earth to *all* mankind, not just to the British.[1]

Born in 1632 and living until 1704, Locke had entered a world in which revolution, religious dissent and colonisation schemes were in the air as well as on the ground. While English and Scottish Protestants had established the plantations of Ireland under Henry VIII, from the seventeenth century onwards the English and Scots began to settle in parts of the Americas and the West Indies where trade in furs, slaves and sugar were to prove so lucrative. Those colonies comprised England's 'first empire' with Locke in the thick of it. It was while employed as secretary by Lord Shaftsbury, one of the eight Lords Proprietors of the American colony known as the Province of Carolina, that Locke drafted (or helped to draft) the *Fundamental Constitutions of Carolina* (1669) setting out a view of how a colony could be governed more equitably than was then the case. Proving too much for the Proprietors, his formulations were never adopted. Colonisation remained a matter of interest, however, and Locke's approach to it was important to the colonists involved in Britain's 'second empire' in India, Africa, South America, North America and myriad small islands, the sprawling empire that from 1788 included Australia.

By the time that Locke's *Second Treatise* was published in 1689, the upheavals of the English revolution of 1688 had left a strong dissenting force in the towns but one shorn of its political rights by the 1689 Toleration Act. Within the parishes administered by the rural squirearchies the established Church of England remained a force to be reckoned with. It provided a kind of balance to the dissenting and sometimes radical politics of their towns, while an increase in the petty powers of landholders was used to persecute the dispossessed in their parishes.[2] It is not so surprising, then, to see Thomas Hobbes' concern to justify sovereignty and Locke's interest in justifying a right to private property. Locke had had plenty of time to consider the nature of a colony; he also had his Carolina experience to draw upon.[3]

In his *Second Treatise* Locke looked to consider not just the government of colonies but the nature of the colonial impulse and its legitimacy.[4] As such, he had to confront the way in which colonists came to own their property and it is this that is important for Australia. His success in justifying the right to colonise was of a kind, Lisa Ford suggests in a detailed analysis of colonial sovereignties, that gave 'impetus to English expansion like no other'.[5] The influence of Locke's ideas, as Eva Mackey has demonstrated, have never lost their political significance. They have remained alive because of the way in which he was able to bring sacred and secular reasoning together to make the taking of land for a colony seem a blessed as well as a legitimate legal act.

Locke's Blessing

In Locke's time, England contained a spiritual world 'filled with magic, astrology, divination, ghosts and witchcraft' against which the words of the Bible provided a certain amount of protection.[6] It was a world in which the Bible was seen as a fundamental account of English history as well as of its culture and customs. Locke's blessing of the inaugurating colonial act of usurpation rested upon Verse 16 of Psalm 115 as his starting point: 'The heaven, even the heavens, are the Lord's: but the earth hath he given to the children of men.' He used these words as the basis for his first proposition, that the one true God gave the land to mankind in common, a sense preserved in England in the 'commons' found still in some old village settlements as well as in law.[7] Equally important is the need to notice that the immediate base of Locke's reasoning lay within precepts embedded in the civil laws of England. On the one hand, he spread the eternal moral mantle of the Christian Bible over the taking of the 'common' lands given by God to all; on the other, he offered a more direct call upon secular legal concepts. It is the two together that legitimated, he argued, the wholesale conversion of colonised lands into a form of property owned by the British Crown.

The Dual Nature of Property

The claim that taking foreign land on which to plant a colony was legitimate arose from a distinction drawn between land and property. By *property* Locke meant privately owned land – with ownership having been earned through the act of applying the labour required to make common land productive. Property therefore consisted of two elements, land and labour, welded together in a way that cast an almost magical cloak over its owners.[8] As many have observed, in English law crimes against property have usually been more severely punished than crimes against the person, a principle still clearly operating in Australia, particularly crimes committed by men against women.

This simple concept of the transformative powers and effects of labour was not Locke's alone. It circulated in France in the 1790s after the revolution there and was discussed by Karl Marx in 1843 when it was already flowing through British colonies around the globe. It became enshrined in British law and by that means, from the first day entered directly into the laws of the Province of South Australia.[9]

Its particularly Protestant cast would make its presence felt in South Australia, the home *par excellence* of dissenting Protestants intent on labouring hard to make a new land productive.[10] Among them were many whose preachers were of the old school with a lively sense of hell and damnation, a sensibility found also among the dissenting German Lutherans settled at Klemzig, Hahndorf, and in the Barossa Valley. Those first German colonists, often of peasant or village stock, were of families who in 1817 had refused their king's instruction to merge their Old Lutheran practices with his Calvinist reformed forms of worship.[11] They were those ready to choose exile rather than conformity; they were colonists stamped by the seventeenth century's concerns that Christopher Hill would describe as those who 'followed the Bible in contrasting the wilderness of the world with the garden of the church, separated by its hedge of discipline and doctrinal orthodoxy' ... those who saw it as 'the duty of the saints to bring the earth under cultivation and to bring the heathen into the church ...'[12] Such dogmas were perfect for colonists taking supposedly empty lands populated by people whose humanity was questioned and who could be described as savages or barbarians.

More directly, Locke's thinking came to the colony via political philosophers like the Bentham brothers, Samuel and Jeremy. Jeremy Bentham's first experience of colonisation had been in Ireland on Lord Shelburne's estates. Like so many of his time, Shelburne was a great improver. He had hundreds of tenant families and sought Bentham's advice on caring for the elderly, the ill, widows, orphans and the able-bodied unemployed. At that same time Bentham inspected Irish poor-houses, and he had had sufficient time to read about the colonies. To him it seemed as though the British empire was full of areas in which his utilitarian principles could be applied.[13] From this fertile time, a direct line of descent can be traced through Jeremy Bentham's disciples to many of the ideas of the founders of South Australia. Bentham was influential in shaping the work of the Welsh utopian industrial reformer Robert Owen, for example. Owen, in turn, was a friend of Robert Gouger (1802–1846), pious Congregationalist and staunch supporter of both pauper emigration and the systematic, planned form of colonisation advocated by Edward Gibbon Wakefield. By 1831 and recently released from Newgate Prison, Wakefield had developed a strong sense of the danger posed to respectable society by increasing crime rates, the emergence of a large urban poverty-stricken rabble, and the political and theological criticisms of active Radical reformers among whom he included some of the Owenites.

Untroubled by the marital transgressions that had landed him in prison, Wakefield's pamphlet *Householders in Danger of the Populace* provides an indication of why his dream for a better world should take the form of transplanting British civilisation into the antipodes without resorting to the pauper emigration that others thought so practical. It was in 1831, too, that Wakefield seems to have met with the elderly Jeremy Bentham, and it was the more utilitarian-inclined among the Benthamites who engaged in turning the dream of a new and better society into reality.[14] Benthamites were the most energetic members of the committee guiding the South Australian Association's efforts to promote the new colony. 'Utilitarians and philosophical radicals', Pike calls them, listing them as 'Dr Hawkins, Henry George Ward, Henry Warburton, Edward Strutt, George Grote, J.A. Roebuck, Aubrey Beauclerk, Matthew Hill, Sir William Molesworth, Dr Southwood Smith and Rowland Hill,' all of whom were enthusiastic improvers, inventors and rationalisers. Many were Dissenters.

Given the lines of thought running from Locke to the colony and Locke's place in the laws of Britain and its outposts, and given its value in justifying colonisation as a righteous act as well as a legal one, it is not surprising to find that Locke's concept of private property as consisting of land plus labour has remained alive and well in Australia, ready for use whenever either the righteousness of colonisation or the ownership of land enters into the domain of public debate.[15] As part of the justification of the colony in London, South Australia's lands were to be considered in law as 'waste'. In his *Second Treatise* Locke had set out his view that in addition to land and labour, colonial property rights were founded equally upon the legal category of 'waste land'.[16]

Waste Lands

The crucial aspect of the concept of waste land under Locke was that it did not have to be empty of persons. If inhabitants could be considered as wanderers rather than as improving their domains by labour, their land could be defined legally as *waste*. In the words of the emigration agent of the colonists, John Brown, the lands of South Australia were 'not occupied according to any law regulating possession which is recognised by civilised people'.[17] Robert Thomas, the fiery printer and husband of Mary who arrived on the first ship of colonists, used the same language even before arriving in South Australia:

> *It is well known that the natives consist of wandering tribes, wholly independent of each other, who continually travel from place to place without any fixed habitation, and, with all deference to superior judgement, I conceive these wandering propensities of the aborigines of Australia be sufficient reason why the millions of fertile acres over which they tread, like the beasts of the earth, unconscious of their value and ignorant of their use, may be taken possession of by a colony of civilised people, without doing them the smallest injury ... what wrong can it do them if others till that which is now a waste, ...?*[18]

Robert and Mary Thomas were among the more thoughtful and sympathetic colonists, concerned for the well-being of the local people they found living on what was now their land. Robert's explicit wish to do no harm was a way of dealing with the unavoidable conundrum of colonisation, of how to reconcile the taking of land and the displacement of its owners with the moral dilemma it posed. His letter shows just how important Locke's resolution of that dilemma was to them.[19]

For South Australia, the legal concept of waste land was carefully inscribed into the colony's originating legislation:

> *The Act of the sixth year of the reign of Her Majesty Queen Victoria ch 36 intituled 'An Act for regulating the sale of waste lands belonging to the Crown in the Australian Colonies' and the Act of*

the tenth year of the reign of Her Majesty Queen Victoria ch 104 intituled 'An Act to amend an Act for regulating the sale of waste land belonging to the Crown in the Australian Colonies and to make further provision for the management thereof'.[20]

Later, the *Australian Waste Lands Act* of 1855 would repeal elements of the earlier provisions governing waste land while keeping intact the validity of the first land seizures. Those first provisions have never died.[21] They were written into the Constitution agreed by the colonies as they federated to form the Commonwealth of Australia in 1901.

Plantation

The use of the term *plantation* when speaking of a colony was touched upon in the chapter describing the ways in which the first colonists looked at and thought about the lands they were taking. In the language of English law and usage, colonies have always been 'planted', a virtuous term describing the act of converting waste land to productive use, a use often implying gardening that harks back to the Garden of Eden. In Christianity's most widely understood origin myth, God himself appears as a gardener, for 'God formed man *of* the dust of the ground, and breathed into his nostrils the breath of life ... And the Lord God *planted* a garden eastward of Eden; and there he put the man whom he had formed' (Genesis 2: 7 and 8). That originary sacred act of God fits well with the colonial impulse of a Christian-driven colonial settlement, sanctifying the transformation of waste land into a garden through planting. It is a vision that sat easily with nineteenth century capitalism.

When, as he wrote his *History of South Australia* in 1893, Edwin Hodder was considering the superiority of his colony over its predecessors the three concepts came together. 'In South Australia', he wrote,

the whole net proceeds of the sales of land being appropriated [as waste] to give a free passage to young and industrious emigrants of both sexes, by which means the capitalists will be ensured an adequate supply of labour. Thus the purchaser does not buy land so much as the facility of obtaining it combined with labour – that which alone makes land valuable [as property]. Here, then, is the first attempt, in the history of colonisation, to plant a colony upon correct principles – to ensure to the labourer employment, and to the capitalist an ample supply of labour.[22]

Set within the context of the gathering forces of a capitalist bourgeoisie, Locke's concept of property re-emerges: it is labour that makes the land valuable, labour that converts God's common land into privately owned property. Young men and women are being planted in the new world to come. Nevertheless, the colonial concept of planting a garden in the wastes and the Wakefieldian utopia of transplanting British civilisation from one place to another to build a new world, cast a benign cloak across the originary violence and displacement without which no European colony could come into being. Today, the term 'property' remains in use in South Australia in the common expression 'They had a property in the Flinders'. Owning a 'property' has remained very different from owning a farm. It is a recognised marker of social status that has grown directly from the original acts of dispossession and 'pacification' through which the first properties were established.

Chapter Eight

The First Degree of Separation

As the comments of the colonial diarists show, so long as the numbers of newcomers seemed relatively low and the real consequences of the survey parties and auctions of their Country were not apparent, relations between colonists and colonised could continue as reasonably friendly. Initially, small groups of Kaurna had settled right beside particular colonists like the Browns, with others living around the Emigrant Location on the parklands, and the reception depot prepared for the arrival of new colonists.

The numbers of Kaurna living around the nascent township increased as presentations to them built up – the clothing, trinkets and ship's biscuit given in return for labour, for water carried up from the river, and as a response to presentations of vegetable foods or flowers. Such exchanges, as well as many acts of individual kindness on both sides, more or less conformed to Kaurna concepts of reciprocity. To some extent they fitted with Kaurna norms governing the appropriate behaviour of hosts to strangers entering their country, and also with a Kaurna sense of the proper obligations regarding the distribution of food and objects along recognised networks of reciprocation. The fit was not good, not properly recognised by the colonists, but in a shadowy sense it was there. That first close residential mingling could not hold.

As initial fears subsided, as the Kaurna quickly picked up the commonplace English of daily life – its greetings and phrases, numbers, basic verbs, nouns and pronouns – they were able to observe more closely the customs and values of the colonists and their technologies. While James Cronk (1811–1904) learned enough Kaurna to act as an interpreter of sorts, most got by with a rickety form of gestures, mimicry and some kind of imagined pidgin English derived from received ideas about how to speak to 'natives' rather than from actual linguistic encounters. Inevitably, pidgin phrases were learned just as readily as correct forms of English, much to the annoyance of the missionary linguists Clamor Schürmann and Christian Teichelmann when they arrived in October of 1838.[1] Eventually, a form of pidgin Kaurna emerged as well as distinctive forms of Aboriginal English.[2] But overall, communications improved sufficiently to allow for the requirements of daily interaction.

*****

Although the numbers of Indigenous peoples living around the rudimentary and makeshift huts of Adelaide increased, the number of colonists increased much faster. The first full year of colonisation, 1837, saw about 2000 colonists on the site of Adelaide, all busy carving out a living on the fertile plain, all anxious to get possession of the land on which their futures depended. During 1838 another 3154 emigrants left England for the colony so that by year's end, nearly 50,000 acres of land (over 20,000 hectares) had been sold and taken up, alienated under the terms of the new property laws established under the *South Australia Act* of 1836.

The rapid influx of colonists in 1837 and 1838 created one of those turning points, a brief moment that could be grasped or missed, a moment from which a different future might have emerged. The numbers of colonists arriving put immediate pressure on the land in ways that they did not yet understand; but this was also a moment of opportunity, an opportunity to put in place the social and moral foundations that might have brought into existence the vision of the enlightened, fair, and peaceful society used to justify the founding of the colony. This was a moment at which the Aboriginal sovereignty of the land under native title was still recognised by the British and certainly had never been conceded to the colonial government. Substantial areas of good land for the use and support of its Indigenous owners *could* have been set aside as had been planned, before it had all been given over to the colonists. But regardless of instructions from London and the December 1836 proclamation of the colony read by Governor Hindmarsh setting out concerns and protections for the local people, the step that would have made a real difference to the better world the colonists thought they were building was never taken.

In designating the land of the colony as legally 'waste' and then opening the new waste lands to purchase by British settlers, the panoply of laws that entered colonial governance from Britain prevented Indigenous peoples from either possessing or obtaining any economic advantage from their own country. Under English law as established through a Supreme Court, any Aboriginal person wanting land had to ask the British governor for it. Had the governor given it, it would be as a grant, not as ownership by right or title deeds. But as was immediately apparent in the years of the governorships of Hindmarsh and Gawler, there was strong opposition to reserving lands for Aboriginal use. During the Queen's Birthday celebration of May 1840, Parroo Paicha known as 'Encounter Bay Bob', a man who had made himself a very useful guide and intermediary to the new regime, did so. Mentioned approvingly for having asked for land to dig, with the Governor saying that he was 'very glad of it', very little came of it.[3] As always, any land granted was never able to support a customary way of life; instead, it was imagined that those receiving it should 'dig', that they should become productive agriculturalists. This was not the intention of the colony's London backers.

They seem to have envisaged a process of colonisation based on the belief that if the land was not exactly empty of people, which they knew it was not, then those people were few and they were 'wanderers', one of those key words that kept cropping up in local newspapers, conversations and sermons whenever the nature of Indigenous society and economy were under discussion. While the colonists would settle on the 'waste lands' of the law and their imagination, sufficient lands reserved for the Indigenous populace to create spaces in which they might live according to their own customs and way of life were never created. The colonial administrators and those seeking to shape a just colony had recognised the need for large areas to be set aside, well supplied with water and game and large enough to allow for the seasonal harvesting and hunting on which people depended. Good country and plentiful. But even the few small reserves put in place were opposed and where granted, were never secure and never sufficient. As late as 1895 when Simpson Newland was suggesting that the long coastal dune system running along the Coorong at the mouth of the River Murray could be made over to the the various groupings of the Ngarrindjeri peoples without much hardship, there was absolutely no support.[4]

In practice, most of the small parcels of 'reserved' lands that came into ephemeral existence were leased to a colonist, its inferior title always subject to being redefined or revoked, never made over to an Indigenous family, and always lying outside the economy of capitalism. It was never intended to be heritable. At best, any reserved lands remained *land* that was only transformed into *property* when a title of ownership transferred it to a colonist. Indeed, most reserved lands were quickly overtaken by the survey and sold to colonists.[5] But more importantly, even where reserved land was cultivated by the sweat of Indigenous brows, their labour never had the magical power referred to by John Locke that converted *land* into the real *property* of the new capitalist economy. When the colonists thought about the future of those being displaced from the land they imagined them as learning to become labourers on land owned by others, a landless labour force. Not only had the transformative power so essential to the creation of property been lost to Aboriginal owners of their own country but at the same time, in becoming a labourer for owners of property, the transformative powers of labouring on land shifted from workers to the owners. Lack of Indigenous interest in working or withdrawal of their labour from the colonial economy was soon to be construed as idleness, laziness, stupidity and the moral corruption likely to lead to theft, pilfering and the pillaging of food stocks. Within the colony a degree of fear circulated.

The consequences of trying to live within the new globalised market economy being rolled out in the colony emerged almost immediately. Not only did the Kaurna people have no access to land or proper wages but early colonial farming practices failed to recognise the difficulties posed for agriculture by the ancient soils of Australia. Early successes were followed quickly by crop failures and loss of soil. Just three years of continuous cropping in the McLaren Vale exhausted what were initially considered as good and productive soils. By the time that sheep and cattle were brought in to stock the new farms and stations (known as ranches in the USA), local food and game supplies around Adelaide had so diminished that there were food shortages. At the same time the grazing habits of sheep and cattle interfered with a great deal of the plant cover and regular regeneration that had kept the country from turning to dust. As early as 1838 some among the Kaurna were looking sick, hungry and poorly nourished, some were selling their tools, weapons and skins to collectors, asking for the money that could be used to buy the food, drink and trinkets that came with the colonists.[6]

Predictably, the efforts of Captain Walter Bromley, first Protector of Aborigines (May 1837–May 1838), both to economise and encourage self-sufficiency by limiting the distribution of government rations to the tasteless oatmeal porridge that was thought to be strengthening but often burnt, led to great resentment. As a result, any meat kept in his own hut was simply taken from him.[7] At about the same time food began to be taken from the huts of other colonists. It was not long before asking for food or money, regarded by the local people as theirs by rights of reciprocity, was construed as begging and regarded as a degrading social nuisance.

Then there were the trees of the parklands so admired by the first shiploads of colonists. With wood being used for building as well as for fuel, one observer noted that while the Kaurna took the branches of the trees for their own huts thus allowing for regeneration, the colonists felled the trunks and grubbed out the roots for fuel so that the parklands around the town were quickly denuded. Sometimes the Kaurna were employed to help them.[8] However, rather than being seen as the inevitable consequence of ending the Kaurna's 'wandering' ways and the colonists' constant need for wood, the blame for the loss of the great trees from the park was sheeted home to the Kaurna. 'They are not only stripping the trees in the same manner,' wrote one angry colonist, 'but are burning down others, and peeling the bark off the finest to make roofs for their temporary huts. If these go on much longer, the lovely spot reserved for the park will be deprived of its greatest ornaments, and we shall look in vain for a shady walk during the summer months.'[9] The parklands given to Adelaide on William Light's township plan remain today, a visual reminder of the way in which colonial administrators were able to make and enforce long-term reservations of land for the pleasure and use of the colonists but were unwilling to reserve significant land for the Kaurna or any other of the owners of the Country on which the colony was being built.

Under these circumstances it was not long before the first purchasers of land about the town were finding that the Aboriginal people living on it could be 'troublesome'. Even with their quick entry into the wood-cutting and wood-selling market and their intermittent use as shepherds, sources of information or as guides, the steady collapse of the Kaurna economy on the plain was making self-sufficiency less and less feasible.[10] Underpinning much colonial thinking about what was best for those being displaced was their belief that the wanderers of their imagination needed to learn how to labour, just as did the respectable poor at home. That there was real labour involved in living within a Kaurna economy was entirely discounted. Their hunting and gathering seemed to happen without effort, without regularity, and with little motivation. The colonists saw freedom as inhering in regular work and indeed, looked on productive work as good, satisfying and blessed. It was the ability to engage in work that had made the men who had become the Protestant middling classes of England. In an argument that would be repeated generation after generation and in place after place, the colonists saw the provision of food that had not been worked for as leading away from self-sufficiency toward the indigence and the dependency they saw as degrading.

Under such conditions, the first close, personalised inter-minglings of the initial moment of colonisation became less and less viable. With such an influx of colonists and the ebbing of major fears, the close contacts that had characterised the earliest days ceased to matter in quite the same way. The uneven reciprocal exchanges between the colonists and Kaurna became truncated as the colonists began to demand labour rather than just accepting friendly help. At the same time the Kaurna and their neighbours quickly appreciated the value of money, the actual cash with which to buy things rather than needing to rely on gifts and goodwill. Once the value of their labour to the colonists was appreciated, the Indigenous peoples living around the town wanted proper recompense. And as more Kaurna, Peramangk from around Mount Barker, Ngarrindjeri from the lakes and Encounter Bay, and people from higher up the Murray River arrived in town, not all the colonists wanted the closeness that living in conjunction with an Indigenous sociality and morality required.[11]

The colonists did not like the way in which Indigenous people were swimming in the Torrens, their main source of water; Kaurna dogs killed fowls and harassed sheep. Attitudes to the nightly dance performances hardened. One early visitor wrote that 'The Corrobbaree was held half a mile from the settlers' houses, as the performers make such a horrid noise that they cannot be tolerated at a less distance'.[12] The same processes were at work among those living around the whaling station at Encounter Bay. As colonists took over the good land and waters there, a man known as Big Solomon did his best to deal with the situation. In a colonial memoir, Simpson Newland described Big Solomon as 'a fine brawny savage, who did his utmost to prove to the whites by argument that they had no rights there.' He remained one of those who 'never took kindly to the whites.'[13] Like him, in Adelaide Mullawirraburka was quite capable of articulating a right to compensation for the absolute loss of their land and did so. But regardless of instructions intended to provide land for the colony's

Indigenous peoples, they got none. What they got instead, at least initially, was Piltawodli, a small patch of land that became known as the Aborigines' Location. It was Interim Protector of Aborigines Bromley who had gathered up those living on lands surrounding the town centre that are now described as the west parklands, crossed the River Torrens and resettled his cheerful flock on fourteen acres just behind the site of the Adelaide Gaol.[14] This was Piltawodli. There he intended to live and teach the skills required to become servants or labourers.[15]

Piltawodli, The 'Aborigines' Location

While it is likely that poor Bromley's success in moving people out of the town centre was a consequence of the fact that he seems to have been leading people from one part of their own Country to another, he was not a success as a Protector. An unsympathetic correspondent to the *Southern Australian* wrote that,

> *The Protector to the Aborigines, instead of being an active, intelligent, and upright man, was an old, decrepit, useless creature, too querulous to have any influence over the natives, too feeble to serve them, and too impotent to excite any thing but emotions of pity from the whites and contempt from the blacks.*[16]

Bromley drowned in the River Torrens in June 1838, to be replaced by William Wyatt who asked again for land to be made available for First Australians and managed to make the Location more habitable. Wyatt set up a schoolhouse and settled in James Cronk as interpreter.[17] With some success in the alphabet and numbers in the schoolroom there was none with Christian evangelisation. Indeed, adults resented attempts to displace their own religious views as well as attempts to intervene in the social practices that Christianity abhorred. And when parents went hunting, trading or visiting, the children went with them, abandoning their lessons without a second thought. In its heyday, there were substantial buildings on the Location forming a busy little settlement. But with difficulties caused for the Kaurna when more unwelcome River people came to town and their children, too, were put into school, the Location drifted until reaching a point early in 1845 that led to all Indigenous children being taught off the Location.

By the time that the first of the missionaries arrived the Kaurna, with no access whatsoever to the fundamentals of good fortune in the new capitalist economy – land and proper wages – were effectively paupers on their own country. But for a short time the presence on Piltawodli of the German missionaries made it a busy little settlement – not a mission or a reserve but nevertheless a place in regular use that the Kaurna could use without restriction.

And so that first moment of close intermingling passed away, ushering in a kind of interlocking separation that would characterise the next phase of the social and economic relations of the colony. Although the local people were never very far away, most were now living just beyond the township. The shift gave them a legitimated place on Country that they regarded as theirs, while their closeness made for a great deal of traffic between the two.[18]

Chapter Nine

Intimations of Unrest

James Ashton, *c.* 1899, *Where reeds and rushes grow*, Art Gallery of South Australia Collection. The reed beds running along the coastal strip from the Pattawilyanga (Patawalonga) at Glenelg to the estuary of the Port River.
Much reduced by this time.

Although the colonists liked to refer to 'our friendly natives' and the 'good Aborigines' who were helping them, relations with the Kaurna land-owners were not always running smoothly. An incident seeming to date from 1837 or 1838 suggests that it did not take long for Kaurna attitudes to the colonists to harden. For it had been then that the young John Adams saw two men coming up into the town from the river looking quite different to any of the Kaurna people he had seen before. Their bodies, he recalled, were covered in fine white down over what was probably red ochre, their heads dressed with feathers. In their hands they carried a 'small dart about 18 inches long', that also had feathers at one end. The two men travelled along Morphett Street, 'light-stepping' Adams called it, 'on tiptoe', looking always at the sky.[1] These men, he learned later, were renowned rainmakers although their progress through the town may have been less benign than it seemed.

Among the Kaurna and those referred to by the colonists as the 'North Men' were ritual specialists who could 'produce thunder, hailstones, rain and so on ...'[2] While usually understood as a method of summoning seasonal rains or breaking a drought, there was another important aspect to the powers of rainmakers – they were specialists who dealt with primordial forces of great and sometimes destructive power. With their carefully anointed and feathered bodies, their decorated feathered 'darts' and their ritualised, ecstatic mode of walking within the town precinct itself, these men may have been intent on a vengeful attempt to call down bad weather upon the colonists as a way of driving them off the land. Later, the missionary George Taplin who worked around the lakes at the mouth of the River Murray, would record just such a use of weather-making, of rain-making as an act of revenge against the colonists.[3]

By 1838 there were other signs of rising dissatisfaction at the way in which peaceful co-existence was working out for the Kaurna. An incident in which a quail-shooter shot and wounded an Aboriginal man, allegedly accidentally, was followed by an attempt to set fire to one of the colonists' huts.[4] Although the reports from Protector Wyatt were generally positive, as time went on the colonists were finding themselves subjected to distinctly unfriendly behaviour and a stream of thefts. By 1837/8 there were, Gara has written, undercurrents of fear and mistrust among the colonists.[5]

At Witonga – The Coastal 'Reed Beds'

As 1838 opened there were a series of incidents at Witonga, the coastal Reed Beds district of colonial Adelaide. Witonga's periodically flooding swamps and lagoons had been intensively used both by the Kaurna and their neighbours. The marshes provided breeding grounds for birds, tortoises, fish and food stocks like the tuberous roots of bullrushes that could be baked.[6] The reeds also provided long straight stems for spears, fibre for the weaving of the elegant baskets and baby carriers used by Kaurna women and the rushes used for roofing the settlers' huts. Draining the marshes in order to plough and fence them had an immediate and inevitable impact on local food supplies. Just as important, the coastal sandhills lying beside the lagoons had been used for burials. As the settlers began digging into the sand and soil large numbers of corpses came to light, their upright positions sometimes interpreted as being buried alive rather than as the consequence of the sanctifying, smoking and drying of the seated body before burial.[7] The desecration of the graves was deeply offensive. It is understandable that resentment should grow among the Kaurna and that resentment could easily lead into dangerous anger.

The colony's surveyor, Colonel William Light, had taken up land near the lagoons and reed beds running parallel to the coast, retreating to it during his last months of life. As the land around the reed beds was being converted to pasture or made over to horticulture and housing, the reeds themselves were being harvested at an unsustainable rate for thatching, destroying the habitat relied on by fish and fowl alike.[8] The Reverend T.Q. Stow's tiny Congregational Chapel on North Terrace, built in 1837, was just one example of the use of 'pines and reeds'.[9] Even Government Hut, the first rather uncomfortable home of Governor Gawler, was built that way – walls of pine cut from the Pine Forest now known as Nailsworth, with a roof thickly thatched with reeds.[10] It would be quite some time before reeds lost their attractions as a roofing material.

By the time that Colonel Light's cottage was set alight he had already lost his first survey office and possessions to fire, was dying of tuberculosis and desperate to provide a home for his partner and devoted nurse, the remarkable Maria Gandy. So his part in the story is a sad one. But the astute Kaurna action against him in attacking the surveyor in charge of converting their country to foreign-owned property shows just how critical the reed beds were to the local economy.

As for Light himself, according to David Elder who drew on Light's diaries, he did not object to Aborigines camping on his property at the Reed Beds but there had been a determined attempt to deprive him of the fruits of his labours – 'they had set grass fires, destroyed his trees, and stolen his vegetables.'[11] 'On Wednesday last a firebrand was thrown in the dry grass immediately to windward for the purpose of setting fire to my house', Light continued, 'There is hardly an hour in the day they are not either lopping down branches, or burning some tree, and it is in vain speaking to them, and at this moment another fire has been kindled under an old tree which I have been obliged to send two men to put out'.[12]

And again: 'Last night', he wrote, 'several garden palings were torn down by them, and a sack of potatoes, the property of Mr Wm Lawes the gardener, stolen. Many of the natives were seen early this morning with potatoes on the end of their spears'. That the stolen potatoes were fixed to the points of spears and brandished at him points to the way in which mockery and incitement were used as a powerful, if misunderstood, challenge to the way in which the rich country around Witonga was being despoiled and ruined.

Light was not the only one to face problems. When Henry Breaker's mother refused food to a Kaurna woman knocking at her door, she was told that her cottage, too, could be burnt down, not such a difficult task when the cottage was built of reeds. The end of December 1839 saw four Kaurna imprisoned for stealing potatoes from Governor Gawler's garden,[13] while Wariato (the first Kaurna woman to be imprisoned) would spend fourteen days at hard labour for taking potatoes from Thomas Payne's garden at the Reed Beds.[14] Four years later, potatoes were still a target. John Adams mentioned how they were stolen from his store by one man lifting potatoes with his feet while another distracted Adams' attention.[15]

These incidents suggest a very different mood from that displayed during the first months of the colony when young Kaurna men had shown Mary Thomas how to light and manage her fire, how to keep the great fires of summer away from her tent, and helped to carry her water up from the creek. The killing of Enoch Pegler shows how the situation was deteriorating.

The Death of Enoch Pegler

Pegler's body was found lying on a path on the northern side of the Torrens River in March of 1838. Pegler was not the first to die at the hands of local people but he was the first of those living so close to Adelaide.[16] According to the newspaper report, the coroner was told that death had been caused by the insertion of a round, sharp-pointed instrument into Pegler's heart causing its immediate collapse. After making inquiries, William Williams (Deputy Store-Keeper General) was able to show the coroner just such instruments, one of wood, the other of kangaroo bone. One of these was said to have killed Pegler. Frederick William Allen gave evidence that a group of about forty Aboriginals had been near the Iron Store at about ten o'clock on the night of the killing, and that they appeared hostile. Some of that hostility was said to be due to the way in which the colonists had killed four Kaurna dogs. Dogs, used for hunting, eating and, in ways that were not always clear to the colonists, were integrated into the spiritual world in which the Kaurna lived.[17] Dogs would prove to be a sensitive issue in the colony, a point around which tensions continue to circulate. Pegler, however, had been drinking while watching a dance performance. Rather than leaving when asked, Pegler had tried to 'insert himself' between a man and a woman but was driven off. When he eventually staggered away, he lay or fell down beside the path, insensible. It was then that 'William' and 'George' were said to have dealt with him once and for all.[18]

Pegler, like many in the colony, had walked north from town to one of the Aboriginal settlements just across the river. He may have gone to watch the dancing or he may have gone in search of sex, but whatever his motivation he had made himself obnoxious and was apparently dreadfully drunk by the time he was asked to move on. At the very least all three elements – entertainment, alcohol and sex – were likely in play. Whatever the reason, in Kaurna eyes Pegler had been an uncivilised, demanding, disturber of the peace.

In a side-effect of Pegler's case, the method of his killing entered into the colonists' understanding of Aboriginal powers. The use of a sharpened stick or bone to penetrate so accurately into the heart as to cause a silent death, and the production in court of what were said to be such tools, cast a new light upon practices of death that the colonists regarded somewhat uneasily as sorcery.[19] It now appeared that the magic and superstitious practices of a supposedly powerless people might have some reality.

*****

For the Kaurna, Pegler's murder might be seen as a symptom of growing resentment about the sexual exploitation of Kaurna women and a growing determination to apply their own Law to the transgressions of the lawless barbarians. Whatever the general or immediate precipitating factors, under Kaurna Law Pegler's killing was entirely justified.

For the colonists, however, Pegler's murder created legal difficulties. Under their own law, all the colony's Indigenous peoples were intended to have the full rights and responsibilities of British subjects. But charging Pegler's alleged murderers under a law of which they were ignorant and bringing them before a jury and court run on principles that they could not understand made punishment unjust and meaningless. The difficulty posed by an action legal under Kaurna Law (always referred to as native *custom* as they were believed not to have laws) but illegal under British law was resolved in this case by resorting to the fiction that the names of the murderers were not known, even though evidence of their names had been given by 'Onkaparinga Jack' – the highly respected Mullawirraburka who was first to be appointed as a Native Tracker.[20] As the local newspaper reported it: 'The Coroner briefly addressed the Jury, who having retired, returned the following verdict – That the deceased, Enoch Pegler, has been wilfully murdered by a native or natives unknown.'[21] With no further action required, the difficulties of applying English law equally to all and the fears raised by the killing were laid safely to rest.

Chapter Ten

The Coming of Colonial Law

In a colony founded explicitly on the careful planning necessary to create a better world it is unsurprising to find that the mother country's rule of law should be installed from its inception. South Australia was one of the few colonies that from its first day was equipped with a Supreme Court and an English judge appointed to it. The judge arrived in April 1837. Based upon an amalgamation of the practices of a number of English courts, the legal structures established through this first Supreme Court relied not just upon a judge and jury in Adelaide but required a network of support from Justices of the Peace (sometimes referred to as magistrates), police and Coroners.[1] In cases distant from Adelaide, a local Justice of the Peace could assume simultaneously the role of Coroner. The powers exercised through these men could be extensive particularly when operating far from town. The autonomy and powers of remote Justices of the Peace bedevilled justice in South Australia just as they did in the other colonies, particularly when they were also pastoralists, miners or members of the police. Although sometimes modified to meet local conditions, in essence the laws exercised in the colony were based on the common law and statutes of England with the highest court of appeal, the Privy Council, located in London. The colonists' commitment to complete separation of church and state ensured that the powers of England's ecclesiastical courts to control marriage were absent, an absence that caused some difficulty for those wishing to sanctify their unions.

As far as the colonists were concerned, the rule of law arrived with them. It was understood as applying right across the colony regardless of whether its lands were known or unknown. In practice, its enforcement followed roughly the limits of the land survey that was required before land could be taken up in an orderly manner – unruly squatting and claiming was to be prevented if the land was to be properly sold. Beyond the surveyed districts the early governments had little chance of enforcing the law and little interest in spending scarce funds on it. It did not mean that the lands beyond the survey were without British, colonial, law. The law was for the whole colony and all were to be equal before it.

The First Judge Arrives

The first Chief Justice appointed to South Australia's Supreme Court arrived in Adelaide in April 1837. Sir John Jeffcott was an Irish Protestant with colonial experience in West Africa plus first-hand experience of English courts of law from having been charged with a murder he had committed during a duel. Jeffcott's opening address to his first court provides some insight into how the coming of English law was to be regarded as a wonderful benefit as well as the foundation of an orderly society. He referred to the great privileges it offered, particularly 'the palladium [safeguard] of English liberty, trial by jury. This valuable institution', he said, 'trial by the grand and petit jury – will from this day – the first on which a court is held in this province – be in operation, and I again congratulate you on it'. With a grand jury beside him, he eventually turned disapprovingly to the seven malefactors delivered from the gaol for trial on that day, 13 May 1837. 'I am sorry to perceive', he said,

> that the list of prisoners is much more numerous than I had expected, and the offences of a graver character than I had anticipated in this early stage of the Colony. It is, however, satisfactory to know, that the prisoner who is charged with the most serious offence in the calendar – I mean the individual charged with Burglary, is not one

of our Colonists, but an importation from Van Diemen's Land. Two others are in the same situation, being Sailors charged with a riot and rescue (i.e. 'rescuing' men taken up by the police) – so that, out of the seven prisoners for trial, only four, or little more than half the number are of the class of the immigrant population, and the offences with which they are charged, are of a comparatively light complexion.[2]

Quoting from Jeffcott's address, the local press waxed lyrical – the court's proceedings were seen as able, in every respect, to 'challenge a comparison with those of a similar class in the mother country'... with the judge commending the gentlemen of the colony for their zeal at assembling so early in the morning.

On that first day, Jeffcott took advantage of a case in which two colonists were charged with theft from an Aboriginal hut to address his audience on the universal reach of the law.

I perceive that two white men, settlers of the labouring class, are charged with the offence of stealing a jacket, and some of their warlike implements (spears and waddies) from some of the aboriginal inhabitants of this Province, and that this theft, petty in its amount, but of great importance when viewed with reference to its consequences was committed in a hut, which these poor natives had constructed for themselves at the Town of Glenelg, in imitation of our huts, being the first which had been constructed by them, a circumstance in itself one of congratulation, as their first step towards civilisation – for you are aware, Gentlemen, that in their savage state they have no fixed habitations, and will have to look to us for instruction in all the arts of civilised life, towards which, this has been their first interesting though feeble essay.[3]

The point the judge stressed at some length was that the coming of the law brought with it a promise that all under its mantle were equal. Its coming, the judge believed, offered the Indigenous members of the new society a new dawn. Jeffcott stated very firmly:

They have been declared British Subjects – As such they are entitled to the full protection of British law, and that protection, while I have the honour of filling the situation which His Majesty has been pleased to confer upon me, shall be fully and effectually afforded them. I will go further, and say, that any aggression upon the Natives, or any infringement on their rights, shall be visited by greater severity of punishment than would be in similar offences committed upon white men. With reference, Gentlemen, to the case which has called forth these observations, I am informed by the Advocate General, that the evidence has not, as yet, been brought into such a form (the persons who are alleged to have committed the offence having only just been apprehended,) as would justify him in preferring a bill before you at this moment. Should the additional evidence which he expects, be available before the close of the Session, a bill will be sent up to you. ... By this means, the ends of justice will be rather advanced, than retarded ... and should the evidence which is expected, lead to the conviction of the accused, it will be my duty to see that they do not escape the punishment which they so justly will have deserved.[4]

In considering the legal ramifications of the jacket's theft it seems unlikely that its nameless owner would have had any real sense of the ponderous steps being taken through the court, particularly as the charge against the perpetrators of the theft appear to have been dismissed for want of evidence.[5] As a first example of the benefits of British law for all, the theft was not perhaps the best but it was an attempt to demonstrate the impartiality of the new law, to advance the claim that it was there to protect Kaurna land ('property') as well as that of the colonists.

While many British lawyers liked to think of their laws as superior to all others, in the early nineteenth century its practices and punishments were harsh: floggings were common for women as well as men, sentences were long, hard labour was very hard indeed for both women and men, and many crimes carried the death penalty. The early colonial courts and punishments retained much of the exemplary public spectacle of earlier centuries. Trials, judgements and punishments were often matters of high drama utilising the arcane latinised language of lawyers, rituals of homage to the judge, with methods of truth-divining and truth-telling having much in common with those of earlier centuries. They were the rituals that helped to establish a judge as one whose special knowledge and powers descended directly from the monarch, who in turn had derived them from God. In 1838 the shift away from public punishments was yet to come and it was some time before hangings and floggings were carried out inside the prison, out of sight rather than in public. The first colonists liked justice to be well and truly 'seen to be done' as it was in the case of Michael Magee, hanged in May 1838 for attempting to shoot the colony's Sherriff. Magee's shot had only grazed the Sherriff's ear, a fact that did not save him from the ultimate penalty.[6]

The First Hanging, 2 May 1838 – Michael Magee

When the day of Magee's hanging arrived in Adelaide, 'nearly the whole population of the colony was on the move by an early hour'.[7] It was the spectacle that attracted them, the spectacle of sure and certain punishment so highly valued in law as a deterrent. The mythical 'Jack Ketch' was an essential part of it. In life, Ketch had been such an incompetent seventeenth century executioner that his name had lingered on within popular mythologies of execution. He became such a terrifying character in the public theatre of death that all executioners were given his name. The horror of Jack Ketch's presence at the gallows tree was accentuated by his blackened or masked face, and the padding of his body to produce the grotesque shape that helped disguise him within his baggy, waving robes.

The condemned man, too, had a well-defined if unavoidable role in the drama of his death being performed that day. Bound, he was taken across to the gallows in a cart in which he was made to stand with a noose around his neck, the assembled crowd following his rough progress along the track toward death. At the gallows stood a priest holding the Bible, whose duty was to the condemned man's soul until finally, at the scaffold, 'Jack Ketch' emerged and tried to do his duty. Failing miserably, he ran away from the scene of protest produced by the swinging, groaning body of Michael Magee until, chased and captured, he was brought back by the police to try to finish his work.[8] It all took some time.

Magee was unfortunate in that he was a Catholic from Ireland where opposition to British rule was causing considerable trouble. Even worse, he was believed or assumed to have been a convict. These two characteristics singled him out from other miscreants as well as from respectable Protestant society. They reinforced the essential Protestant nature and goodness of the good colony as well as the inherent criminality believed to be embedded in the Catholic Irish.

The Murderers of Two Shepherds Come Before the Law

While the agitation around the Witonga Reed Beds that saw Colonel Light constantly harassed was related to the rapid rate of the colonial incursion into the marshes, and while Enoch Pegler's murder, most likely due to his unwanted attentions to a Kaurna woman, the killing of William Duffield and James Thompson in May of 1839 reflected the increasing pasturing of sheep and cattle on country just beyond Adelaide town's limits. There was a spreading anger circulating not only among the Kaurna but also among their neighbours – those whose country was also threatened by the survey as it was rolled out north and south. The Wirra men who killed the shepherds William Duffield and James Thompson in May of 1839, a year or so after Pegler's murder, faced a very different court and a hardening public opinion. Rather than having their crime ignored by a polite legal fiction, as in Pegler's murder, the colonists were now fearful.

Out one day shepherding sheep on farms established on the upper Torrens River just six miles (c. 9.5 km) from Adelaide, William Duffield and James Thompson were killed by people said to be Wirra men. The method used to kill Duffield was the same as that used to deal with Pegler, this time as described by the victim on his deathbed: a long sliver of bone had been inserted upwards under his ribs while two men held him down.⁹ In order to capture the guilty parties, the government decided to withhold the distribution of the rations that depleted local food stocks had made necessary. Until the culprits were handed over all colonists were instructed to co-operate with the government's decree by refusing both food and employment to all Aborigines. The move from individual to collective punishment, illegal under civil law, created great resentment among its targets and such controversy among the colonists that the instruction had to be rescinded.¹⁰

Eventually three men were charged with murder – George, Peter and Williamy.¹¹ They were sent to trial before a crowd of 'eager spectators'.¹² George, whose real name was Bakkabarti Yarraitya was convicted of killing Duffield while another of the men, named as Wang Nucha, more properly Parutiya Wangutya, was convicted for the killing of James Thompson. These two men were hanged in public as a warning to others. The newspaper reporter claimed that the men were utterly terrified at their fate and protested against it, 'exhibiting none of that stern determination which despises to show a fear of death – a characteristic of the natives of some countries.'¹³

One of the differences between the killings of Pegler and the two shepherds arose in part from the fact that the shepherds were not ex-convicts or Catholic Irish but employees of an established landowner. Shepherds were particularly vulnerable to attack as, in the absence of fences, they followed their flocks, working alone or in pairs on largely uncleared lands. The targeting of the shepherds by Bakkabarti Yarraitya and Parutiya Wangutya was a direct response to the impact of colonisation. The murders also signalled to the 'practical men' among the colonists that there could be trouble ahead. As fear rippled around Adelaide, swift and exemplary punishment to demonstrate the powers of the new regime seemed a sensible approach. And so, they were tried under British law, found guilty and hanged.

Consequences

As the death penalty was carried out, the settlement at nearby Piltawodli, the Aborigines' Location, was filled with lamentations that continued for many days. Clamor Schürmann witnessed the hangings, an event that, he told George Fife Angas, had 'passed without further disastrous consequences.'[14] Nevertheless, consequences there were and they trickled on into 1840.

After the exodus from the Piltawodli Aborigines Location as the bodies of the dead were carried home for their funeral rites, Indigenous life in town appeared to return to a form of calm but it was superficial. Word of the colonists and the hangings seems to have spread. Toward the end of the year a large group of hostile 'East' men arrived with grievances that were freely expressed. As they walked aggressively through Klemzig, the German village of Lutheran refugees established just outside Adelaide, they threatened the colonists with their spears and made themselves obnoxious. Among a later group of newcomers was a man who had taken the name 'Captain Mitchell'. He was one among a number of drovers from New South Wales who worked under British overseers. To the locals, he was known as the man who had stolen the wife of a 'North' man and killed her husband. More importantly, he was believed to have once killed a white man. While in Adelaide 'Captain Mitchell' is said to have speared another, Hugh Burns, the captain of the *Giraffe*; he later gave himself up, was released after four days and then disappeared. Clearly a man not to be meddled with, his challenging assumed name and his claim to have killed a European add up to an expression of real power as well as real anger.

When the southern aurora turned the night sky swirling pink in February 1840 it was taken as a bad sign. 'The natives of all three tribes were most disturbed', said Schürmann, as they believed it to be a harbinger of a plague [named as *koko*] which would destroy them all.'[15] Whether the *koko* plague stood for syphilis, a new wave of smallpox, or as a metaphor for the colonial presence is not clear. Kaurna statements about the earth tremor that followed not long after were more direct. It had been caused by 'a black man living far to the North who had dived into the earth', they said. The tremor was the sound of the earth itself, calling for graves, for the blood of revenge.[16] There were reports, too, of Kaurna threats to poison the waters of the River Torrens on which all depended, as well as tales of colonists being murdered with the killers escaping by transforming themselves into she-oak trees. These and similar stories circulating around the town show an Indigenous world in fundamental disarray in which the earth itself is angered, its powers being called upon to help return it to stability. They provide an indication of the fear and anger around Adelaide in the aftermath of the hangings and a realisation perhaps of the scale of the disaster that had befallen them. Other methods were more direct.

From 1839 and into 1840 the hostile use of fire as an effective weapon of war increased. To the immediate north, attacks on property around Modbury (c. 15 km from town) and then Lyndoch (c. 45 km north of Adelaide) built up. Police records show that by 1840 a station just east of Lyndoch was attacked by fire. Mr Beames, the hut-keeper there, found himself 'surrounded by natives who set the grass on fire, by which the tents were burnt, a cask of gunpowder exploded, and the hutkeeper was severely injured. In addition, the whole herd of cattle was dispersed and 30 of their number [were at the time] still missing.'[17] There were damaging fires in other parts of the district and further out with all, rightly or wrongly, attributed to Aboriginal incendiarism. In all, the fires of the summer of 1840 amounted to a determined effort to discourage colonial settlement.

This was just the kind of response that George Fife Angas had wanted to avoid. It was precisely why he had put so much effort into ensuring an early missionary presence. Two Lutheran missionaries had arrived with Governor Gawler at the end of 1838. Despite its focus on equality, South Australia's leading legal historian, Alex Castles, described colonial law as it was from 1837 to 1850 as 'very much a hit and miss affair'. Governor Gawler was to test it to its limits.

Part Two

Governor Gawler Arrives

Chapter Eleven

Governor Gawler's Time in the Colony Begins

When, on a fine Friday in October of 1838, the *Pestonjee Bomanjee* sailed into Holdfast Bay with the colony's second Governor on board the colonists were glad. About five hundred people went to Holdfast Bay to greet him. As his party travelled from the coast up to Adelaide some of the more energetic ran beside his horse, cheering him along.[1] The divided administrative powers of the first colonial government that had pitted the first Governor, Sir John Hindmarsh, against the Commissioner of the South Australia Company in such a way as to create the unseemly factions, jockeyings for advantage, complaints, vitriol and fisticuffs that had led to Hindmarsh's recall, were now to be administratively united in the person of Colonel George Gawler (1795–1869). As a professional soldier, Gawler could be expected to sort out the difficulties in bringing the colony's land under survey more rapidly than Hindmarsh had managed to do, and thus its rapid sale and improvement. He could be relied on, too, to get the faltering economic underpinnings of the colony working again although in due course his unconventional financial methods would lead to his removal too.

Equally important, Gawler was a godly man. His reading of William Paley's influential book, *View of the Evidences of Christianity* (1794), had led to his desire to become a true Christian, a desire that dramatically changed his life. An anti-slavery campaigner and heterodox Anglican, Paley had led a revival movement based on the idea that the proofs of religion could be seen in the wonders of the natural world, a world that could only have been created by design, by a creative intelligence. The transformed Gawler 'was soon noted for his piety and works of active evangelism within and beyond his regiment'. In 1820 he married Maria Cox, 'a lady as religious as himself.'[2] The governor wanted, Maria Gawler wrote to her sister, to make South Australia 'a Bible colony' and she was certainly the one to help him.[3]

Governor Gawler came of military stock, descended from men who had fought in Britain's colonial service over several generations. In Adelaide the class tensions then developing in Britain as industrialisation gathered steam were also visible. They were reflected in official concern with making sure that their status as representatives of the British Crown was maintained and visible to all. With the unseemly ructions of the Hindmarsh years only just behind them, the Gawlers set out to give the governership some dignity and to ensure that colonial manners should not become too relaxed. On arrival they found that the first 'government house' was but a small slab hut of elementary construction. Mary MacLeod, wife of James, was one of the party accompanying the Gawlers out to Adelaide. She recorded how she 'was invited to pitch a tent beside it [the governor's hut] and teach piano and painting to the Gawlers' children'. Construction of a more solid residence began almost at once so that the Gawlers could live and entertain as their status suggested they should. The first official reception for some hundred of the 'better' colonists illustrates the separate spheres of colonial women and men's lives taken directly from the practices of English society. It was conducted in full English dress along entirely formal lines. In Mrs Gawler's 'drawing room' reception for the women, she was attended by a maid-of-honour with a lord-in-waiting to announce the guests by name; the men attended the Governor's separate *levée*.[4] Visiting cards were required for entry. When a mercifully cool Christmas day arrived, the Gawlers dined in style on roast beef and plum pudding as, in one version or another, South Australians were to do for many years to come.[5]

Maria Gawler is sometimes thought of as rather too concerned with the niceties of social distinctions and rather too anxious to evangelise, yet her piety, her evangelism and her concern for those they referred to as 'heathens' give some insight into how the great political currents of her time appeared on the outskirts of the emerging British empire. She shared the imperial fascination with the natural history of the new worlds they were making, she insisted on joining her husband on an ill-fated journey of exploration to the River Murray, and she put considerable effort into collecting curiosities and preparing bird skins for her mother and friends in England. The explorer, Edward Eyre, sent skins to her from his Moorundie outpost on the River Murray while other specimens came in from those living around the outskirts of the town. One gets a glimpse of her temperament in a letter to her mother after the birth of one of her children: 'I have now beloved Mother six darlings by God's grace to train for heaven and six I doubt not are safely folded in the arms of their Saviour.'[6] Such trust in the enveloping personal presence of her God was found in many of the colonists. It is not so surprising to find her translating concern for the Kaurna into efforts to get clothing for them (they were already forbidden to enter the settlement while unclad), to establish a school, to provide employment and of course, to help them to learn how to keep themselves clean. So in addition to policies aimed at rectifying the colony's parlous economy, one of the first things the Gawlers did was to introduce themselves and their entourage with a feast for the Kaurna.

*****

Just two weeks after Gawler's arrival, officials, colonists and the vice-regal party met and socialised with the Indigenous peoples living around the town. Martha Berkeley painted a finely detailed watercolour of the event (mentioned briefly in chapter 6) that Clamor Schürmann described in his diary:

> On the first of November was a festival for the natives such as they have never had before in their entire history. His Excellency the Governor provided a lunch for them consisting of roast beef, rice, biscuits, and tea. For such festivity, suitable finery was required, which was supplied to most adults. Many of the women received a woollen blanket, and of the men, 15 to 20 were strikingly dressed.

As a head covering, all wore a blue soldier cap with white edging. Instead of jackets, half of them wore red, the other half blue, sailor shirts. The latter had a yellow apron strip of calico around their body and a violet-coloured sash around the shoulder, while the red-shirted ones had violet aprons and a yellow sash. Among them were two outstanding, clever personalities, King John and Captain Jack. Their very colourful red shoulders were further decorated with a bunch of variously coloured ribbons, and likewise the right sides of their chests. On the right arm, each had three strokes like a caricatured sergeant. The outfits gave them the appearance of warriors, and each carried his winda (spear), his waddi (club), and his wommera in his hands.

At one o'clock the procession moved toward the appointed place, where a considerable number of Adelaiders awaited them. Mr Wyatt, their Protector, led the procession. The uniformed men marched two by two, the others, including women and children, walked in a casual manner. Arriving in front of Government House, on a signal from Mr Wyatt, everyone swing their caps and shouted 'Hurrah!'. Some distance away stood His Excellency in full regalia, catching everyone's eye. As the Blacks became aware of the colourful gathering, they were startled and halted, until Mr Wyatt convinced them there was no reason to be frightened, and persuaded them to march on. Arriving in front of His Excellency, they halted and again cried 'Hurrah!'. The Whites formed a great circle around them, and the Governor made a speech, which was interpreted by Mr Wyatt.

After shouting once more, they settled down in a semi-circle to their meal. Nearby a target had been erected for them to show their skills with their spears after the meal. Such a joyous day had to finish on an appropriate note, and this was achieved by their performing war dances. The English call these dances corroborees.[7]

Mary Hindmarsh's unfinished sketch of the day shows some of the guests wearing the red shirts handed out to them. She shows, too, a little monkey chained to a log that Tracey Lock-Weir identifies as probably belonging to George Milner Stephen, the then Colonial Secretary who eventually became a popular faith healer.[8]

Such was the success of this first gathering that it became an annual event timed to celebrate Queen Victoria's birthday each May, drawing in people from a number of the neighbouring regions. In recalling the 1850s and '60s, one colonist noted how people from the lower reaches of the Murray River travelled up from their Country to Adelaide via the tiny township of Clarendon. There, beside the Onkaparinga River and before travelling the final twenty-five kilometres into town, they staged a grand corroboree at which King Rodney, his wife, Queen Charlotte and daughter Princess Amelia (Ivaritj) were all present.[9] By then, colonial attitudes seem to have become rather sceptical. The *Register* reported that

> *a vast concourse of holiday-makers attended at the Location grounds [in Adelaide], to see the annual distribution of bread, beef and blankets, to those dingy denizens of the forest, who chose to own allegiance to the Queen [Victoria] and devotion to a 'tuck out', by paying on her birth-day a visit to the representative, and accepting from her bounty a two-pound loaf and a piece of beef ...*[10]

By the 1850s, attitudes were hardening to the degree that Edward Snell would write in his diary:

> *A grand carnival among the blacks to day, a lot of bread, beef bones and blankets given away by the governor [by then Sir Henry Young]. Went into town to see them and precious set they were and dressed in the most ridiculous manner possible, some had their hair and faces painted red, one fellow had a sort of pig tail made of the feathers of some bird, one or two had gaudy red and yellow handkerchiefs wrapped round their bodies, some had nothing but a dirty shirt, and others blankets and kangaroo rugs, one ugly looking customer was buttoned up to the chin in a black dress coat, black trowsers and a silver watchguard round his neck. There was a display of*

fireworks at the government house in the evening and the blacks had a corrobory at the [South Australian] Company's mill ...[11]

The intricately worked head-dress Snell described as, 'a sort of pig tail made of the feathers of some bird', can be seen in William Cawthorne's picture of an Aboriginal family in which the parents are looking away from the painter as the children play. This quiet family scene in which the painter seems relatively distanced from those he is painting is very different from the great oil paintings of the settlements around Adelaide made in 1850 by Alexander Schramm. In Schramm's picture the Kaurna are arranged in camp so as all are visible to the eye of the beholder, allowing the eye to move right into the lives of the people being portrayed. Schramm's painting is right in the viewer's face while Cawthorne's is distanced, much less intrusive. While both painters have provided later generations with valuable images of Aboriginal lives during the earliest years of colonisation, the differences between them reflect not just differences in the skill of

Aboriginal Family, undated, by William Anderson Cawthorne.
People of the Adelaide region. Cawthorne describes the feathered head-dress of the man in several accounts of the dances he saw.
Courtesy Mitchell Library, State Library of NSW

the artists and the medium they use, but differences in the impact of colonial government on Aboriginal lives together with the increasingly watchful attitudes of the colonists.

Inevitably, Gawler's consideration for Indigenous interests, shown in suggesting the use of Kaurna place names rather than their British replacements for example, earned him a good deal of criticism: '... his paternal benevolence towards the Aboriginals', they thought, prevented 'efforts to discipline them for their own good into habits of prudence and hard work.'[12] During his governorship the contradictions on which 'the Bible colony' was being built became all too visible. But like so many others, this was never a lawless colony but, as has already been shown, one in which right from the start the laws of the mother-country were installed with considerable pride.

Chapter Twelve

The Massacre of the Survivors of the Wreck of the *Maria* 1840

Things were changing in 1840. Until then each attack on life and property around Adelaide had been understood as a singular event, as exceptions to the peaceable relations that the colonists were quick to reassert as the normal condition. The 1840s are also the years that historians mark out as coming closer to a stage of colonisation that, when considered through the lens of frontier warfare, is understood as a short-lived transitional phase leaving peace in its wake. The news that the survivors of the shipwrecked *Maria* appeared to have been killed reached Adelaide in July of 1840, causing great consternation. Usually referred to as the *Maria* massacre, this largest single killing of colonists in Australia created fear and horror in the other colonies as well as around Adelaide. It was particularly unsettling because the passengers of an earlier wreck, that of the schooner *Fanny* in 1838, had been kindly treated and helped to safety.[1] Now there were rumours of ten or fifteen dead, including women and children.

The Finding of the Bodies
First news of the killings emerged from information provided by a Ngarrindjeri/Kaurna man known as 'Encounter Bay Bob' whose real name Schürmann gives as Tammuruwe Nankanere, son of Tungaranwe.[2] News had come to him from two visiting Milmenrura or

'Big Murray' men (generally considered as a grouping within the larger Ngarrindjeri/Ramindjeri people) that perhaps ten men, five women and some children had been killed somewhere along the Coorong at a place two or three day's walk south of the mouth of the Murray River.[3] Through Tammuruwe the rumours had reached Police Sergeant Macfarlane at Encounter Bay and Dr Richard Penney, surgeon to the Rosetta whaling fishery. They were told that there were definitely no survivors.

Tammuruwe's information led to an immediate search-party setting out. As guides and interpreters the searchers took with them Tammuruwe himself (Encounter Bay Bob), Bob's brother Caldecotte, known as One-arm Charley, and Wira Maldira (a man named as Encounter Bay Peter) who knew the country at the far end of the Coorong and also understood the language of people referred to as the Milmenrura. Although Simpson Newland described 'One-Arm Charley' as a tall, morose, and fierce man, a haughty warrior who always concealed the remains of the arm mauled by a shark when he was a boy, all three men served as reliable and necessary guides to those searching for the dead.[4] These men were crucial to the success and safety of the search party, the more so as the Milmenrura dislike of the colonists and their herds had given them an early reputation for ferocity.

The search party's access to a long spit of land bordered on one side by the sea and on the other by the lake known as the Kurangk-Coorong, was complicated by the shoals and treacherous tides at the mouth of the River Murray. As the drowning of Judge Jeffcott and his companions in 1837 had shown all too clearly, the sea mouth of the River Murray was exceptionally dangerous. Had they been able to move from Encounter Bay through the Murray mouth directly to the lake they would have had an easy route to the Kurank-Coorong. Rather than face the dangers of entering the lake system through the Murray's sea mouth, a boat and equipment had to be carried overland to Goolwa, a tiny settlement on the south western bank of Lake Victoria (now Lake Alexandrina), the inner side of the Murray's mouth.

SEX AND SAVAGERY IN THE GOOD COLONY

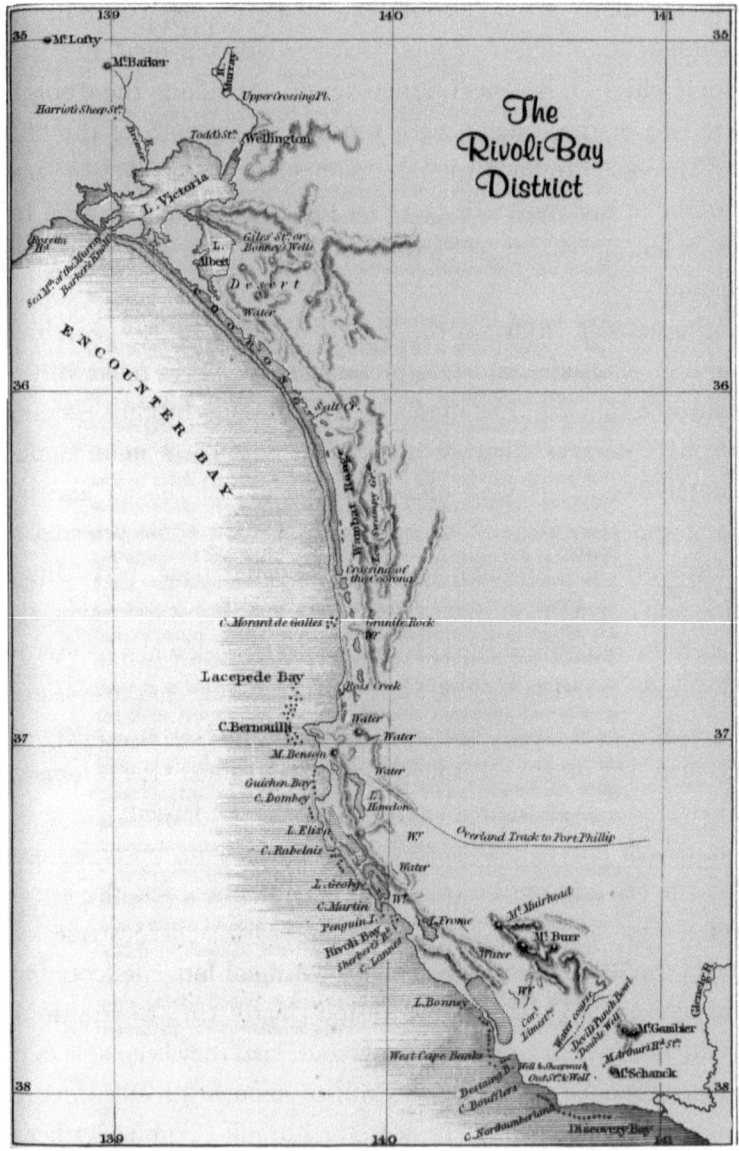

Map of the Rivoli Bay District. From: Francis Dutton 1846/1978, *South Australia and its Mines, With an Historical Sketch of the Colony Under its Several Administrations, to the Period of Captain Grey's Departure*, London: T. and W. Boone. Facsimile edition, National Library of Australia, facing page 94.[5] This map gives a clear picture of the lakes around the River Murray at its dangerous mouth and the narrow strip of water running parallel to the coastal sandhills.

THE MASSACRE OF THE SURVIVORS OF THE WRECK OF THE MARIA 1840

From Goolwa a small boat could travel, as W.J.S. Pullen and his party did, through the channel around Hindmarsh Island, past the shifting shoals and shallows surrounding the small islands of the lake and so on into the long spit of water shown on the map as the Coorong, more properly, *Kurangk*. Once into the waters of *Kurangk* the searchers had to rely on the information that had come to Tammuruwe Nankanere (Encounter Bay Bob) from Milmenrura men and on the ability of the guides to speak the language of the people they came across so as to avoid hostilities.

When found, the bodies of the dead were reported as dismembered, badly bashed and in one case, reduced to a skeleton.[6] The blood-stained clothing of many of the bodies had been removed. Later the search party would see people wearing clothes taken from the dead, while other possessions of the dead were found in some of the Milmenrura huts. Edward Frome's sketch of the huts shows how substantial they were. Frome also shows the great size of the sandhills separating sea from lakes that made the search so difficult for horses and anyone not knowing the country, especially when locating the inconspicuous sources of fresh water that remain there still.

Edward C. Frome, 'Native village on the Coorong deserted by the Milmenna tribe after the murder of the crew of the *Maria*, burnt by me Oct. [18]40. Watercolour on paper. Frome was Surveyor-General of South Australia. Courtesy Art Gallery of South Australia.

Captain Pullen's report described the finding of the bodies:

> ... *the sight I witnessed was truly horrible. There were legs, arms, and parts of bodies partially covered with sand, strewed in all directions, and in one place was a body with the flesh completely off the bones, with the exception of the feet and ankles* ...[7]

For the colonists, these were frightening reports indeed, the more so as their perceptions of their own role in the founding of the colony were so deeply embedded within beliefs about the peacefulness of settlement and 'our friendly natives' on whom, despite the killings of Duffield and Thompson and despite the fires of summer, they had come to rely. It became clear that although the *Maria* had been wrecked, all on board had reached shore safely and with local guides were attempting to walk north toward Adelaide. Then they had been killed. Suddenly the colonists were faced with descriptions of groups of people who were far from friendly, together with graphic images of what might be expected if anyone should fall into their hands. Here was a very definite suggestion that the colonists might face real resistance. The searchers could do little more than bury the bodies, return to town and report to Governor Gawler.

In his introduction to Pullen's published report on the finding of the bodies, Governor Gawler noted that

> ... the tribe of natives by which the murder described by Mr Pullen appears to have been committed, is not connected with the tribes with which the colonists are in familiar intercourse. From the first discovery of the Province, this tribe inhabiting to the south-eastward of the Goolwa and the sea mouth of the Murray, has been little known, and when known has been remarkable for its ferocity.[8]

This was the report, publicly circulated, that formed the background to public discussions of what was to be done and of Governor Gawler's widely criticised decision that nothing but exemplary punishment, illegal under British law, would suffice.[9] The Milmenrura were to be considered as living outside the area of settlement and thus as aliens who were *beyond the protections* of colonial law.

Retribution – Major O'Halloran's Punitive Expedition

The members of the party of mounted police sent to deal with the Milmenrura were commanded by Governor Gawler's newly appointed Commissioner of Police, Major Thomas Shuldam O'Halloran, with Inspector Alexander Tolmer as second-in-command.

Like Gawler himself, both were professional military men by training, and able to use military tactics against the Milmenrura. Both went on to have established careers in Adelaide but at this time, the twenty-five year old Tolmer had been in the colony for just five months, O'Halloran for seventeen.[10] With them as they searched again for the bodies of the dead and for those who had killed them were Captain Nixon piloting the cutter, the crew of the boats, Captain Pullen who had first discovered the bodies and Mr Bonney, possibly Charles Bonney who had arrived in Adelaide with cattle driven overland from Victoria, passing inland from the Kurangk and around the Murray's lakes.[11] Wira Maldira (Encounter Bay Peter) was there as guide and interpreter.

Eventually they caught sight of a group of Milmenrura running away from them. Setting out in pursuit, O'Halloran described the capture of this large group:

> ... we rode hard upwards of two miles before we neared them, when they took to the high sand-hills that are in many places covered with thick scrub. I, however, threw skirmishers out from the coast to the lake, and we thus kept those steadily in sight whom we first saw; and the result was, that by evening, and after very great fatigue and exertion, from the hilly, scrubby, and sandy nature of the country, we contrived, without injury to any, to capture thirteen men, two lads, and about fifty women and children.[12]

Those who fled into the lake were also captured. In all, a search of these people and their numerous huts revealed quantities of clothing and objects clearly belonging to the dead. It is difficult to understand quite how sixty-five prisoners could be taken unless they had somehow been persuaded to stop running or had been herded into some kind of locality from which there was no hope of escape. They were, O'Halloran reported, 'carefully secured and guarded during the night, but the women and children I liberated; the latter, however, remained near the men till the evening of the next day.'

Next morning the search for further culprits began. There was an attempt to catch 'a number of ferocious characters with European clothing on and who were chiefly the murderers, according to the statement of the captured natives'.[13] Two men were chased into the lake, shot at *for the first and only time*, wounded, who nevertheless managed to escape. More women were captured, more relics of the dead discovered. O'Halloran fired the huts containing clothing of the dead.[14]

According to O'Halloran's report, his captives were now alarmed. They pointed to one among them, a man O'Halloran named as Moorcangua, as responsible for earlier killings in the district and told him also that one of the *Maria* murderers could be found across the lake. Two unnamed captives accompanied Charles Bonney and Encounter Bay Peter to the camp of these people in an attempt to deceive the man, named by O'Halloran as Mangarawata, into accompanying them back to O'Halloran's camp. In this they succeeded. O'Halloran described the man lured into his camp as having 'the most ferocious and demon like countenance I ever beheld'. He now had two culprits, one of whom was connected to an earlier crime rather than the killing of the *Maria* people, but neither of whom, he said, denied their guilt. After a summary trial and 'the unanimous declaration of all the gentlemen around me, as well as of the Encounter Bay blacks,' the two men were declared guilty and hanged, an act that left in its wake a sustained hatred and distrust of colonial police.

The crowd of captives who had been forced to witness the executions were then set free. Those watching were told not to touch the bodies but to let them hang until they rotted. Which they did, most likely because their terrible deaths had thoroughly defiled the locality. Their bodies are those that Edward Frome sketched when he was in the area six or seven weeks later, mapping the land around Lake Alexandrina.

*****

The pitiful figures hanging over a shallow ditch are named as Moorcangua and Mangarawata, two of the four men who fell victim in 1840 to the first official punitive action against the Indigenous peoples of the colony. Neither men were guilty. The names of two of the actual murderers are said to have been Pallarynaka and Poreilpeepol. One of the Indigenous men accompanying O'Halloran's party was the Ngarrindjeri man referred to in the report as Encounter Bay Peter. It was he who duped Mangarawata into coming into O'Halloran's camp. Within the clash of conflicting political allegiances that grew out of differing assessments of where a viable future lay, the complexities of the political and trade arrangements operating among the Milmenrura and their Ngarrindjeri neighbours, and the attempts of individuals to build fruitful or protective alliances with the British – Encounter Bay Peter's readiness to deliver someone as a Milmenrura murderer into the hands of the English makes a good deal of sense.

Frome made two other pictures of his visit to this sad place. One shows the burning of a 'look-out' that he came across in the sandhills and set fire to; the other is of a small settlement nestled into the shelter of the Kurangk's great hills of sand that he also fired.

As Frome rarely painted Aboriginal people, his record of the punishment meted out to the Milmenrura and his own fiery contributions to it might justifiably be seen as an indication of the impact of this very significant event.[15] His personal acts of revenge, taken in the absence of anyone who might have been involved or who might have challenged him, give an idea of the level of fear and uncertainty gripping the colonists as well as of the government's determination to do whatever was necessary to stamp out any retaliation from those who had lost their Country and were losing their livelihoods.

It had fallen to Gawler to determine the form that a response to the killings should take. His controversial decision to authorise a punitive expedition rather than a search, capture and trial in a court of law shows how limited the borders of the zone or reach of British law could be, and it illustrates how uncertain its protections and justice would become. It was a clear demonstration that when tested, the new law and Judge Jeffcott's doctrine of equality did not apply equally at all. Gawler had reached his decision under considerable pressure from land-holders and many of the public. He consulted his Council, he considered Emmerich de Vattel's influential *Law of Nations* (1760), he discussed matters of citizenship and its limits, and he took advice from Judge Cooper who seems to have favoured Blackstone's view that prior law remains in place until challenged or conquered.[16] In this line of argument, Milmenrura law was still in place because their Country had not yet been settled. That legal fact meant that the Milmenrura could be defined as *aliens* who were, by such a definition, outside the reach of the protections of British law. Instead, they were people with whom the colonial government could go to war.[17] This, Gawler had done. Based on such legal reasoning and information available to him, Gawler opted for exemplary punishment rather than investigation, capture and trial by jury.

Questions about the legitimacy and morality of Gawler's decision were framed in terms that by 1840 had already emerged around other killings and other crimes involving First Nations Peoples. Framed as a debate between unrealistic 'philanthropists' who lived safely in town and 'practical men' who had hard work to do and a colony to govern, the unblinkered realists considered that the best way forward was to give a forceful demonstration of the powers of the new regime. In a memorandum to his governing Council after the hangings of Moorcangua and Mangarawata, and after reading the signed reports of those involved, Gawler responded to his critics by saying:

> *I consider it my duty to have no share in that unhealthy sentiment, by some persons miscalled philanthropy, which, under the apprehension of exercising cruelty, would allow impunity to wanton crimes. Whenever such are committed, whether as in the present case by the blacks against the white population, or, as in future cases that may occur within the limits of the Province, by Europeans against the Aborigines, I will most certainly, as long as I have the honor to be at the head of this Government, use every exertion in my power to bring such wanton offenders to formal and condign [ie fitting or deserved] punishment.*[18]

Nevertheless, with Gawler acting on a war footing but without a declaration of martial law, the rule of law underpinning a superior civilisation had faltered at its first major test.[19]

Frome's small drawings of the men hanging and the burning Milmenrura settlements in the sandhills are a reminder of how important it was to the colonists to have visual images of their superiority, their ability to pillage with impunity, and to possess an aestheticised picture of the theatrical violence of the new order. Frome's pictures gave him a personal record of the subordinate place of the Indigenous peoples within the new world he was helping to build, as well as an image of his own heroics. But they can also be thought of as a way of recording an image of an extra-legal collective punishment in a form the colonists found safe and satisfying. Frome has pictured the terror that the more 'practical' of the colonists sought to instil in the Milmenrura mind. At the same time he offers an image of colonial control that he, as the leading surveyor of the colony, was just then intimately involved in rolling out over the country of the Kaurna, Ngarrindjeri, Ramindjeri, Milmenrura and those living near them.

Frome's pictures remained in his notebook, not circulated until many years later. But there is another image of the punitive expedition at work that also offers some insight into the ways in which the colonists were thinking about the lives they were fashioning within the colony and the land they were living upon.[20] Although the hangings were carried out at a time when a great many educated people learned to draw and to use water-colours, no amateur painter is known to have accompanied the punitive expedition. The oil painting, *Major O'Halloran's expedition to the Coorong, August 1840* by an unknown artist is more likely to have been worked up in Adelaide from descriptions of the events it describes rather than being an eyewitness's account. Nevertheless, its composition and imagery offers a glimpse of the thinking of the painter and the times.

Unknown artist, *Major O'Halloran's expedition to the Coorong, August 1840*, Artist's name given as U for unknown. Could George Hamilton have been the artist? Courtesy Art Gallery of South Australia.

The artist has left no doubt as to the moral righteousness of the expedition – the colonists ride the white horses, their Aboriginal guides and interpreters the brown and black ones. Behind the police party walks the crowd of captured women, children and some spear-carrying men – so many more of them than there are police. Their huts nestle under the trees while in the distance there appear to be men running away, up the steep side of the sandhill. The artist shows the two boats authorised by Gawler to support the land searchers, while in the foreground stands a mortuary platform of the kind used by people living around Encounter Bay and the lakes.

The mortuary platform appears in the picture as an ethnographic detail that gives veracity to the scene while emphasising the barbarity of the people who used it, their utter difference from the Christianised civilisation of the colonists. This is a detail that should not be overlooked. The centrality and significance of the ritual handling of the body of the dead in Christian narratives of the crucified Jesus (of his being taken away to be washed, anointed, shrouded and carefully laid to rest in a mausoleum or cave) shows how burial practices can become highly significant markers of cultural boundaries. It is the Christian context that gives the defiling of the bodies of Moorcangua and Mangarawata shown in Frome's sketch its disciplinary significance in the eyes of the colonists. To the British, the hanged men were alien outcasts, more so even than criminals tried and hanged in Adelaide, whose bodies were not left to rot on the scaffold but buried, usually within the prison precinct rather than in consecrated ground to be sure, but buried nevertheless. It is unlikely, I think, that the unknown painter of Major O'Halloran's punitive expedition at work was using the Ngarrindjeri burial platform to indicate the refusal of the proper obsequies to the dead; more likely that it was intended as a more general marker of the strangeness of Ngarrindjeri cultural practices. But that should not prevent reflection on how the hangings might have appeared to those watching at the time. For those Ngarrindjeri living around the lakes and along the Kurangk, the barbarity of the mode of death – execution by a method formerly unknown to them – might well have been as confronting as the desecration of leaving unprocessed human men to rot on the end of a rope, a nineteenth-century image familiar from the lynchings in America as well as from the scaffolds erected at cross-roads in England from which the criminal dead were left to rot.

It certainly deprived the two men of the attentions proper to the dead that Milmenrura and Ngarrindjeri burial rites demanded. Their bodies would never be carefully smoked and dried, never lie upon the platform prepared for them, their spirits released, their bones painted with ochre, cared for by kin. If one would speculate about how this manifestation of British power appeared to the Milmenrura and the Lake peoples, about how they saw this early ripple of colonial terror slowly spreading across their Country and what lesson they might have taken from it, it was more likely to have confirmed the barbarity and unpredictability of these harbingers of the new order rather than to demonstrate their superiority. But as an act of power and terror, it was exemplary and widely approved. The colony's Advocate-General, the Scottish lawyer William Smillie, was clear enough: 'Aborigines would be subjected to "measures summary and severe ... adopted to terrify the whole tribe by a sense of our power and determination to punish".'[21]

Chapter Thirteen

The First Missionaries – The Dresden Lutherans

As with the laws of England, Christian missionaries came early to South Australia, an essential part of George Fife Angas's plan to make his colony a place of peace rather than conflict. In the 1830s Christian missions to colonised outposts of empire generally focused on the spiritual needs of the colonisers. Concern for the Christianisation of colonised peoples, however, came in the wake of Britain's emancipation of slaves and from the knowledge that colonisation generally could, and did, lead to great harm to those subjected to it. By the time that South Australia was created colonisation's ill-effects – the violence, political corruption, depravity, drunkenness and sexual licentiousness found in colonies like New South Wales – were widely known. This was what George Fife Angas wished to avoid. As early as 1835 he had already formed his view that missionaries needed to learn the local language so that Indigenous peoples could read the Christian gospels in their own tongue (as Protestants did) as well as to receive the new knowledge brought by colonists – how to raise crops, build huts, wear clothes and for the young, to learn to work as labourers.[1]

Having had trouble in recruiting trained missionaries in England, Angas had been delighted with the discovery of the Dresden Lutherans, the more so as there were also other German religious refugees interested in settling in the colony who would arrive at about the same time. All four of South Australia's first missionaries – Christian Gottlieb Teichelmann, Clamor Wilhelm Schürmann,

Heinrich August Eduard Meyer and Samuel Gottlieb Klose – were Dresden trained and good linguists.

The Evangelical Lutheran Mission Society of Dresden offered its students a curriculum covering pastoral skills, Lutheran theology, Greek, Hebrew and other languages (Schürmann, for example, learned Chinese).[2] Most importantly, the Dresden emphasis included the practical trade skills required by those settling in a colony. And like George Fife Angas, they carried a strongly Protestant belief in the formative moral value of honest labour. Schürmann, Teichelmann, Meyer and Klose knew this perfectly well. Their task was therefore a dual one: to teach the skills of labour as well as those of Bible literacy.

Teichelmann and Schürmann had the good fortune to sail out to the colony on the *Pestonjee Bomanjee* with Governor Gawler. With theological interests in common, the two Dresden missionaries managed to convince Gawler of two contentious answers to two very contemporary questions: were the Aboriginal peoples of Australia fully human, and was Kaurna a real language? These questions circulated in the colony for many years.[3] They were matters of great interest for they bore upon what, if anything, could or should be done for Australia's First Nations peoples. Based on their reading of the Bible, however, the Lutheran missionaries had already reached a conclusion on both issues: as God's children, Aboriginal Australians were indeed fully human and they could certainly be raised up out of what were seen as their degrading customs and erroneous beliefs. And as for their language, the Kaurna spoke a language that, like all others, was 'not the product of human art, but the gift of God'. As such, it was on a par with all other of God's languages; it was not to be destroyed and was perfectly suited to evangelising. Only if they understood Kaurna, these first missionaries believed, would they be able to teach the reading and writing that would open up their pupils' hearts to the Bible's message, as well teaching them the skills required by the new world they had to live in, those of domestic service, farming and building. Through speaking to the Kaurna in their own language they believed that with rational discussion and evangelisation, true conversion might take place. Once ashore, therefore, Teichelmann and Schürmann's first priority was to learn Kaurna.

The missionaries had been instructed also to take an interest in the social lives of the Kaurna (and any other peoples they might meet) in order to provide sound information relating to current discussions at home in Germany.[4] Among the questions being discussed was why some societies, like those in Australia, had not moved away from what they referred to as 'superstitions' toward a true religion like Christianity; they took it for granted that technological advances, monotheistic religion and a morally good society progressed together; and they believed that the societies that they saw in Australia and similar countries were living examples of human society as it was when first it came into being in a distant past. Stone tools were important in this imagery as they were imagined as being a technology of people living close to the animals from which humans had evolved. They were societies that had been left behind in the past. While their descriptions of the people they worked among were intended to encourage the fundraising efforts of their home congregations, the fundamental purpose of the Dresden interest in gathering sound information of Aboriginal life and customs was driven always by the hope of religious conversion. Teichelmann, Schürmann, Myer, and Klose, as well as those from the other denominations who followed them, wanted to know how best to woo Aboriginal Australians away from lives they regarded as the epitome of sinfulness.

Schürmann's first hope was to find out whether the Kaurna had a supreme god of some kind, one that could be directly assimilated into Christian monotheism. Quite early he found a Kaurna name that he felt could be used as roughly equivalent to Jehova, *Munaintyerlo*, but the fit was not good and it had to be abandoned.[5] Teichelmann had expected to find the Kaurna worshipping idols – that decisive Protestant marker of Catholicism as heathenism – and was astonished to find that they had none. They seized, too, on the Kaurna practice of circumcision as a point of similarity, to point out that like them, Jesus had been a circumcised man even if modern Lutherans were not. One difficulty here was that the point was lost on the neighbouring Ngarrindjeri at Encounter Bay who did not practice circumcision, a difference causing the Kaurna some mirth. Increasing anti-Semitism in Europe, however, meant that the links between Aboriginal religious practices and those of European Jews would remain an issue in the colony for many years among both German and English evangelisers.

Although those first Lutheran missionaries were educated in an era in which radical secularism and politics prospered in parallel with the religious revivals that men like Paley, Gawler and George Fife Angas exemplify, they adhered to ideas about the malleability of human nature that had descended from the Enlightenment philosophy of John Locke. More than many who came later they were less likely to see people of differing cultures or races as enduringly different, but they did think of them as inferior. Like Locke, the German missionaries also believed strongly in the power of teaching to fill and shape the human mind, as well as in the universal rightness of the Protestant beliefs and customs they sought to instil into it. Indeed, Locke's notion that the human mind at birth was an 'empty cabinet' that needed to be filled by knowledge and moral values acquired throughout life, was alive and well in secular attitudes to education as well as in beliefs about the opportunity for moral reform found among the colonists and missionaries in South Australia.

The missionaries were fortunate that senior Kaurna men living intermittently on the Piltawodli Location were prepared to help them. One man, referred to by Schürmann in his diaries as Munnitya Wattewattipinna, emerged as a major teacher, mentor and facilitator. Mullawirraburka, Ityamaiitpinna and the traditionalist Minno Gadnaitya Kadlitpinna – painted in full dress by George French Angas a few years later – were also there; later they were helped by Tilti Midlaitya whose name they translated as 'Native Cherry' followed by the sequential name of his place in the family, fifth child.[6] Teichelmann eventually formed the view that the first success in attracting the Kaurna to settle on Piltawodli, the Aborigines' Location, rested upon their sense of entitlement – that they liked the idea that they were to receive some form of compensation for the loss of their Country and livelihoods.[7] And it is likely that the chosen Piltawadli site was one linked in with their customary kin and religious networks.

Schürmann's diaries give a vivid picture of daily Kaurna visits and his efforts to learn the language. It was at Piltawodli that in the light of the full moon, they first saw the *Kuri* danced. At Piltawodli they were taught Kaurna, there that the Kaurna provided some of the labour of daily life; there, too, that they persuaded some visiting boys to wash their faces with soap for the first time and in what must have been a mighty effort, it was there that Teichelmann managed to comb the hair (usually worn greased, ochred and with mudlocks) of one their young visitors.[8] In this small attempt at introducing new forms of grooming and hygiene, the major project of re-shaping the Kaurna body that would shortly need to be covered with clothing in order to enter the town, got under way.

Evangelisation and the Time 'Before'

It is easy to understand the fascination of these early missionaries with the culture they aimed to supersede. They felt they were looking at themselves as they might have been before time began its inexorable march through history, progress and into the present, while the customs and supposed moral failings of the Kaurna verified the evangelical sense of moral superiority as well as confirming the righteousness of their actions. They were perfectly aware of the moral failings to be found among their fellow colonists, but they also had a strong sense of the way in which, in industrial British cities like Manchester and London, the progress of civilisation could bring moral degradation in its wake.

Although Adelaide was without the convicts and military governments of Sydney, there was nevertheless plenty of evidence of the drunkenness and disorder found in the eastern colonies. The loose behaviour Schürmann and Teichelmann deplored among the colonists – the brothels, sexual licentiousness, drunkenness, gambling and the fighting that Judge Jeffcott also so deplored – could not but have an effect upon Kaurna life, as did the provision of government rations, the gradual adopting of clothing, the steel axes, and the glass flakes used for ritual incisions. Despite arriving so soon after the initial settlement, in the missionaries' eyes Kaurna life was no longer pristine. Schürmann, particularly, was desperate to see how life had been lived before it was contaminated by progress and industrialisation, the time before the Kaurna became known to civilisation.

It was not until September of 1839 that Schürmann's wish to travel across the countryside with local people was finally granted. Invited by two young men, Tuitpurro (whom Schürmann called 'brother') and Kudnaipiti, he and Teichelmann joined a group of thirty or forty people, among whom was the greatly respected Tidlaitpinna. They were setting out with their dogs to hunt for kangaroos. 'I have the desire', Schürmann wrote, 'to observe the life of the natives in their natural state, convinced that I would get a better insight into their nature and that it would provide a good opportunity to learn their language.'[9] It was their 'nature' that was at stake here: once it was known it could be addressed, moulded and changed for the better.

On this first excursion Schürmann was able to see how a kangaroo was killed and roasted with hot stones in an earth oven, how a sausage was made from its blood and roasted, how the animal was seasoned with leaves from a small gum tree, and how the cooked animal was jointed with portions of the meat being taken back to the camp for the women, children and the men who had not taken part in the hunt. He also noticed how the huts were built to face away from any wind and learned how to reinforce his own to make it more effective; and indeed, he improved his understanding and fluency of Kaurna. In his diary he wrote that he enjoyed what he called the gracefulness and decency of his Kaurna hosts and that his five days spent with them gave him cause to hope that their spiritual awakening had begun.

Although Schürmann called Tuitpurro 'brother', not surprisingly, the social conventions underpinning the lives he was observing and sharing were still opaque. While he observed the way in which those in camp were provided with meat by the hunters, he was not aware of the kin and marriage responsibilities that determined how the sharing was done, which portions of meat had to be given to whom and, looking at it from the other side, who received which portion from whom. He could not know why his numerous attempts to have some share of the kangaroo's tail were refused, always politely deferred until 'later'. He does not record who received the tail, nor by whom the tail was given, although the distributions of meat were surely socially determined – that is to say that the distribution was based on entitlement, not personal generosity or whim. They were not gifts in the English sense of the word but an example of the way in which food and other items were distributed so that all might share.

Schürmann took food with him when he set out with his Kaurna patrons, and although willing to share the very popular hard ship's biscuit that he carried, he ran short. He was relying, really, on being provisioned by his hosts. At this stage at least, the scale and nature of proper exchange relations were unknown to him. Ignorance of the proper way of entering into exchanges could not do other than help to shape Kaurna impressions of Schürmann and Teichelmann as persons and it is indeed an illustration of grace as well as of politics that their social deficiencies were overlooked and their status grew to be positive. He records that a young man, Nanto Kartammera, who was 'sometimes wild and obstinate', agreed to share Schürmann's house although it seems unlikely that he would have become as useful around the house as Schürmann was hoping.[10]

Learning To Labour, Learning To Be Like 'Us'

The changes in the lives of the Indigenous peoples sought by missionaries and Governor Gawler alike can be seen in the speeches addressed to them on the occasions at which the Governor provided food, clothing and blankets to those living around the new town of Adelaide. Gawler's three exhortations all took the same form: become good white men by living as they do. It takes the nineteen months between the 1838 and 1840 exhortations before the moral values and individual behaviours (infanticide, wife beating and drunkenness) enter into the public address. But the addresses provide a picture of the scale of the total transformation of body, custom and society required by the government and missionaries alike. Fighting between 'tribes' and within them are of course mentioned from the first, as is the need to build huts, to work, clothe the body, and love God. No more wandering about and don't fight back if injured.

The 1838 Address

Black men – We wish to make you happy. But you cannot be happy unless you imitate good white men. Build huts, wear clothes, work and be useful. Above all things you cannot be happy unless you love God who made heaven and earth and men and all things. Love white men. Love other tribes of black men. Do not quarrel together. Tell other tribes to love white men, and to build good huts and wear clothes. Learn to speak English. If any white man injure you, tell the Protector and he will do you justice.[11]

The 1839 Address

This time, events began with a salute and fireworks from the ships anchored in Holdfast Bay. A short account of the May 1839 exhortation appeared in a Sydney newspaper:

They gathered between Government House and the Torrens. A speech was interpreted by the Protector. The Governor 'assured the aborigines of the friendly disposition of the white men towards them, exhorting them to adopt the habits of civlised life, to work, to build huts, to wear clothes, to live like the white men, and be their brothers'.[12]

On this occasion each person present was given a 'bright pewter plate, having a device of the Queen [Victoria], and the letters of the alphabet inscribed on it', plus blankets and clothing. The aim was to restore peaceable relations after the unpleasant events (among other events, the hangings) of that year. In the 1940 address, the moral force of colonisation and the discipline being applied as the government tries to encourage a sedentary way of life is brought to bear more explicitly:

> *Black men – These which you have just heard, are the Commandments of Jehova who made the sun, and the earth, white men, black men, and every thing – you must obey them always with all your hearts.*
>
> *You must not steal. You must not quarrel and fight and kill each other. You must not kill your children. You must love your wives and be kind to them.*
>
> *You must love Jesus Christ the Son of God with all your hearts. He sees you every where – he is always with you – he is able to save you from every thing bad and to give you every thing good. You must not be drunkards – getting drunk will soon make you ill and kill you. Besides which – you must live in houses, as King John, Captain Jack, Tommy, and others are doing. If you will try to build houses, white men will help you. Encounter Bay Bob wants some ground to dig – I am very glad of it – I will give it him, and some to any of you who will dig it.*
>
> *You must do what Mr Moorhouse [Protector of Aborigines] and Mr Teichelmann and Mr Schürmann tell you, they love you and wish to make you happy, and white men and black men will be brothers together.*[13]

Once this speech had been translated into Kaurna and repeated by Schürmann the Indigenous guests gave three cheers, perhaps because the incomprehensible speeches were over, and proceeded to their dinner.

The clarity of the reform intentions is very striking. Here we see missionary and government speaking with one voice. Live and be like 'white men'. The need to live in a monogamous Christian family in which women are not to be treated badly and all children are to live under the guidance of the husband, is also clear. Equally striking is the absence of mention of property ownership from the earlier addresses until, in 1840, it appears within an uncontested colonial project as within the Governor's gift.

And finally, it was apparent to the colonists by then that the Kaurna had clung to the notion that they were living on Country that belonged to them, that they despised labouring for others and found it demeaning. Each Kaurna person was responsible for him- or herself; each was independent. Those men known by the missionaries were very helpful at times but the regular daily and seasonal labour required to establish a self-supporting mission was regarded with contempt. None of which was helped when, despite promises, the government refused to provide seed for land prepared for sowing under mission supervision.[14]

Conversions and Consequences

In those first few years the Dresden missionaries made no converts to Christianity; nor could they ameliorate the effects of colonisation. With their knowledge of Indigenous languages they often found themselves as unwilling observers of punitive actions against the people they wished to convert, found themselves caught up too as interpreters in the courts, witnessing both the brutality of settlers and the often gross lack of justice meted out by police and the courts. Despite their intentions, their experiences in Adelaide, Encounter Bay, and later around Port Lincoln challenged not their faith but their belief in the value of a self-supporting mission project under such circumstances. They came to see that the fundamental fact of colonisation – the total loss of land and the dispossession of a people – had consequences that could not be easily ameliorated. Nevertheless, their efforts to evangelise, their learning, and their relations with the people they worked among had consequences for the Kaurna.

Very early on a kind of rough consensus emerged between the main players. Missionaries, the colony's philanthropists, and government officials all came to agree that the only hope of introducing the Kaurna and others to the structures and practices of the new society lay with the children. It was absolutely clear that up to a point parents were happy that their children should learn to speak and read English and to be housed and fed. But as soon as children needed to learn their own

Law and customs and to pass through the educational stages of their own society, as soon as their parents needed to travel to hunt, trade or to participate in ceremonies, the children would be removed from school, re-joining the way of life that the colonists and the missionaries saw as mired in sin. This point of view transformed Indigenous parents into a social problem in need of fixing. Separating their children from them appeared as a straight-forward solution.

It was also apparent that, with so many of the Kaurna and their visitors living beside the colonists, the less welcome customs of the colonists were causing trouble. Disease, alcohol and hunger were causing problems among the Kaurna. The solution to those problems was formulated in terms of a need to separate the Indigenous peoples from the intemperate or criminal colonists by establishing mission settlements completely separated from the evil opportunities of the town.

And finally, while the need to educate remained paramount, government officials, particularly Governor Grey who succeeded Gawler, rejected the idea of educating people in their own language. Both believed that learning to read and write in a language so soon to be superseded was wasteful and would cause problems later. Their solution was to insist that schooling for the children should be in English from the start.

These three solutions to the problems created by colonisation – removal of children from their families, separate settlements for Indigenous people, and the education of children in English rather than in the languages spoken within their families – were to remain fundamental to the thinking of governments and churches with only the German missions retaining an interest in language and translation. But the missionaries were not the only people interested in taking up Aboriginal children and removing them from their families. Motivations varied but Aboriginal children were vulnerable because they carried with them colonial hopes for the new future – they were not part of the past as were their parents but living on the borders of the present and thus of the new future. They were easy to kidnap or lure away, with the added advantage that they could be useful. Pastoralists sometimes took some, droving parties took some, sometimes children were wanted as servants, sometimes for sex and sometimes as pets. Most commonly, such children were described as being saved or rescued.

Chapter Fourteen

Eyre's Children

Taking children from their families as the explorer Edward Eyre did is a practice deriving directly from the era of slavery. From the time of Britain's first empire, the enslavement of Africans and others began to be justified by claims that white skins were a sign of inborn superiority. So from the years of Britain's first empire, racism and slavery developed hand in hand, attaching easily to the monotheism of Christianity to form the concepts of whiteness and Christianity that shaped the political and social beliefs of many of South Australia's early colonists. Although the British had abolished the slave trade and later, the use of slave labour in their West Indian colonies, the great demand for the products of slave labour and the accompanying doctrines of free trade ensured that slavery continued to flourish across the globe. It remained the basis of the economies of the American colonies, even those like Texas where all the cowboys are remembered and portrayed as white-skinned, never as enslaved Africans. In the world the colonists left behind and in the world that they would have to trade into, slavery was not hidden, was still the subject of violent argument and would continue to form the motor of an expanding capitalism in Australia as elsewhere. By 1834 when the *Slavery Abolition Act* passed through the English parliament, however, the dark skin-colour of the slave was serving to distinguish them from the 'free' labour force of Britain. The 'free-born Englishmen' whose labour conditions were often so appalling that it was cheaper to hire them than to have to house and feed slaves, had come to be considered first and foremost as 'white'. This reflected a distinct shift from earlier perceptions of skin colour that had been in place until the sixteenth century when Europeans described themselves and others as having differently tinted 'complexions'. The tints recognised had ranged from black to white with the middle ground, olive-coloured or red or even greenish being seen as best.[1]

Slavery was a practice with which the colonists were perfectly familiar. As mentioned in Chapter 3, George Fife Angas had owned 121 slaves whom he freed when government compensation became available to him. The nineteenth century saw a whitening of a British populace that was far from uniformly pale, but instead reflected the consequences of the large numbers of dark-skinned people who had lived and worked there for centuries.[2] Charles Darwin, for example, learned his skill in taxidermy from 'a negro living in Edinburgh'. His teacher, John Edmonstone, was a freed slave who had belonged to Darwin's uncle. The emphasis on *free* labour was one aspect of this whitening at work and very important to the founders in establishing South Australia as a colony of freedom as well as of peacefulness. The assumed whiteness of that free labour force accounts in part for the pervasive horror attached to rumours of 'white slavers'. The concept of a *white* slave cut right across the hierarchy of skin colours used to define concepts of race in which white, British, men stood as the only truly 'free men' in a world they ruled. They were the free men of *Rule Britannia* who would never be slaves. Even with slavery abolished by the British it remained an active force in the global capitalist economy coming into being during the nineteenth century. And of course, following abolition the money paid to British slave-owners in compensation for the loss of their human assets flowed into the colony of South Australia just as it did elsewhere. George Fife Angas was only one of the beneficiaries of compensation for loss of slaves, as were other well-known people among those who planned and came to the colony – Raikes Currie, Jacob Montefiore, Anthony Musgrave, Edward Stirling, Augusta Sophia Young and others.[3]

The English arriving in South Australia in 1836–37 had never known a world in which their economy was not underpinned by the labour of slaves. Their own economy benefitted enormously from the vast trading profits that flowed into Britain through trafficking in human beings through slave markets, and the plantations built and staffed by them. So by 1836 slavery had not gone far away but was close and well-known. Aboriginal children in South Australia were being kidnapped, stolen, sold, handed on, or given away as presents just as earlier, slave children had been in Europe.[4] And when in 1966–67 Australian pastoralists were finally obliged by law to pay real wages to their Aboriginal workers, a good many of them preferred not to employ them at all. It is just that the comforting belief that there was never any slavery in Australia has meant that the traffic in children, the refusal of wages for adults and the removal of civil rights according to skin colour were not regarded as practices of slavery. Because child stealing has become such a continuing and destructive element of the policies and practices through which successive governments have sought to improve the lives of Indigenous Australians, it is important to look back at it and try to see how it came about, why aspects of it endure, and why from the colony's beginning it had an immediate veneer of goodness. Edward Eyre, later a governor of colonial Jamaica, did not think of the children he travelled with as slaves.

*****

At least seven children travelled with Eyre at some time or other: Wylie, Cootachah (also known as Yarry), Neramberein, Joshuing, Unmallie, Kour and Warrulan. Eyre took Kour and Warrulan, son of Tenberry of Moorundie on the Murray River, back to England with him at the end of 1844 'to be educated'.[5] In his published book about his time in Australia, Eyre also mentions an un-named small boy living with him, with his father's permission, in March of 1843 at Moorundie.[6] Whether this was Warrulan or another child is not clear.

Edward Eyre is one of South Australia's most admired explorers, subject of biographies and the author of widely read accounts of his life. If South Australian children know little of their colonial past, they are more likely to know of Eyre than anyone. His *Autobiographical Narrative*, written in 1859, includes an account of the first two of the children he took in when he was just twenty-two years old. Camped on the Goulburn River in June 1837 Eyre had met up with Yaldwyn's drovers who were travelling with 'two little black boys' who were about eight years old at the time.[7] 'The children had come', he wrote,

> *with some man from the Murray, had remained at Mr Yalbone's [Yaldwyn's] when he crossed the Goulburn [river]. The overseer did not know what to do with them so I at once attached them to my own party. Both, said Eyre, were perfectly naked and seemed very hardy as well as full of life and spirits. They were allowed to occupy a corner of the tent at night but if it did not rain preferred always sleeping by the fires, turning first one side to get warm, then the other. They soon got reconciled to their new master and were made very happy in such garments as we were able to supply them with. Young as they were, too, we found them very active and useful, especially in tracking lost animals, though they did not like going out in the cold mornings when the frost was on the grass.*[8]

One of the boys was called Cootachah but the name of the second child remains lost in the intricacies of Eyre's cramped script. The editor of the manuscript suggested that the name might be Joshuing. Rather than leave the child nameless, most writers have settled on that until his real name can be recovered. When Eyre left the Goulburn River for Melbourne both boys went with him.[9] In Eyre's eyes, he had adopted them. Today's concept of adoption, implying the taking of a child into a family as a member of it, masks the real nature of the relationship being established, one in which a child's new father is also their 'new master'.

When Eyre took the boys to Van Diemen's Land (now Tasmania), in both Launceston and Hobart Town the novelty of their presence in his party came close to receiving the sort of attention given to the 'wild savages' who so fascinated English and American fairground crowds. Roslyn Poignant's detailed description and scholarly analysis of the way in which, later in the nineteenth century, Robert Cunningham was able to abduct adults and young people from northern Queensland for display in carnivals and exhibitions in America and Europe shows how popular exhibited humans could be and equally, how easily people could be taken from their country to be used as merchandise far from home.[10] Cunningham exhibited his stolen people as 'wild', as real 'savages' and perhaps inevitably as 'cannibals'. As Eyre would note, by the time of his own arrival in Van Diemen's Land there were no wild dogs, nor were there Aborigines, all of whom, he believed, had been systematically slaughtered into extinction.[11] In this he was not correct, but nevertheless, the arrival of wild dogs from Australia along with two young examples of a people thought to have somehow just become 'extinct' in Tasmania meant that Eyre and the boys made quite an impression. From Launceston, Eyre and the boys went by coach to Hobart Town where they again attracted much public attention as they visited the theatre with him and then the parade ground to see the troops perform their drill exercises.

From Hobart the three of them embarked for Sydney where they stayed with Eyre as preparations were being made for his overland journey to Adelaide. When, on 21 December 1837, Eyre left Sydney to try again to find a droving route through to Adelaide three Indigenous boys went with him, Cootacha, 'Joshuing', and Unmallie, a young man from near Gundaroo where Eyre had once owned land.

Amazingly, when Eyre and his herds reached the Murray River, among the large number of Aborigines living there were the parents of the two young boys still in Eyre's care.

> *The father of one of them especially shewed a great deal of feeling and tenderness. The tribe encamped around us for the night and when the next day we crossed the river and moved on for a mile or two they still followed and again encamped with us. It was only natural that they should, but I did not quite like it and I was moreover, afraid of losing the two boys. By being very civil to the parents and making them sundry little presents they were however inclined to acquiesce in the children remaining with us.*[12]

Eyre's own account of what took place is puzzling because of the way in which each explanation of his actions seems clear but is not. On closer reading the whole passage begins to carry an aura of subterfuge, or perhaps reinvention or just faulty recollection. Eyre seems to have bought off the anxious parents, for example, saying that the parents were willing to part with their children for a consideration, that they were bartering their children away. Given the age of the children, the joy of their return and the great strength of family feeling demonstrated by the parents and kin, such an interpretation seems implausible. Then, in a passage written long after the event, Eyre said he was afraid of 'losing the children', still aged only eight or so, to their rightful families, families who wanted them back. Why *was* it that Eyre was so keen to keep the children with him? [13] Of the feelings of the children he had nothing to say.

One might have expected that the educated son of an English vicar who aspired to be a gentleman, one able to trace a family line back to the Norman conquest, a young man then of twenty-two who was reared in a world in which the Christian concept of family formed the foundation of middle class concepts of society, one who proclaimed firmly his belief in the power of kindness to win alien hearts and who condemned the use of violence against Indigenous Australians – such a one, surely, would have leapt at the opportunity to perform such a wonderful and unexpected act of restoration?

The editor of Eyre's *Autobiographical Narrative*, Jill Waterhouse, responded to Eyre's account of the boys' life with him in this way: 'Eyre was genuinely and even selfishly fond of the boys, allowing them to sleep in his tent if they wished and keeping them with him, even when it was possible to return them to their affectionate parents. Apart from the amusement of their youthful company and their value as trackers and interpreters in the bush, Eyre liked having Aborigines about him when he returned to civilisation.'[14] But why? Were they a kind of trophy that demonstrated his personal success in dealing with Aboriginal people, of the value of using kindness rather than force? And why were they always children rather than young men with greater strength and skills?

In the phrasing Eyre used to describe how the children came into his care, as in 'so I at once attached them to my own party', he is deliberately trying to distance himself from the more commonly used colonial phrase of 'picking up' Indigenous children, a widespread practice that carried less benign associations.[15] The motives given for the stealing of Aboriginal children vary – sometimes the child was said to have been rescued in the aftermath of fighting, for example; sometimes a child was just 'found' alone in the bush (a very frightening scenario to the colonists, but sometimes less so to Indigenous children), while at other times the child was rescued from the evils of living with their parents in conditions thought of as squalid or immoral. Sometimes the children were seen as bright with potential for civilisation if only they could be taught and brought to the Bible; other times they were required for work, their age making them more amenable and less able to abscond (especially when they were taken far from their own country), while sometimes they were required for sex, with girls sometimes dressed as boys in order to deflect comment.

So there are still a number of questions. Why was Eyre taking children into his life; why did he refuse to return the children to their families on the river; even if the parents were willing to barter or sell their children, how did Eyre feel about buying them; and what is the best way to describe the 'picking up' of these children and 'adopting' them? There are answers to be found but to see them more clearly we have to look first to the customary practices of European slave owners that were the antecedents to the 'picking up' of Aboriginal children in Australia to see what they are. And then, in the next chapter, we will need to consider the British *cult of the hero* and its concepts of masculinity.

*****

Eyre's taking up of Aboriginal children to some extent replicates the older European practice in which the very wealthy took a male child slave into the household, dressed them in finery, played with them, allowed them a certain degree of social license (cheekiness, joking, sweetmeats) and had them in attendance as small pages at social gatherings. They were a marker of status and wealth. And even though they were often boys, often the young domestic slaves were associated with women. They appear in portraits as the attendants of such people, as in Van Dyk's portrait of Henrietta of Lorraine (c. 1634–35). The artist shows the slave page, his status marked by a golden chain wound around his shoulder and under his arm.[16] The value and status of such a slave attendant is shown by the way in which one would be added to a painting where no real child existed. Painters of the seventeenth and eighteenth centuries also pictured young slave pages with their masters, some of the paintings offering at least a suggestion of a sexualised interest.

Their privileges indicated that they were not just servants. In the hierarchy of absolute power that slavery conferred upon slave-owners the sexual use of slave children needs to be considered, especially along the boundaries of social categories where these small 'pages' lived, partly in and partly out of the social domains of their masters. For some years privileged child-slaves in European households lived between the world of slavery, the realm of service that utilised non-slave servants, and the world of aristocratic 'society' that required labour and service to maintain their status. In other words, they lived at the social border that separated slave from owner, not out of slavery but not in the domain they served. When boy slaves were serving women owners, they were often treated as pets, at least while they were young.[17] There are many examples of Aboriginal children being taken into colonial families, especially small children, who later found that they were not part of the family at all, but servants of it. The two children taken up by the Mortlock family as they established their huge pastoral holdings provide just one example of children trained for servitude, no matter how well they were treated in some respects. In Europe or England, when child slave pages reached puberty they were despatched to the stables, traditionally to work as young grooms but sometimes as gardeners on the large estates being established.

Small Indigenous grooms can also be seen in colonial paintings from South Australia. S.T. Gill painted the departure and return of kangaroo hunters showing 'grooms'; another is visible in Alexander Schramm's picture of the Gilbert family as they established themselves north of Adelaide.

S.T. Gill, *Kangarooers Returning*. Clearly part of a series (or pair). The small boy holding the stirrup cup is pictured at the far right-hand side.

S.T. Gill, *Setting Out for the Hunt*, 1840s. 'Pencil and watercolour sketch showing a group of men and dogs assembled on the road in front of a house. Four of the men are on horseback and are pictured being served drinks by an aboriginal servant. Courtesy State Library of NSW.

Eyre did not treat his young 'adopted' boys as members of his family. They may have shared a tent with him when they were young but they were supervised by his overseer, a man who was known to be a serious drinker when opportunity arose. Eyre treated the boys much more as amusing pets with whom he played when he felt like it. And they were able to work, which they did. In this, he was within the established traditions of slave ownership and perhaps in one sense, a man of one kind of property. But like other young men of his social background and time, Eyre faced another problem. In the rough and tumble of colonial life, how did one become a real man?

Chapter Fifteen

Becoming a Man

Respectable manhood early in nineteenth-century England required both property ownership and that an adult man should live at the head of a family household.[1] A man who did not establish a family, like the writer and politician Thomas Babbington Macaulay (1800–1859) for instance, could find their status questioned. In Catherine Hall's view, 'In remaining single Macaulay was putting his manhood at risk. Having a wife, children, and household – dependants who demonstrated one's status as *independent* – 'was an essential element in achieving it'.[2] As a young man of his era and social class, Eyre's lack of property meant that the essential legal, moral and gendered link between property ownership and masculinity was indeed qualified. It was a lack that drove many a man out to the colonies but for those without access to inherited property or capital there was another way to adult manhood, open to those who could grasp it. The heroism open to the successful explorer was a particular kind of *heroic manhood* that could bring glory and status, and sometimes fortune.[3]

Eyre had thought about heroism already by 1838. As he set out overland on his droving journey to Adelaide he had asked himself,

> *Would the price be worth the cost when attained? Time only might reply, but one thing I felt quite certain of – that the vigor of body, activity of mind and energy of will could never have been imparted to man to remain unexercised or to be suffered to become enervated thro' idleness and inactivity.*[4]

Eyre had the qualities, his South Australian biographer said, 'that make a man a hero in an empty landscape or amongst primitive peoples', qualities that 'may destroy him amongst demagogues and politicians,' as perhaps they did.[5] Eyre's entry into to what he saw as the great opportunities of the Australian colonies was therefore driven not only by the economic and religious pieties of the 1820s and his need to find a fortune, but also by the sense that, for him, in order to become a man and enter manhood proper, he had to find a wife. Without her he could not be the head of an idealised, patriarchal family.

The land required to start off Eyre's journey toward respectable English manhood was, however, not cheap. His great chance came when the South Australian colonists decided that the need for a droving track leading from the north of South Australia to the Swan River Colony in the far west was sufficient to justify an expedition of exploration. This was a major undertaking into country of which nothing was known except that it was extremely dry. Just back from a journey to Western Australia by sea, Eyre seized his day. By chance, he had brought with him from the west an Aboriginal youth known as Wylie who could act as guide on the long trek westward. The initial stages of the journey saw his party reduced until it consisted of his overseer Baxter, Wylie, and the boys Neramberein (who had been 'picked up' in the district around the Murrumbidgee River), Cootacha, then known as 'Joey', and 'Yarry'. Wylie was, of course, going towards home to Western Australia, but the other two boys were already very far from theirs and heading even further away, entering a country of which they knew nothing and with which they had no ties.

On 29 April 1840, the two younger boys accompanying Eyre and Baxter across the top of the Great Australian Bight would go no further. They absconded in the night, shooting Baxter when he tried to stop them. According to Eyre, after Baxter's murder, Neramberein and Cootacha ran into the desert, shadowing Eyre and Wylie for some days, apparently hoping that Wylie would join them. They had reason to think that he might do so as Wylie had been party to an earlier incident in which all three had abandoned Eyre, but were then persuaded to continue on with him. But this time Wylie stayed. Eyre did not entirely trust Wylie, believing that he had been involved in some way in the events that led to Baxter's death, although he also believed that the driving motive had been theft rather than murder.

In the description of Baxter's murder given by the colony's early historian, Edwin Hodder, Wylie is said to have called out to Eyre, using a purely slave vocabulary, 'oh, massa massa, come here'.[6] This phrasing now seems rather unlikely as the term 'boss' was more commonly in Australian use, but it illustrates the pervasiveness of patterns of thinking and vocabulary anchored in the practices of plantation slavery. When Clamor Schürmann spoke later to people around Port Lincoln about the fate of Neramberein and Cootacha, he said that they had heard that 'two strange young men, carrying a peculiar kind of nets or netbags, had been killed by the Kukatas, in the belief of their being *Purkabidnis*,' mythical giant black men who lurk in the shadows of the night.[7] In the Ngadju-Mirning version of Baxter's murder, recorded in the 1990s by Arthur Dimer, it was Eyre himself who had killed Baxter in a fit of rage because Baxter was drunk. Neramberein and Cootacha had then fled in fright only to be speared by the Mirning people who were observing the expedition's progress.[8] Even with Wylie to help in locating water, Eyre's decision to continue westwards after Baxter's murder, when food was short, water locations unknown, and with no local guide, was risky indeed.

Eyre was now left with just one companion and many very difficult miles before him. It was the account of his travails as he forced his way westward across the top of the Great Australian Bight towards King George Sound that provided the material for Eyre's legend. The image of a sole white man trekking across endless bare, waterless desert and sandhills 'alone' with his trusty black servant was the stuff of legend and it served Eyre well. The many illustrations of the two struggling on are entirely imaginary.

Eyre became famous not just for his ability to endure endless hardship but also for the way he was able to forge a friendship with Wylie. Although commonly spoken of as a boy, Wylie's age is unknown.

Entirely imaginary: 'Eyre's Journey to Albany', 1891,
Print published on New Year's Day in the *Illustrated Australian News* supplement titled: 'The story of Australian exploration.'[9]

Most likely he was indeed young when in May of 1840 he sailed away with Eyre from King George Sound to Adelaide, but just how young remains uncertain.[10]

Eyre's decision to carry on across the Great Australian Bight with only Wylie to help him places him in the company of a group of men who sought their glory through unrelieved pain and suffering. The Christian tradition of the sinfulness of the body and its desires, requires control and disciplines anchored in sometimes violent strictures applied from outside the body. In this he, to some extent, mirrored the practices of those pilgrims and penitents who lashed the body or approached a sacred site on their unprotected knees in order to approach a state of penitent purity. Like the penitent pilgrim, the nineteenth century hero triumphed over the body, over starvation, thirst, sexual desires, exhaustion and sickness. Eyre and Wylie were only saved from death by the chance discovery of a French whaling ship anchored off Esperance. They were taken on board, fed, rested and re-provisioned. After the raging heat of earlier months they then faced a dismal wet and cold winter in order to struggle on to complete what Eyre had set out to do.

The best explanation for Wylie's decision to stay with Eyre under such forbidding circumstances lies in his personal decency, coupled with a determination to get home to King George Sound that equalled Eyre's desire for recognition as a hero. What seems to emerge from Eyre's journals and reports is a relationship between the two based on a series of mutual obligations and a willingness to work together toward what was, in the end, a shared goal.

Accounts of Wylie's recognition by family and friends at King George's Sound and word of his return to his people are touching. Death ceremonies had already been performed for him, his people believing him lost for ever. In thanks for his loyalty and help, Eyre arranged a pension for him. Newspaper reports of their safe arrival went eastwards, occasioning much celebration. A medal from the Royal Geographical Society would follow. Eyre had indeed achieved the reputation of a hero and it helped him to get work.

In October 1841, when Eyre had returned to Adelaide by ship, the governor of South Australia appointed him as magistrate and Protector of Aborigines at Moorundie on the River Murray near the crossing-point at Blanchetown. It was not much, but he was on his way. By 1846 he had secured a more lucrative appointment in New Zealand, and later the series of postings in the Caribbean that led him to Jamaica where his extreme brutality in putting down a revolt of former slaves rather sullied his reputation. And finally, by 1850 he was able to marry Welsh-born Adelaide Frances Ormond (1826-1905) and start a real family of his own. Manhood had been achieved.

*****

But manhood has not precisely the same meaning as masculinity. In the dictionary sense *manhood* refers to the state of being a man, the *social* status achieved through property. *Masculinity*, on the other hand, means being 'of the male sex' and has come to have more of the meaning of how men behave, how they present themselves to the world as 'real men', as bearers of the *qualities* of maleness. Although the two are intimately entwined, it is masculinity that highlights the sexual practices of men and Eyre's practice of picking up small boys and attaching them to himself as he moved about the country with droving parties.

In colonial South Australia, as in the other colonies, forms of masculinity came into play that were only available outside of England at that time, forms that had consequences for the women and children whose subjection to them was so important. Colonial concepts of masculinity were shaped in part by the beliefs and gendered structures of British society but it was in the colonies that the relations of power underpinning them were most clearly and perhaps most fully realised. For it was only in the colony that men had such unrestrained access to women who, along with their families, were being turned off their Country, and only in places like South Australia that the practices of slavery, like the kidnapping of children and the use of unpaid labour, could be smothered by beliefs in free labour, equality under the law, and the supreme value of Christianisation and British civilisation.

Colonial forms of masculinity have to be set within the context of violent dispossession and sexual practices that, within polite society went unspoken but not unknown. As the land survey and land-grabs washed across South Australia, Eyre set out to make his future in just that highly sexualised and violent culture, one that characterised the colony in the town of Adelaide as well as regions beyond it. Violent sexual practices were enhanced and magnified; they were treated as a normal part of war, the war they denied having. There is nothing explicit in Eyre's published memoirs that can tell us, really, how he reacted to those violent sexual forms of masculinity swirling around him as he travelled around New South Wales, south to Port Phillip Bay, and then around the river systems leading into South Australia. And as the originals of his diaries have been lost there is little chance of knowing if he ever wrote about what he really thought and did.

It is hard not to wonder why the two younger boys decided to leave Eyre and to kill Baxter in the process. On Eyre's public testimony, Joey and Yarry (the younger of the two) had been with him for several years and he had always treated them well. They helped willingly with the work of droving and tracking. But according to Eyre's account of the events leading up to Baxter's murder, the Aboriginal boys were driven by greediness and their lust for large quantities of food. Given Eyre's concept of the need to discipline the body, his need to conserve his supplies and his ability to exist on little more than hard tack, the boys might indeed have been hungry.

Certainly, Neramberein and Cootacha took off with guns and as much food as they could gather up. Eyre thought they may have wanted to return across the desert to Fowler's Bay and safety, a very reasonable ambition given the circumstances. After following Eyre for several days, calling to Wylie to come to them, they vanished, to be seen no more. This account is open to an interpretation, unstated by Eyre, that the boys were treacherous in their loyalties, ungrateful for the kindness of Eyre. The treacherous nature of the Aboriginal people of the colony was a constant theme in newspaper reports of incidents of violence. Indigenous violence appears as an innate characteristic of a people that marks them out as 'savages', as a people lacking the Englishman's love of truthful straightforwardness; it denies and covers over any right to resist the stealing of their land by the colonists. It also denies the boys the right to make their own judgements about how best to survive.

The difficulty with Eyre's report about the death of Baxter is that he was understandably anxious to clear his friend and overseer of any act that might have disrupted relations within the small party or that might have led to the young men wanting to kill him. He may also have wanted to ensure that Baxter's earlier role in raising the boys was seen as benign. Baxter, however, was a well-documented heavy drinker as well as someone taking an undue interest in Aboriginal women. During Eyre's 1840 attempt to find the good country everyone believed lay just beyond the salt lakes to the north of Adelaide, Baxter had captured an Aboriginal woman while Eyre was away from camp and kept her with him for two days before giving her presents and letting her go. On Geoffrey Dutton's account of Baxter's action, there had been no ill-treatment of the woman, a statement unlikely to be true. Dutton's understanding of the event was perhaps conditioned both by his admiration for his hero and by the reconstructed myths of peaceful colonisation that were well-established by the time in which he was writing. The consequence of Baxter's time in control of Eyre's camp and the capture of a woman was that on his return, Eyre found he had to deal with 'about thirty natives with spears, looking exceedingly hostile and warlike'.[11] They were clearly angry about the kidnapping and imprisonment of the woman and looking for vengeance; it may have been difficult to convince them that the woman had been well-treated. So at the very least, Baxter's drinking as well as his relations with the boys could have been at issue on the journey westward.

Set against the context of the colonial forms of masculinity and the enhanced violence it permitted, Eyre's claim that he and Baxter had always treated the boys well cannot be taken at face value. While some like to think that Baxter misinterpreted Eyre's instruction to him to keep any Aborigines with him until he could return, his readiness to capture a woman rather than a man and to restrain her in his camp rather than entering into negotiations with others nearby raises the possibility that she was not well treated at all. As for the boys – who can say whether Eyre's interest in them was sexual or not? Just as the question of why Baxter 'restrained' the woman he took into his camp needs at least some consideration, Eyre's practice of taking young boys rather than adult men into his household can be thought about not just as an attempt at forming a family or the acceptable independence of manhood but also as a venture into the practices of colonial masculinity that swirled about him as Indigenous Country was converted to colonial property. From very early on, the actual processes of conversion of land from Country to British property created moral problems for the colonists and increasing resistance from those facing such terrible losses.

Chapter Sixteen

Heroes & Myths

The imperial cult of male heroes as supermen as it is practised still today is based on the myths of the colonial explorer and men like him. It displays and justifies a class structure and forms of masculinity that make possible the competitive and destructive economic practices now known as 'neo-liberalism'. Charles Sturt, Edward Eyre and John McDouall Stuart, South Australia's best known explorers, are among the mythical heroes of a colonial government because they have a particular function that exceeds the value of their powers of discovery. South Australia's colonial heroes are harbingers of a world to come: the colony will be built upon the land they see. They have the fantastic powers of endurance, and the special knowledge and technical skills that allow them to look out into the remote distance, to see emptiness and 'tame the natives', to describe and name the spaces of what will become the map of their new land. Where they go, law and civilisation will follow regardless of the consequences to those whose country they are taking.

Such men are history-makers whose names will live on. Henceforth, all who follow them onto the new lands will tell of how that First Man had arrived there, the Being who 'opened up' and 'cleared' the land for the invaders. In this sense the explorer becomes a character within narratives that anthropologists refer to as *foundation myths*. The journeying explorer becomes a character in a great epic, his heroic 'firstness' serving to block out the reality that he was by no means first at all, that the country was occupied, not empty but known, mapped and put under production by others, and that usually he needed those others to sustain him, as well as to show him the way to his 'discoveries'. The images of Aboriginal men like Wylie and Tenberry who supported Edward Eyre and others like him become the imaginary 'good natives' of colonial fictions, those who appear to have recognised the forces of progress, those who are kind and helpful, not wild or savage.

Colonial foundation myths are interesting because through them we can hear the voices not just of explorer-heroes but of a society speaking to itself. We can hear voices that tell the people of today about their origins in the past in ways that help to make both past and present acceptable. To achieve this ability, the facts of the individual explorer's fraught travails need to be organised into a recognisable story of heroics, survival, and the triumph of the will that draws on earlier, traditional conventions that give to a personal story a sense that within it there is some kind of a more universal drama being played out. In that mix of personal truth with universal truths lie the makings of myth. Mythical narratives are powerful ways of knowing the world because they appear to offer access to some kind of fundamental truth about its nature, of how it came into being, perhaps, and what people want to believe about their society. And sometimes they provide a way of thinking about what people would rather not know. Myths change over time, they may become more important or less, elements may drop out or be added in, but mythical thinking is basic and common and usually believed to be true, whether it is or not. Any challenge to major stories about the beginnings of the world or, in this case, the beginnings of the colony of South Australia, will be greatly resented by those whom they comfort and support, particularly men.

Australia's foundation or origin myths are important to women in part because they speak so directly to men about being men. They offer powerful models of being in the world that speak of the ways in which a truly manly man can or must live – the courage, the honour, the loyalty, the self-control, the willingness to sacrifice the self for God and country, the physical ability to succeed where others might fail. Such men are heroes indeed. As with other mythical creatures the hero is something of a shape-shifter, his nature changing to match political and social interests. It did this toward the end of the nineteenth century when the hero's characteristics changed just as Britain was becoming less religious and more involved in the nationalist struggles of Europe and empire.[1] Nevertheless, whether a hero's cult embraces religious, military or nationalist heroics, women are often absent or marginal. When they do appear they are safely under male control. If they are not, they become a threat. In colonial Australia's myths of origin, the land itself often appears as female, as an unpredictable vicious female force that is crying out for male control.

The Conquering Hero in the New Land

Exploration is a concept as well as a deed, for with the explorer's travails come the possibilities of personal heroism, a necessity that is expressed in the explorer's aloneness, his solitude in the landscape, his control of those men making his solitary journey possible, and his valour. In nineteenth-century England and its colonies, the person of the hero was literally heroic and worthy of worship. Nowhere was the adulation of the colonial hero more visible than in the public recognition given to those who were successful, or nearly. You can see the processes of acclamation at work in South Australia in the grand and luxurious subscription dinner held to honour Edward Eyre's journey westwards in 1840–41. Eyre's efforts were acknowledged by the singing of the old Templar hymn 'Non Nubis Domine'.[2]

> *Not unto us, O Lord*
> *Not unto us, O Lord*
> *But to Your name*
> *But to Your name*
> *May all the glory be*

Although less triumphal than the musical acclamations that came later, it expresses one of the characteristics of the early Victorian hero as Thomas Carlyle (1795–1881) – author of *On Heroes, Hero-Worship and the Heroic in History* – would have understood him, his committed selflessness and his humility.³ The glory was to God. Later, as the nature of the hero shifted focus, the musical offerings at their public dinners celebrated both empire and a nostalgia for England – 'Rule Brittania' was one of the favourites – while others took a more sentimental tone. But for the hero himself, he, rather than God, became increasingly the focus.

The shift in emphasis can be seen at the public dinner given in 1862 to mark John McKinlay's safe return from his unsuccessful search for the lost explorers, Burke and Wills. Both McKinlay and A.W. Howitt, who was on Cooper Creek some years later, believed that Burke and Wills' companion, Gray, had been eaten by the Dieri or a related people.⁴ On his arrival at the Mill Inn in his hometown of Gawler (just north of Adelaide), the welcoming band struck up not the quiet hymn to humility that was played for Eyre but the stirring 'See, the Conquering Hero Comes' from Handel's *Judas Maccabeus*.⁵ It was played again at the official public dinner held at the Pier Hotel in Glenelg to mark the same event.⁶

John McDouall Stuart, who was returning from crossing the continent from south to north, had an even more glorious reception. As he was carried towards Adelaide in a litter in 1862 the rural populace turned out to cheer him on his way while in Adelaide, a great procession of excited well-wishers, bands, and contingents of freemasons paraded into the city to welcome him. After lengthy congratulatory speeches given in his honour, the Ancient Order of Foresters conferred upon him the laurel crown of the victor. For John McDouall Stuart, too, at the public banquet that followed his crowning, the military band of the West Adelaide Rifles would play again 'See, the conquering hero comes'.⁷ So there is no doubt that to the colonists of the time, men like Eyre, Stuart, as well as McKinley who had tried and failed, were accorded the title, the status and the adulation granted to the hero. They played an important part in the well-established British cult of the hero.

The Cult of the Hero

Shortly after South Australia was colonised, Thomas Carlyle's lectures on the hero electrified the intellectual world of London. Carlyle believed that in Britain the significance of heroic acts for history and progress had been forgotten and needed to be restored. Carlyle's concept of the hero as a kind of engine of progress was widely discussed at the time; it is the person of the hero as Carlyle described him and wanted him to be that helps in understanding the significance of the heroic explorer as a character in Australian foundation myths. For through the person of the hero, Carlyle was describing a way of thinking about men, virtue, and truth that became so entrenched among his peers that it could be described as a cult – a nineteenth-century English 'cult of the hero' that South Australia's colonists were familiar with and participated in, just as they were familiar with the idea of worshipping or reverencing such a person. Within that cult was also a minor strand of thought offering models of heroism that emphasised spiritual strength rather than the physical. Put forward by women writers in novels (often anti-Catholic in concern), they were looking for a truly Protestant heroism, one that opened it up to women – as once was the case among the ancient Greeks – as well as to the unpropertied and labouring classes of men. Always a minor genre in England, the female hero vanished without trace in South Australia. Within the cult of the hero that came to Adelaide with the colonists, if their heroes were less than gods they were certainly more than men – exemplars, powerful, creative and much more.

Of course Carlyle had his own list of heroes, some of whom were the subject of his lectures, but he saw all of them in these terms: they were, he said, 'the leaders of men, these great ones.' They were

> *the modellers, patterns, and in a wide sense creators, of whatsoever the general mass of men contrived to do or to attain; ... We cannot look, however imperfectly, upon a great man, without gaining something by him. He is the living light-fountain, which it is good and pleasant to be near ... a flowing light-fountain, as I say, of*

native original insight, of manhood and heroic nobleness; – in whose radiance all souls feel that it is well with them.[8]

Carlyle wrote his lectures at a time when heroes were being widely discussed in Britain, a time in which the hero had become 'a major Victorian preoccupation.'[9] In them the hero usurped the creative fecundity of women. His sentiments were shared by his fellow Victorians to such an extent that, Edmund Gosse believed, admiration had turned 'from virtue into a religion, and called it Hero Worship.'[10] From 1830 through to the 1880s hero worship in England was intense – just the years in which explorers were travelling across Australia, just the years in which Eyre and Stuart were carrying out their attempts to travel overland from Adelaide to the Swan River Colony in the west and from Adelaide to find a route through to the northern coast. Although none of Carlyle's heroes was an explorer, aspects of the cult readily envelop the characters of Eyre and Stuart, pointing not simply to their religious and mythical qualities but also to their relationship to ideas about manliness at a time in which those ideas were changing.[11] It was the driving force of the heroic dream that sent forth the explorer of unknown lands. The imaginary figure of the explorer contained within it the promise of exemplary manhood, a manliness to be achieved through the performance of the most extreme of manly qualities, the total subjugation of the body to the will. As new norms of self-regulation were being established in England, the Victorians had to guard themselves against a series of newly discovered sexual perversions and curb their violence.[12] Just how that subjugation was achieved is a matter of some interest. How was it to be done, and why?

Body and Will

Something of the importance of subjugation emerges in the way in which the triumph of will over body draws a particular kind of response from modern writers as well as those of the nineteenth century. Such is the seductive power of the hero's body that in a considered evaluation of Eyre written in the 1980s, the South Australian writer-poet Geoffrey Dutton would try to capture something essential about Eyre's journey westwards through a characteristic he described as its purity.[13] 'The purity of the heroic act remains', he said, 'with everything else gradually stripped away; finally there is nothing but Eyre and Wylie, walking beside their stumbling horses, collecting dew with a sponge, eating the roots of trees.'[14]

Here Dutton portrayed the travails of the explorer as a mortification of the flesh to a degree that leaves behind only some kind of pure essence of being, a 'purity' of body and soul that has come from the torments of flesh denied everything. This is a vision of man as will, of the body as irrelevant except as a capsule enclosing it. Such mastery of the body is definitive. In it, the god-like persona of the explorer-hero is revealed although not that of his guide. Wylie's dogged support for Eyre was recognised and publicly applauded, but it is Eyre's body and will that is celebrated. On reaching the west, Wylie disappears into his old life with a pension from Eyre but almost no biographical traces. Eyre stands alone as the solitary hero whose force drove them forward. Eyre is the man, Wylie the 'young man' who accompanied him, his status as servant well captured in the various drawings of the partnership. Wylie is known as knowledgeable and faithful perhaps, but never quite the man his master was. The essence of manliness is will; the will revealed through travails and transit is Eyre's alone even though Wylie is often pictured with him.

Eyre's own writings refer to the bodily mortifications and determination that drove him forward as his 'duty' rather than his purity. Today, a reading of the literature about Eyre, and his own accounts of his actions, leaves in its wake a sense of a man whose determination to discipline his body was a driving force, much as it had been for Charles Sturt who preceded him in South Australia when rowing heroically up the Murray River against its flow in order to get safely home, as well as for John McDouall Stuart, travelling some seventeen years later, whose privations entirely ruined his health. Such extreme tests of the will are not necessarily best described or explained as having been driven by a sense of duty, important as duty was to the Victorians.[15] One should look also to the ways in which during the years of Eyre's youth new forms of British masculinity were emerging, a masculinity shaped by Protestant doctrines of rationality, free will, and the discipline that aimed to eradicate emotionality from the male *persona* by allocating it to women, a re-writing of the nature of gender based upon an ancient strand of Christian distrust of the body. It was sometimes expressed in later novels as the Englishman's typical 'stiff upper lip' and in Australia as the colonial man's disconnection from his emotions or feelings.

Eyre's addiction to controlling his body through restricted intakes of food and water, a restriction courted at every turn, leaps from the pages describing his decisions to keep going westwards across the edge of the Great Australian Bight, regardless of the safety of his companions as well as of himself. Perhaps, like Daisy Bates camped at Ooldea much later, he believed that 'the simpler our needs, the nearer we are to the gods.'[16] Most certainly Eyre came very near to meeting his. His endurance, like that of many other of the explorers, was contrived, the product not just of ignorance of local water and food supplies (an unavoidable failing he was aware of) but of that dogged determination to push the body not just to its limits but to extinction, if that was what was required – to journey to the limits of life. It is a testing of the will, of its mastery over the body, rather than the performance of a duty.[17] In Eyre's case, he transmuted that mastery into the religious and political language of a loyal servant's duty to his Queen.

Stuart's follies were similar. Each of his journeys was undertaken with very limited provision for food, water, or repair of equipment, his hardships increased by systematic under-provisioning. Even his well-funded final push across the continent to the northern coast was beset by poor provisioning, poor quality horses that had to be abandoned or sent back, poor equipment all round. He was ravaged by scurvy on a number of occasions but took little care to guard against it, lost his sight intermittently and frequently lost time by having to rest. He often lacked the strength to sit on a horse; on his final journey home he was carried the last six hundred kilometres on a makeshift litter. Descriptions of Stuart's journeys often include a statement that 'he never lost a man', but he certainly ruined the health of a number of them and his own never recovered.

Those reading the accounts of the journeys of Eyre and Stuart cannot but be impressed with the hardships both endured. Yet both were reckless as well as determined. In travelling in summers, travelling without guides, in leaving behind equipment that more careful men might have insisted on taking, in refusing to accept setbacks that might have caused delay, both regularly courted disaster. That both men lived to tell their tales is indeed a tribute to their tenacity but many of their heroics involved overcoming avoidable, self-inflicted disasters, or rescue.

What are we to make, now, of those headlong marches into bodily ruination and possible death, journeys marked by the defining *travails* of the hero cult, but one in which many of them are self-inflicted? Is the body of the Protestant explorer – both Eyre and Stuart being raised within Protestant homes – particularly prone to the taming of the will through bodily mortification or does the mortification of the body live mainly within the Catholic or Orthodox forms of Christianity, as a penance or punishment for sin? Or is there a more secular male body emerging in the middle of the nineteenth century, alongside its old roles, one that also needs discipline applied to it by the self in order to eradicate any unruly desires emerging from it? To make any sense of a consciously poorly equipped venture onto country that is known to be harsh and often apparently waterless, one needs some understanding of the darker reaches of Christian teachings as well as of the processes by which middle- and upper-class boys were made into colonial men. For a good many of them, heroic endurance was supplemented by the unrestrained violence involved in securing access and control of country that was not theirs, violence that is particularly visible along the stock routes passing through country watered by permanent rivers.

Part Three

Trouble on the Murray

Chapter Seventeen

Fear Rising

By 1841 Lake Bonney on the River Murray was at the north-eastern boundary of what were effectively the 'settled areas' of the colony, those in which the colonists and the governor saw themselves as living peaceably on Country with its Indigenous owners.[1] But the presence of numerous pastoralists pushing out from Adelaide in search of good land did not make it safe.

The First Incident – Attack at Lake Bonney
On 16 April 1841 an overlanding party led by Henry Field and Henry Inman was attacked near Lake Bonney, two hundred or so kilometres north-east of Adelaide.[2] In a major engagement, people known as the Maraura succeeded in scattering five thousand sheep and eight hundred cattle with, according to official statements, only one Maraura man killed.[3] Already Inman had a barbed spearhead embedded in his back acquired seven weeks earlier on the Murrumbidgee River. Since then, Inman and Field's drovers and herds had been harassed by the river peoples, Inman said, all the way along the Darling River and on to the Rufus. The Maraura or their allies, who had speared several of the drovers' sheep on the Darling, followed their progress until on 16 April 1841, a sizeable force of thirty or forty of them appeared across the river. More, Inman said, were concealed in the scrub. Although the visible men appeared to be unarmed, their weapons, he said, were hidden in the long grass. Believing hostility to be in the air, Field and

his party refused to allow Maraura men to approach their camp – they do not say how. As the herd moved off, signs given to the drovers led them to believe that there would be fighting further along. As a result, firearms were prepared and primed, ready to meet the large group of Maraura waiting for them in the scrub. Three to four hundred of them, Inman believed, were shouting and beating their waddies together to make it clear that the herds were not to pass. In this they were delivering a warning that was disregarded.

When the fighting began, many of the drovers' guns failed to fire or fired badly, so that they found themselves first encircled and then attacked. Two shepherds were speared, one of whom died, the other being captured. Once the droving party had retreated safely to the river, Henry Field rode off to seek help. Henry Inman, still very ill from his spear wound, rode for a week to reach the station of a Mr Hallack. In the absence of their leaders, the shepherds moved their flocks onward to Narcoota Springs, an important well-used watering hole on the overland track between Adelaide and New South Wales. At the springs they met up with Mr Bagot and Mr Hawker who were able to take over the flock for the last stage of the journey to Adelaide. And somehow, the captured shepherd also arrived at Naroota, having escaped or perhaps having been allowed to leave.

Although the sheep arrived safely in Adelaide with the remainder of the party alive, and although Inman recovered from his spearing, the battle (or 'incident' as it was often described as) saw a clear victory go to the river peoples, with a clear loss to the colonists. Their failure was put down to the poor state of their firearms and the great numbers of the enemy. The 'natives of that district,' Inman wrote, 'do not seem to have much fear of firearms, and are in such numbers that, when determined on fighting, it is no easy matter to keep them at their proper distance.'[4] It would not be for some years that greatly improved guns would make a decisive difference to the outcomes of major attacks like these.

Despite Inman's wounds from the undescribed incident on the Murrumbidgee, despite the spearing of sheep and persistent 'annoyances' all along the river, Inman concludes by stating that 'on no occasion during the journey was any act of violence committed by us on the natives; on the contrary, we universally treated them with kindness, but still with that caution which was necessary for the safety of the party, and the property entrusted to our care.'[5]

With arguments about the legitimacy of Governor Gawler's response to the *Maria* killings still exercising the public mind, and fears heightened by Inman's report of a major battle on the upper Murray, the drovers sought more government protection. The furore generated by Gawler's punitive action taken against the Milmenrura on the Coorong meant that this time he wanted to be more cautious.

The Second Incident – Major O'Halloran's First Attempt to Recover the Lost Stock

Although Major O'Halloran was placed in charge of a small contingent of police and volunteers, due to humanitarian opinion in Adelaide, rather than punishing any perpetrators his orders were to retrieve the lost stock and prevent more violence breaking out. O'Halloran did not like his instructions. Like many in the colony he was of the opinion that a severe lesson delivered now would save many lives in the future.[6] Before this lesson could be delivered, when his party was just fifty miles short of Lake Bonney, an order to return to Adelaide reached him. Governor Gawler had been recalled to England and replaced by George Grey. So they returned to town empty-handed.

The Third Incident – Inman, Field and Hawker Attempt to Recover the Lost Stock

In response to O'Halloran's recall, Henry Field (later a successful pastoralist) and Henry Inman (later to join the police force) put together a group of volunteers whose stated intention was to recover the missing stock. In fact, it was they who would deliver O'Halloran's lesson. James Hawker was one of them. His diary records the fighting that followed and the six or eight Maraura who were killed.[7] The stock lost from the previous herd, however, were still missing. The lesson delivered, the men returned to town with the stock remaining on the loose.

The Fourth Incident – O'Halloran And Moorhouse Set Out to Protect Langhorne's Herds

When news came in May 1841 that Charles Langhorne and his herd was approaching the unsettled river country, demands for government protection grew louder. Newly appointed Governor Grey was reluctant to provide it.[8] In his view the Indigenous people of the colony were protected by the same laws as everyone else and could not be treated as aliens with whom the colonists were at war.[9] By the time he consented to the sending of an escort to protect the herds, an escort to be led by Major O'Halloran but accompanied by Matthew Moorhouse in his role as Protector of Aborigines, Langhorne's droving party had already been attacked. Losing at least five of their own men in the fighting, the Maraura had killed four of the drovers.

Although news of the attack was not yet in O'Halloran's hands, the party assembled was a large one. At Governor Grey's insistence the volunteers were sworn in as special constables with all the legal responsibilities as well as the powers that such a role devolved upon them. Even so the expedition was referred to by the Unitarian historian Edwin Hodder as setting out to 'chastise marauding natives', that is to say, a punitive expedition. It was funded by donations from the more prosperous and more concerned of the colonists.[10] The South Australian Company, for example, gave £10 toward its costs, others gave biscuit, flour, tea, salt pork and beef, sugar, tobacco, a tent and tarpaulins, and gun-powder. The quantity of alcohol donated seems surprising perhaps, but the colonists were thirsty men.[11] For the expeditioners there was a cask of ale, two cases of gin, and two gallons of rum.

They set out at the end of May 1841 with the volunteers accompanying O'Halloran organised along military lines. They fell into two groups: a mounted contingent that included Captains Beever, Inman, and Ferguson, plus Messrs Berry, Hawker, Langhorne, H. Field,

J. Fisher, Barber, Brown, Tooth, Whitpine, S.K. Langhorne, Daniel and E. Oliver. Those travelling on foot (more accurately, by wagon) were Messrs Martin, Gatwood, Dennis, Pavlin, Head, Day, Diprose, Deverill, and Taylor.[12] The names published in the Adelaide newspapers are important because of the way that, when things turn nasty, the names of those involved can be very difficult to determine. None of the police party under O'Halloran's command is named although Inspector Tolmer, formerly a soldier with considerable battle experience in Europe, is mentioned in O'Halloran's later report of the venture. Tolmer had eighteen mounted men under his command.[13] In all, O'Halloran said, there were sixty-eight men 'including officers'.[14] At least one Aboriginal man from Adelaide went with them but is not named in the newspaper reports.

As the expedition approached the upper reaches of the River Murray, there were a number of attempts by local Aboriginal men to get some insight into the intentions of such a large party. Although presenting themselves as friendly well-wishers their visits were reconnaissance missions aiming to deceive the intruders in one way or another. There was no attempt to dissuade the colonists from advancing further; indeed they were encouraged forward with indications that the lost herds were still alive and that the guilty parties were those living further up the river. The account of these encounters in O'Halloran's report is necessarily slight, his aim being to establish that they had indeed followed Grey's orders and that with Moorhouse's help, attempted to get into friendly relations with the local people. But a consequence of them is that despite being described as intelligent, the Maraura men who approached them appear as, at least, untrustworthy, and at worst, as treacherous. Despite information from their Aboriginal contacts that the sheep were still alive and roaming, the sheep were in fact dead and had been so for some time.

As with O'Halloran's report on the state of the bodies of those killed on the Coorong, he includes a description of the state of the battleground on the Rufus River. He discovers the body of one of Langhorne's men, named as Mr Martin, still guarded by his injured bulldog. He described Martin's body as badly battered, his entrails removed, as were his thigh bones. Such treatment of the body was bound to horrify the colonists; it also fuelled accusations that these people were cannibals. The other three bodies had vanished, a fact that might also have raised the spectre of cannibalism. The battlefield itself was strewn with the various equipment of the drovers, guns, flour and dead animals, as well as large numbers of clubs and flesh encrusted spears. O'Halloran and Langhorne both believed that another attack had been imminent and that only the arrival of the detachment of police and volunteers had saved their lives.

From O'Halloran's report it appears that those who had dealt so effectively with Langhorne's men were well aware of the approach of this new party of colonists and had no intention of leaving the field. When Tolmer led his detachment of mounted police across the river, O'Halloran's men remained on the opposing bank. They then swept along the river on horseback, up toward Lake Victoria. O'Halloran's party was lured into the pursuit of a group of about thirty Maraura men, crossing the Rufus at its junction with the lake, only to find that after a chase, some of their quarry had taken to their canoes and all were well away and beyond reach on the far banks of the lake. Tolmer was equally unlucky. As the Maurara lit fires to warn their neighbours of a hostile presence on their country, the colonists retreated to their fortified camp. O'Halloran believed that the lives of Langhorne's surviving men had been saved by their arrival.

By the end of the day, some of the stolen cattle had been retrieved but the flocks had gone and no prisoners had been taken. In explaining the failure to take any prisoners, O'Halloran wrote:

> *In a country such as we have gone over, intersected by rivers, lagoons, and creeks, and thick with polyginum [sometimes polygonum] scrub and high reeds, it is next to impossible to surprise any blacks, for all know the approach of a party from the time they make the river, into which the natives plunge, all at once escape to the opposite side, and is there secure from all danger.*[15]

Like others who engaged with the Indigenous owners of the country around the Murray–Darling confluence, O'Halloran found the local people competent swimmers, proficient in the handling of their canoes, well-armed, fearless and determined. The thick reedbeds of the upper Murray, like those found in the coastal lagoons near Adelaide along the Onkaparinga River and throughout the lakes at the mouth of the Murray, offered protection and safety from marauders. O'Halloran had always believed in the need to use force, the need to demonstrate the abilities of the new order sweeping the country. 'The cruel tribe we are now surrounded by are very numerous', he wrote, 'and have doubtless become emboldened by having defeated three successive parties of Europeans, and having also escaped punishment from any detachment …'[16]

Most of those travelling with him would have felt the same. Governor Grey's restrictions upon their actions were a frustration; the successful action taken by the Maraura to evade such a large and well-equipped party of colonists was a humiliation that fed into that frustration, building up fears in Adelaide that demanded a sterner response. Langhorne omitted the Maraura deaths from his report to O'Halloran; O'Halloran omitted them from his report to Governor Grey. Governor Grey was aware of the killings, however, for they were recorded in the report submitted to him by Matthew Moorhouse, Protector of Aborigines. O'Halloran's actions in the field also aroused considerable alarm among the humanitarian residents of Adelaide. They believed that everyone fell under the jurisdiction of the law and that a government could not properly go to war against its own people.[17] The legal question of whether they could or not may seem arcane, but it arose again in 2022 when it became a live issue under the radically conservative, evangelical, Liberal-National government led by Scott Morrison.

A Minor Incident Elsewhere – Trouble at Mt Dispersion, 18 June 1841
While O'Halloran was out searching for Field and Inman's sheep, reports of the loss of large numbers of sheep and the killing of the

shepherd on Mr Dutton's Station about 100 kilometres north of Adelaide caused further alarm.[18] The *Southern Australian* told its readers:

Our opinions as to the decided steps which should be taken in such cases to convince the natives, that neither the lives, nor the property of the whites, are to be trifled with impunity, have been so repeatedly expressed, as scarcely to need re-iteration. Seriously do we deprecate on the part of the settlers, any resort to those unhappy measures, which have been so unfortunately adopted towards the Natives in New South Wales and Van Diemen's Land, but fearfully apprehensive are we, unless some decided steps are speedily adopted, with the view of putting an end to these acts of aggression, that the settlers will be tempted in many cases to take the law into their own hands. This is an evil, we are fully persuaded, which every right-minded individual would deprecate, and which we hope to see every means at the command of the Executive employed to avert.[19]

Reports like these fed into a rising wave of fear. They led to more demands for effective action.

Chapter Eighteen

Lake Victoria and the Rufus River – Prelude

Like the people known to the colonists as the Melmenrura who lived around the Coorong, the people living in country watered by the intersection of the Murray and Darling rivers were hostile to colonists and determined to drive them off. They had already adjusted their tactics in ways that undermined the effectiveness of the colonists' guns and were less fearful than the colonists would have wished. When harassing the drovers they stayed out of range until after the guns had been discharged before rushing in to launch their spears while the shooters reloaded; alternatively, they dropped to the ground as the guns discharged before rushing into spear range or engaging with the shorter fighting spears and clubs used in close combat. Such very determined attacks on droving parties travelling along the rivers had given the river peoples a reputation for ferocity and treachery ('treachery' or 'treacherous' being the word used to describe Aboriginal tactics designed to defend their own country), for the river people believed that they were the rightful owners of the rich country the colonists believed was theirs already.

Like the country around the lakes at the mouth of the Murray, the junction of the Murray and Darling rivers created a mass of creeks, swamps and lakes that provided fish, birds, meat and a vast stock of plants for both food and medicinal purposes. They supported riverine economies of plenty. Those living there made the solid bark canoes capable of carrying twelve or fourteen men seen by the first British to

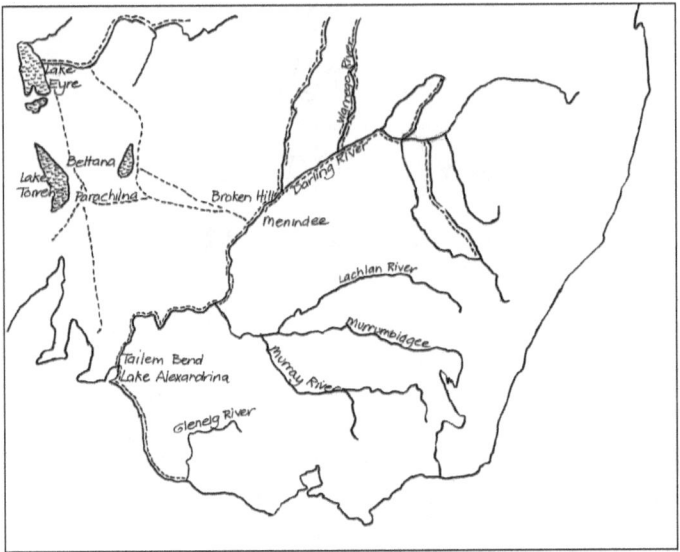

The Murray-Darling River system and its tributaries. Indigenous walking tracks along the rivers are shown by a broken line. The Murray flows into Lake Alexandrina and then to the sea at its mouth. The much smaller Rufus River lies around the junction of the Murray and the Darling.

pass by.[1] Built from the bark of the great River Red Gums they were heavy but long-lasting. Those great canoes would be crucial to escaping across the lakes from pursuers left stranded on the banks. The more domestic of canoes described in 1838 were 'constructed of a large sheet of thin bark, about fourteen feet in length, and two and a half feet in breadth, round at both ends, with the edges elevated about an inch at the stern, and gradually rising forward to a foot at the bow; towards the stern was the remains of a fire-place in a small mould of damp earth, on which muscles [sic] had been lately cooked.' And the river peoples used huge bird and fishing nets 'made of cord as thick as garden line, with meshes well finished'.[2] It was in this region, too, that Charles Sturt had reported seeing excellent made pathways, some wide enough and clear enough for the drovers to get their bullock wagons along them.

But if the people were war-like, their Country was enticing. This was country and water that the colonists would lust after; it was the country that made possible the droving of animals from the eastern colonies into Adelaide and the huge profits to be made from selling them into a market that was short of meat and equally short of breeding stock.

Although the water levels of the big rivers fluctuated according to season and rainfall such highly productive country was able to support large numbers of people for long periods of time. When Charles Sturt passed that way in July of 1838 he saw 'below the Darling ... a succession of lagoons backing flats of considerable extent, on which we found abundance of food for the cattle ... [lake Victoria] is a very pretty sheet of water ... on all sides of it the natives are very numerous'.[3] Later, Edward Eyre saw six to seven hundred people camped around Lake Victoria and the Rufus River in May of 1842, all feasting on the plentiful fish and birds.[4] Even accounting for exaggeration Lake Victoria operated as an important trade and ceremonial centre. The region provided opportunities for the exchange of news and information and, as the herds moved through, the planning of tactics. Although Strangways reported that the Aboriginal people living along the Hume River at the eastern end of the overland droving track were 'rather shy', a fact he put down to their encounters with Major Mitchell who had travelled through there some years earlier, he described those around the crossing-place on the River Murray as 'much more numerous and troublesome, besides being expert thieves.'[5] They were the people who had troubled colonial intruders as early as 1830.[6]

The people living along the rivers, the Maraura, Parkinji, and their allies, were described by colonists like Charles Sturt as big people, taller and more evidently muscled than the slightly smaller, wirier people living further up the Darling. They were strong and healthy with good white teeth – and they were numerous. Again and again, Europeans passing through remarked on the large numbers of people gathered there, even after earlier smallpox epidemics had taken a severe toll. Archeologists have shown that the high population densities of this region stretch back millennia.[7] They have recorded huge numbers of burial sites, middens and campsites around Lake Victoria and the rivers.

*****

Joseph Hawdon and Charles Bonney were hailed as heroes when they and their herds managed to reach Adelaide by an overland route that followed these rivers. They had got their herds through without fighting although not without some tension. Some of the Murray people, usually referred to then as Maraura, were clearly hostile, others 'more friendly and, indeed, in some cases too familiar'.[8] Such familiarity – walking in and out of the drover's camps at will, touching their equipment, inspecting the weaponry and assessing the calibre of the men – was often a prelude to theft or to demands that the drovers preferred not to meet and might well herald less friendly action.

Charles Sturt, along with a party including Finniss, McLeod, and Giles Strangways, had followed Hawdon's 1838 route into Adelaide.[9] In June of 1838 Edward Eyre also travelled this way. He and his herds met with some hostility at the Rufus River. By April of 1839 McLeod and McPherson arrived in Adelaide from New South Wales with 500 cattle and 1000 sheep, reporting a 'rencontre' in which forty unidentified Aborigines had been shot.[10]

Rather than pacifying the river peoples, the lessons the drovers sought to teach them had made the journey increasingly dangerous rather than safer. So it is hardly surprising that Alexander Buchanan's drovers, coming through later in the same year, found the river people very hostile indeed. Buchanan's drovers survived at least six clashes in the Lake Victoria–Rufus River region. His diary records that five or six Aboriginal people were killed in just one of those incidents. Neither the nature of the fighting nor the Aboriginal deaths were admitted in public although they were well enough known through the informal channels of popular discourse.[11] With successful drovers relaxing in the pubs and brothels of the town, it was impossible to keep the details of life on the overland track quiet. Besides, drovers and pastoralists were widely regarded as heroes, the men of stamina, determination and self-sufficiency who were building the colony from the ground up.[12] They and the early drovers were the men who would be idolised in later years as 'overlanders' in poetry, music, legend and yarns, men whose lives and the way they lived them would feed into the mythologies of 'the Australian legend', a legend expressing particular attitudes to the land as a place of men and manliness, a place without women in which men could be free to act as real men.

There is no doubt, however, that right across this country its Indigenous owners were very hostile to the rapidly increasing numbers of herds and drovers using the well-watered overland river route. The increasing use of the track meant that as early as 1838, sly grog shops set up to benefit from the drovers' thirsts were in business along the track's eastern approaches.[13] With colonists in Adelaide desperate for meat and stock, they were anxious to have an easy route for those willing to make the journey, 'to *finger-post* the route as far as possible', as one journalist put it.[14] Maraura attacks on the would-be finger-posters were the prelude to those that ended with the deaths of so many people at the Rufus River.

The Rufus River was not a great river like the Darling or the Murray, more like a creek. But its path through a complex network of intermingling channels and swamps emerged close to a narrow Indigenous crossing-point used by drovers to get their flocks across the river. At such a point the droving parties became particularly vulnerable. The profits available to those able to get their stock through to Adelaide were such, however, that the droving parties were prepared to do whatever had to be done to get there.

Chapter Nineteen

Massacre on the Rufus

When news came that herds were approaching the river country again, this time under the command of William Robinson, pressure for protection was again brought to bear on Governor Grey. He attempted to deal with his legal and moral misgivings by placing the Protector of Aborigines in charge of the twenty-nine men he authorised to protect the drovers. Barnard Shaw, sub-Inspector of Police, was appointed as second-in-command. Three Aboriginal men accompanied them as guides, interpreters and go-betweens, one of whom was known as Pangke Pangke.[1] Protector Moorhouse had the task of preventing bloodshed but his orders stated that if his party was under threat of attack, he was authorised to hand over command to sub-Inspector Shaw. With these instructions in hand, on 31 July 1841 the men rode out of Adelaide. Moorhouse found the country around the upper Murray almost empty of people; only the aged, the very young and the infirm remained; everyone else had gone up river to join the attack on the approaching herds.

Moorhouse's arrival at a gathering of people near to Lake Bonney caused panic, women grabbing their babies and running for the safety of the reedbeds. Moorhouse was warned to go no further up-river as the people were angry and preparing for battle. At this news two of the Adelaide Aborigines fled, the third one remaining only because Moorhouse 'did not suffer him to escape'. In other words this man was restrained in some way that was not mentioned. The situation was now very tense. A sheep was speared overnight, the spear left in its side – a clear warning to the colonists that there was trouble on the way. Nevertheless, Moorhouse persuaded three people from this group at Lake Bonney to travel with them to act as negotiators or interpreters. To try to head off any treacherous action from their interpreters, they were told that they must sleep within the men's camp with the others as anyone seen beyond it would be shot. After some shooting exercises intended to impress upon the Aboriginal contingent that they were safe from attack by their own people and would be protected, they marched on toward Lake Victoria, eventually coming upon a large contingent of armed Aborigines as well as Robinson and his herd.

The Precursor – Robinson's Battle
Robinson and Levi's well-armed party of twenty-six men had left Gundagai on the Murrumbidgee River on 1 July 1841. With them travelled 6000 sheep, 14 horses and 500 cattle. By 27 August 1841 when Moorhouse's group of men met up with them at the Rufus River they discovered that a major battle had taken place just the day before. According to Robinson's account, on nearing the Rufus River, they had encountered a large group of Maraura who blocked their passage and refused to disperse when instructed to do so. Robinson collected his sheep and cattle into a defensible position and then, when the approaching Maraura were within twenty yards or so, Robinson's men fired upon them. As the Maraura retreated, Robinson's men followed. In this account, about fifteen were killed and injured. Later accounts say five Maraura men were killed, ten injured.

Whether it was after this battle or that of the following day, Philip Levi is reported to have told Mr A.T. Saunders that in the affray (on the Rufus) they had killed a bearded woman, thinking that she was a man. After death he held her head while another member of the party cut it off, and they brought it to Adelaide as a curiosity.[2] Dorothy Roysland recalled that in her youth, 'The river bank had broken away so that you could see all their bones. You could dig the skeletons out whole, and in those days it was no crime to sell the skulls as souvenirs for seven-and-sixpence each. It was a common sight to see rows of these skulls on the riverbank barges, and the Aborigines used to come up and scowl at them.'[3] It is a claim that fits well with scientific and public interest in the anatomy of Indigenous Australians, the distribution of hair that appeared to link them to the animal world, and the size of their brains. Next day, Robinson and Levi met the Moorhouse party, newly arrived from Adelaide.

Massacre on the Rufus

Both Robinson's men and those with Protector Moorhouse and Sub-Inspector Shaw were now on the Rufus, Robinson looking for the best place to get his herds across the river, Moorhouse instructed to prevent violence erupting while he did so. Within an hour of meeting up, a large group of Maraura men, women and children appeared on the Sydney side of the Rufus.[4] The men were drawn up in a line, quivering their spears and shouting at the drovers. Three of them approached the colonists with a demand for biscuit, tomahawks and other items, requests that I assume were refused. At this point neither spears nor the lethal fighting clubs (waddies) had been thrown, no move to attack had been made, nor was the way of the colonial party blocked.

Nevertheless, believing attack from the approaching Maraura to be inevitable, Moorhouse handed over his command to sub-Inspector Shaw of the police. Whether this constituted an abrogation of his own duty has been often debated. But in doing so without attempting to negotiate he took the step that enabled the violence that his presence was intended to prevent. It is likely that his position as Protector was severely compromised by his position as leader of a force of men looking to fight. Whatever factors shaped Moorhouse's thinking on the day, step aside he did. For those wanting to deliver an effective lesson, the opportunity was too good to miss, and Robinson was not the one to let it pass. Before Shaw could issue his orders, Robinson's men began to shoot, driving the Maurara into the river. From the other (western) side of the river, the police contingent joined in.[5]

The Maraura were caught in the relentless cross-fire that led to so many deaths – thirty to forty according to Robinson with a similar number wounded.[6] Among the dead were the women and children seen on the opposite bank as well as Maraura men; Moorhouse believed thirty had died; others thought more.[7] Hawker believed that Robinson's men were all 'picked marksmen' whose skills contributed to the great number of dead – more than had been reported, he believed. Robinson also stated that two women, a boy and a man known as Pul Kanta were captured. One of the women was claimed by Pangke Pangke, the other liberated. When Pul Kanta, the man taken as a hostage, attempted to escape he was shot in the left arm and lower jaw, then recaptured. Whether Robinson's statement is correct or not, it was certainly not the final episode in what had been a very nasty full-scale battle.

Once the shooting stopped, Maraura women were brought to the camp of the victors. 'The women were brought afterwards with a desire to promote friendly feeling, and the men had intercourse with them', said Mr Phillipson from Robinson's party.[8] More details of the consequences for those women who survived the battle are given in the thoroughly researched accounts gathered together in *Survival in Our Own Land*.[9]

Moorhouse reported rather differently. First, he reported that straight after the 'affray' one of the shepherds asked to have sexual intercourse with the woman assigned to Pangke Pangke as his 'wife' but was refused. Regardless, this shepherd took the woman from her hut, 'much against her will'. A second shepherd then also raped her. By Moorhouse's account, about fifty surviving men, women and children were camped just half a mile away from them. The shepherds went to them and asked for the women, promising meat and clothing in return. When Moorhouse arrived in the camp, three women were being raped by the shepherds with several others standing around watching. Mr Phillipson reprimanded the men who said in reply that they would do as they wished. While the sexual violence of the colony is generally attributed to the appalling nature of drovers and other rough and tough characters in the bush, on the Rufus the indifference of the wealthier and more educated leaders of droving parties that accepted sexual violence actually facilitated it. Either Robinson or Phillipson could have stopped the rapes – they were armed, they held the purse-strings and could withhold or dock wages as they did for other crimes, like stealing. But they did not. In effect they authorised the rape of the women. It is unlikely, of course, that they themselves were always as chaste as they appear in reports of their heroic efforts to bring peace.

Moorhouse continues his report:

> *There were several natives accompanying me from Lake Bonney to Adelaide; but I doubt whether they will reach Adelaide, on account of the incessant application for their wives by the Europeans. When I left the party I placed a sentry at the native hut during the night, and ordered every person who visited the females to be taken in charge by the police.*[10]

Perhaps it was the best he could do, but the likelihood of the police protection being effective seems remote; the Indigenous women were left to their fate.

Moorhouse also reports that he had asked whether the attacks on drovers were due to their behaviour with women but says they replied 'no', that they wanted sheep and clothing from the rewards given to them for the use of their women.[11] There is little doubt, however, that previous experience of the treatment of women by the men of droving parties had been a major factor in causing the violence.

For many years the death toll on the Rufus meant that many of the children were left fatherless, with many of the women wearing the distinctive mourning caps of white gypsum over their shaven heads, caps that marked their status as widows and the funeral rites that should have taken place. Tom Gara has documented a shocking drop in population from the 1850s onwards.[12] It would be surprising, too, if the rape of the Maraura women by the victors had not left behind a trail of venereal diseases, together with the consequences for health already all too evident in Adelaide and Encounter Bay. Grey's instructions to the colonists, good intentions, and his appointment of Moorhouse had had no effect on the outcome of the expedition apart from casting a legitimating veil over a major battle.[13]

Chapter Twenty

After the Rufus

It was inevitable that word of so many deaths should provoke horror and determined criticism in Adelaide as well as calls for an investigation.[1] A Bench of Magistrates that included Major O'Halloran and Edward Eyre was set up to hear evidence from those concerned, with Captain Charles Sturt presiding. Equally inevitable was that the evidence given was coherent and repetitious to a degree that suggests at least some prior consultation and co-ordination among witnesses. By the hearing's end the numbers of dead had shifted from the initial report of fifty (always likely to be an underestimate) to thirty. In addition, the merciless killing of so many Maraura women, children and men had been reframed as 'merciful': it was accepted that there had been absolutely no provocation, either sexual or physical, by members of Mr Robinson's party; there was no recognition that the colonists had been warned of trouble ahead, warnings that

'Old Mrs McKinley, who died at the age of 104 and was buried at the side of our house. As a young woman she had escaped the massacre at the Rufus Creek by swimming away with her son, then a tiny baby, carried on her back'.
Dorothy Roysland 1977, *A Pioneer Family on the Murray River*, Adelaide: Rigby.

they had chosen to ignore but that might have signalled a desire to negotiate. Moreover, Matthew Moorhouse's actions in trying to prevent conflict, as well as his decision to hand command at such an early stage to Sub-Inspector Shaw, were commended. The rape of the Aboriginal women by the victors was mentioned, passed over, and faded from history despite being well-known at the time. Robinson, whose attack was described by later diarists as 'revenge', went on to earn himself a reputation for ruthlessness in his dealings with Aboriginal people.[2] 'He was not shy in using his gun … and was not a man to be trifled with', wrote Skye Krichauff in discussing his later activities on Yorke Peninsula.[3]

As a sop to philanthropic opinion in Adelaide, and also to reinforce the image of the colonial government as a force to be reckoned with, it was at this time that Edward Eyre was appointed as both magistrate and Protector of Aborigines and posted to Moorundie (near today's Blanchetown) on the River Murray in 1841.[4] To ensure peace, two policemen went with him. Twelve soldiers and a non-commissioned officer from the 96th Regiment who earlier had seen the deadly and vicious action against the Aborigines of Van Diemen's Land were sent there too. Governor Grey sent another fifteen men of the 96th Regiment to Port Lincoln under Lieutenant Hugonin. Their actions there justified the description of the regiment by Lester-Irabinna Rigney as 'infamous'.[5] How the Moorundie contingent behaved is less clear although there were said to have been complaints of boredom among the soldiers so perhaps it was indeed quieter.

Rather than settling on the disputed lands around the Rufus, Eyre chose to make his base at Moorundie on land he selected because of its great beauty. While travelling along the river in 1839 he had seen what he called a 'natural avenue' of trees that reminded him of the parks and gardens of England.[6] His first weeks were given over to clearing land for a garden, building a cottage, and walking in his gracious tree-lined avenue. Having come to Australia to make his fortune he had at last achieved his goal. He had become a well-pleased 'man of property'. Eyre's property lay upon Ngaiawung Country, a people with strong political links up and down the river, people who traded with the Ngarrindjeri living far to the south around the lakes and coast at the mouth of the Murray. There the Ngaiawung had important roles in Ngarrindjeri ceremonial life as well as trading connections. Decades later at Moorundie, R. Brough Smyth saw a Ngaiawung 'canoe dance', with two rows of men, bodies decorated with red and white ochre, swaying gently, singing as they paddled while dancing.[7] It is not surprising to find such an important part of river life as the canoe immortalised in the ceremonial practices of the river peoples especially as the great canoes had been such an effective method of escaping the colonists and their guns.[8]

Eyre lived at Moorundie from 1841 until 1844. He is written into South Australian histories as a heroic explorer and as the man who brought peace to a troubled region, doing it through kindness and negotiation rather than through brute force. In an early account of the colony's settlement, the *History of South Australia*, published in 1911, John Blackett wrote that in bringing about a better understanding between river peoples and the colonists, Eyre was 'eminently successful'. Blackett goes on to say: 'He obtained the confidence and the goodwill of the natives and had great influence over them, travelling alone from wurley to wurley and from tribe to tribe up the Murray and the Darling.' Blackett's opinion rests on Eyre's own assessment of his success. He makes this clear by quoting Eyre directly:

> *Said he: 'I have gone almost alone among hordes of fierce and bloodthirsty savages, as they were considered, and have stood singly among them in the remote and trackless wilds when hundreds were congregated around without ever receiving the least injury or insult. In my first visits to the more distant tribes I found them shy, alarmed, and suspicious. But soon learning that I had no wish to injure them they met me with readiness and confidence. My wishes became their law; they conceded points to me that they would not have done to their own people, and on many occasions cheerfully underwent hunger, thirst, and fatigue to serve me.'*[9]

Later authors agreed. Geoffrey Dutton wrote that, 'Eyre had immediate success in restoring good relations between the Aborigines and the settlers', noting also that Charles Sturt had seen Eyre's Moorundie outpost as beneficial and that 'parties of stock were passed down the Murray in perfect safety.' On his first venture into unmapped country Charles Sturt, along with the surveyor, John McDouall Stuart, had passed through Moorundie on their way up-river in August of 1844, with Eyre providing them with a safe passage for the next stage of what would turn out to be an ill-fated journey. Furthermore, Sturt said, any acts of violence or theft by the Indigenous peoples of the district resulted in the perpetrators being delivered up to Eyre, so that 'instead of the Murray being a scene of conflict and slaughter, its whole line is now occupied by stock stations, and tranquillity everywhere prevails'.[10] By this time, however, the country around the Rufus, the Murray and the Darling was thoroughly depopulated. So many killed, so much defilement, so much that many had left. Later assessments of Eyre's role in bringing peace were less fulsome. Foster and Nettelbeck point to the unpublished reminiscences of Henry Melville, who put peace down to the consequences of the terror.[11] Others thought the same.

But as Blackett noted, Eyre 'obtained the confidence and the goodwill of the natives], if not of all of them. The man who helped Eyre to negotiate the difficulties of the post-massacre situation and who developed a degree of confidence in him is known as Tenberry (1798–1855). Described in 1853 as a 'fine, plump, and muscular fellow, he had two wives and was at that time in mourning for a son'. Tenberry was also called Memparnimbe, the father of the child Memparne, and sometimes Worrammo, a reference to his left-handedness. The 'father of' patronymic was applied only to the first child. Warulan and Timarro were both younger than Memparne. Eyre gives Mooroondooyoo Bookola as meaning Old Man of Moorundie.[12] A distinguished man of great authority, Tenberry was crucial in conciliating Eyre's way.[13] He lived around Moorundie for many years, spoke good English and was undoubtedly crucial in negotiating some kind of peaceable relations.[14] A Ngaiawung man, Tenberry was appointed as a 'Native Constable'. He clearly believed that the best interests of his people lay in establishing effective relationships with the new order.[15] Reflecting Eyre's acknowledgement of his relationship with Tenberry, there is an engraving of him as frontispiece in Eyre's book, *Manners and Customs of the Aborigines and the State of Their Relations with Europeans*. It was published in London in 1845 on his return there. Drawn by George Hamilton, the image is of Tenberry in a monogamous-style family with a single wife clad in the rather Romanised style of cloak used to cover her body, and one small boy holding a spear, possibly Warulan, the child Eyre took back to England with him.

Like the Government Resident in Port Lincoln, at Moorundie Eyre had the power to punish local miscreants. Some of the steps Eyre took as he set out to take control of his district in 1842 are mentioned in his letters to Governor Grey.[16] In one, Eyre records the case of a workman who had acquired an Aboriginal man's trousers from him without payment; this man had also extracted a pair from Tenberry. As no reason is given for these incidents it is impossible to know whether they were thefts or part of some other transaction. Eyre did not lay charges against this man but dismissed him from government work. Then early in 1842 Tenberry's eldest son was punished for stealing flour. Eyre put him in leg irons on board the launch *Water Witch* moored on the river, and intended to refuse to give him flour at the next distribution of rations. Tenberry is said to have been taken to see his son in irons but, in an enigmatic comment Eyre wrote that once on board, Tenberry had not taken much notice of his son.

In the course of the year, Eyre reported four cases of petty theft and listed the punishments meted out:

1.	Neiuta stole a small quantity of flour	handcuffs for 24 hours & no flour at next issue.
2.	Tolperoo (a boy) attempted to steal a handful of sugar	12 lashes
3.	Paneranaby stole a quart pot from Koami	hand-cuffs until Monday & then 24 lashes in front of 'the assembled natives'.
4.	Neiuta for attempted but unsuccessful theft of a small quantity of flour	50 lashes because it was a 2nd offence

Eyre does not say who delivered the lashes or whether they were delivered all at once or over a number of sessions, but as he had both soldiers and police stationed at Moorundie, I assume that one of them meted out the punishment rather than forcing a relative of each miscreant into the role of flogger as Governor Grey had recommended for transgressors in Port Lincoln. I have not been able to determine how the lashes were delivered, whether they used the methods of the Adelaide Gaol (a cane or whipcord soaked in water) or whether they used, as was the case among the pastoralists, a stock whip.[17] In his memoirs, Henry Melville described how whippings were carried out on pastoral properties:

> *to the uninitiated I must explain that a stock whip has a thong about twelve feet long with a handle about fifteen inches and when well applied leaves its mark on the hide of a bullock. [S]o the darkie's hide suffered considerably.*[18]

So whether the cane, the official whipcord or the stock whip were in use at Moorundie, the punishments were substantial and made it plain that even small offences would lead to violent retribution from Eyre.

The peace of the Murray lands for which Eyre is so widely recognised was built on a number of factors, only one of which concerned his repeatedly expressed faith in the power of kindness and gift-giving. In the first place, the people he presided over were suffering from the after-effects of the slaughter of women, children and men on the Rufus and the rape of the surviving women. The wives of the dead and the mothers of children were in full mourning; the scale of the deaths inevitably influenced the demographic structure of the surviving people.

Old and respected leaders as well as young men were gone. Just as importantly, the unrestrained violence of the colonists had been revealed, a violence that made clear the other side of the coin of kindness that Eyre proclaimed. In this sense, the peace along the Murray was the peace that follows a wave of destruction – a peace built out of shock, exhaustion, horror, despair and fear. Eyre might speak of his friendly reception as he travelled across those lands, he might picture the people happily feasting on the rich produce of the country, but such a picture has to be matched against that of a grieving, reduced, and raped populace.

The massacre on the Rufus was the largest so far conducted by colonists, greater than the Myall Creek massacre in New South Wales in 1838 that had seen participants taken to court; it would not be equalled until 1928 when the waves of killings known as the Coniston massacre of central Australia were carried out by a similar coalition of pastoralists and police. The wave of terror rolled out from the Rufus massacre was reinforced by Eyre's punishments at Moorundie. They were visual proofs of his power. It was backed up by the dozen or so armed troopers and the two police officers living at the Moorundie Barracks making it less surprising than it seems that he was 'feared as well as loved'.

There was also the work of disease. Disease has always been understood as both a weapon and consequence of war, regularly carrying off far more soldiers than those dying amid the smoke and guns of the European battlefields, just as it would do during Britain's venture into the Crimea in the 1850s. Its effects in the colonising of lands long separated from the germs of the Euro-Asian mainlands were equally well-understood. Eyre recorded that when he arrived at Moorundie in October of 1841, just two months after the massacre, the people there were all healthy, 'almost free of disease', he said. But 'by about October 1844, because of their frequent dealings with the town and nearest pastoral stations, they had contracted the most horrible diseases.' As a result at that time most were ill, some had died, only 'a few of those who frequently had intercourse, of every age and gender, were altogether untouched by this disease in their bodies.'[19] While an epidemic of syphilis could be deadly as well as crippling, gonorrhea produced the infertility that was so important in producing the absence of children so often recorded by those travelling through. Then there was tuberculosis carried by those sent out to Australia with the hope that a drier climate would lead to a cure; and conditions like pneumonia and sepsis that developed in the wake of other diseases. As well as being depleted in numbers, the River people around Moorundie were becoming as sick as those living around Adelaide. By 1851, the Protector would report that three quarters of the women and men of the Yorke Peninsula were infected and very ill indeed, infected initially by colonial men.[20]

Douglas Pike's view was that Eyre had not needed to do much at Moorundie to create peace as, after his appointment, 'both the overland [droving] routes fell into disuse ...' In his last quarterly report as Police Commissioner, O'Halloran wrote under the heading 'Overlanders': 'None have arrived from the neighbouring colonies of late but eight men and one woman started a short time since from Adelaide for Portland Bay' [in Victoria].[21] It was perhaps just as well that the overland traffic in herds had withered away just as the river peoples' capacity to oppose it was so greatly reduced.

Given the need to come to terms with the great disruptions facing the river peoples at a time of violence, fear and sickness, it is not surprising to find that, as in Adelaide, fears for their personal safety, their futures, and the disruption of their social lives by so many deaths were translated into powerful images of a world out of control. The disruption of the natural cycles and linkages of daily life produced by the colonists was sufficient to trigger fears of retribution, of a world turned vindictive, of forces unleashed from the controls that should have preserved its order. This is what Eyre records:

> *Anything that is extraordinary or unusual, is a subject of great dread to the natives: of this I had a singular instance at Moorunde. In March, 1843, I had a little boy living with me by his father's permission, whilst the old man went up the river to hunt and fish. On the evening of the 2nd of March a large comet was visible to the westward, and became brighter and more distinct every succeeding night. On the 5th I had a visit from the father of the little boy who was living with me, to demand his son; he had come down the river post haste for that purpose, as soon as he saw the comet, which he assured me was the harbinger of all kinds of calamities, and*

more especially to the white people. It was to overthrow Adelaide, destroy all Europeans and their houses, and then taking a course up the Murray, and past the Rufus, do irreparable damage to whatever or whoever came in its way. It was sent, he said, by the northern natives, who were powerful sorcerers, and to revenge the confinement of one of the principle men of their tribe, who was then in Adelaide gaol, charged with assaulting a shepherd; and he urged me by all means to hurry off to town as quickly as I could, to procure the man's release, so that if possible the evil might be averted. No explanation gave him the least satisfaction, he was in such a state of apprehension and excitement, and he finally marched off with the little boy, saying, that although by no means safe even with him, yet he would be in less danger than if left with me.[22]

Although Eyre offered no further commentary on this incident, moving straight on into a discussion of sorcery and witchcraft, it reveals a good deal about the fears circulating around the river lands in the wake of the killings on the Rufus and their aftermath. Their hope is placed in the people to the north, the not yet settled lands where order and their real Law still prevailed, where the powers of the non-colonial world were still active, still nurtured, and still understood. As the cultivated, intelligent intermediary for his people described by those who knew him at Moorundie, Tenberry must have known and sorrowed for his people and his country and the changes being forced upon them all. The photograph of Tenberry said to date from 1847 shows him as an older man, his eyes so very mournful, his life in tatters by then, his children dead, wives gone, and standing there with no clothes, a very clean beard, and looking like the specimen of scientific interest he had become. An exceptionally sad image of such a remarkable man.

After Eyre

The artist William Cawthorne visited Moorundie after Eyre had left to return to Adelaide. Cawthorne made a sketch of Nulgta, one of the men living around Moorundie at the time, showing his head-dress and body scars.

'Tenbury (at *c.* 60) Chief of the Murray Bend tribes. 1847. S. Australia'. Albumen Print. Courtesy Pitt Rivers Museum (PR 1998.249.33.1 and Mannum Aboriginal Community Association, Inc.

Cawthorne, who had a great deal of sympathy for the plight of the Indigenous peoples of the colony, also prepared a painting of the Rufus massacre. Drawn from descriptions rather than life, he shows the Maraura caught between the drovers and the police, some of them in the water.[23] He shows large numbers of armed Maraura massed together, caught in the cross-fire. At the same time, he has minimised the numbers of colonists – there were many more of them than he shows – creating an impression of the few against the many and in the process emphasising the deadly capacity of superior weaponry. This may be how he heard or understood the accounts of what had happened, or it may simply have been too time-consuming to get the numbers right. What is missing altogether from the picture are the women and children mentioned in reports. The small figure at the rear of the Maraura contingent might well be a recognition of their presence, an indication that in Adelaide, the presence of women and children among the men was known.

William Cawthorne, 'A fight at the Murray'.
Courtesy State Library of NSW

'Conflict on the Rufus, South Australia', Engraved by Samuel Calvert from a sketch by W.A. Cawthorne; published in
The Illustrated Melbourne Post, 1866.
Courtesy State Library of Victoria

In Samuel Calvert's engraving, made from Cawthorne's painting and published in 1866 when reminiscences of the frontier life of the old days were becoming popular, the presence of women and children on the battlefield reappeared although they are still few. Calvert has retained the small figure at the back of the central mass of Aboriginal bodies and added some more clearly defined Aboriginal figures to the foreground. They add an element of menace that was lacking in Cawthorne's painting, heightening the effect of relatively few mounted colonists facing a very large number of Aboriginals.

Once the inquiry into the massacre was over and Eyre was installed at Moorundie as magistrate, the Rufus River massacre settled quietly into the past, not forgotten but set aside until literary accounts of the 'old frontier days' like those written by John Wrathall Bull and Simpson Newland, became popular; and from time to time the massacre appeared in newspapers as in the engraving printed in *The Illustrated Melbourne Post*. But neither was it prominent. A newspaper mention of the massacre in 1934 written by Archer Russell took the form of a recollection given to him in conversation with an 'old-timer':[24]

> *"Yes', he answered. 'I used to hear the old dad speak of it at times. But that's the sort of thing one likes to forget. It was little to our credit.'*
>
> *'You know,' he went on, 'this place used to be a favourite camping place of the overlanding cattlemen going down to Adelaide on their way in from New South Wales. Somewhere about the [eighteen] forties, I think it was. It was also the main camping ground of the Rufus River blacks – big, dangerous fellows they were, an' full of the devil.*
>
> *'Well, the inevitable happened – the nigs got flinging their spears about, an' they clashed. But the cattlemen fought 'em off, an' sent word through to Adelaide, an' that was the end of 'em – the blacks, I mean. A big mob of police came up, ran 'em into the gooseneck of the river down there, an' butchered 'em off.'*
>
> *'What, all of them?'*

> 'No, two got away, so the old dad said, a young gin with her piccaninny. Swam across the river with the kid on her back. Some gin she must have been. That was the last of the Rufus River blacks. They were all buried in the gooseneck down there.

The woman who got away is perhaps Mrs McKinley pictured at the beginning of this chapter, a woman Archer Russell may well have met in the years he spent around the river. Like the unfortunate woman beheaded after earlier fighting, Mrs McKinley has not removed her facial hair but wears it without concern. Its presence was just one element of differing attitudes to the body and the ways in which hairiness was and remains such a problem for non-Indigenous Australian women.

More recently, historians have again drawn the terrible killings around the Rufus River to public attention, working from new sources, offering new perspectives, attempting to present more realistic accounts of the colonisation of South Australia.[25] Yet it is not an easy task. Take Edward Eyre's appointment as magistrate at Moorundie on Ngaiawung country, for example. After so many killings, after so much rape, how could one man bring peace to the river?

Edward Eyre has entered history in Australia as an indefatigable explorer, the man who walked across the top of the Great Australian Bight in order to find a route from Adelaide to King George Sound in Western Australia; a hero indeed. The literary scholar Kay Shaffer came to consider that Eyre's reputation as explorer rested upon 'an experience of failure blown up to typically Australian epic proportions.'[26] In that epic, as in other epic Australian failures (like Gallipoli in the first of the European World Wars) Eyre appears as a hero. In England he is remembered differently. There he is known for the harshness of his methods in putting down a revolt of freed slaves in 1865 in order to preserve the colonial authority of the British Crown. His actions in Jamaica split the humanitarian movement into his supporters (like the historian, Thomas Babbington Macaulay) and his critics (like John

Stuart Mill and Charles Darwin), turning friend against friend, ally against ally. The West Indian descendants of those involved speak of Eyre's time as 'the killing time'; he is known as a monster who lashed, burned and destroyed those who sought no more than justice, while the man Eyre hanged, George William Gordon, is honoured as a National Hero.[27] Perhaps the two aspects of the man epitomised by Geoffrey Dutton in the title of his book, *The Hero as Murderer* – the bringer of peace and the terrible avenger of anti-colonial revolt in Jamaica – are not really so very far apart.

Part Four

Toward the South-East

Chapter Twenty-One

Wellington

Just after the fighting on the Rufus River, Protector Moorhouse received instructions that he should leave the party heading for Adelaide to travel instead to Wellington to investigate the killing of the drover, George McGrath. Moorhouse and his sister held at least 122,500 acres (*c*. 50,000 hectares) of good Ngarrindjeri country including some of their important fishing grounds. With its coastal and riverine resources, bird life, plentiful stocks of reeds, rushes and vegetable foods, Ngarrindjeri country was said to be the richest in Australia.[1] Whether it was or not, theirs was a bountiful country in which the river, lakes and Kurangk-Coorong underpinned a flourishing fishing, weaving and canoe culture.

Wellington, where Protector Moorhouse went to speak to Police Corporal Mason about McGrath's death, was the colonists' town that had grown up at a Ngarrindjeri crossing-point on the River Murray. The rickety Wellington ferry established in 1839 was on the track linking Adelaide to Port Phillip Bay in Victoria. Travellers and drovers alike used it to get across the Murray. At the time of McGrath's murder this traffic was increasing and the colonists were moving rapidly southwards in search of good land.

As a land-holder and Protector, Matthew Moorhouse was well-known on Ngarrindjeri Country. On his arrival from the Rufus the people living around Wellington agreed to help in finding McGrath's murderers. In return, they would receive blankets. Just to make sure,

Sketch Map showing Wellington just at the point at which the Murray River feeds the lakes through which it reaches the sea.

Moorhouse refused to distribute the blankets until the murderers were in his hands.[2] Despite Moorhouse's need for help in identifying and locating the killers of McGrath, the unquestioning reliance placed on Ngarrindjeri guides and negotiators at the time of the *Maria* killings seems to have been replaced by a less trusting attitude. Wariness was inflecting colonial attitudes despite the very real contributions of negotiators and intermediaries like Tammuruwe Nankanere/'Encounter Bay Bob' and 'Big Solomon'. One of McGrath's murderers was identified as Wirra Maldira, possibly the man who had helped entice one of the

Milmenrura murderers into their pursuers' camp; another was named as Wek Weki, and both were identified in the courts as Ngarrindjeri men. But the initial search for the murderers of George McGrath was unsuccessful even though Wirra Maldira (Encounter Bay Peter) was well-known to local colonists and had been seen around various properties. It was three years before he came before the courts.

Chapter Twenty-Two

1842, Murder of George McGrath

Wira Maldira/'Encounter Bay Peter', the Ngarrindjeri man who had helped the colonists to locate the *Maria* dead and then to deal with those accused of having been involved in the killings, came before the Adelaide court early in 1845 referred to in a headline as 'A Native from Lake Alexandrina'. He was charged with murdering George McGrath who had been killed on or about 2 June 1842.[1] Three years is a long time to have spent in trying to capture the killers of a man who had no particular status or significance in the life of the colony. It indicates the importance placed on tracking down and dealing with any sign of resistance to colonisation, an importance often expressed as 'teaching them a lesson'. It was not that the police did not know who they were looking for nor that he was still living in the district. Wira Maldira had been seen a number of times, but always seemed able to vanish among the islands and swamps of the lakes. Whether George Mason had a role in searching for him or was protecting him in some way is not clear.

*****

George McGrath had been one of the many men who formed a floating, often anonymous workforce who had to accept any kind of work and wage, living as best they could, largely on hope. He had arrived in South Australia with a herd brought from Portland Bay in Victoria. Although his name suggests he might have been Irish, possibly Catholic and thus possibly a convict, his murderers were pursued. McGrath's willingness as well as his need to take on four local Indigenous men as guides for the long journey from Adelaide back to Portland Bay and the closeness of the interactions between the men in his party offers an insight into the kind of relationships that could emerge among those yet to find a financial toe-hold in the colony. Newspaper reports of the trial of McGrath's murderers describe the men camping for the night around a fire, sleeping close to each other, waking to pass around a pipe of tobacco, of sharing it – a kind of coalition of the socially excluded. But these were not the relations of equality between men. Nights were dangerous times along the track. Perhaps McGrath and his companions Chace and Pugh calculated that it was better to have the four Ngarrindjeri guides safely in sight, where they might be watched. For there were suggestions that earlier in the day McGrath or perhaps one of the others travelling with him had taken a woman away from one of the Ngarrindjeri men. There were also suggestions that the guns of the drovers had been an enticement for the attack and that rations promised in return for help had been withheld.

In the event, the drovers had slept, and at some stage in the night Wira Maldira and his companions, named as Wekiweki, Koorykownimmi and Pantowyn, had made a determined assault upon them. George McGrath had been killed with a blow from a club while the badly beaten William Chace and William Pugh (or Pew) had fled, abandoning their guns, gear and blankets, desperately hoping to find their way to McLeod's station house in search of help. In 1845 all those involved came before the court. Wira Maldira was convicted and hanged. Wekiweki received a lesser charge and a death sentence that was commuted to a term of imprisonment. Later he was pardoned.

Newspaper reports of the trials show that the judge relied on an account of the night's events provided by Chace that was supplemented by those given by the two young Ngarrindjeri men who had been involved in the attack, Pantowyn and Koorykownimmi. They had been taken to Adelaide, bathed, trimmed and neatly dressed in order to appear more as if they were of the 'civilised' rather than the 'savage native' category. In return they were not prosecuted. Just as was the case when Wirra Maldira wrongly delivered two men to O'Halloran's party searching for those who had killed the passengers and crew of the *Maria*, the use of evidence from the two younger men against Wirra Maldira and Wekiweki had the potential to cause discord and resentment among the Ngarrindjeri, the potential to create a sense of grievance and injustice that could ripple around through the community, causing trouble.

In the published notices of the murder and trial, the claims expressed in the mythological mantras of *our peaceful natives*, and *there was no war in South Australia*, and later, the question, *why didn't THEY fight back*, were crucial to the way the colonists thought about themselves and what they were doing. The early arrival of South Australian law, Jeffcott's sentiments of equality before it, and the importance of being a lawful and thus a just colony had not been swept away by Gawler's lapse from its principles in the *Maria* case, nor by the volunteer posse sent to the Rufus. It remained crucial to have any resistance to colonisation dealt with as it should be, for responses to it to be legally correct and proper. So three years was not so long to wait in order to put McGrath's murderers on trial.

What had emerged in South Australia by the time of McGrath's murder was that the mantle of English law covering the whole of the colony and all those living under it had fragmented. Within the law there now lived an incubus, a zone in which acts illegal in law could be carried out lawfully – if they were considered necessary or unavoidable. Although the violence of dispossession might be untrammelled it could now be construed as both necessary and acceptable, as a form of action that was not-illegal. The Rufus River massacre took place in this zone of not-illegal violence that had been authorised by the Governor of the colony.

Such shadowy legality meant that in districts distant from Adelaide the violence of dispossession was not simply out of sight of the forces of law but tolerated within it. In such a conflicted approach to the new law of the land and the colonists' doctrines of peaceful settlement, it was useful to have resistance perceived and understood as isolated incidents or as attacks explained as being provoked by individual acts like, 'they raped his wife earlier in the day' – which in McGrath's case was perfectly plausible. It was also useful to think that peace would come as soon as people realised how they had to behave to the colonists. It was the heartfelt desire for peace that made it difficult to think of the Indigenous people as fighting a war against them, a guerrilla war perhaps, one in which the destruction of flocks, horses and property loomed as large as major attacks on individual colonists.

McGrath's murder breached the conventional assumption of the peaceable nature of the colony's Indigenous peoples, and it took place on Country that was being taken from its owners at a considerable rate. There was increasing unrest in the colony as settlers pushed out from Adelaide, southwards toward Mt Gambier, north through the Flinders Ranges and over to the Eyre Peninsula where resistance from the Battara and others was fierce. In this expanding colonial domain and coming as it did in the wake of the fighting on the Rufus River it was inevitable that McGrath's murder at Murundundungah (McGrath Flat) should lead to calls for firm action. The murder challenged the law under which all now lived and it stated clearly that all would be treated equally. The prosecution of his killers, no matter how flawed by language difficulties, cultural misunderstandings and doubtful evidence, bolstered the colonists' sense of order and lawfulness. It reassured them of the justice and righteousness of their project.

Yet for all that equal treatment, Alan Pope's analysis of police and court records from the first decades of the colony shows that of the nineteen incidents in which colonists were charged with either the assault or murder of an Indigenous person, only one was found guilty. He was hanged. On the other hand, Pope lists nearly eighty Aborigines before the court for killing colonists. Of these, twenty-three were executed and one died in custody.[2] Because of language difficulties and also because of concerns about if, how or when English law should be applied to Indigenous subjects of the Crown, some of those charged with murder or manslaughter were discharged, particularly in the earlier years. Such 'leniency' and failure to deliver a lesson on the power and expectations of the new regime provoked immediate claims that if law was failing to punish miscreants, retribution would be taken by the settlers themselves. This was a claim repeated and repeated as settlers spread out. It was one of those polarised either/or claims that allowed those in favour of teaching the First Australians a lesson that they would never forget to ignore alternative strategies emanating from Adelaide. The numbers of those charged and the outcomes of the trials offer an insight into how the law was brought to bear on Indigenous people unequally, into how, from the start, its protections were rarely available to a colonised people. The readiness to execute, too, is striking, even though Judge Cooper's published remarks on the need for knowledge of British law or custom and his insistence on adequate interpretation indicate the way in which the law acted as a brake in some instances.[3] Those early cases establish patterns of racialised violence backed by government that not only had consequences for those immediately subject to it and for those exerting its force, but also for the nature of the society and the practices of the governments that would be built from them. These are matters that became clearer and clearer as more and more Country was put under colonial title.

At the time of McGrath's murder, Ngarrindjeri Country lay on the edge of country that was reasonably easy to police under law. Further south lay Tatiara Country that was not. Like the Milmenrura they had a reputation as fierce and dangerous.

Chapter Twenty-Three

Cannibals at the Margins of Society

When asked whether he thought that since the attack on the peoples living around the Rufus River other droving parties would now be able to travel safely, Robinson's answer was 'no'. He did not think the 'natives were yet intimidated' and that people using the route who did not have sheep or cattle would be murdered. When asked why, he answered: 'I think they would eat them.' He continued:

> I have heard, from what I consider good authority, that they are cannibals. I do not think any party, to bring over stock now, should consist of less than thirty men.[1]

Robinson's claim that the river peoples were killing drovers in order to eat them was not a fact but an example of how the imaginary cannibal was used to justify the violence of colonisation. As a potent mix of fact and fantasy the idea of the cannibal monster had fascinated Europeans for centuries but the horror attached to it became much stronger in the nineteenth century as racial theories became more and more important and as violence increased.[2] In Australia the use of cannibalism to discredit the quality of Aboriginal society and people has never died. Belief in an Indigenous cannibal past holds sway, with old references to cannibalism in newspapers and diaries treated as fact rather than fantasy.[3] Most recently the image of the Indigenous cannibal of the colonial past was called up once more by Hugh Morgan of the Western Mining Corporation. He made public claims about

Indigenous cannibalism to help justify the mining industry's campaign to oppose and discredit Aboriginal claims for landrights.[4] Morgan's allegation was supported by very conservative Christian members of the mining lobby who, in a somewhat perverted proposition, asserted that while the invasion and colonisation of Australia may indeed have required a degree of violence, in exchange it has given Aboriginal Australians the great gift of Christianity.

A measure of the enduring public fascination with transgressive cannibalism can be seen in the popularity of Herbert Basedow's book, *Knights of the Boomerang. Episodes from a Life Spent among the Native Tribes of Australia*. It is one of a few supposedly first-hand accounts of Indigenous Australian men baking a corpse, the smell of roasting human flesh, the noisy munching of those feasting on the body and other details. First published in 1935 (after the author's death), it was reprinted in 2004 and again in 2010. Basedow inserted a chapter on cannibalism into his manuscript in order to help with sales. Entirely fanciful, it marked the end of Basedow's more scientific work and of his humanitarian hopes of improving Indigenous lives by racial policies.[5]

Better known, perhaps, is the scandal caused by Daisy Bates when late in her life, she published *The Passing of the Aborigines* in 1938. Her claim that Aboriginal women ate their babies ensured good sales and supported mission fundraising campaigns. Drawing on earlier concepts of horror, it was an old slur put to use to clinch an argument or make a case. In 1865-66 claims circulated in Australia that the drought was so bad that northern Aborigines were said to be eating their babies.[6] But Bates is a readily available source for more recent popular conviction of the reality of Indigenous cannibalism even though in other contexts many of her readers would regard her as eccentric at best, at worst slightly touched if not crazed. Bates' life was indeed a fascinating one – the tale of the penniless young Irish girl struggling to find an independent life in the colonies, her bigamous marriages, her long Edwardian dresses, her adventurous visit to the north of Western Australia and her camps at Fowlers Bay, Eucla and Ooldea where she tended her 'dying race' beside the railway line linking Adelaide to Perth.

Bates' anthropological writings were less known than her journalism and her book until the distinguished anthropologist Sally White looked at Bates' notes and edited some of them for publication.[7] White concluded that, 'Though Mrs. Bates' observations and descriptions are of great value, she seemed incapable of making logical deductions from these.'[8]

Bates was a great storyteller. With little or nothing by way of an income, her public writings, her prolific journalism and *The Passing of the Aborigines* were aimed at earning money. She had a very good idea of what might sell and cannibalism was one of the topics she used regularly. She published 'Cannibal Aborigines' in Melbourne's *Australasian* in 1928.[9] The claims she made in 'Cannibal Aborigines' are extravagant; but her statement that no-one will admit to ingesting human flesh when asked, that it is always the 'other fellows' who are guilty of such appalling behaviour, is an example of how cannibalism often tends to disappear the closer one gets to it.

In her early West Australian anthropological studies Daisy Bates made few references to cannibalism. At one stage she noted: I travelled in the train from Geraldton with two cannibals from the district east of Lawlers. Sally White commented on this paragraph: 'Mrs Bates was probably reflecting the views of the Aborigines of the western part of Western Australia, who believed the people of the desert to the east of them to be savages and cannibals'. Although we can learn of cannibals prowling along Indigenous boundaries we still do not see the cannibals themselves. Bates' earlier manuscript for the unpublished *The Native Tribes of Western Australia* was more careful about cannibalism, but it is *The Passing of the Aborigines* with its scandalous allegations of women feasting on their babies for which she is mostly remembered.

As Andrew Lattas has shown, fears and allegations of cannibalism in Australia were crucial in creating the sense of savagery used to justify not only the initial violence of colonisation but also to magnify the sense of radical cultural differences that serve to intensify the racial hierarchy on which a new and modern society was being built.[10] The image of the Aboriginal as a cannibal monster was black, his face ugly, his women even uglier (unless very young when she tended to be seen as lissome), his nature violent to a degree that questioned his humanity. Here is a damaging mythical image of the cannibal body applied over and over again to the Aboriginal people of Australia.

Accusations of cannibalism serve to blot out an inconvenient truth about the reality of colonisation, the truth that it is not a peaceful process and that it cannot be accomplished without violence.[11] Allegations of cannibalism deflect attention away from the savage nature of the colonists themselves. It was a colonist, for example, who had an Aboriginal man's head hung on a nail in his hut, just as later a pastoralist in the Northern Territory was famed for his collection of Aboriginal ears, nailed to a post or a door.[12]

Robinson's public claims about the dangers of cannibals along the overland track from Sydney to Adelaide are not innocent mistakes based on ignorance but indicate a clear strategy in play in dealing with the official investigation into the Rufus River massacre: first, destroy, then discredit, and finally, deflect attention away from the real causes of hostility – a 'look over there, nothing to see here' tactic in the war for the land. The claim that only large parties of colonists would be safe on the track – at least thirty men – is being used as an indicator of the very great danger surrounding the rich, well-watered river lands and the colonists' equally great desire to settle upon them.

With the first phase of the strategy, to *destroy*, carried out already on the Rufus, the label of 'cannibal' was intended to *discredit* Indigenous opposition to colonisation, to reveal the depths of savagery to be found in the local riverland peoples, to present them as utter barbarians, undeserving of concern or sympathy from any ill-informed Adelaide humanitarians who might think of taking an interest in what was happening. The allegation of cannibalism was also crucial in the third phase of the strategy. It *deflected* attention away from the real cause of any continuing danger along the post-massacre droving track – the determined resistance to colonisation on the one hand, and on the other the untrammelled violence of drovers and the punitive massacre facilitated by Governor Grey. It shifted attention instead onto the supposedly inherent cannibal nature of the people living there, raising the possibility that they were barely human at all. It certainly raised the level of fear in Adelaide as it brought the South Australian experience into line with the cannibalistic tales circulating in the eastern colonies. Rising fear lowers public resistance to actions that would be illegal or condemned under ordinary conditions. As more and more Country was taken from its real owners the fear-effect became more and more important in shaping attitudes to the violence being deployed as colonists moved outwards from Adelaide onto new Country. In colonial eyes, cannibals lurked at the edges of the colony. At the time of the Rufus River massacre, the rich river country had been beyond the limits of the survey line and largely policed by posses of volunteers, pastoralists and their employees. So the thought of a fierce, black, monstrous people, living around the margins of their civilised society, a people who would actually eat the bodies of those working so hard to give them the gifts of modern civilisation, of true religion and its peace – created a fearsome, awe-filled, horrifying image indeed.

As settlement expanded during the 1840s there was such resistance that the colonists found themselves fighting on several fronts. A major front had opened up on the Eyre Peninsula, there was trouble in the northern Flinders Ranges and on the Yorke Peninsula, and there was fighting and harassment in the south-east on the Bugandik and Tatiara lands, still considered 'new' and still under violent dispossession by pastoralists arriving from the eastern colonies as well as from Adelaide. Robert Leake, for example is said to have lost forty sheep one night and in 1845, a thousand. Huts or houses were built as fortresses with attack in mind.[13] This was a wild country indeed, just the kind of place to be inhabited by cannibal monsters.

Cannibals on Tatiara and Bugandik Country

Accusations that the Tatiara people were cannibals emerged in the press with the 1846 killing of Richard Carney, a shepherd travelling near Lake Mundi close to the colony's eastern border. Although three men were said to have been involved in Carney's murder, the police caught only one, a man known as 'Tatty' Wamboureem, 'Tatty' being probably an English contraction of Tatiara. The report of the murder provided by the *South Australian Register* concluded with the statement that: 'some civilised natives had informed Mr Cameron he [Carney] was killed about the 11th Nov., cut up, and eaten by the natives in that neighbourhood. The natives materially assisted him in his endeavours to apprehend 'Tatty', having promised them blankets &c. for their efforts.'[14]

By the end of December, the allegation of cannibalism, allegedly laid by 'civilised natives', had become more elaborated. 'We have been enabled to gather the following additional particulars of the murder of Carney by the natives in the neighbourhood of Lake Mundy', they said,

> ... the unfortunate man, whilst in friendly conversation with the prisoner and his lubra was pierced through the side with a barbed spear, and tortured by its being drawn to and fro. When the prisoner was thus employed, the lubra commenced beating him over the head with a waddie; and to complete the details of the most horrid murder ever committed in this province, or perhaps any other. Whilst the deceased was yet in the agonies of death, his murderer, looking him steadfastly in the face, imitated his agonising gestures, and the woman commenced disembowelling him, in order to consummate [sic] the bloody deed by a cannibal feast.[15]

In this gruesome scenario, the alleged cruelty of Carney's death and the subsequent eating of his body was picked up and circulated by other colonial newspapers where it bolstered its fellows in the already circulating mythology of cannibalism in eastern Australia.[16]

The claim that cannibalism had been involved in the murder of Richard Carney was followed by a supposedly eye-witness account in a letter to the *South Australian Register* from Kenneth Campbell of Mt Carmel, County Grey (on Buandig Country) in which he shifted the allegation of cannibalism from an individual act to a general practice of the Tatiara. The gruesome details he provided had, the *Register* said, 'fully convinced us that this revolting usage is generally prevalent in the Tatiara country and its vicinity'. The journalist went on to state as fact that the people living around Mt Muirhead had their eye on a very fat woman whom they were trying to purchase with a view to eating her, offering in exchange two lean women.[17]

It is hard to know why a reasonably reputable newspaper would have published such nonsense. The intention may have been to whip up public support for increasing a police presence in a region known to harbour all sorts of criminal colonists, or perhaps to offer the public a justification for the violence of dispossession. Whatever the reasoning at the time, the allegations of cannibalism among the Tatiara and Buandig emerged at the height of British expansion onto their Countries and settler violence against them, with the Cameron family, who by 1851 held over 250,000 acres (c. 101,171 hectares) 'of the richest land in the South East', among those at the fore of it.[18] The map below shows how the good lands around the River Murray were snapped up early by the canny and privileged.

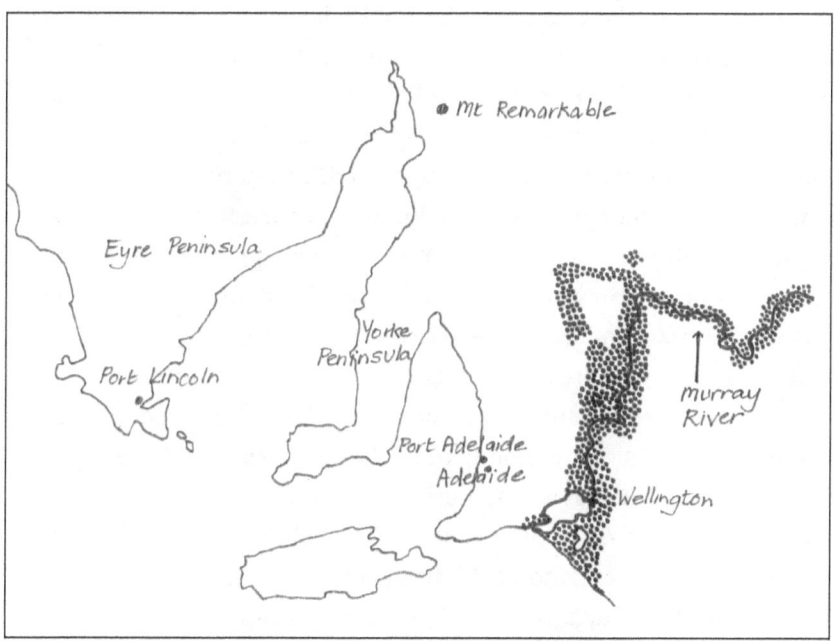

'The Province 1850', showing the early clustering of pastoral leases along the River Murray and the lakes at its mouth by 1855. Tatiara country lies south of this area. From: Griffin, Trevor and Murray McCaskill 1986 (eds), *Atlas of South Australia*, Adelaide: South Australian Government.

Although arrested, the accused cannibal, Wamboureen, never went to trial because no-one could speak his language, although Duncan Smith was able to ascertain that Carney had had sexual relations with Wambareen's wife.[19] After fifteen months in gaol awaiting trial, Wamboureen had to be discharged, an outcome that led once more to public concern that the failure of the legal system to punish Aboriginal miscreants would lead to settlers taking the law into their own hands.[20] This they undoubtedly did.

Truth, Fiction and Cannibal Tales

The allegations of cannibalism circulating in the colony were not based on fact but on fascination and the use of accusations to justify the 'clearing' and 'quieting' of the country. In Australia, as has been shown by Tracey Banivanua-Mar's research in Fiji (often referred to by the British as 'the Cannibal Isles'), colonial cannibalism fades away, vanishing over the horizon as the investigator approaches closer to it.[21] According to his own account Robinson's allegation was based on a 'good authority' who remains anonymous; the case for Carney being eaten relies on information from 'some civilised natives' (anonymous) who told Mr Cameron (hearsay only) who in turn told the newspaper reporter; while the story about an attempt by people near Mt Muirhead to exchange two thin women for one lusciously plump one, so obviously linked to fantasy, nevertheless serves to bolster the colonists' claims that Aboriginal men treated their women with violent contempt. There are no verifiable accounts of any of these tales. W.H. Leigh's claim in his reminiscences that the body of the botanist Richard Cunningham, lost in New South Wales, had been eaten, however, was known to be false. Those who finally found Cunningham's body simply reburied his remains and set off for home. Written years later, Leigh's allegation of cannibalism illustrates the way in which accusations float around in colonial mythologies, a horror story ready to be attached to any passing body as and when required.

Because of the marketing and political value of such tales, it does not really matter whether the claims are true or not. This is because they address fears and beliefs that exist in the imagination quite independently of any proofs. In reality, the best documented incident of cannibalism in colonial Australia concerns not an Indigenous person but a Tasmanian convict, the notorious Alexander Pearce who was prosecuted in 1824; photographs of his skull can be seen on the internet. On the whole, English law tended to make cannibalism illegal *unless it was necessary*; in Pearce's case it was not.

Fascinating Cannibalism

While much written about cannibalism in the nineteenth century was fantasy, the strength of public interest in the cannibal and the desire for the imaginary cannibal to be real can be gauged in part through the huge crowds attracted by displays of supposedly 'real cannibals'. Roslyn Poignant's careful, detailed and moving account of the ways in which several groups of people kidnapped from Palm Island in Queensland by R.A. Cunningham in the 1880s and '90s were taken around America and Europe to be marketed and exhibited as cannibals (as the word made flesh), serves as a revealing if horrifying demonstration of the fascination with the fantasy of the cannibal that was so widespread that good money could be made from it. What was it that made the cannibal so fascinating on such a large scale?

One factor perhaps was the massive eighteenth and nineteenth century exodus of populations from Europe onto supposedly empty lands or to the lands of supposedly inferior peoples. With the impact of colonisation on colonised peoples only too clear by the nineteenth century, mythical social horrors to be found among colonisation's victims may have helped to assuage European Christian consciences. Poignant argued that the Western obsession with the consumption of human flesh reflects the way in which it had come to mark an absolute boundary between the civilised self and the cannibal other.'[22] Her argument is important because it points to the way in which the two images, the civilised colonist and the savage cannibal, are bound together tightly. By not being a cannibal, the colonist is at once more civilised and superior.

The reality was, that Europeans, no matter where they lived, were familiar with their own forms of ingesting the body parts of other humans. A range of body parts – some taken from executed criminals because they were held to be more powerful: blood, placenta and the well-known 'mummy' said to have been imported from Egypt – were all dispensed by doctors and druggists. These were common treatments that were never connected to cannibalism. English law also recognised the consumption of human bodies as legal in times of need, as among members of Sir John Franklin's ill-fated voyage through the Arctic seas in 1845. Due to being cast up upon deserted islands or coasts, mariners often found themselves in need as did those caught up in famines or in towns surrounded by hostile soldiers who were trying to starve them out.[23] In all these cases, the horror of cannibalism was far from anybody's mind.

Nor did Christians consider the imagery of the rites of the Eucharist by which the body and blood of Christ were taken directly into the body of the communicant as a cannibal ritual, although often enough it has been discussed. Indeed it has caused huge splits among Christian congregations, some of which were active among Adelaide's Christians. While some opt for the Eucharist as symbolic, others maintain its absolute reality. The Australian poet Les Murray (1938–2019) for example, maintained that the bread and the wine taken during this rite are truly transubstantiated, that is, in taking the blessed bread and wine into their body they are taking in the body of their God to truly become the body and blood of the man they know as Christ their Saviour. God and person become as one. Such powerful imagery, such widespread practice, such holiness, and such a presence of the sacred within the individual person cannot be thought of as only symbolic – it is actively transformative. In this way of thinking the eucharistic meal is *not* cannibalism but a mystery. Looked at from outside, the rite offers a positive image of the ingestion of the flesh of Jesus the Man that is not-cannibalism (as in the negative form of a positive photographic print).

In summary, the European and Australian fascination with cannibalism might have arisen from all or some of the practices of their own society and religion and from its practical political uses as a way of damning those accused of it. I am not speaking here of those societies in which the eating of human flesh is seen as sacrifice, or as a way of gaining power from enemies, or as a respectful way of keeping parts of the dead close and dear. What is often missing from the panoply of human behaviour is the practice of eating human flesh in order to gain access to protein – except in countries like England where it is permissible if necessary, or in the United States where there is no law against it.[24] That acts of cannibalism cause so much legal trouble today, even when the victim consents to be killed and eaten, is a measure of how effective erroneous nineteenth century beliefs have been that the ingestion of human flesh was a definitive marker of the savagery of *other* cultures. Not *ours*.

Part Five

The North and Eyre Peninsula

Chapter Twenty-Four

Port Lincoln

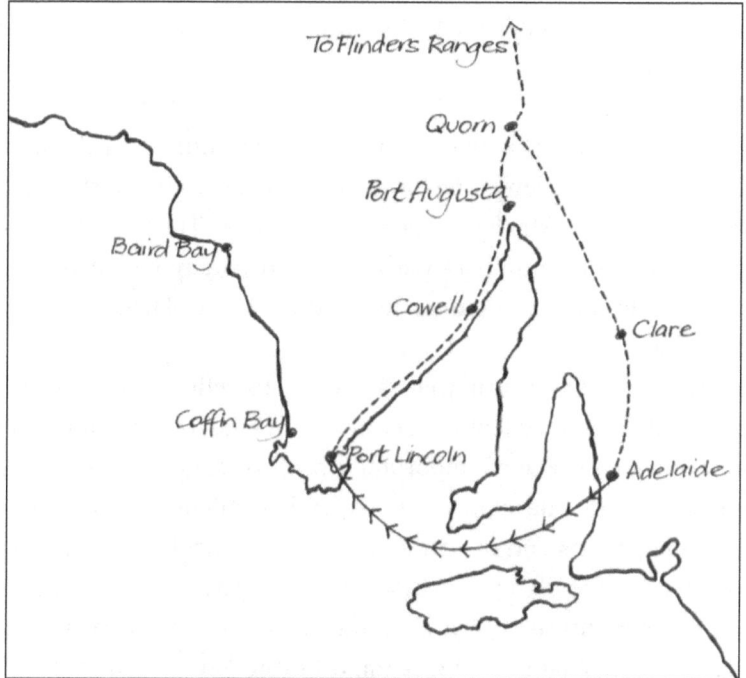

The shortest and safest route from Adelaide to Port Lincoln was by sea. The overland route remained dangerous for some time

Port Lincoln was settled early but it was very small. Around 1840 there were just 220 settlers and 30 houses clinging to the small open bay on the coast of Nawu country with a few more further inland.[1] The town had a few police under Sergeant McEllister (later to become a

Member of the Legislative Council), a rudimentary gaol, a doctor (Dr Harvey), a magistrate (Matthew Smith), and his clerk, (John Irving Barnard). The Government Resident was Charles Driver. The peninsula standing behind the town was large and relatively dry although there were small lakes, creeks and springs that were quickly taken up by anxious pastoralists. Their early hopes were thwarted by overstocking and farm practices that denuded the land, turning much of it to dust. The long coastline, however, provided the good fish stocks on which many people relied so that with little by way of viable tracks a large number of tiny ports and jetties servicing the substantial coastal traffic eventually came into being. But the absence of passable tracks leading out from Adelaide made Port Lincoln seem remote even though reasonably accessible by boat.

Even so, communications between Adelaide and Port Lincoln were slow, while bad weather could make the sea journey difficult and unpleasant as well as long. The harbour was so open that during storms shipping had to seek safer moorings elsewhere. The combination of unequal population numbers with slow and patchy connection with Adelaide made the few colonists living there feel isolated, uneasy and prone to fear.

There is one key factor that is crucial to reflect upon in understanding not just the violent history of the invasion of the peninsula but the way in which it shaped important aspects of the way the colony was governed, ways that have proven remarkably resilient. This key factor is that, small as it was and remote as it felt, Port Lincoln was established entirely within the realm of British law cast across the whole colony – law emanating outwards from Adelaide, reaching over to Port Lincoln and out from it. That is why it is important to keep in mind that Port Lincoln was not at all like one of those wild towns of western America where there was only the erratic law of the gun. The representative of the colony's Governor (the Resident) who in turn represented the Queen, arrived more or less with the settlers. And with the Resident came a magistrate and the enforcers of law, the police. They were the three arms of government that were intended to produce the rule of law and its peace, to ensure that the laws made in parliament provided each subject of the Crown with justice. In Port Lincoln these three aspects of government would eventually be supplemented by the 96th Regiment of the British army. Port Lincoln was no frontier settlement beyond the reach of law, but a settlement governed by it.

People of the southern areas of the colony, showing Eyre Peninsula under Indigenous occupation. This map also shows the salt lakes that rarely contain water. Based on Horton, David (ed.) 1994, *Encyclopaedia of Aboriginal Australia*, Canberra: Aboriginal Studies Press.

The unknown country of the Barngarla, Nawu and Wirangu people of what is now the Eyre Peninsula provided a powerful incentive for those who would, or could be, first to locate those crucial sources of water and to apply for a 'special survey' of the land surrounding them. But it was not to be straight-forward, as the land was inhabited by people who had had long experience of the habits of European and American seafarers and were not happy to see more arriving. Although Clamor Schürmann described the local people as relatively shorter than Europeans (*the tallest and strongest of them would present but a poor figure among a regiment of grenadiers*) and less well-built than the Kaurna and Ngarrindjeri people around Adelaide, they were sufficiently strong to make their presence felt – their weaponry was formidable and they had the numbers.[2] They did everything they could to drive off the colonists.

*****

Over the past few years the history of the colonisation of the Eyre Peninsula has been comprehensively re-examined. Professional historians working in and outside the universities have had to face the rise of Aboriginal historians wanting to record their own histories, their connections to Country, and to record histories that speak of the violence that forced away so many of the survivors of it. And they wanted their oral records respected and included. Those new histories and perspectives have been of great value. And so the story of the colonisation of the Eyre Peninsula has had to change. It is not a pretty one and inevitably it is contested.

It is striking to see how, even now, talk of massacres, shootings, and local resistance too easily provokes a polite unease and sometimes a drift towards unmistakably and familiar defensiveness – 'times have changed', or, 'that's just what everybody did then', 'what else could they do?' or, 'what's past is past – everyone (i.e. First Australians, not the invaders) has to move on.'

*****

The Eyre Peninsula is the district that has been described by both the colonists who lived through its early years and, in the more recent reassessments of Indigenous and non-Indigenous scholars alike, as having developed a scale of violence that might be described as war, and sometimes even as a 'race war'.[3] For the rule of law on the Eyre Peninsula fractured early, just as it had elsewhere. Given that the law defined the Indigenous landowners as fully British subjects rather than aliens, it follows that the war for the lands of the Eyre Peninsula was a *civil war*, a war of one category of British subject against another. As it appeared to at least some of those present at the time, the crucial parties in that war were not workers rebelling against English aristocrats or Catholic Christians against Protestant Christians. Rather, some were fighting for their homes and way of life, others fought for the right of their own superior white race to displace them. The prize was of course, the land.

As more colonists arrived on the peninsula, once again shepherds, isolated settlers, drovers and their flocks, and travellers out searching for land or water found themselves vulnerable to attack. The first wave of violence, often dated to 1842, actually began several years earlier with the Indigenous landowners wasting no time in their efforts to convince the settlers to leave. They created sufficient fear to cause the population of the small town of Port Lincoln to decrease rather than grow, while many of the earliest property owners had to abandon their holdings. It was one of those abandoned holdings that helped Mortlock build up the huge acreages that became Yalluna Station near Tumby Bay, just as another of them became the basis of Andrew Tennant's pastoral empire and prosperity. Tennant's methods in dealing with local opposition were mentioned earlier but he was far from the only settler to act with such violence.

The colonists in Port Lincoln were nervous, however. When they sought more police, Governor Grey instead sent Clamor Schürmann as a deputy Protector of Aborigines. Schürmann arrived in Port Lincoln in 1840. All the early German missionaries faced many difficulties in South Australia but of this first generation of evangelists, it was Schürmann who became most involved at the interface between the new world of the colonists and the reality of the violence that the gift of Christianity had brought with it. Often required to interpret, he sometimes found himself attached to parties of a militia or police posse setting out to deal with unrest. Sometimes he was required to interpret for those from Port Lincoln whose court cases were heard in Adelaide, with the sad duty to do so for Ngarbi, who was eventually hanged in Adelaide as a lesson to the people of Port Lincoln. Later, in an attempt to demonstrate the superiority of colonial law and its powers, hangings on a purpose-built mobile gibbet allowed the punishment to be delivered closer to the place in which the offenders' actions had occurred. Fourteen Indigenous men would be hanged on the Eyre Peninsula as their attempts to drive off the colonists intensified.[4]

Schürmann's unwilling official attachments to various punitive expeditions led to threats against his life. One can see why it was that his presence should be seen as treachery by those he was intending to protect. With evangelisation impossible he left Port Lincoln in 1846 to go to Encounter Bay where conditions were also unsatisfactory. Returning to Port Lincoln in 1848 with his wife and a new appointment as interpreter, he intended to start a school in which teaching would be in Barngarla. This he did until it was taken over by Archdeacon Hale of the Church of England who had established the mission station at Poonindie where, as in Adelaide, instruction was to be in English. Disheartened and seeking a less compromised life, Schürmann went to minister to a Lutheran congregation in Portland, Victoria.[5]

Nevertheless, before setting aside his mission he had spent many years in Port Lincoln, learning languages, noting cultural practices and trying to dissuade the Nawu, Barngarla and their neighbours from actions that he knew would bring down upon them savage retribution. In this task he often failed. In living through the years of the wars from 1840 onwards his diaries offer a great deal of information about his hopes, fears and observations. Because Schürmann had nothing to gain from downplaying the numbers of the people killed and injured, and because he had little to lose by mentioning the roles played by individuals, his descriptions of the fighting are likely more reliable than accounts prepared by some those more directly involved in it. If not providing the whole truth (who could?) and if his perspective and religious beliefs sometimes operated to frame his understandings of the situation too narrowly, his diaries are more reliable than many other sources, reliable enough to take from them his descriptions of several incidents. Each illustrates something of the ways in which the war for the lands of the Nawu, the coastal and inland branches of the Barngarla, and of the southern Wirangu was so fiercely fought.

Chapter Twenty-Five

'Dead or Alive Without Discrimination'

Nine Men Come Into Town

Clamor Schürmann arrived in Port Lincoln shortly after the spearing of Frank Hawson, a young boy. Due to the spearing, relations between the Nawu and the colonists were understandably somewhat distanced, with the colonists discouraging visits from the local people who were, Schürmann records, already 'regarded as a nuisance'.[1] As a result, he had had difficulty in making contact with the local Indigenous people he was being paid to protect even though he knew that they were living relatively close to the town.

So when, on 8 October 1840 nine men walked into town, among them several older men, their beards wrapped with grey fur and plaited at the ends, Schürmann was delighted. He went to meet them at six o'clock on the evening of their arrival, as did some of the small police force. After some initial discussions Schürmann was asked to leave so that the visitors could sleep. When Schürmann returned to their camp in the morning all had disappeared. The police had taken them into custody, not without bloodshed. Dr Harvey, called to treat them, found the men 'bloody from their wounds' ... locked in a small cell which he described as a 'subterranean dungeon' and 'crying like children.' Harvey, who had taken them some of the onions they loved as a gift, left the cell door open so that they could leave, which they did.

Schürmann goes on to say that these were men who had had nothing to do with the attack and spearing of young Hawson and there was absolutely no reason to believe that they had. When he wrote to Protector Moorhouse in Adelaide, Schürmann pointed out than none of the nine resembled those described by the Hawson boy who was still alive although gravely ill from his spear wounds. It was the kind of incident that did little to calm the situation and nothing to overcome the image of the settlers as dangerously unpredictable and violent. From the colonists there were renewed calls for police reinforcements.

Schürmann's diary entries of these days paint a picture of an inflamed situation in and around the town. Already, theft had become a weapon of war with food and clothing being taken from the gardens and homes of the colonists, a practice that was later to increase to a level that made it a significant part of the effort to drive out the colonists. The scale of thefts of food stocks and clothing indicates that those concerned had understood that food supplies like flour, sugar and potatoes were in short supply due to the long delays and irregularity of the arrival of supply ships; while the destruction of gardens, including Schürmann's, indicates their awareness of the importance of vegetables like potatoes in mitigating the problem. The thieves were regarded as 'loafers' who, if allowed to go unpunished, would become 'cheeky', thus embittering the colonists, as indeed they did.[2] Schürmann's efforts to gather up old clothes from the colonists to be given to the Nawu women whose bodies were entirely unclad failed completely as well as generating some hostility toward him for asking.[3] So already, in 1840, antagonism was high and checks on the ways in which the Nawu and Barngarla might speak and behave were coming into practice (they were not to 'loaf' but to work for rewards).

Similarly, the hundreds of Nawu people said to be living near Coffin Bay were already, C.C. Dutton told Schürmann, 'not to be trusted'. These were small indications of the levels of tension in the district – colonists living in town did not want unknown Aboriginal men prowling around at night. The police were not too fussy about how they dealt with those who fell into their hands. It indicates, too, that the practice of punishing directly and collectively rather than individually through the courts was already regarded as normal and acceptable even though Port Lincoln fell under the mantle of colonial law and as noted above was equipped with a magistrate as well as police and a gaol of sorts. The gaol was, as the 'nine men' found out, more properly described as a dungeon; eyewitnesses speak of 'tumbling' the prisoners down the steps, 'sometimes in leg-irons locked onto a bar 7 feet long'.[4]

The Killing of Frank Hawson

Understandably, Frank Hawson's murder had created a great deal of concern in Port Lincoln. He had been speared on a property relatively close to the town where his parents seem to have been working as shepherds. The murder of such a young boy in October 1840 was uncharacteristic (Hawson's age given variously as twelve or nine years), occurring just a year or so after the establishment of a formal settlement at Port Lincoln.[5] It was said that while shepherding the flocks of his parents he had refused food to a group of Battara people.[6] The Battara were already involved in attempts at theft, in sheep-stealing and in burning the few fences built with so much effort. Edward Eyre, who was in Port Lincoln on his way west at the time of Hawson's death, knew that already there had been unrecorded shootings around the town and that outside it, sheep were being speared and stolen. Indeed, the killing of Frank Hawson was preceded by an attempt by his elder brother to use his gun to frighten off a group of men who had arrived at their hut.[7] Although later accounts suggest that previous relations between the family and local Aboriginal people had been amicable, even if true, the fears of two young boys left alone at a distance from their parents and facing a hostile group of armed men are understandable. The attack certainly increased the level of fear among the colonists. Despite weeks of searching those involved in the killing of the boy were never found.

At Biddle's Station, Long Pond – 29 March 1842

A determined full-scale attack on the four people living on Long Pond Station led to the deaths of James Rolles Biddle, Elizabeth Stubbs and James Fastings, a shepherd. Elizabeth's husband was seriously injured but managed to drag the bodies from the burning station house. As with the killing of Frank Hawson, the killing of a woman was and remains a rare event, even on the Eyre Peninsula. In this crime a man named Ngarbi was implicated, as he had been in the deaths of John Brown and his shepherd, Lovelock, a little earlier. He was one who went through the court processes. He would be hanged in Adelaide in July of 1843. Another of those involved, Nultia, would be 'hanged on 7 April 1843 upon a scaffold symbolically erected outside Biddle's ransacked hut, 20 miles from Port Lincoln.'[8]

In response to the attack on Biddle's Station, the Government Resident, Charles Driver, organised a party of men to locate and punish those who had been involved in the killings. Schürmann was instructed to find local Aboriginal men who could be used as trackers, which he did. Led by the Government Resident, the party of eight mounted colonists, Schürmann and six Indigenous men from their camp at Wanelli began their search on 2 April 1843. Although Driver was uncertain about whether the trackers were reliable they managed to locate a group of men who were seen to be sitting down in the distance. Approaching quietly they came up upon them causing them to flee, leaving only four men and a few women behind them. Then, Schürmann said,

> *Driver ordered Stewart to shoot the native nearest to us. I asked Driver why he ordered the man shot, when he was unarmed and could have been taken prisoner. He said that he didn't want any prisoners, since they were useless.*
>
> *Shots were fired at three of the fleeing natives, but none fell. However, our trackers told us that Nulta and Mulya were wounded. On top of the hill we found a woman who was in advanced stages of pregnancy, trying to hide in the hollow of a tree, and I asked the Sergeant if he was going to shoot her.*[9]

Back at the first campsite they found four more Indigenous men who immediately fled; a fourth man was encircled, who, protesting his innocence, was told to put down his spears. This was Ngulga, who was brought back to town but feeling unsafe, quickly departed. When news of the attack arrived in Adelaide, demands for revenge amplified.

Hugonin Arrives – 17 April 1842

Under pressure, by 1842 Governor Grey, a devout Anglican, was ready to send Lieutenant Hugonin and about fifteen men of the 96th Regiment to quell local resistance.[10] This was a regiment with a reputation for ruthlessness forged in Van Diemen's Land at the time of the great cross-country sweep that saw so much death. The regiment arrived in Port Lincoln on 17 April 1842. As Grey intended the army to be seen as peace-keepers whose role was to assist the police in protecting the colonists, Hugonin was also appointed as a Justice of the Peace, one of the inappropriate melding of military and civilian roles disparaged in Adelaide but remaining a general practice.[11] Clamor Schürmann, working in the district while Hugonin and the 96th regiment were there, said that Hugonin was under no illusions as to the nature of his duty. '[H]e said had been ordered to "take the whole of the Port Lincoln natives either dead or alive without discrimination".'[12] Their job was mass murder. They did not do it single-handedly but needed to form posses of police, Indigenous trackers and armed volunteers.

Schürmann agreed to accompany Charles Driver and Hugonin as interpreter, as well as to help in identifying those *not* involved in the murders on Biddle's Station. As was common practice among police and pastoralists alike, their guide was 'a single native ... brought in from a far tribe', a man whose interests lay entirely with those he was serving.[13] When the posse came across a group of people who were fishing near Coffin's Bay, they were encircled by the troops despite protestations of innocence that were confirmed by the guide. They had had nothing to do with the spearings, they said. Regardless, a soldier fired at Yumba but missed him. A soldier then fired at Schürmann's friend Nummalta who shortly after died from a bullet wound to his abdomen. With his head lying in the lap of his friend, Nummalta had asked Schürmann for a handkerchief with which to cover his face. Schürmann had known Nummalta for over a year, he said, 'and he was always so good and open ... It was like a knife in my heart to see this innocent man shot, and I could not hold back the tears'.[14] Hugonin refused to discipline the soldier involved, claiming that Nummalta had been shot in self-defence, a statement that to Schürmann's mind, was wrong. Finding his position as interpreter compromised he left Hugonin and his men next morning. On 9 May Schürmann discovered that the following men had been shot: Ngulga, Munta, Tubu, and two children Tyilye and Tallerilla (about 10 and 12 years old). Driver told Schürmann that 'the butchery will continue until they hand over the guilty ones'.

In a later foray into the countryside to deal with the murderers, Hugonin led his men and volunteers toward an estimated one hundred Aboriginal people gathered on the coast near Port Lincoln. As Hugonin moved in, all but some old men, women and children fled. With the nearly empty camp surrounded, two men were shot on the shore and, according to Hugonin, two more were wounded. It is surprising that a group of experienced soldiers facing a crowd of perhaps one hundred people could aim so badly that only two were killed and two wounded. None of these people was part of the raid on Biddle's Station which, Schürmann's contacts said, had been carried out by inland people, known as the Yurarri.

The Attack on Pillaworta Station in May
Hugonin's raids and reprisals led directly to an attack on Pillaworta the property belonging to Charles Driver, the Government Resident. The soldiers guarding the station were forced off, the huts plundered. When Schürmann was called to Pillaworta to interpret he found that the head of Ngulga, a man shot by the soldiers, had been stuck on top of a post, a clay pipe between his teeth.[15] Where the heads of the dead were removed, they were often placed into collections, not all of which were scientific.

*****

The raids and reprisals did not stop and the killings were often brutal. The spears used against the colonists were often barbed, the muscles of the throwers well-developed and their aim accurate. Several of the Aboriginal men who actually lived to be taken captive were taken to Adelaide for trial, although not always convicted. For those sentenced to death, the government's policy now was to hang them near the site of the offence and to try to round up their families and friends to watch them die. In pursuit of their belief in the deterrent value of a public demonstration of colonial power and the horrors of the awful spectacle of death, they built the portable gibbet that could be carried by boat to the most appropriate tiny port and then carted inland as needed. As in the case of the *Maria* massacre, sometimes the bodies were left to rot.[16] Those whose offences were less serious were publicly whipped. For theft and an attempt to strangle a policeman, Nante received three months in gaol and seventy-five lashes delivered in front of the gaol in Adelaide.[17] In Port Lincoln, Driver made great use of the lash; some of the pastoralists, like Mortlock's shepherd, made use of poisoned flour and damper. But the violence continued. When John Charles Darke, leader of a privately funded exploration party was killed in August of 1844 by the outwardly friendly Aboriginal people met the day before, they had erroneously assumed that the men's fear of guns and refusal to eat the food given to them meant that they were unaccustomed to dealing with colonists. This was most unlikely given the years of fighting, poisonings and violence then taking place and the customary travels and networks of all First Australians. It was a common misjudgement of the early colonists that Country seeming remote to them was not so to those living on it.

*****

As these few incidents selected to illustrate the nature of the war for the Eyre Peninsula show, the fighting there was terrible and brutal. It continued into the 1860s. The last hanging of an Indigenous man for murdering a colonist took place at Venus Bay in 1862. Overall, of the total number of people hanged during the colonial period, nearly half were of First Nations.[18] In addition to the deadly work of the 96th Regiment, the killings there involved pastoralists, their workers, and as noted, government officials including the most senior representative of the British government, the Government Resident. Charles Driver was the son-in-law of the early pastoralist, Henry Hawson, and the owner himself of a pastoral property.[19] Driver's role in the war for the Eyre Peninsula was crucial. Sometimes he led the reprisal parties himself while others were carried out by the militia or organised through his office as local representative of the government.

Driver's claim that after the hanging of Ngarbi in 1843 hostile incidents were 'annoyances' rather than attempts to intimidate was not correct. Violence continued on William Pinkerton's Stony Point Station near Lake Newland, as it did elsewhere. It was in May of 1849 that five people were poisoned on Mortlock's Station. Two boys, Karakundee and Yurdlarir, with Puyultu and Ngamania (whom I assume to be their parents), and the baby, Pirrapa, all ate poisoned flour stolen from the hut of Patrick Dwyer, Mortlock's shepherd. As Police Inspector Alexander Tolmer arrested Dwyer, it seems clear that Tolmer favoured the view that Dwyer had set the trap that had snared the flour-thief and left five people dead. It was Charles Driver who released Dwyer on the grounds that there was no direct evidence against him, allowing him to evade prosecution by taking passage on a ship heading for California.[20] Mortlock, however, had told the initial investigating police and the local magistrate that arsenic had been used in dressing the sheep, a process involving immersing a sheep in an arsenical dip. There was therefore a direct link between Dwyer, arsenic and those who had been poisoned. When Matthew Moorhouse (Protector of Aborigines) arrived to investigate he, too, confirmed the use of arsenic, considering the absent Dwyer to be guilty of murder.[21] Driver's reluctance to hold Dwyer until further investigations could be carried out is an example of the difficulties faced in providing justice for Indigenous people murdered by the colonists, a failure that could only increase the violence directed against them. Dwyer's crime was, after all, indiscriminate mass murder.

Some of the violence circulated as myth – the cannibalism story of how John Hamp's head was cut off and cut up to be roasted in a camp oven was one of them, while the cycle of 'true stories' about a group of

'DEAD OR ALIVE WITHOUT DISCRIMINATION'

Aboriginal men being driven over the cliffs to their deaths near Elliston is another. These stories are examined in detail in Foster, Hosking and Nettelbeck's *Fatal Collisions*. While they highlight a local propensity for telling yarns, they also point to the decapitation of an Aboriginal man by soldiers in May 1842 that was seen by Schürmann. In writing about this incident Nathanial Hailes described a young man of about eighteen, intellectual and a fierce fighter who was terribly wounded in 1842:

> *The horsemen left him, as they supposed, dying, but on their return found that he was still alive, that he had crawled several paces, and rearmed himself with abandoned weapons. He was at last despatched and his head chopped off with a hatchet. The trophy was borne to Port Lincoln where I had an opportunity of inspecting it. As the head rolled out of a bag, and I recognised the lofty retiring forehead, I said to myself, 'if that man had been born with a white skin he would have been a hero'.*[22]

He would indeed.

Chapter Twenty-Six

Poonindie

The story of Poonindie mission station is both enlightening and very sad. It tells of good intentions, hard work, education and its solid foundations of land and paid labour; and of how those foundations were undermined, first by the imposition of a destructive disciplinary regime and then by ecclesiastical greed. At Poonindie young Aboriginal boys and girls from around Adelaide were to be completely transformed from savagery into civilised, Christian, English-speaking women and men. They had to learn how to not-be themselves in order to survive at all. That stripping away of the self, begun in early schooling in Adelaide, must surely have been a traumatising experience. But for it to take place so far from their own people as to make them unreachable, with their mothers and fathers, sisters and brothers, cousins and friends – all far away – must have been appalling. The first small contingent had come from Adelaide. To get to their new home on the Eyre Peninsula required a land journey north then onwards by sea. Walking home by a land-route was out of the question. This was the well-intentioned settlement, Poonindie, on the eastern coast of the Eyre Peninsula, far enough north of Port Lincoln to make walking into town a problem for any potential escapees. The story of the rise and fall of Poonindie has been richly documented by Peggy Brock in *Outback Ghettos. Aborigines, Institutionalisation and Survival*.[1]

*****

Poonindie, the Church of England's first mission station in South Australia, was established by Archdeacon Mathew Blagdon Hale

(1811–1895) with the support of the colony's first Anglican bishop, the high churchman Augustus Short (1802–1883).[2] Founded in 1850 when the country close to Port Lincoln was considered safe, Poonindie stood at the half-way mark used by historians to separate the shifts in the social fabric from its early-Victorianism (c. 1830) that distinguish it from its later, highly industrialised, and racialised imperial forms. Poonindie's establishment on the cusp of those changes meant that the ideas that drove it, as well as the personal and religious formation of the two men who founded it, are characteristic of the privileged men of the slightly earlier era. The story of the people at Poonindie is therefore partly one of how the tensions between the attitudes of its founding era and those flourishing during the hardening of attitudes toward the First Australians after Hale's departure to Perth in 1856 were to bring about its downfall. Its history also shows how the ideas and policies of its later years were built upon a set of beliefs about the nature of masculinity that undermined those of the young men and women being mission-trained for entry into the new world of a colonial society.

The Civilising Values of Cricket

Archdeacon Mathew Hale and Bishop Short had arrived in Adelaide together in 1848 with money, friends and access to the ear of government officials. Hale was able to buy the lease of the land on which his mission, known officially as 'the Native Training Institution', was to be established on the eastern coast of the Eyre Peninsula.

Both men had been shaped by and maintained the principles of an education that formed the bodies and minds of the men who were destined for the church, the law, and the administration of the growing empire – Short at Westminster school and Oxford, while Hale was a Cambridge man. In addition to theology, their learning was based in the languages and knowledge of the Greek and Latin classics, rather narrow, and undertaken in a somewhat leisurely manner compared with the much wider reading in philosophy and literature required by the great educational institutions of mainland Europe. What was hoped for in these educational practices was the creation of the pious gentlemen who formed part of a ruling elite, an amalgamation of the landed aristocracy, major land-holders, and the wealthier merchants, bankers and traders of a rising upper middling-class.

Both Thomas Arnold, the famous head of Rugby School in England, and Thomas Hughes, who described Rugby as it was between 1834 and 1842 in *Tom Brown's Schooldays*, were interested in the ways in which a proper manliness could be inculcated into young men. Arnold's system of disciplinary prefects and severe physical punishments bolstered by team sports and fierce competition was directed to that end. The fictional Tom Brown, on the other hand, had to abandon competitive sports like these in order to become a decent man. By 1879, Hughes had rather given up on the values of competitive sport. In *The Manliness of Christ*, Hughes would write that, 'Athleticism is a good thing if kept in its place, but it has come to be very much over-praised and over-valued amongst us'.[3]

Whether educators of ruling class boys believed that more or less sport would produce the type of masculinity that was both pious and competitive or pious and more co-operative and sensitive, cricket emerged as the gentler sport of England's wealthy landed and financial gentry as epitomised in the exclusive Marylebone Cricket Club, the owners of Lord's cricket ground. Cricket became a hallmark of social superiority, the mark of a gentleman (if you knew you had been bowled 'out', you walked off the field whether the umpire had called you, or not) and of civilisation itself. Both Bishop Short and Archdeacon Hale came out of this tradition and it guided their hopes for the type of man and woman that they wanted to create at Poonindie.

The distance between the practical labour in which they trained the young people under their tutelage and the leisurely and false amateurishness defining the sportsmanlike behaviour of the English cricketers did not prevent the successful establishment of cricket at Poonindie. That other hallmark of the gentry, style of dress, is visible in Crossland's portraits of Samuel Kandwillan and Nannultera that can be seen on the web. Kandwillan's portrait is one of very few to provide a picture of the kind of transformation sought by Mathew Hale. Every inch the gentleman, Kandwillan was a reliable worker, spoke excellent English, was an eventual convert and preacher – a man trusted to stand in for Hale when he was away. He and Nannultera were part of the team taken to Adelaide to play in a match against St Peter's College that they won.

At Poonindie, faith in cricket, the game of the ruling elite, was defined as amateur and gentlemanly. The game of cricket exemplifies an important strand of nineteenth century educational practice that stood in sharp contrast to the prefects, bullying and caning that Hughes described at Rugby in the 1830s. Both aimed to produce manhood and forms of pious masculinity as well as the sense of superiority characteristic of the English upper classes.

Village Life

Hale intended Poonindie to be a Christian village. In order to provide security of tenure for those living there he bought the lease and nearby land on which it was to be built. In Poonindie village, English customs, Christian religious beliefs and the skills required for labouring could be inculcated in an environment in which the inhabitants would be safe from backsliding into the barbarism of their parents and safe, too, from the evils brought about by close contact with the colonists.[4]

Most colonial missions were intended to be or to become self-supporting. This meant that those living there had to support the mission staff as well as themselves. Where mission funds could be extracted from local or English and German congregations they were used in a variety of ways, but much of the work of clearing land, building houses and sheds, ploughing, planting, harvesting, shepherding, and caring for animals had to be done by those living on the mission. It follows that the young women and girls had to undertake the care and support of their brothers, cousins and husbands as well as the families of the missionaries – they had to cook, clean, iron, sew and mend their own clothes and those of the men, look after any babies and younger ones, milk the cows, make bread and on occasion, be sent out to work as servants.[5] In 1852, for example, mission women also worked as household servants for Hale himself, for Minchin the schoolmaster and for George Wollaston, Poonindie's overseer.[6]

As at other mission establishments, life was shaped by the bell. In speaking about the daily round at Point Pearce on the Yorke Peninsula, later to be home to many of the Poonindie people, Lewis O'Brien stated simply that 'You live by the bell.'[7] By 1859 Poonindie's church bell rang out for rising from bed, shaping the day in accordance with the conventions of time that structured the colonists' world – prayers at seven o'clock each morning, then breakfast, then farm work for the boys.[8] At eleven the women and children assembled for school. Dinner was at midday. In the afternoon there was sewing for the girls as well as reading and writing. After the evening meal the boys began their lessons until at eight o'clock, the bell rang again for evening prayers, then bed. I assume that the girls spent the time between breakfast and their lessons engaged in cleaning of one kind or another.[9] They were learning the domestic skills required of good wives.

The Family
The family was absolutely central to the evangelical mission to Christianise the other peoples of the world. It was through the family that Protestant concepts of a true Christian life were expressed in actual behaviour. At its core lay the virgin woman as bride, monogamy and a set of gendered social roles and laws establishing the patriarchal rights of men over women that mirrored those of a patriarchal image of the One God. The village layout of Poonindie was intended to facilitate family life with married couples getting a cottage for themselves. By 1852 four of the highly valued Christian marriages had taken place, while five more were recognised as 'man and wife' without being solemnised.[10]

Hale was a godly family man who, greatly disturbed by the loss of his first wife, reached the age of thirty-seven before marrying for a second time. His new marriage took place just before establishing Poonindie and he went on to raise eight children.[11] His was the kind of happy middle-class marriage and family life that he hoped he could create at Poonindie. In such a union the husband held sole sexual rights in his wife, the right to control, use or spend any monies she might have, and the children were his, not their mother's. In such a marriage the wife lost her personhood – legally she lost the civil rights granted by her birth by becoming absorbed within the male who henceforth spoke for her. The influential eighteenth-century legal scholar, William Blackstone put it plainly: on her marriage a woman suffered a 'civil death' that was written into the law of the land.[12] For eighteenth-century women, as for those who came later, the marriage contract was an agreement that transferred her from father to husband and then to cease to be, an institutionally endorsed negation of freedom. Divorce required an act of parliament. Despite the challenge posed by women writers like Mary Wollstonecraft, whose declaration that men and women were equal in the eyes of God caused a great stir, women continued to be thought of as subsumed within the male and often, as male property. Marriage law from Britain had not only entered the colony but was unchallenged by pillars of the Anglican church like Hale and Short who gained much power through controlling marriages. Marriage was central to their notions of Christian conversion. It meant not just attending a different sacred place and learning its rituals, prayers and hymns but a whole new way of life.

Given the general acceptance of these views it is not surprising to find that critical accounts of Indigenous life in the colony should focus upon the nature of Aboriginal marriage customs and the nature of the lives of the Aboriginal women subjected to it. With little real information to hand and a set of preconceived ideas about the high status of Christian women within the English family and society and the low status of Indigenous women within theirs, the status of Indigenous women was a flash-point for racially biased interest and crude criticism. Colonial righteousness and a sense of superiority were bolstered by an unshakeable belief in the marital and sexual horrors from which Indigenous women needed to be rescued.

The problem was that Aboriginal women did not share the colonial view that they were little more than beasts of burden, subject to sexual mistreatment and barbarous rites, and likely to be beaten for minor misdemeanours. Had the colonists looked more carefully around them in Adelaide they would have seen that Kaurna women were independent, autonomous, enjoyed a degree of sexual freedom, were able to share childcare and had important roles in crucial ceremonies, in controlling births and in family life. The concept of a monogamous family in which a wife was legally consumed by the person of the husband and subject to his outright control was entirely foreign to them. Instead, the missionary demand for monogamy and subordination to men meant a massive loss of autonomy for Indigenous women and a big shift in how men thought about their wives.

Mission monogamy also meant an equally massive new restraint upon the sexual lives of men, as well as the loss of access to the extensive networks of exchange that were based upon control of marriages. Indigenous men were being forced to relinquish their customary methods of control over women through control of their daughters' marriages, receiving instead a set of Christian gender relations that theoretically assigned one woman to one man. In the process of these changes, the patterns of responsibility for caring and nurturing in Indigenous family life did not follow those of the British model. Under British law a man governed his wife through control of women's reproductive potential as well as through removing her fortune, if any, and excluding her from as much education as possible. This was not the case in Indigenous cultures where polygamy was usual.

Like their British sisters, colonial wives in South Australia were almost constantly pregnant, bearing large numbers of children, many of whom died. Aboriginal wives, on the other hand, were able to space their pregnancies and were therefore less likely to end their lives in childbirth or through being worn out by the effects of constant childbearing. When it came to sex, there was little difference in overall practices. The licentiousness the British associated with polygamy, ritual sexual ceremonies and sexual exchanges of women by Aboriginal men was paralleled by British men's easy access to extensive networks of brothels, street-working sex workers, to servant girls and to very young girls and boys.[13] Such practices made the concept of illegitimacy useful in preserving fortunes and an apparent moral rectitude; but as in many other polygamous societies, in Aboriginal families *all* children were legitimate, part of a wide network of kin and social relations on whom they could rely.

Even though arranged marriages remained common in Britain for many years, Protector of Aborigines Matthew Moorhouse and Archdeacon Hale saw it as essential to break down Aboriginal marriage and family structures, particularly older men's power to arrange the marriages of their daughters as well as other sexual practices deemed barbaric. Committed to improving the lives of future generations, the Protector and the Archdeacon were quite happy to insert themselves into the role of the patriarchal marriage-controller that they so deplored in Aboriginal society, just as they were happy to arrange marriages for the Adelaide school students in their care at a very early age. They wanted to prevent the vitiation and corruption that Moorhouse had seen in previous years, 'either by being drawn away again to their former wild habits of life or by associating with the dregs of the population of this city.'[14] While their proposal to marry off girls of fourteen to boys of sixteen without parental consent was not approved by the government, nevertheless a number of such marriages were arranged. The earliest of them (October 1851) was that of Neechi and Kilpakto, then that of Narrung and Manyatko and that of Kandwillan and Tandatko.[15]

Educated in Adelaide at the school for Aborigines, Kandwillan was literate, a good student and went willingly to Poonindie. As with Neechi and Kilpatko, Kandwillan and his wife Tandatko had difficulties in finding a way of putting the new moral and sexual order into practice. Eventually, Tandatko complained to Hale about Kandwillan's behaviour while he had been in Port Lincoln. With Hale unwilling to commit Kandwillan's offense to his diary it is hard to know what to make of this incident. That Hale considered the offense 'so immoral as to merit dismissal' from Poonindie is not really a very good guide to whatever it was that Kandwillan had done.[16] News of the offence seems to have reached Poonindie in advance of the returning offender as Kandwillan was stopped at the river to prevent him entering the mission until later in the day when Hale, a Mr Haslop, and the young men walked across to the burial ground to meet him. There, amid the terrible symbolism of the site of death, Hale dismissed Kandwillan from Poonindie.

'Many of the boys shed tears,' he wrote in his diary, 'nor could Mr Haslop or I refrain from doing the same ourselves.'[17] By the next day he had relented. 'My sense of grief and suffering has been very great over Kandwillan. His poor wife was inconsolable, she sat out of doors in the cold and wept nearly the whole day.' Hers was a clear act of mourning and grief, one anchored in her own social practices rather than those of the mission. So was the silence that fell across the day. Hale must have repented of his righteous haste in casting out the miscreant. Next day, he wrote that: 'Seeing how much punishment had been felt by all and hoping that enough had been done as a warning. I received joint petition of all the boys together, I consented to receive him back.'[18] Kandwillan had learned his lesson, he was back with his wife and in 1853 he and Tandatko were baptised into the church by Bishop Short. Tandatko died in 1856; Kandwillan remarried, his new wife dying in 1858. Kandwillan followed his wives 1860. He had survived just a decade of Poonindie's protection and training, his wives even less. Such very young people.

All accounts of Mathew Hale mention his kindness and untiring care for others, whether Aboriginal or not. In his willingness to impose such a penalty upon a transgressor whose abilities and co-operative nature he had so highly valued, the disciplinary nature of the Christian village and the rather Old Testament wrath of its patriarch in casting out his prodigal son stands revealed. At Poonindie, Hale and those who succeeded them had extraordinary powers that came at the expense of the rights and needs and hopes and pleasures of those living there. It is easy to forget that while in Poonindie's case, the first generation of young people seem to have gone there willingly, perhaps in adventure but almost certainly without knowledge of the distance and separation involved, the village was nevertheless just one node in a network of control and conversion spreading across the colony.

Later

In the end, the colonists wanted the land that had been cleared and made productive by the Aboriginal residents of Poonindie. In 1861, part of the land was sold to John Tennant, the Scottish settler who had arrived in 1839, whose daughter would marry William Ranson Mortlock who also held land in the district, and whose son, Andrew, would become a large land-holder and member of parliament.[19] Years of agitation from colonists wanting the rest of Poonindie's well-developed land followed.

By 1896 all the land had been subdivided and sold to them, as had Poonindie's plant and machinery, all bought for the mission by Hale, paid for through donations and more importantly through the labour of those living there. The transfer of Poonindie's title had to be achieved through legislation. First the South Australian parliament passed an Act in 1895 that declared Poonindie's lands to be crown land. As a result the government of the day was able to transfer the land to 'the Right Reverend John Reginald Harmer, of Adelaide, Doctor in Divinity, Sir Samuel Davenport, of Adelaide, K.C.M.G., and Edwin Gordon Blackmore, of Adelaide, Esquire, as joint tenants for an estate in fee-simple.' The Act gave them the power to do whatever they wished with the land.[20] Although the Act also specified that the money paid for the land should be used to benefit of 'aborigines' and 'half-castes' it failed to limit its use to the people to whom it had belonged, the people of Poonindie to whom Hale had gifted the property. Instead, Poonindie monies could be used right across the colony, as the Church saw fit.[21] It is not surprising that once inside Church coffers it effectively vanished. Despite holding money that should have been devoted to the welfare and resettlement of Poonindie's people, the Church of England took no further interest in supporting them. They were left to fend for themselves with no land, no homes and with the value of their labour discounted. Poonindie's 'Christian village' had produced paupers.

The loss of land at Poonindie was not unique. In colonial Victoria, New South Wales and the Northern Territory, Aborigines were also regularly dispossessed, refused access to land for farming and repeatedly re-colonised.[22] But Poonindie could have had very different results. The three men required by law to manage the dispossession – Harmer, Davenport and Blackmore – were all educated, respected, respectable citizens of the colony, while the governor, Thomas Fowell Buxton, who had to approve the legislation on behalf of the Queen, was a member of a distinguished family widely known for its philanthropy, its sustained support in the great campaigns to abolish slavery and its many contributions to important humanitarian reforms.[23] In her letters to her mother from Adelaide, Maisie Thomas described Harmer as 'a dear old duck' and there is little doubt that as a person, he was.[24] Davenport was one of those who had managed to buy early a 'special survey' of 4000 acres, his son selecting land for him near Port Lincoln. That land, however, was quickly exchanged for land closer to Adelaide near today's township of Macclesfield. He became a major property owner; his tenants he treated well, along the lines of a country squire as he played an important role in the political and community life of the colony. Augustus Short remained bishop until 1882; he was followed by George Kennion, then, from 1895 until 1905, John Harmer.

When Archdeacon Hale left Poonindie for his new appointment in Western Australia he left behind him a hybrid form of community, one engaged within the colonial economy that had been built upon the dispossession of its Indigenous people. Hale's purchases of land for the mission's people meant that the colonial transformation of Indigenous 'Country' into English 'property' took place at least in part for the benefit of the people taken to live there. Hale's determination to educate and teach the skills of farming and domestic maintenance and his practice of paying wages and allowing for work to be done outside the mission meant that when he left, he left behind him a relatively prosperous and independent people. For many years Poonindie's income from outside wages for seasonal labour, crops, flocks, wool, and from the sewing and domestic labour of the young women had supported not only the Indigenous workers on the mission but helped to pay its various employees and support the missionaries and their visitors. Whatever personal difficulties were created by placing young women and men into a closely regulated and supervised village life, the place itself was a quiet financial success due to the paid wages that were central to it. And this was despite the ways in which the farming methods of the early colonists often spoiled the land rather than making it productive. As mentioned earlier, much of the Eyre Peninsula was ruined by pastoral settlement. It was not good pastoral country; mining was ephemeral and the weather unreliable. Now they grow wheat, other cereals and canola in huge paddocks while Port Lincoln relies on fishing and recently, vines, organic foods and tourism. But it took some time to work things out. Much of the labour continued to be done by Aborigines.

Poonindie's people possessed skills and a willingness to work that meant that their labour was in high demand outside the village. The biographies collected up during later years show how very resourceful those people were. When forced off Poonindie some went westward toward what would eventually become Koonibba near Ceduna, some to Point Pearce on Yorke Peninsula, some back to Adelaide or to the Murray River, and some went eastwards toward the people of the Flinders Ranges now known as the Adnyamathanha.

But there was a second factor involved. The resident mission managers who followed Hale were not as committed as he had been; the quality of managers sent there deteriorated. The process that Peggy Brock described as an increasing use of 'the language of the asylum and the prison rather than that of the Anglican parish', originated in the quality and type of manager sent by the Adelaide bishops.[25] The shift in the concept of the mission endeavour from independent living to disciplinary centres of control drove many of the institutions that were to follow. What becomes visible for the first time in the shifts in the staffing and management of Poonindie is the outline of a distinctive 'mission zone' of governance characterised by the exclusion of the civil rights of those living there and the transfer of legal powers from government to mission staff that would expand and flourish over many years. When, in old age, Hale received a letter from one of Poonindie's residents about conditions there he was very distressed.

Chapter Twenty-Seven

In and Around the Flinders

The Flinders Range is the most northerly segment of the line of gentle hills running parallel to the colony's coast but those of the Flinders are craggy and rocky, cut by gorges and sandy creek beds that are often dry. Those travelling north from Adelaide or Port Augusta see them first as a startling blue eruption into the flatness of the country surrounding them while at dawn the ridges stand out as black against burning red skies. The gorges and gullies provide shade as well as waterholes. Adnyamathanha Country, the country of the 'Stone People', was very desirable. The Adnyamathanha people of today have formed a political and social conglomerate of peoples whose country included the northern Flinders and the country east and west of the range; people who speak variations of the same language and share similar social and cultural practices.

In addition to some good water sources the people of the 'stone country' had one priceless resource: the deposits of a highly prized, glistening form of red ochre that drew trading parties from Australia's far north coast down to the carefully guarded Pukardu in the Flinders Ranges. The trade in ochre ensured that Pukardu was not just at the southern end of a major transcontinental trade route but that the northern Flinders Range was neither isolated nor remote in First Nations terms but integrated into a network of trading and ceremonial tracks and waterholes that linked them to people further east and west as well as those further south. This most valuable trade route

SEX AND SAVAGERY IN THE GOOD COLONY

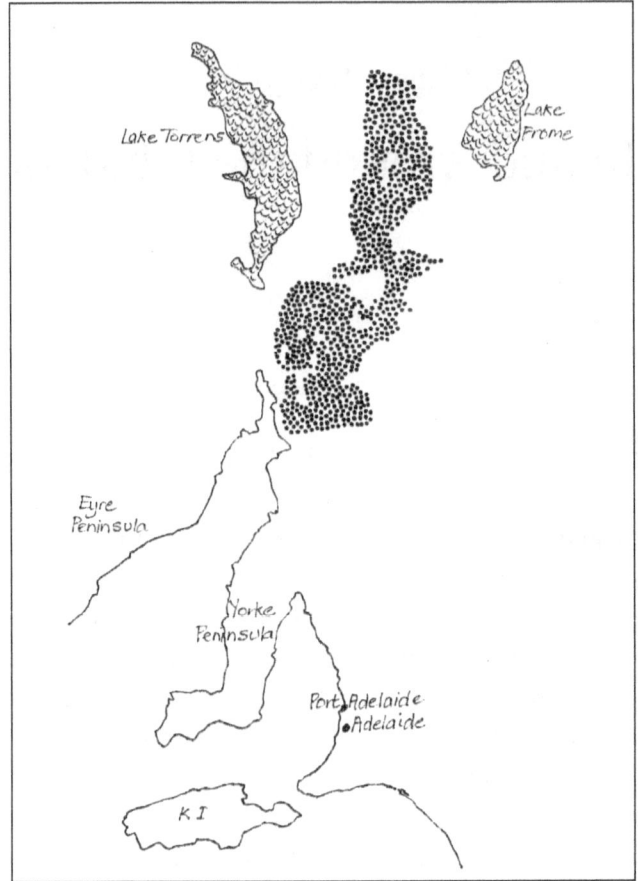

Early colonial pastoral leases in and around the Flinders Range showing two of the salt lakes characteristic of the region that are usually dry.

began towards the Gulf of Carpentaria in the north. Northern trading parties leaving for Pukardu had to wait for good seasons and the water flows that meant they could follow the rivers and creeks south. On the way the traders could carry out or join in ceremonial rites; and as not all along the tracks were friendly they had to be prepared to fight. Early descriptions of the ochre trading parties spoke of large numbers of men and at least some women passing along the way. To get to the Flinders from the Gulf country and then return carrying large and heavy packages of ochre could take years. The ochre trade survived settlement until eventually the arrival of the narrow trainline heading up to Oodnadatta allowed trading parties to board the wagons, sometimes unobserved, sometimes with permission. This trade was one Indigenous economic institution that the pastoralists eventually had to accept. Pastoralists had to decide whether they wanted to provide a couple of sheep to passing traders and allow them access to waters that they regarded as theirs, or whether they would rather have the sheep killed anyway, the flocks disturbed and their shepherds and labourers harassed. Along this route Lake Kopperamanna, later to become the site of a mission station, also operated as an important trading centre. Through it many goods flowed south to the Adnyamathanha – the prized pituri grown around Boulia waterhole in Queensland, axes and the blanks carved from the special stone from which they were fabricated, secular and sacred ceremonies, dances and songs, pearl shell ornaments, and much more.[1] The Diyari living in the Lake Eyre basin traded pubic tassels and woven net bags (they were excellent weavers, making long fishing nets for use in the lakes and rivers) as well as the red ochre they had brought up from Pukardu in the south, getting hardwood tools and weapons in return.[2] A major trading hub, Adnyamathanha country was not simply good for the colonists' cattle and sheep but good for the Adnyamathanha people too.

*****

Converting Adnyamathanha Country into pastoral leasehold property is usually dated to the 1850s although well before then there had been a number of colonists out and about, searching for mineral resources, water sources, possible fodder stocks and testing the responses of local people to their presence. Edward Eyre and one of the children he had taken up, Cootacha, had looked over parts of the Gawler Ranges and the country between the salt lakes before heading back to Port Lincoln and then on to his long journey to the Swan River Colony with Wylie and Baxter. Eyre's reports on the potential of the north discouraged settlement for a while but were ultimately shown to be wrong.

As dry and isolated as this country seemed from the perspective of those living in Adelaide, there were always small parties of men (like Eyre) who were ahead of the settlers, seeking the advantages of being first. Some were working for southern pastoralists or land speculators, sometimes they were mapping or gathering geological samples. Occasionally there were solitary travellers using Indigenous pathways coming in along the rivers from the eastern or south-eastern colonies. They may not have been many but they were there and their presence could not be kept secret from the custodians of the Countries they were traversing. Some of these men left resentment and troubles in their wake which meant that while, once again, those coming after them often thought that the fear and hostility their presence caused was simply due to the first sightings of men with strange animals and pale skin, this need not have been the case. And in any case, news of the colonists, their horses and their guns travelled along trade routes in advance of their actual appearance.

The several branches of the peoples known now as Adnyamathanha stood right in the path of these northerly incursions. The colonists had fought their way north, first from Adelaide to Gawler, then into the enticing Clare Valley, seen by pastoralists as early as 1839 when John Ainsworth Horrocks took up land there, establishing the village of Penwortham; by 1844 colonists were on the well-watered patch of country surrounding Mount Remarkable. By 1846 the most northerly property was a cattle run belonging to Alexander Campbell and Malcolm Gillies at the foot of the mountain. In the language used to cover the violence associated with their presence they and the nearby White brothers had 'much difficulty with the Aborigines'.[3]

The White brothers' property east of the range at Charlton (later Wirrabarra), was described by Frederick Hayward as having good soil, good timber for fuel, building and fencing, and plenty of water for stock and wildfowl. A paradise, he called it, and highly desirable. At this time, the colonists' pursuit of Aborigines by armed men on horseback led to the spearing of one of the shepherds working on the Hill River Station near Clare, while the 1846 murder of two shepherds on Andrew Tennant's Mt Arden Station (north of Quorn) led to him abandoning it.[4]

Tennant was attempting to drive sheep overland to Port Lincoln where he intended to take up new land. By February of 1846 both his shepherds and their sheep had disappeared. In April, a police search found fifty of the lost flock, along with some clothing thought to have belonged to the shepherds. The 'northern blacks' who were said to be the culprits had kept the sheep carefully penned in folds. The police came upon their camp where they were 'regaling themselves upon divers [sic] roasted legs and shoulders.' Those 'who surprised the natives in their retreat', they reported, 'were glad enough to satisfy their hunger from some of the ready-cooked joints, and subsequently committed to the flames the spears, shields, and implements which the blacks had abandoned in their flight.' According to newspaper reports of the search, at this point, 'The difficult country around Mount Arden discouraged the police from following the Aborigines further. 'The retreating blacks set fire to the country behind them, in order to retard and baffle their pursuers, employing also some of their number as look-out men to signal any hostile approach.'[5]

The reported facts seem oddly anodyne, a cheerful account of lost sheep found, a feast, and fleeing natives. A closer reading suggests that the camp surprised was sufficiently established to contain a sheepfold and men with a quantity of weaponry. There is no comment on the fact that only fifty of a large flock had been located, no explanation of why the police put no further effort into locating the bodies of the lost shepherds. There is certainly no mention of any shooting, although the spirited defence put up by the 'northern tribe' in firing their country suggests that they were determined to discourage any further pursuit. The absence of any mention of women and children in a reasonably well-established camp also seems odd. Many colonial accounts of hostilities describe the presence of women both in hunting parties and in the war zone and indeed, their rape afterwards (as on the Rufus River). The account published in the *Adelaide Observer* asks the reader to believe that police and settlers were on something of a jolly romp or a boys-own-adventure that was followed by a feast of mutton at the Aborigines' expense and a tactical withdrawal that should be seen as success rather than as failure. One cannot now say that shots were fired, people killed or women captured but as the area around Mt Remarkable and Mount Arden Station was in the process of being made safe for colonists making it unlikely that the pursuit of the killers of the shepherds was terminated with a picnic. The failure to pursue is more likely to have occurred because those surprised in their camp had been 'taught a lesson' of some kind.

At the end of the year two Aborigines were said to have been killed for driving off 400 sheep from the Crystal Brook Station of William Younghusband and Peter Ferguson. In this case, Protector Moorhouse's investigation increased the number of Aboriginal dead from two to three and found the actions of the Aboriginal transgressors to have been justified. Nevertheless, they were still dead.[6] The taking of new land always led to renewed calls for more police protection as well as expressed fears that the failure of policing would lead to pastoralists having to take matters into their own hands. In 1848, more fighting around Mt Remarkable led to a police station being established there. Even so, the colonists were now spreading out toward the more northerly reaches of the Flinders and the surrounding country. The names of many of the stations they established there remain well-known today, stations like Moolooloo, Umberatana and Aroona and Pekina.

But by the 1850s a wave of colonial entrepreneurs in search of land had located the best waters around the Flinders Ranges and achieved changes to the Waste Lands Act that made squatting easier, along with the option of leasing land rather than its outright purchase. The map above (Map 27:1) shows the way in which by 1855 lease-holdings had snaked along the ranges where the best water supplies could be found. It took a little longer to understand the value of saltbush as fodder but once that happened the drier country on either side of the Flinders Ranges also became valuable as property.[7]

Lying just to the north of Wilpena Pound, the early days of taking control of Pekina and Aroona in 1850 are well-known through the diaries kept by J Frederick Hayward, a great friend of the White brothers at Charlton. An Anglican by affiliation, Hayward arrived in the colony in 1847 aged twenty-four. He was a big strong fellow standing 6 ft 4 ins (193 cm), the type of young man identified by Governor George Grey as being bound to get on in South Australia [where] *every requisite for human happiness can be gained by industry and perseverance. In no country can such requisites be obtained without, and in many not even with, these qualities.*[8] Hayward worked hard, he persevered and he got the land he needed for prosperity. He got his start by being willing to accept unfavourable wages. As a result he found work immediately on arrival. He went as overseer to Price Maurice's head-station, Pekina (between Orroroo and Booleroo Centre) that had been carved out of Nukunu Country. Pekina Station was then on the most northerly boundary of the sheep farmers while the Welshman, Price Maurice (1818–1894) was already one of the wealthiest of the pastoralists. It was there that Hayward learned his trade and mastered the practicalities of settling onto new land. He is known today for his untroubled diary entries describing the steps he took to deal with any opposition from local Indigenous owners.[9]

Chapter Twenty-Eight

Hayward and McKinlay

Because he left a diary, Hayward's record of his life in Australia has been widely commented upon. In his well-known history of the Flinders Ranges, Hans Mincham paraphrased Hayward's words, but even so, they show a young Englishman taking to colonial life with a certain gusto. 'When Hayward went to Pekina,' Mincham wrote,

> *Aborigines and dingoes often made off with from eighty to a hundred sheep, and on one occasion they drove away about four hundred. Hayward always kept an Aboriginal tracker from another area on the station to help in searching for stolen sheep. They usually, it seems, arrived at a native camp to interrupt a glorious feast of mutton, but in time to save most of his sheep. Rarely did Hayward catch any able-bodied men, but he invariably made a fire and burnt every waddy, boomerang, and spear left by the fleeing tribesmen.*[1]

It is doubtful if the statement that Hayward rarely captured any Aboriginal men is correct unless the implication is that he shot rather than captured them. Like John McKinlay (a man who was 'no stranger to violence'), who was with Hayward during a major massacre, Hayward has entered history as a hard-working pastoral pioneer whose success is emblematic of his type.[2] On his English descendant's website they put it this way: 'Frederick Hayward was a notable figure in the development of South Australia's great staple industry [wool] and his name stands high on the roll of pastoral pioneers. He returned to England in 1864 a wealthy man, purchased a fine estate at Limpley Stoke [near Bath] which he named Aroona after his old South

Australian Station and lived there until his death close to his 90th year on 8th April, 1912.'[3] They go on to write of how well loved he was in the village, that he was referred to affectionately as 'squire' and that for many years he served as a warden of the Anglican church of St Mary. Respected and esteemed by all, with a large family as well as a large fortune he epitomises provincial respectability and English values. In this he was typical of many of the earliest settlers who had come to make their fortunes in a colony. Once made, few questions were asked about how their riches had been accumulated; had questions been asked, little notice would have been taken of stories of daring adventures and fierce or wily natives.

*****

Hayward, Tony Hull has written, set out to clear Aborigines right off Pekina Station. The use of terror as a way of dealing with opposition to colonisation is by no means a modern idea projected backwards onto the early years of colonisation but was recognised and understood by those using it at the time. In their volume of Indigenous recollections of dispossession in South Australia, Christobel Mattingley and Ken Hampton noted that Hayward was quite clear about it, referring explicitly to the role of terror in dealing with local opposition:

> *Each petty tribe on all sides of Pekina, and there were a number, had to be terrified before their depredations ceased, and that pretty well lasted all my sojourn, say three and a half years.*
>
> *These campaigns against the niggers gave a zest to the wild life I led. At first their craft and cunning in stealing and concealing their line of march and camp were too much for me, but a very few pursuits ('campaigns' I used to call them) brought us equal ... There was an excitement to this 'nigger' tracking that was not wholly disagreeable ... and in after years [I grew to] deplore that no such excitement remained.*[4]

Hayward enjoyed the chase, just as Police Inspector Tolmer did when he joined Major O'Halloran in Port Lincoln 'in the hopes of having a brush with the blacks and some exciting fun'.[5] Hayward went first to Pekina to learn his trade, then to Aroona where he could apply what he had learned.

While at Pekina, Hayward attempted to have several Aboriginal offenders dealt with by the law but his methods meant that in a court of law he had little success. When he captured an alleged sheep stealer named 'Charlie' and took him in to the magistrate at the mining settlement of Burra, Hayward rode while his captive walked, secured with one of the heavy bullock chains used to join yoked bullock pairs into a team. This mode of moving Aboriginal captives about the countryside was used to maintain and reinforce the superiority of the captor riding on his horse. Even so, there were many police reports of captives escaping by various ingenious means. But it was cruel.

The long forced marches of prisoners led to swollen feet and joints while the weight of the chains produced blistering and raw open sores. Later, neck chains were used on the basis that they were kinder as they left the hands unshackled – an assertion that ignored the blistering, bruising and straining on the necks. On this occasion Charlie reached Burra. The magistrate, however, wanted an assurance that Hayward would promise to get his captive safely home, which was refused. Again, we see in action an example of the way in which great violence took place within the reach of the law but that equality before it faded outside Adelaide to a degree that left a man like Hayward's prisoner liable to personal punishments. Even a 'not guilty' verdict could leave a person stranded, sometimes hundreds of miles from home or in Charlie's case, three days' walk away through country not his own.

While at Pekina Station Hayward also looked around further north, searching for good waters that could be acquired under lease. Eventually he took a half-share of Aroona in partnership with the wealthy and well-connected Browne brothers, doctors who had moved into the more lucrative field of pastoralism.

Aroona

By the time that Hayward and four thousand or so sheep droved up from Encounter Bay arrived on Aroona in 1850, his ideas about how best to build up a profitable sheep station were based on three years of experience. It was the creation of terror through violence that made Hayward successful in securing his flocks. The raids on his Pekina flock had persisted, Mincham records, until 'every tribe was terror-stricken, or other settlers crept farther north'.[6] In his diary Hayward records the way in which he had tied up a cattle thief that he had captured and flogged him with a stockwhip.[7] On Aroona, at the edge of settlement and facing harassment of his flocks from those feeling the brunt of their presence, he set about creating the terror he had found so effective at Pekina. He whipped anyone he thought might be responsible for stealing sheep, considering a dozen cuts as merciful. Similar claims were made by Thomas Brown when recounting the punitive expedition launched in response to the killing of his young brother, James, in September 1852. James' body had been defiled – his genitals cut off and put into his mouth, most likely as a response to the casual violation of the bodies of Aboriginal women by those engaged in converting country into property.

After describing the violence that followed, Brown has no hesitation declaring that in leading the killings he had been fulfilling his God's command. Brown's description of his collective vengeance upon those who had killed his brother shows how religious beliefs were used to veil the extent of the violence that created the terror that led eventually to a 'quieter' time for the colonists. In Brown's case he quoted a verse from Genesis 9, an Old Testament chapter well-suited to colonists building a new world. It was verse 6 that Brown cited: 'Whoso sheddeth man's blood, by man shall his blood be shed: for in the image of God made he man.'[8] This is a verse used by many to establish the death penalty for the crime of murder as being God's will, with man being made in the image of God and on occasion, standing in for Him. Here we see the justification of revenge and the law taken into private hands, a system of law that in other countries would be described as lawlessness or feuding perhaps, or banditry or gang warfare. It was the opposite of the ideals of a civilised nation in which people lived by the justice of the rule of law. Public debate about the use of the death penalty in England had been going on for many years by the middle of the nineteenth century and the numbers of crimes to which it applied had been wound back. William Wordsworth's poem arguing for its retention, 'Sonnets upon the Punishment of Death' (1841) argued for the older, Biblical, value of the death penalty that assumed the divine source of all government as, in an individualised way, did Brown. Others, like Charles Dickens and William Thackeray for example, were repelled by the spectacle of public executions with Thackeray seeing it not as an expression of the sacred in man but as violation of the sacred.[9] In England, 'home' to so many of the first colonists, there were many moves toward prison and penalty reform during the first half of the nineteenth century that were generally resisted in the Australian colonies. South Australia was no different.

Massacre

By 1852 the hostility generated by Hayward's unchecked reign of violence led to the killing of the shepherd, Robert Richardson, and the apparent mutilation of his body. It also led to the planning of a full-scale attack on Hayward and his property. News of the hostile gathering of Aboriginal men came to Hayward through 'a friendly native', most likely one of those brought in from elsewhere to provide just such a conduit for valuable information. Together with one of his shepherds and two stockmen from neighbouring Oraparinna Station (now part of a national park) Hayward set out at dawn to raid the sleeping Aboriginal camp. The number of people shot was disputed but according to Hayward himself the number of dead started at fifteen; later accounts reduced the number to one. It is only as a result of the careful research published by Robert Foster, Rick Hosking and Amanda Nettelbeck that it is now clear that Hayward's first estimate of the numbers of Indigenous dead lay between forty and sixty.[10] Such a massacre could not but have effects on the Yura peoples and their neighbours. Once the shooting stopped, Hayward heard from the survivors still in camp that Richardson's murderers were not among the dead. As Richardson's murderers were still at large, an unworried Hayward reported the fighting and sought police assistance in catching the culprits.

Enter McKinlay

The next episode in this story therefore began some weeks later with the arrival of a contingent of police from Adelaide. Their task was to capture the real murderers, one of whom said that Richardson had killed his brother and that his death was a response to his murder. The police party included Hayward, William Marchant from Arkaba Station, John McKinlay who had cattle resting on a property just north of Aroona, one of McKinlay's stockmen, and Peter, one of the Aboriginal men from another district whom Hayward found so useful.[11] The two men accused of killing Richardson were duly captured, passing their first night chained to posts in the rudimentary hut on Oraparinna Station where all were sleeping. Their attempt to set fire to the roof failed, although Hayward said that in a fit of rage McKinlay attacked one of the prisoners with an axe, the victim saving himself only by grabbing a tin dish and placing it on his head to protect it.

Later, McKinlay joined those searching fruitlessly for Burke and Wills on the flood-plain of Cooper Creek. John Bailey suggests that the grave McKinlay found in 1861 was probably that of Charles Gray, who had died on Burke's march toward the Gulf of Carpentaria. But McKinlay believed, or said he believed, that the man in the grave had been murdered by Aborigines and eaten by them. According to Bailey, McKinlay called the place Lake Massacre and then killed 'a line of Aboriginal men he said were threatening him.'[12]

Nearly sixty years later, the Catholic Press of Sydney would offer its readers a further account of the cannibalistic natives of the northern ranges:

> Towards the end of October, 1861, John McKinlay, and W.O. Hodgkinson, as second in command, set out from Adelaide to search for Burke and Wills, whom Brake had reported as lost. Crossing Lake Torrens, the party made for Cooper's Creek. After passing

through a country dotted by small, shallow lakes, they reached a water-course, and on the banks of this stream found a battered pint pot and a recently dug grave. This was the grave of poor Gray, ... but a blackfellow who came to McKinlay's camp had a wonderful story to tell about it. He told them that a party of blacks had attacked a camp in which were four white men. Three of these had been killed and eaten, and the fourth was buried in that grave. The native had marks of a bullet wound on his body, and said that a pistol and other articles were hidden in the creek close by. He offered to fetch the hidden articles, but next morning he brought with him a whole tribe of his fellows, who attacked McKinlay's party. The leader was obliged to order his men to fire at the blacks. It was some time before they were driven off. McKinlay felt certain that the native's story was a true one, so he sent Hodgkinson back to report that Burke's party had been killed and eaten.[13]

Excerpts from McKinlay's diaries give a clearer picture of his thinking at the time of his discovery but make no mention of any shooting.[14] Although McKinlay's reputation in the colony was high, hints of violence surround his name. One historian of the colony, Reverend John Blackett, says only that McKinlay and his men 'were in danger from hostile natives'.[15] On an 1865 journey to the Alligator River region in the Northern Territory, Blackett says that McKinlay and his party 'were attacked by natives, who were repulsed without serious results'.[16] McKinlay died at the small township of Gawler, respected for his integrity, with a mountain named after him. Mt McKinlay was more properly known as *Warna*, an important site for Adnyamathanha women, given the name not just of the 'white male "explorer"' referred to by Cliff Coulthard, but one who had driven them away from their country with such terrible violence.[17]

A reminiscence of McKinlay, signed only JHG, was published shortly after his death in Gawler's *Bunyip* newspaper of 11 September 1874. After mentioning McKinlay's kindness to boys, the author illustrates McKinlay's pluck, 'his command over man, his fertility of resource, and presence of mind.' Written in a jolly style, the incident revolves around a 'favourite blackboy', Tommy. The 'jealousy' of the others (or possibly his role in keeping his patron informed and receiving privileges in return), had made Tommy hated to the degree that when he was alone one day he was very badly beaten. In response, somehow McKinlay got all those concerned, some fifty of them, the author claimed, into the wool shed. Ranging them in a line he demanded that the culprit should be given to him for punishment. Although he was allegedly alone and the others were many, McKinlay responded to their refusal by taking the waddy, 'from the man at the head and knocked him down, next his fellow, and so, doubtless amid many a wild shriek and frantic struggle, continued the merited chastisement till they were piled, every man of them, pell-mell upon each other on the floor.' The author goes on to praise McKinlay's 'manly cheerfulness of disposition.' In the eyes of JHG, and as was described in chapter five, McKinlay was a hero. McKinlay had, JHG wrote,

> broken the silence of many dim tracks, and entered, first of his race, into many a solemn forest. There remained only the last journey to the most silent and mysterious, yet most travel-worn, of all regions. For his earthly travellings he was always prepared, nor was he unprepared for this. 'Abiit ad plures' [Petronius] he has gone over to the great majority; he has joined the famous nations of the dead. God rest him. The hic jacet of his tomb is writ above a noble man.

The obituary published by the *South Australian Chronicle and Weekly Mail* of 4 January 1873 mentions McKinlay's time as a pastoralsist on the Darling River in the 1840s 'when nothing but ready resource, unflinching firmness and fearlessness, enabled Europeans to hold their own against the savage tribes whose territory they were occupying ... the shepherd kings had to guard themselves and their herds against all enemies.' McKinlay and his brother, the writer said, were 'thoroughly understood by the natives. They found him kind and indulgent when they acted honestly, but they knew how quickly he punished treachery and murderous violence, and many are the stories now extant of his dealings with the wild sons of the forest. The Darling country, however, became as safe and as quiet as other portions of the colony.' On the Darling, McKinlay was greatly feared. He had taken up land near Lake Victoria in 1848, a beneficiary of the fighting on the Rufus River. McKinlay is quoted as saying 'that the Aborigines "came down upon the half-protected stations and livestock of the settlers, committing frightful murders and destroying their flocks and herds to an alarming extent. The blacks in fact took possession of the country, threatening to utterly exterminate the white man, and establish a perfect reign of terror".'[18] So terror was a strategy understood by both parties to the war for the land. Yet the number of Indigenous deaths far exceeded those of the colonists.

Remembered explicitly as an explorer, McKinlay's pastoral investments were not always successful. His portrait looks as if it is a companion piece to one of John McDouall Stuart who worked so hard to get across Australia from south to north – a man armed with a gun, looking into the future, and pointing into the unknown.

McKinlay's presence intersected with Hayward's again in the narratives of other incidents on his property. When two Indigenous men taken from Hayward's property to Adelaide by the police were released because no-one spoke their language, Hayward refused to travel to town to give evidence. The men were discharged and set off on the long walk home. Hayward records that when they reached McKinlay's run, an unknown person killed them. As these murders left Hayward's shepherds living in fear of retribution, it seems safe to assume that either Hayward or McKinlay was their murderer. If not all new landowners were prepared to be as ruthless as Hayward and McKinlay, and many were truly concerned about the welfare of those they were displacing, it is also the case that Hayward was not the only man who believed in violence and terror as the only way to advance settlement – he could muster plenty of help when he needed it. There were fortunes to be made from land once it was securely in colonial hands.

A wealthy man, Hayward was greatly respected in Adelaide. His virtues are extolled in Cockburn's *Pastoral Pioneers of South Australia*.[19]

Ready to raise a family, he married and retired to England in 1864, naming his large and comfortable house 'Aroona' after his station in the Flinders. There he was referred to as 'the squire'.[20] He and his wife, Ellen Margaret Litchfield, had eleven children of whom eight survived, at least one of the boys coming to South Australia.

*****

Yet we know from his diaries that both fortune and respectability were purchased by the relentless murder, sexual violence and terrorisation of all those unfortunate enough to live upon land he wanted to convert to grazing. We also know from his diaries that his actions did not trouble his conscience and that he rather enjoyed the thrill of the chase. Hayward's unguarded descriptions of his life in South Australia have been comprehensibly examined by Robert Foster, Rick Hosking and Amanda Nettelbeck in their *Fatal Collisions*.[21] The detail of his reminiscences, they suggest, may have resulted from earlier diary entries, although no such document has been located. But certainly his published account of life in the Flinders Ranges bears few marks of censoring.

Foster, Hosking and Nettelbeck also note the way in which the violence of dispossession is often laid at the feet of convicts, ignorant shepherds or people coming in from the other less humane colonies. Yet in truth, as in Hayward's case, most often the violence is associated with wealthier and educated colonists – with the upper classes, not the lower. The prosperous and well-educated do not always take part in the violence as Hayward did, sometimes preferring to keep their hands clean, but it is they who enter government and have the power to disseminate doctrines that first encourage and then justify or protect its practitioners. They have the power to stop it, but they don't.

In South Australia the first fortunes were made by the first to arrive. They were the fortunate ones who had bought rights to land before leaving England, had family or money behind them, or were able to invest, improve and sell out before moving onto new ground in order to repeat the process. Whether the first fortunes came from urban development, pastoralism, agriculture or from mining, those with some money already were best placed to make the kind of profits that set up people like Hayward, Tennant and Mortlock for life. Hayward was no working class struggler nor a small merchant capitalist but an educated man from an established provincial English background. He worked initially for those wealthier than he, people well-connected to the more privileged class of colonist. That respected and influential men like the Browne doctors and Price Maurice were willing to work with men like Hayward and McKinlay as their properties were made safe from First Nation retribution provides an example of the ways in which racial violence and upper class toleration of it was at the heart of the colonial enterprise, no matter how much it was disguised.

Chapter Twenty-Nine

Women and Children

The treatment of women and children was a sensitive issue for both Frederick Hayward and Thomas Brown. Hayward said he never shot children, a fact known, he claimed, to the people whose camps he raided, so much so that his policy led to fleeing men carrying a child with them as protection. Brown described how, at the time of a savage massacre, the women and children were separated from the men, kept safe until the shooting was over. In part, their statements reflect a sensibility to the criticism that such killings could provoke in Adelaide. Hayward, perhaps, used his claim to deflect public attention away from the brutality of the terror he was using to take the land, perhaps also to rehabilitate or create a reputation that was more suitable to his later life as a village squire. The Biblical avenger Thomas Brown was perhaps more troubled by shooting defenceless women and children, perhaps more troubled also by possible repercussions.

Records of other incidents in the colony show that the killing of children during punitive raids was not always a matter of particular concern. On George Alexander Anstey's Station on the Yorke Peninsula, for example, when the unarmed Nantariltarra went back to his camp to fetch a child left behind in the rush to avoid George Penton's posse, George Field had no hesitation in shooting him as he ran away and made no attempt to rescue the small child who fell from Nantariltarra's arms into the bay and drowned.[1] Field was unlucky in that the shooting was scrutinised by the law. But while the Aboriginal evidence against him was clear, the requirement by law for the corroboration of all Indigenous evidence before the courts (there were difficulties with the oath, as Aboriginal witnesses were unable to swear meaningfully on the Bible) was not forthcoming.[2] So Field became yet another of those whose violence was protected by the processes of the law, one of those who contributed to the great statistical disparity between the numbers of Aborigines prosecuted for the murder of colonists and the number of colonists prosecuted for murdering Aborigines. And certainly neither Hayward nor Brown seemed to have feared prosecution for their killings.

In later years, hopeful settlers riding through the colony's north would remark on the absence of women and children in the Aboriginal camps, an absence put down to the slow processes involved in 'fading away' that was part of the explanation for the calamitous drop in Indigenous population numbers seen right across the colony. More realistically, their absence could have been caused either by the flight of women from the camps as strangers approached, or, it might be that as well as the impact of sexually transmitted diseases the shooting of women and children in the course of 'settling down' the country had been severe enough to have an impact on the ratio of men to women in the population.

That both Brown and Hayward felt a need to say that they did not kill children and in Brown's case, that he kept the women and children safe, points up the moral issues surrounding both the status and proper treatment of colonial women and children, and the important role of women and children in defining colonial superiority in its contrast with Indigenous savagery. The savage nature of the violence used in taking the land was itself a challenge to the notion that savagery lay always with the other side – it kept alive the possibility that colonial righteousness was not entirely well-founded or secure. Reading Thomas Brown's account of the revenge killings that followed the murder of his young brother, his God-driven terrible anger might be seen as driven in part by the realisation that he had been driven into the savagery he might otherwise have deplored. Hayward's account of his raid and of men running away bearing children has no such intensity in it. It fits much more easily into a colonial yarn, a mythical retelling that presents the narrator once more as hero.

*****

Inevitably, the violence of colonisation threw up questions about who was really the savage – the real owners of the Country being taken over, or the civilising colonisers taking it from them? This was a constant problem for the first generations of colonists, first because they preferred to believe that they came with peace in their hearts, that they wanted peace, and that it was easier to believe that any violence was fragmentary and short-lived. And second, despite rhetorical strategies that used language to downplay any unfortunate incidents ('our peaceful natives', 'a brush with the natives', or, 'an affray in the north'), a Protector sent to discover the causes of the 'trouble' and to check the supposed numbers injured, the realities involved in securing colonial possession of life and property were not so much secret as hidden in plain sight because so many colonists chose not to look.

Constant calls for more police, for example, are an indication that 'settling' the country was not going so peacefully; claims that large flocks had been driven off and generally declared lost forever indicate active targeting of colonists at a vulnerable point; the deaths of shepherds and other hands (of C.H. Dutton and his flock on the way overland to Adelaide from Port Lincoln, for example), the attacks on property and the use of fire as a weapon – all these actions made it plain that there was resistance to the colonisers and indeed, that there was fighting severe enough to qualify as war. Even as news of some of the worst killings of Aborigines reached town and information about the actual nature of fighting was suppressed or reconstructed, even as vociferous criticism of police, pastoralists and government emerged from Adelaide, it was difficult to retain full confidence in the distinction between *our* superior civilising way of life with only necessary and lamentable violence and *their* debased savagery and barbarous customs. The difficulty of maintaining that crucial moral distinction of superiority is most apparent when it came to Indigenous women.

If Indigenous women were seen as morally debased and at risk of violence from Indigenous men, what were the colonists to think of their own men, sometimes even pillars of the church, who were quite prepared to shoot defenceless women and children? This is the logical and troubling moral issue raised when fleeing women were mown down in dawn raids and their children dealt with likewise. The claims of men like Haywood, Brown and Tennant occurred within this context highlighted some fundamental moral issues. Although as front-line invaders they were regarded as heroes, they also needed to try to re-establish themselves as decent Christian men who were, indeed, protectors of those poor despised Aboriginal women, men who would hold their fire if women and children might be harmed. It was not just a culture of secrecy that played down the violence but a broader set of moral mythologies that meant that for the perpetrators some kind of personal redemption was required.

A second pillar of the image of colonists as bringers of civilisation rested upon Indigenous children and here the impetus provided by evangelical Christianity is even more visible. The saving of Indigenous children from savagery and barbarity through the attempted destruction of the Indigenous family was carried out relentlessly, backed by both church and state. It took place within a religious and evangelical political context in Britain in which improving the lives of children came to lead calls for substantial social reform. Education, working hours, wages, safety and working conditions were all under critical scrutiny. So the child as unstained hope for the future had already emerged, justified by Bible texts and cemented into political demands. In the colony, the child was also seen as the bearer of the utopian hopes for a better future with Indigenous children attracting intensive interest across religious, humanist and philanthropic associations. It drove the early interest in education as creating a pathway forward to their future. In colonial South Australia, as hopes for Christianising Aboriginal parents faded with the failure of the early missionaries, the Aboriginal child still had to carry the burden of building the new Christian world that their own parents had rejected. 'Saving' Aboriginal children, educating them for their future, and sending them to England to be educated into their world-to-come was one way of fulfilling the utopian fantasy for the Indigenous future.

The image of the Indigenous child in a civilised future was very popular in Victorian England. It appears in evangelical literature, in children's fiction (e.g. Charles Kingsley's popular *The Water-Babies* (1863) in which Tom loses his chimney-sweep's blackness by diving into the water and a new world), in the taking up of 'found' children to be civilised within colonial families, as well as in the doctrines leading to the founding of Poonindie Anglican mission on Eyre Peninsula. The children taken into Poonindie will speak English properly and have a degree of literacy and numeracy; they will be children with some agricultural or domestic skills who are clean, brushed, happy and fetching and in due course, married monogamously. This early colonial vision of the civilised Indigenous child has endured, appearing in hundreds of mission and government publications as well as in popular magazines like the *Woman's Weekly* until, in the 1950s, those children

Agnes Newberry (Peg) Orchard (1899–1984), 'Self Portrait', Picannin Series 1, 1950s. Private Collection.[3]

became the adornment of kitsch ceramic plates and illustrations in books that attempted sometimes to link this attractive 'wild' child back to an imagined Australian 'stone age' of a past that had never really ended, and indeed, to the natural world of plants and animals – back to where they started.

The importance of children in the 19th century as bearers of hope and the future can can also be seen in Eyre's hopes for Warulan, son of Tenberry of Moorundie. Warulan may have been only six or seven when he was farewelled by his family at Port Adelaide and sailed for England in the care of Eyre and in the company of a boy travelling with Anthony Forster, a man who later returned to forge a prosperous career in the colony. A Methodist 'New Connexion' preacher and mission supporter, Forster 'liked to think of South Australia as a "land of peace, of plenty, and of good order ... of chapels, bibles, and religious enjoyment".'[4] Eyre's supervision of Tenberry's son and his belief in the value of improving children through English civilisation was not unusual at a time in which education was widely perceived as the key to a proper place in the world. Eyre may have heard of Robert FitzRoy's attempts with children from Tierra del Fuego taken up in 1828 or '29 during a naval survey of the southern seas and of how they were presented at Court.[5] Charles Darwin on the *Beagle*, who witnessed their return home, was shocked at the way they so quickly gave up all they had learned in England, surprised at their enjoyment of nakedness. But Eyre and Forster held great hopes for the young men travelling with them.

Tenbury's family and friends accompanied Warulan from Moorundie to Adelaide, walking the hundred or so kilometres easily as they had taken to doing when visiting Adelaide for the Queen's Birthday celebrations. Two reports of the sailing of the boys appeared in Adelaide's newspapers. The first, given to a meeting of the 'Friends of the Aborigines', mentions the steps taken already toward more civilised manners; the second, written by a journalist for the general public, stresses the jollity of the day.

Mr Eyre (late Resident Magistrate at the Murray, now on the point of a voyage to England, with a view to the renovation of his health), was among the number of distinguished guests. He had with him two fine native boys, whom he is instructing, and has handsomely equipped for the voyage. The worthy magistrate spoke frequently to the Murray natives who lined the fence [the family and friends of Warulan], and it was most pleasing to notice the respectful deference observed by these natives towards Mr Eyre, as also the kind amenity of the latter in replying to their many inquiries; there were none of the clamorous interrogatories of savage life, but the quiet mode of category and subdued tone which are associated with ideas of civilisation and refinement.[6]

YESTERDAY was quite a gala day at the Port. The occasion of this was the embarking of the passengers by the Symmetry, *by which ship several old and respected colonists leave on a visit to their native land.*

The excitement was materially increased by the fact that, by this vessel, three of the aborigines are proceeding to England, and in consequence of this a body of the natives, upwards of one hundred in number, proceeded to the Port yesterday morning to say good-bye to their old companions. Two of the natives go along with Mr Eyre, and the third with Mr Fo[r]ster. Mr Eyre kindly presented each of the natives who visited the Port with a piece of bread, and other presents were also given to several of them. A great number of them afterwards went on board the Symmetry, *where they were kindly treated by Capt. Elder, who, along with his passengers, and many of their friends and acquaintances, were on board. They afterwards returned to the shore, and proceeded to Adelaide, the children in drays, and the men and women on foot.*[7]

In England, Eyre sent Warulan to the Friends' School in Saffron Walden because of the way in which the Friends believed that there was 'God in every man, in every woman, and every child, negro slave, and native of whatever race.'[8] In doing so, Eyre was drawing on the extensive network of humanitarian Quaker merchants that had been instrumental in the successful campaign to abolish British slavery – the Gurneys, Cadburys, Rowntrees and others with Backhouse and Walker in Tasmania taking a considerable interest in the welfare of First Nations peoples there. Some were already in Australia feeding reports on Aboriginal well-being back to England. One way or another, Warulan's life in England was under the supervision of Quakers. Eyre's posting to New Zealand in 1847 as deputy to Governor Grey led him to put Warulan into the care of Dr Thomas Hodgkin, whose interest in anthropology included the possibilities inherent in educating the 'sons of chiefs' to provide the leadership that would help to bring civilisation to those living without it.[9] By this time Warulan was about ten or twelve years old, while aspects of the behaviour of young Kour, who had also left Adelaide with Forster and Warulan, had led to his being sent home. Warulan was not considered a good student, one of his faults being that he had no memory, a surprising criticism of someone born into a culture in which memory was essential – it is a failing that suggests unwillingness rather than incapacity. His summer holidays were spent with Hodgkins, he was taken to visit the Queen, his head was examined by phrenologists, until finally he was apprenticed to a saddler and harness-maker in Banbury. Eyre believed that Warulan should remain in England regardless of any wish to return to Australia. He did not want him to take up his old childhood life on the Murray again, he did not want him to 'revert' as had the Tierra del Fuegans and others like them. Warulan died in 1855 in Birmingham – he was about nineteen years old. His father had wanted to visit him but could not.[10] He too was now dead, as were most of Warulan's siblings, most likely caught by the epidemic of venereal and other contagious diseases unleashed through the permanent presence of the British settled onto the Murray lands.[11]

Part Six

The North-East

Chapter Thirty

Into the Dry Lands

The north-eastern segment of the colony was vast, differing greatly from the country to its south. The move into it was driven not only by the search for grazing land but also by a thirst for mineral deposits that might deliver the mighty profits like those then flowing from mines around Kapunda and Burra Burra. Until the discovery of coal (1888), oil and gas fields (1960s) and uranium (1970s), the little copper-mining town of Blinman (operating from 1862) more or less marked the most northerly of the mines but the region was considered hopeful by all concerned.

Beyond Blinman lay the 'far north', a natural stage onwards from the outlying reaches of the Flinders Range. The first pastoral claims were based on the waters and food stocks produced by several good seasons, their first sightings of lakes seething with bird life and fish and also, of the healthy, strong First Australians who often gathered in quite large numbers. But ignorance of both the fluctuating nature of the seasons and the intermittent nature of surface waters would cause massive financial losses to many of those investing in the vast holdings required there for both cattle and sheep. As later generations would learn in primary school, in England the carrying capacity of land was calculated in number of beasts per acre but in Australia it had to be done in number of acres per beast and those beasts needed water. The sheer scale of the herds and the market value of any stock that reached

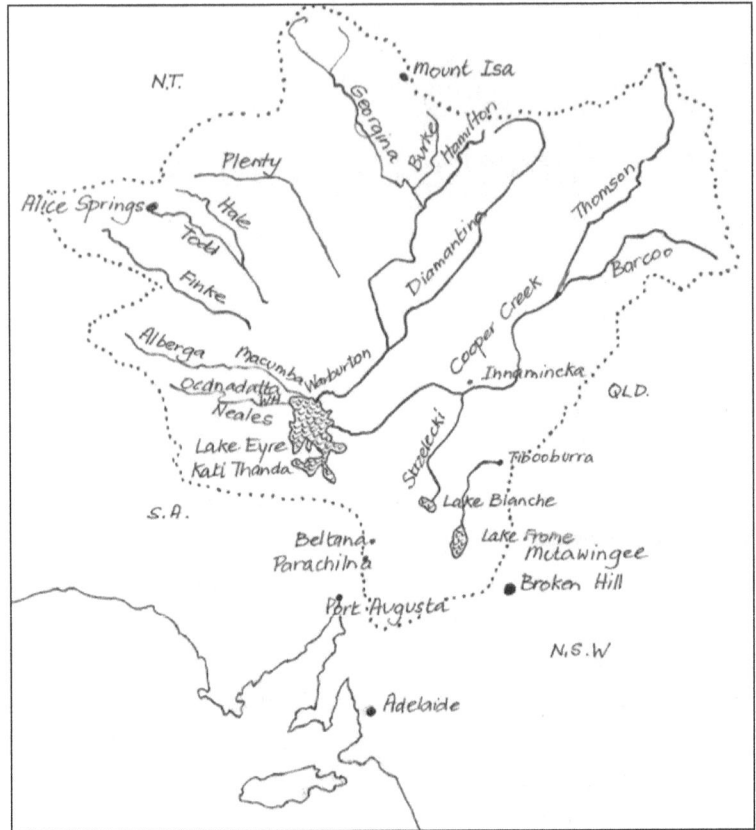

The Lake Eyre Basin showing the major rivers draining towards Kati Thanda-Lake Eyre, none of which are permanent. The map also shows that the rivers that provided trade and ceremonial routes are connected with regions now in other states. Beltana and Parachilna are in the north of the Flinders Range.

Adelaide's sale-yards alive lured pastoralists and investors northward.

Country in the north-east differed greatly from the ranges, hills and plains further south. It was shaped largely by the basin surrounding the huge salt lake lying fifteen metres below sea level, Kati Thanda-Lake Eyre. In the lake's basin there were two main sources of water bolstered by one of lesser reliability. First were the artesian waters. They came up from far below the earth, ancient waters, sometimes scalding hot, sometimes cooler, sometimes undrinkable, sometimes useful for animals. Some of it emerged at such pressure that the colonists found occasional springs on the tops of barren cliffs. The mound springs rising west of Kati Thanda-Lake Eyre that helped John McDouall Stuart get across the continent in 1862 are part of this system, one so ancient that fish and other animals had evolved to live in them. Their apparent permanence attracted colonists. Later, bores would be sunk into waterholes and springs to tap into the stores of artesian water lying below. Vast as they were, the waters of this 'great artesian basin' have been depleted both by pastoral usage and more recently by uranium miners at Roxby Downs and by the loss of surface waters.[1]

Otherwise, the basin relied on a second source of water: rain that arrived from far away, channelled along creeks that led into the rivers leading toward Kati Thanda-Lake Eyre. These waters arrived only if there had been major deluges far from the basin itself – such rains were neither annual nor dependable. Kati Thanda-Lake Eyre fills rarely, perhaps once in twenty years and then not in full. This is not easy country, yet it has been inhabited for thousands of years, probably much longer, supporting a good life for those who knew it.

In a good year it was transformed. The desert flowered, rivers, creeks and lakes filled with highly evolved desert fish, frogs and specialised crustaceans like shield shrimps, while insects, small marsupials (this country is generally too dry for kangaroos), reptiles and birds all bred rapidly and en masse. They were the golden years, one or two of which were witnessed by the first colonists to reach there. Living on such country required great skill and detailed knowledge of every aspect of the land. Life and livelihood rested on highly adapted forms of production that were not extractive, that did not deplete the essentials of life, and of course, on the mobility and ability to move away when seasons changed and water dried up. Then, both plants and animals retreated (frogs buried themselves and hibernated) to wait for better times.

Because it was sporadic, a third source of water, that of water falling as rain directly into the basin, was less important but always welcome. Falls average around 125 millimetres a year. Local rain could fill shallow clay pans, small depressions in creeks that ran rarely and not far, lying in crevices in among rocks, perhaps. But high summer temperatures mean that any surface water evaporates at startling rates – 2.5 metres per annum. When and if it came rain falling on ancient clay soils could make the country boggy and dangerous to sheep, cattle and horses but perfectly accessible on foot if necessary. Once pastoralism arrived it would become common to see animal skeletons around water holes, springs or claypans, animals that had not died from thirst but from being stuck in the mud around them, unable to move. Pastoral exploitation of such country was at best blundering, often destructive and frequently depleting. It was also staunchly resisted by those living on it already.

There are a number of dimensions to the colonisation of what came to be called the colony's 'far north', dimensions that turned sporadic resistance toward determined warfare. The first of these was that although low population densities offered a good life, it was possible for large groups to gather together when the season permitted. There were far more First Nations Australians resident in the north-east than there were pastoralists, explorers, missionaries and assorted others. And as was often noticed, those people were strong and healthy, well able to fight. Had they known their real strength, colonists remarked, they might have taken even more decisive action. A certain amount of the behaviour of the pastoralists aimed to prevent them gaining that understanding. Acts intending to demoralise, humiliate and demonstrate the unlimited and remarkable powers of the new regime were phrased as usual as 'teaching the blacks a lesson'. Terror, as pastoralists knew from the taking of the Flinders Ranges to the south was not only common but cheap.

A major trade route ran north-south across the north-eastern lands, used by those from the far north wanting the red ochre from the Flinders Ranges. Passing through Diyari and Yantruwunta country it went on southwards to Parachilna. Along this route Lake Kopperamanna (later the site of a Lutheran mission) operated as an important trading centre. As mentioned earlier, through it flowed many goods – the prized pituri from around Boulia waterhole in Queensland, axes and the blanks carved from the special stone from which they were fabricated, secular and sacred ceremonies, dances and songs, pearl shell ornaments, and much more.[2] There were also well-known routes leading east and west that connected them to others and helped to define Diyari country – they lived roughly between what are now the towns of Innaminka and Oodnadatta but in touch with many others.

Although appearing to the colonists as isolated country, as remote and next to empty, this was far from the case.[3] The Diyari lived surrounded by many other people and languages, some on good terms, others not. They were far from isolated, living within an extensive web of social, ceremonial and commercial connections that pulsed with the seasons. All this meant that they could call on others to discuss what should be done about the invaders and to muster men who were prepared to drive off the flocks and herds as well as the horses, to protect their waters, to burn the huts and yards of the pastoralists, steal the stores on which the colonists had to rely and, if necessary, to show their intent by killing those attempting to steal their country.

Another factor affecting the Indigenous response to colonial invasion of the far north was the impact of its timing. In the first years of the colony the colonists assumed that the local peoples they encountered around Adelaide had no real knowledge of British ways and habits. While this was only partly so, most local people there lacked the experience of actually living with invaders face-to-face for any length of time, or of living within a colonial order that was overwhelmingly detrimental to their daily lives. Initially, therefore, knowledge of the implications of pastoralism among the Kaurna and Ngarrindjeri was limited.

By the early 1860s, when the push into the north-east was gathering pace, this was far from the case. It was not just that information was coming up from the south as colonists moved northwards through the Clare Valley and then into the Flinders Ranges, but that it was coming in also from the east (from western New South Wales), along segments of trade routes like Yandama Creek.

At the same time, exploration out from the northern coast of Australia was proceeding inland from the seabord. The permanent waters of the Victoria River, noticed in 1839 by John Lort Stokes on the *Beagle* and investigated further in 1855 by A.C. Gregory, was a constant enticement and not only to John MacDouall Stuart who finally found his way across the continent from south to north in 1862. In 1862 also, Queensland moved its inland boundary slightly westwards to capture many of the waters and pastures of what is now called the 'channel country', ancient floodplains cut by rivers like the Georgina, the Diamentina and the Cooper. As a result, Queensland cattle were being moved steadily onto the new border-lands of their colony, not always a happy process, nor one that could have remained unknown.[4] In 1863, with many Adelaide eyes on the waters and harbours on the northern edge of the continent, the Northern Territory was attached to South Australia to form the 'great central state' of colonial Australia on which so many utopian as well as political and financial hopes were pinned.[5] It too was to be administered from Adelaide.

As more and more colonists arrived such shifts were bound to be disruptive. While information about the colonists reaching the Diyari people might have been fragmented or distorted, the Diyari and their neighbours could not but be better informed than were the Kaurna and Ngarrindjeri facing the first of the colonists' ships in 1837. The people of the north-east were living in a world in which information about the nature of the new men, their violence and the consequences of their herds would govern their own responses to colonial incursions. While many of them might not have seen colonists before, neither were they living in ignorance of them, their horses, and their habits. Charles Sturt, for example, had spent considerable time around the upper reaches of the Cooper Creek in the far north-east of the colony in 1845. And it is likely that then, as later, the arrival of colonists was preceded by their cats to form the first ripple in what would become a wave of feral feline incursion that has proved so destructive to native wildlife.

Because the peoples of the north-east had access to more information about the consequences of colonisation than had those who had faced up to the first colonists around Adelaide, the taking of Diyari Country was more complicated. First there was the war for the lands, the methods of 'clearing' them, and the role of the police. Then came the unexpected arrival of two separate sets of German-speaking missionaries, one Lutheran, one Moravian. Until finally, there was a peace brought into existence through the violence itself and the policing practices that accompanied it.

Neither staunch condemnation from colonial voices in Adelaide nor the decent behaviour of some pastoralists in offering a haven of sorts could alter the forms of engagement that came to characterise so much of the life of the colony. As in the more southerly districts, the wars for the lands of the far north were being waged on behalf of the new world that was being built in a new land, the society on which the hopes and the future of the colonists depended. The move into the north-east began from the most northerly of the stations established in the Flinders Ranges. After several good years, pasture was plentiful, there was water in many of the lakes along with the rich fish and bird stocks that came with it. Lake Blanche on Pirlatapa country looked magnificent. On it John Baker established his Blanchewater Station.[6] In 1865 there would be a newspaper report that only two men of the 'Blanchewater tribe' were still living, Jemmy Midnight and Blanchewater Billy.[7] This would mean that after just seven years of colonial occupation the property had been 'cleared' to make it safe for its new owners. The absence of Lake Blanche's Indigenous owners was ascribed to the 'Saltwater Blacks', a name used for those living east of Kati Thanda-Lake Eyre, the Diyari and their neighbours. But it was not they who had driven off or killed the people of Lake Blanche but the colonists sweeping onto their country, covering their water sources with leasehold properties and bringing in very large numbers of stock.

Diyari Country

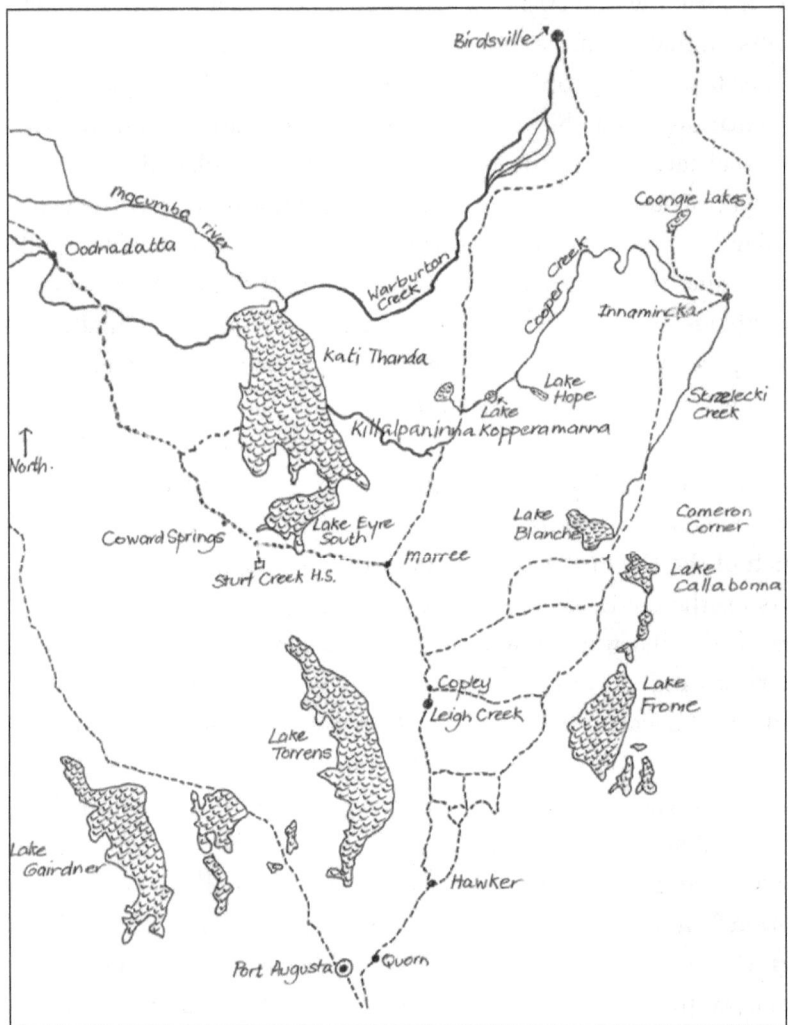

Sketch of the north-east country of the colony to show the main places mentioned in this and subsequent chapters. Lake Hope is fed from Cooper's Creek. Tracks are shown by broken lines, the creek beds by a solid line. Lakes and rivers are all seasonal with most of them dry or salt for many years before sufficient water falls in catchment areas lying far beyond the basin to flow along the Cooper, Macumber, and Waburton Rivers. The Strezlecki River that waters Lake Blanche must wait on water to flow down from the Cooper.

Diyari Country might have been difficult for the colonists to live on but for those with the flexibility necessary to follow and conserve the always ephemeral water supplies it was good country offering a good life. Dibana's recollections of that life as it was towards the end of the nineteenth century, told to the anthropologist Ronald Berndt, offers some sense of how life around Lake Hope and Lake Killalpannina (marked on the map above) was being lived at the time of colonisation, of how their life appeared to them, of what it was that those men fought so hard to protect. Dibana speaks as an old man looking back, as if he is watching a film of his life in which he is also a leading actor.

> *Today the sun is good. The sun is warm and makes my body feel good. I lie on my back with my hands behind my head – and my face is shaded by the shadow thrown by my hut.*[8]

Thus began Dibana as he thought back to his birthplace near Lake Killalpannina, his life around the lake, and of his father's life there too, to construct an account of just one day:

> '*I am married to Miribani, who is a Diyari of the Bandubina (Pando-Lake Hope) country, with the frog as mardu and the dog as bindara. She is a strong woman with a firm body and breasts still rounded, whereas many other women's are sagging; she has given birth to four children – two boys, Malgilina and Jelubirnana, and two girls, Milamirini and Guragurarini.*
>
> '*My eldest son is nearly ready to go through his first test to make him a young man ... My eldest daughter Milamirini is married to Galdrigaldrina, a man I do not like, as he talks too much and does not give me, his father-in-law ... the portion of food due to me by kinship obligation. My eldest daughter is now pregnant ...*
>
> *The sun becomes warmer, and I think it better that I move into the shade. I very much like to look down from this hill on to Lake Killalpaninna, made by the muramura Darana in the Dreaming.*[9] *I feel cool when I look down at the children bathing and playing in its waters.*

Now look! There is my wife. She comes with a skin full of water. Now she will cook the fish, and we will eat. We men caught many fish with the nets yesterday; the yellow-bellied margara is the best ...

My wife and I have our morning food alone. My eldest son has gone out to kill goanna, while the two youngest children play in my mother's camp nearby.

Some of my friends pass by my camp and talk a little. It is a good day to go out hunting, and I will go when I have put out some of the fish to dry so that they will not get rotten. My wife and I talk about our children, and of our eldest daughter who will soon have a child, which will make us both grandparents. We laugh over this conversation. Then we both talk about the second wife, and how she will gather more food. My wife says that she may get jealous, but that it will be all right if I do not sleep with the other too much. So I promise her, and my wife laughs and teases me.

I tell her about the mindari ceremony which was held last night to which she did not go.

My mother brings over to our camp the two youngest children, so we stop talking ... my wife gives them her breasts.

Then I take down the fish from the back of the camp and take them over to my youngest sister's place, where I sit down to prepare them for drying. I cut the fish in halves and remove the bones, fat and eggs, eating the latter. I take off the scales, and we lay the fish on a skin for the sun to dry. She will watch them and keep the dogs away. Later, when they are dry, they will be put into a net bag, hung in a tree, and kept till the fish in the Lake are finished. ...[10]

'When I return to my camp I see that my wife and mother have gone out to gather seeds, so I take up my spears and club and walk along the water's edge to an open plain. I walk along following the tracks of a wallaby, in the thick bush near the inlet of the creek. Here I see four wallabies; I poise my spear in readiness and throw it, hitting one wallaby in the neck. ... I slit open the belly of the wallaby and remove the entrails ... swinging it over my shoulder I carry it back, holding my club and spears in one hand.

> *I return about mid-day; my wife is grinding seeds of the nardoo bush for a damper. She is pleased with the catch ...*'[11]

And so the narrative continues, one of very few to give a picture of the pleasant life of those living to the north-east of the Flinders Range before the effects of the presence of pastoralists, their law, or German missionaries. As with so many recollections of past ways of life, Dibana's sun was shining on that day; it had been a year of plenty, with goannas, hopping rats and bandicoots, as well as fish for eating and drying.[12] Looking back, Dibana would also speak of aspects of Diyari life that the missionaries abhorred, of ceremonies they disliked and condemned, and much else. He records a picture of how daily life and religious and ceremonial life fit together.

*****

For a long time the standard account of the Diyari people and their way of life was Samuel Gason's, *The Dieyerie Tribe of Australian Aborigines: Their Manners and Their Customs*, published in Adelaide in 1874. Population estimates are tricky but by the time of his writing Gason said there were about 230 Diyari in the region, plus another 800 of their neighbours whom he names as Yandrawontha, Auminie, Yarrawaurka and Wongkaooroo who together spoke languages that were mutually intelligible.

Gason had arrived on Diyari country as a mounted police trooper when little more than twenty years old. Of the twelve years he served in the colonial police force before resigning at the age of 31, about 6 or 7 were spent around Pando-Lake Hope on Diyari country. Gason is believed to have learned to speak the language of the people he policed and also noticed their sign language, used over long distances as well as during the periods of silence that accompanied mourning and the tests involved as young men gained ritual knowledge. There is some suggestion that Gason took part in secret male ceremonies, a claim often made by colonists but which, given the violence in the north-east during Gason's time there, seems doubtful. His book was and remains reasonably well-regarded, although Gason had only contempt for the people whose lives he described. As it is very much a book written through the eyes of a policeman it needs to be read with care, particularly the early pages.

Of the Diyari, Gason wrote: 'A more treacherous race I do not believe exists.'[13] He went on to say:

> 'They imbibe treachery in infancy, and practice it until death, and have no sense of wrong in it. Gratitude to them is an unknown quality. No matter how kind or generous you are to them, you cannot assure yourself of their affection. Even amongst themselves, for a mere trifle, they would take the life of their dearest friend, and consequently are in constant dread of each other, while their enmity to the white man is only kept in abeyance by fear. They will smile and laugh in your face, and the next moment, if opportunity offers, kill you without remorse. Kindness they construe into fear; and, had it not been for the determination and firmness of the early settlers, they would never have been allowed to occupy the country. The tribe is numerous, and if they knew (and it is feared they will eventually learn) their own power, the present white inhabitants could not keep them down, or for one day retain their possessions.
>
> They take delight in lying, especially if they think it will please you. Should you ask them any question, be prepared for a falsehood as a matter of course. They not only lie to the white man, but to each other, and do not appear to see any wrong in it.

On the positive side he recognised three virtues in them: their hospitality, their respect for the elderly and their kindness to children and parents.[14]

*****

Unavoidably, Gason's assessment of the character of Diyari people as treacherous, violent and deceptive was formed in the context of the first impact of pastoralism and the war for the land and waters in which he was involved.[15] Expressed so pungently, his views of the Diyari provide an example of how, looked at through the lens of colonial invasion, images of the savagery of the enemy were used to eclipse the origin of the savagery unleashed by the colonists. Tactics that the pastoralists and police might themselves deploy in a situation of invasion are, when used against them by others, put down as defects in character common to their race. The culmination of Gason's career would come in 1874 when he was posted to the Telegraph Station at Barrow Creek just before the attack on it by the Kaytetye in 1874.[16] Before that, though, the people of the north-east had turned their country into something of a war zone.

Chapter Thirty-One

War in the North-East

Imaginary picture of the 'Night Attack of the Natives Near Lake Hope [Perigundi]', Samuel Calvert. It shows three men lying in their swags around a camp-fire, hopelessly outnumbered by local men attacking. In fact there were nine armed pastoralists with one at least sleeping under a wagon. The key issue is that all were sleeping in hostile territory without a watch being posted. Published in Melbourne, 24 March 1866. State Library of Victoria.[1]

The fighting in the far north of South Australia arose in part from the speed and scale of the colonial incursion. Blanchewater Station, established in 1857, covered 200 square miles around the waters of the lake, (c. 52,000 hectares). Umberatana, established in 1858, eventually ran 26,000 sheep, while in the same year 528 square miles (c. 137,000 hectares), became Paralana Station, leased to the brothers John and William Jacob, then stocked. In 1859 Mundowdna waterhole was put under lease, becoming part of Mundowdna Station lying east of today's town of Marree. Further north, Lake Hope was put under lease in 1861, while in 1863 a collection of leases to the west of Lake Eyre made Anna Creek the largest station in Australia, a title it still holds.[2] And so it went – a decade of invasive pastoralism on a grand scale that relied on small-scale, isolated patterns of daily management. This was a vast area in which its most precious communal waters were being privatised.

As the government granted leaseholds over land further and further to the north, as each lease was taken up and stocked, so trouble dogged the new owners. At stake were the major water supplies that in good years sustained large numbers of Indigenous people coming face to face with the courageous and daring colonists who would 'require great judgment and determination' if they were to deal with them. It was not just the water. These leases and others like them took vast areas of country out of local production and use. They forced local people to compete with sheep and cattle for both water and food, leaving them to subsist on whatever animals and plants of the badly depleted food stocks once sheep, cattle and horses had had their fill. Most of these properties were over-stocked and over-grazed. With the arrival of drought the situation worsened substantially.

By the time the colonists' eyes had turned first to Lake Blanche and then to Lake Hope further north, the good seasons of the first few years were already fading. In 1862 significant water sources were drying up and the country was in ferment. Blanchewater Station had little water for their flocks with sheep being stolen by large groups of the men travelling south to mine the valuable ochre available in the Flinders; on their way back they would do the same. Mundowdna was under constant attack with station workers threatened and cattle killed; eventually it was burned down.[3] The owners took the hint and left. In

1863 Paralana was attacked with stock losses and harassment of their herds becoming a great annoyance.[4]

In 1863, also in the very north of the Flinders Range, in an attempt to deal with the perpetrators of such attacks, the police eventually confronted a group of about forty Aborigines near Mt Deception (c. 19 kilometres west of Beltana) killing an unrecorded number of them. The people of the Flinders Ranges still retain oral records of a massacre near Beltana involving members of one of the ochre expeditions during November of that year. The police account of the episode established that the trouble began when a group of Aboriginal men refused to allow shepherds to water their sheep at the important waterholes on Warioota Creek, 'saying that [the] water was theirs'. Estimates of the number killed on this occasion vary. Years later, the Blinman mine director T.A. Masey stated that '11 blacks were killed on the spot, and it is said that 40 or 50 other died of their wounds before they reached their own territory'. The event was significant enough for the local police corporal to claim that 'the late affray at Beltana will be a check to their visits for a time to the sheep districts for the sake of plunder.'[5]

In January of 1864 a man known as 'Pompey' was said to have killed one of Samuel Stuckey's shepherds, Bobby Minchin. Known as a 'saltwater man' from the north with a reputation as a troublemaker, more importantly 'Pompey' was considered to be 'the leader of the Saltwater blacks', possibly the Diyari.[6] In killing Pompey, Stuckey had thought he was delivering a necessary lesson and carrying out something of a public service. Much to his surprise, Stuckey found himself tried for murder in Adelaide and although the distance and time involved meant that there was little likelihood of a guilty verdict it was a great inconvenience and an expensive exercise. By 1865 Stuckey's prosecution and costs were known to Aboriginal people travelling in the far north. John Jacob referred to that knowledge when writing to ask for police assistance on Paralana: 'The natives take advantage of the great trouble and expense that Mr Stuckey was put to to defend himself', he said; they 'reply to any threats held out to them, that they will tell the Police.'

In April of 1865 John Jacob described the local people as 'very destructive'. His stockmen said that over sixty cattle had been killed and that one of his shepherds, William Harris, had been threatened by a group of Aboriginal men who had taken five of his flock from him. A second shepherd, Jarrold, was missing from Paralana, his flock scattered, some left with broken legs and some killed.[7] Eventually he, too, was found dead.

Calls for police protection grew louder, with William Jacobs asking for a Protector as well as more police to deal with the violence. The argument supporting calls for protection for both pastoralists and those seeking to protect the local people from violence again rested on the claim that if the law was not brought into force the pastoralists would be tempted to take the law into their own hands. It was far too late for this – they had long ago succumbed to the temptation of direct punitive action, often collective. Police Trooper Poynter at Lake Hope sought extra stocks of ammunition. In Adelaide, Police Commissioner Peter Egerton Warburton said that he expected pastoralists to look after themselves, a tacit acknowledgement of the violence required to establish peaceful occupation.

*****

From 1862 in the midst of this turmoil and in partnership with Thomas Elder, Bedford Hack and Henry Dean were managing vast amounts of land around Lake Hope. They were the men who had to oversee the initial work of building cottages, yards, sheds and wells as well as manage the droving of stock – all the work involved in converting land from Indigenous usage to a profit-making business enterprise.[8] They were also the men who had to confront any opposition to their presence face-to-face, as they 'cleared' the land to make its conversion to property possible.

Henry Dean had learnt his trade on Blanchewater. Then, the lease was being stocked by the slightly dodgy John Baker who earlier had been involved in a shady mining deal.[9] Little is on the public record of Dean's earlier life before his arrival there in 1857, just as little is recorded of how Blanchewater Station was 'cleared', the absence of

Aboriginal people there was assigned to their fighting with the Diyari rather than the methods of Henry Dean and his men. It is likely that Dean's later actions around Lake Hope had grown out of experience and knowledge gained at Blanchewater Station when it was still the most northerly outpost of the colony and well out of sight of those in town who might protest. When he attempted to move stock north to Lake Hope in search of water he and his men were staunchly, if unexpectedly, resisted.

As Dean and nine pastoral workers were sleeping in the heat of a December night in 1865, the people around Perigundi-Lake Hope attacked.[10] In Adelaide first news of the attack was published on 30 December 1865 under the heading 'Outrages in the Far North'. Henry Dean had been speared in the face, others travelling with him so badly beaten that one of them, Charles Neuman, died later from his wounds. Their horses were driven off, leaving them stranded at what was then the extremity of northern settlement. Some of the attackers at least were the people who had come to be known as Diyari.[11] They were, John Jacob had written in a letter to Thomas Elder, the 'fine powerful race of men; very courageous and daring', and there were many of them. Historian, Philip Jones, says that the 'saltwater blacks' responsible for the attack, who included the Diyari, were able to muster large numbers of 'hostile and well-organised' men in a campaign that continued beyond the drought of 1864–5 and into the 1870s'.[12]

*****

It is hard to say when the attack on Henry Dean and his posse properly began, for resistance and terror were widespread. But its immediate causes are well enough known as they were published in Adelaide's newspapers. The almost elegiac tone of sadness that, once again, such violence was marring the peaceful settlement of the colony was bolstered by statements reasserting the right of settlers to protect 'their property against native depredations'. By 1865, the strong sense of entitlement expressed in the report was part of a well-developed strategy intended to deflect public concern away from the violence on which the peace of the colony was being built.[13] Yet the violence was often in plain sight, as it was in the newspaper reports of the attack on Henry Dean and his posse. Like the headline 'Outrages ...' the sequence of events described as leading up to the attack made it all plain enough.

Henry Dean had written to his partner and financial backer, Thomas Elder, saying that because there had been no rain, both grass and water were in short supply.[14] As a result Dean planned to move the cattle 'to a place called Cooraminchina where both feed and water were plentiful, but where the blacks were also plentiful – rather too much so to be pleasant.'[15] So Dean knew that his move to Cooraminchina could be a provocation and that he was likely to strike trouble. Presumably he felt armed men on horseback would be able to deal with it.

He did not arrive unheralded for his intentions were already known. 'Feeling compelled to defend the property entrusted to his care', the newspapers reported, 'Mr. Dean burnt down three of the aboriginal camps; after which four men followed the aboriginals up the country until the neighbourhood of Lake Hope appeared to be pretty well cleared of them.'[16] Reading these accounts now, despite the sometimes benign language used, it seems clear that Henry Dean had instituted a search and destroy mission on two fronts. First he or his men burned their homes; then he drove away the survivors (or shot them). The newspaper's report continues: 'Unfortunately, however, [in burning the camps] the station hands only shifted the danger – they did not get rid of it.'[17] Follow-up was required. With four men despatched initially, Dean and eight others followed as they all moved north. That a counter-attack should have surprised them is a measure of the degree of complacency of their right to be there as well as of the confidence that their burnings and shootings had indeed made the land safe. They failed to set a night-watch and were attacked while sleeping.

While Dean records the burnings and clearing out of the people as the act of a dutiful employee, it is the detail of his methods and their consequences that are left vague, left to the imagination of people who had been hearing about the violence for years. What Dean's four men did as they 'followed the aboriginals up the country' as they 'cleared' the land, is not specified, nor is any account of the actions of Dean's own party of eight given. Neither is there mention of the women and children who must certainly have been living in or near the camps being burnt. But whatever Dean and his men were doing, it had led to the effective, targeted retribution described in the *South Australian Weekly Chronicle* and other Adelaide newspapers during which only 'one native [was] shot dead' by a Mr Rooke, a claim that would generally be considered as questionable although in this case, it may be the result of sleeping confidently without weapons within easy reach.[18]

Henry Dean never really recovered from the serious spear wound to his face while the others also carried scars from the fighting.[19] Most of those surviving the attack moved on to other work or to other, safer, colonies. Although those men were replaced, in one sense the attack was successful with the Diyari and their allies staying on their Country, fighting for it still. The attack on Henry Dean was one of those that had led Mounted Constable Samuel Gason to label the Diyari as treacherous, although why he should do so when the colonists in the Flinders district and on Eyre Peninsula did not hesitate to launch night-time attacks upon sleeping Aboriginal camps seems something of a puzzle.[20] For Gason, as for many of the colonists, 'it had become a question whether the settlers should drive the blacks away, or whether the blacks should drive away the settlers.' The implications of such a struggle were perfectly clear to readers in Adelaide.

*****

In Adelaide, humanitarian and religious concern for the Indigenous populace was sustained. The governments of the 1850s and '60s were unwilling to fund too much assistance. It took a good deal of effort by the Aborigines' Friends Association to establish Raukkan (Point McLeay mission station) in 1859 on Lake Alexandrina at the mouth of the Murray River for the Ngarrindjeri people and others living with them. Yet in the midst of the fighting in the far north and in the fullness of summer heat, two sets of missionaries arrived at Lake Hope within three weeks of each other, each amazed to the find the other. There were four members of the strongly evangelical Moravian church who had trekked overland from Melbourne, and another four who had come up from Adelaide who were Lutherans trained at Hermannsburg Mission Institute in Hanover. The Moravians had been motivated in part at least by the kindness shown to the lost explorer John King on Cooper Creek. To the Moravians such people seemed worthy of the Christian gospel and also seemed unthreatening. The Hermannsburg Lutherans were looking to save new souls. On arrival all were exhausted and both faced the daunting task of convincing an enraged populace that not every newcomer on their country was dangerous and hostile to them. The Moravians eventually settled forty-five miles to the north-west at Lake Kopperamanna, the Lutherans went on to Lake Killalpaninna which still had some water.[21] Not without great difficulty the Lutherans went on to establish a long-standing relationship with the Diyari; the Moravians eventually withdrew.

Part Seven

The Overland Telegraph Line

Chapter Thirty-Two

The Silence of the Lands, 1870

As the party of telegraph linesmen left Adelaide in August of 1870, travelling north to begin the work that would join Australia into the new telecommunications network encircling the world, Alexander Russell, Anglican Dean of Adelaide, addressed the 'modest crowd' assembled at St Paul's on Pulteney Street to offer a prayer for their success.[1]

The Blessing
To bless the moment of such an important beginning as that of the Overland Telegraph Line so carefully planned and managed by Charles Todd, the Dean chose not simply to bless the line-party and their endeavours, but to restate and elaborate a commonly used Biblical justification for the colony. Quoting from the well-known verse of Genesis 1:28, he spoke of how the Christian God instructed his servants to replenish and also to *subdue* the earth. 'Thy holy voice has taught us that it is given to man to replenish the earth and subdue it', he said, 'and we adore that Providence which, in fulfilment of Thy Word, uttered in old time, has sent us hither to rescue this land from *silence* and *desolation*, and turn it to good and profitable uses.' Here, the word desolation takes on a theological resonance spread around its more secular meaning of utter devastation. Here, desolation refers to a land without God, an absence of the God of the Old Testament. His reference to the land's *silence*, with its companion word, 'empty'

The route of the Overland Telegraph Line from Adelaide to Palmerston (later Darwin) Based on the map provided in Tony Roberts 2005, *Frontier Justice. A History of the Gulf Country to 1900.*

and their relationship to 'nothingness', was one that was there at the beginning and has lived on, thoroughly embedded in colonial experience of the desert lands of 'the Centre' as well as shaping concepts of the pre-colonial time before they came.

The Biblical origins and theology surrounding words like 'desolate' and 'silence' can change as circumstances change but these words and their use have been tenacious. Their Biblical framing is often forgotten or unknown, or regarded as having lost significance in a more secular, modern, world. But the early colonists did not live in a secular or unreligious world but rather in one in which the institutions of the Church of England, with the monarch at its head and the secular concepts of liberalism and democratic government creeping into it, had been accompanied by a revival of Christianity, and a revival of evangelicalism. Furthermore as, along with British Catholics and Dissenters, the Jews of Europe and England were also emancipated, there was a backlash of anti-Catholic distrust in Protestant England. In mainland Europe, anti-semitic persecution led in part by Bavarian Catholics and the Vatican rose up.[2]

For most of the British colonists the world of the nineteenth century remained imbued with strongly held religious beliefs that circulated right beside claims for freedom and emancipation, not just from men wanting the right to vote but, more alarmingly for the churches, from women chafing at their political and social voicelessness. Although the Bible's historical veracity was under challenge, its texts, music, language and rites permeated society as a whole, not just the world of believers. 'Desolate' and 'silence' were words with a secular meaning but in the colony they were freighted with biblical resonances that gave them sometimes the quality of a charm. They were words that continued to call up their theological underpinnings. So it is pleasant to read Dean Russell's prayers and sermons now, giving the modern reader a glimpse of the nineteenth century colonial religious world of which he was clearly a wonderful exponent.

His prayer illustrates the flavour of colonial Adelaide's Anglican beliefs and the relationship of the established church to the enterprise of colonisation, as well as the Dean's preference for praying in the language and cadences of the King James Bible. 'O Almighty God and Heavenly Father,' he said,

We give Thee thanks for the mercy with which Thou hast visited us. Thou hast watered the furrows of the land. Thou sendest rain into the little valleys thereof, and art giving us the promise of such blessings as in the years that are gone, so that the little hills shall rejoice on every side; the folds shall be full of sheep; the valleys also shall stand so thick with corn that they shall laugh and sing. And now we commend to Thy merciful care those of our brethren who are going far away into those regions of our land which are still waste ... So we Thy people and sheep of Thy pasture will give thanks forever ...[3]

Prayers and sermons like these offer glimpses of how a congregation was expected to understand moral and social conventions that elsewhere can be unspoken or overlooked because they seem simply common sense or natural. In Dean Russell's prayer, his reference to the righteousness of the duty to replenish the land (that is to say, to fill the land rather than leaving it empty) and then in a verse well-adapted to the colonial enterprise, to the companion duty to subdue it in its sixteenth century sense of 'bring under cultivation'; his joyful benediction on agriculture and the colonists' success in bringing waste lands of desolation and silence into the fold, and description of his congregation as the sheep of Christ's pasture, all draw on the common ways of picturing Christ so familiar still from Psalm 23, from innumerable stained glass windows in Britain, the Americas and Australia, from hundreds of Christian books written for children – the image of Jesus as the shepherd of his flock. Beneath his watchful, loving eye, sheep may safely graze. His image as shepherd is ubiquitous and powerful, as are those of Jesus as the Paschal Lamb, sacrificed and saving souls.[4]

Deeply embedded within the enterprise of colonialism in South Australia in which so much of the land was first turned over to sheep and in which for many generations it was the custom to speak of a person being 'on the land' (raising sheep) or 'having a property' in a particular place (and raising sheep), the pastoral imagery of the Judeo-Christian religious traditions was alive and pervasive. It also expresses the millennial essences of the Judaic and Christian promise, the promise of the New Man who will usher in the new world to come, the promise of the awaited Messiah, with Jesus himself often referred to as the Lamb of God (John 1:29 and in the prayer of Agnus Dei). This fundamental pastoral concept has never shifted, never lost its relation to the pastures green of a new land in Christian utopian thinking and the hope for that one day in which a man will come to show the way.

'Pure, Manly, and Christian Lives'

Dean Russell's blessing drew directly upon the pastoral well-springs of the making not just of the world of the Bible but the world that these new men were building in the present. He urged those leaving Adelaide to work on this grand project, to 'offer prayers, especially intercessory ones [the prayers to a deity on behalf of others]; to cultivate purity of speech' and to remember Sundays as a holy day on which to read the Scriptures and to pray. But most importantly, they were to lead 'pure, manly, and Christian lives'.[5] He trusted, he said, that they would be saved from danger in their intercourse with the natives, and hoped their influence over the latter might be used for their good.[6]

Both Dean Russell and Charles Todd, the man responsible for getting the line built, knew the realities of male lives in the country across which the line would pass. Each tried to prevent the sexual exploitation and violence that was only too likely to occur as the line parties, the flocks intended to sustain them, and their equipment moved right across the continent. Russell called upon the popular sense of a chaste Christian manliness backed by a concept of shared humanity and the uplifting effects of Christianity. In ecclesiastical terms, the Dean's call for manliness and purity was a call for the manly imitation of Christ, a popular theme in the religiosity of the time that flourished particularly strongly in the second half of the nineteenth century.[7]

Charles Todd, leader of the telegraph project, was a staunch and active member of the Congregational church.[8] His own hopes for the practices of Christian purity and manliness among his men as well as his intention to avoid unnecessary violence were translated into practical effect – they were written into the instructions given to the overseers of each party.[9] Todd tried to control the violence and predatory sexual relations of the frontier by regulation, by writing moral behaviour into contracts of employment. Apart from those engaged as guides, he said, the men of the line parties were to avoid all contact with Indigenous women. At the same time every effort was to be made to avoid provoking trouble – Aboriginal campsites and burial grounds were to be left alone and violence exercised only as a last resort.[10] Todd's message was repeated as his men mustered before departure – in addition, they were exhorted to keep clear of public-houses on the road to the north and to stay close to camp for their own safety if for no other reason.[11] Based on Alfred Giles' diaries, historian Philip Jones believes that on the whole these exhortations achieved their purpose.[12]

Whether it was phrased as the duty to civilise or an opportunity to prosper, both the Anglican Dean and the project leader recognised and endorsed the colonial project, the taking of the land, the 'opening' of what were described as silent wastes to the forces of production and profit. In their eyes it was the great Australian adventure, a vision of the telegraph line that has survived. In Glenville Pike's words written to mark the line's centenary, it was 'epic'.[13] It made manifest the Biblical subduing of the waste land, the heroics and hardships of the 'first men' that would feed the memory and legendary retelling of the feats and ways of life that made men into *real* men. The men who laid the Overland Telegraph Line fit well into the heroic, pioneering mould, popular then and now.

Chapter Thirty-Three

Building the Line

The overland telegraph line was designed to utilise a series of repeater stations in which messages coming in could be relayed along a single wire in both directions. Through its connector point on the north coast it would link into a global communications network that allowed for rapid transmission of messages to and from overseas. The South Australians had added the Northern Territory to their colony in 1863 and fought hard to have the telegraph link come through to Adelaide rather than Perth or Sydney. It linked them into this wider world directly as well as providing first access to news from 'home'.

Three thousand kilometres of line was to run right across the continent, to be built in three parts: a northern section, a southern section (to be built by Edward Meade Bagot who held a lease over the important waters of Dalhousie Springs, now Witjira, from 1872) and a government-built central section running north from Port Augusta to Attack Creek in the Northern Territory where north and south would meet. Line parties would move north from Adelaide to Port Augusta with another group working from a base just north of Port Augusta toward the centre. From the far north the line parties would move south from Palmerston (later Darwin) on the coast to meet with those coming up from the south. While the southern line parties setting out overland travelled north from Port Augusta, largely following John McDouall Stuart's route of 1862, for the southward-travelling line parties it was more difficult. Before they could start, all workers, equipment, provisions and animals had to be shipped up to them from Adelaide. The ships carrying supplies went first from Adelaide to Sydney, then north along the east coast, around the tip of Cape York and onwards either to Palmerston or to the partly concealed mouth of the Roper River.

W.A. Crowder's diary of his 1871–72 journey from Adelaide to meet the northern line party in the Territory gives an idea of the scale of it: 'We had a tremendous load; horses in the fore hold & bullocks aft, all the deck taken up with drays and other necessary things for the Expedition, & Fodder to be used on the journey; so that we had to hang on by the rigging in going from one end of the vessel to the other.'[1] As the country south of Palmerston was such as to make transport of stores and equipment from a ship to the line parties inland arduous, the northerly line parties quickly began to use the Roper River to get to and from the inland segments of their line as quickly as possible. They unloaded at the great slabs of rock blocking the river that came to be known as the Roper Bar. For all line parties, though, supply lines could be uncertain. In country in which the trees suitable for telegraph poles were often very scrubby, supplies of usable timber were almost always a problem with timber-cutters ransacking the country for miles around.[2] When sheep and horses died and food stocks dwindled, line parties could face starvation.[3] This was a huge operation to run from Adelaide and full of danger.

Although remote from Adelaide, the coast of the Northern Territory was mapped and known to European mariners and traders. Several attempts to establish permanent settlements there had failed due to ignorance of the difficulties of growing food crops in a monsoonal climate, and the health risks of contaminated waters and tropical diseases. But the apparently permanent waters of the Victoria River in particular had been quickly identified as offering possibilities for pastoralists, fuelling dreams of untold riches to be made in the north. From earlier mapping expeditions the colonists of South Australia also knew that the coastal regions and islands of the north could be densely populated, that the people were strong and ready to stand their ground.

There had been a punitive expedition launched as early as 1828 to respond to the spearing of a soldier from Fort Wellington on Iwaidja country on the Coburg Peninsula. An eyewitness to the shootings at that time thought about thirty men were killed in retaliation for the one man injured.[4]

The colonists had tried to establish a settlement on the Coburg Peninsula. Harden Melville's painting of the situation at Port Essington in the 1840s shows the fine strong men he saw there and illustrates the sexual relations that formed a backdrop to colonial settlement.[5] He pictures some of the men wearing clothing, others not, and shows women sitting behind them, one with a child with paler skin, a comment on local sexual relationships. Right in the background, outside the back of the hut serving as a hospital, are two lightly sketched European men.

Never successful, Port Essington was abandoned well before the Overland Telegraph Line was built but it left behind people who had first-hand knowledge of the ways of foreigners.

Previously part of New South Wales, distance from the government in Sydney and the brutal westerly expansion of pastoralism from Queensland towards the Territory meant major incursions of stock and well-armed drovers, and fighting. By 1863 when the Territory became part of the colony of South Australia much of it had become a wild no-man's-land – violent, debauched, shameless and largely untroubled by law or edict. The South Australian government in Adelaide was not much closer to the northern coast of their new lands than Sydney but they took a greater interest in the Territory because they too believed the myths of fortunes to be made in the north by those willing to grasp them.

Boyle Travis Finniss was sent from Adelaide to the settlement at Palmerston/Darwin as government Resident and Protector of Aborigines in 1864. Like the line parties that would come in the 1870s he, too, had been entreated not to antagonise the local people, to make sure suitable land was reserved for their use, and to introduce them nicely to the benefits of British law. Camped in a small settlement at the mouth of the Adelaide River, however, Finniss' surveyors soon found themselves dealing with thefts of food and gear, the spearing of a horse, and the killing of a shepherd. His term in office had ended in great hostility, the 'friendly feeling' that had been hoped for transformed into fear, guns and a bloody punitive expedition.[6]

By 1869 when George Goyder was sent to make a proper survey of the town and to bring a semblance of order to the speculative grabbing of land by Adelaide investors, there was plenty of evidence that a colonial presence along the north coast was unwelcome and being resisted. There was the death of John William Ogilvie Bennett and the wounding of William Guy at the hands of a group of Woolna men in May of 1869, and just a week later another Woolna attempt to drive off Goyder and his men. They surrounded their camp with fire.[7] Goyder reported that the attack on Bennett was entirely unprovoked: 'the only possible cause having been Bennett's sending away of an old man whom previously he had found to be "very troublesome".' He did, however, mention incidents of the deliberate destruction of canoes and burial sites, and of how some Aboriginal men had been killed. The arrival, in May 1870, of a large group of Woolna at the colonist's compound demanding not only food but women, suggests that the uneven nature of sexual relations was causing anxiety among the Woolna gathering around Palmerston.[8] Samantha Wells' research suggests that licentiousness may indeed have caused grave offence. 'Many of the diaries and journals written by those attached to Goyder's survey party,' she notes, 'stress the debauched behaviour of the party which was constantly prevalent in the camp due primarily to boredom and the consumption of massive amounts of alcohol.'[9] By 1871 Alfred Giles recorded that his survey party had been attacked on the western branch of the Roper River and that the practice of taking hostages for safety or when searching for thieves was well-established.[10]

From the 1870s such incidents were common although not universal. In the eyes of the young Crowder, attached to a line party as a cadet, the six Indigenous men hailing them as they sailed up the Roper River to begin work on the northern section of the telegraph line 'seemed very friendly,' he wrote, *and are fine men about 5 feet and 10 inches to six feet high. They brought off some Tortoise shell fishing hooks & turtle shell & twine, I got one hook. The sailors played music and danced, the natives imitating them which was great fun. They had their fill of biscuit and meat. Then the sailors dressed them up in old clothes, and they quite pleased. They were taken off again about 12 a.m. They had no weapons, but two of them had spear wounds.*[11]

Despite such encouraging encounters, first attempts at colonisation in the Northern Territory foundered. The men of the line-parties faced people with some experience in the ways of the colonists and on the whole were unhappy if not actively hostile. Those were the conditions known in Adelaide that had informed the preaching of the Dean of Adelaide to the departing line-party. As the line-parties moved north they were following not only in the path of John McDouall Stuart (attacked a number of times) but meeting considerable local resistance. The provisions of the line-parties, their equipment and their animals were regularly pillaged. In January of 1872 Crowder noted: 'Mr Patterson was telling us that if they left a dray behind on the journey overland the natives chopped and hacked it all to pieces & they saw some doing so but they were off before they could be shot at.'[12]

Along the Line

In addition to the line-parties moving north, the tracks of their wagons and stock and the building of the fortified repeater stations close to crucial water supplies created a route to the hoped-for riches of the north that could be followed by all sorts of interested and hopeful people. Hawkers, for example, moved along it to offer supplies to the line parties; drovers used it, those searching for land to buy or lease, and those reporting on the progress of the great technological feat being rushed across the continent went along it, as did criminals and those wanting to benefit from the opening up of new lands and opportunities in the Territory. First Nations peoples living around the line had to deal with an increasing flow of intruders, some of whom were none too scrupulous and many of whom were fearful and unafraid to shoot.

Once the line went through, the rapid influx of new claimants to the country either side of it, and the lure of the first gold finds at Pine Creek in 1872 (and in the 1880s at Arltunga near Alice Springs) meant that pressure from miners, pastoralists and traders on the Indigenous custodians of the country and its valuable water supplies increased dramatically. Inevitably, conflict increased too.

At Charlotte Waters repeater station, just over the southern border of the Territory, overt hostilities began in April 1871.[13] The removal of the line party's valued supplies by the local people and the failure of the colonists to observe the traditional courtesies expected of strangers had created such bad feeling that the line party had to commit two men of their small workforce to guarding their camp. In a discussion of two versions of an attack on the line party written by Randall R. Knuckey, Ingereth Macfarlane noted that while Knuckey's original diary focused on lack of provocation and the firing of a warning shot, his later account mentions that the shot he fired from his Snider rifle (designed for use by big-game hunters in Africa) injured the shoulder of the old man leading the attack.[14] The Snider was a terrible weapon, much favoured by punitive parties in northern Australia although the large bullets of the later, longer-range Martini-Henry were even worse.[15] The local people used fire, clubs and spears as weapons; they attempted to steal or injure the horses, but still the line-building continued. There is no mention of massacres in this area nor of sexual encounters although women were part of the labour force working for the telegraph contractors' employees. Local women herded the goats, some worked as cooks and probably helped with washing clothes.[16] In the 1920s both syphilis and gonorrhoea were rampant right along the line.[17]

But in July 1872 when the brothers John and Jim Lewis were running a 'pony express' between the two ends of the unfinished line and camping on the site of John McDouall Stuart's misadventure at Attack Creek, they faced a barrage of spears from men who had approached them apparently unarmed. The attackers 'were only stopped by a volley of rifle fire at close range.'[18] If they were using Snider rifles it is unlikely that such a volley created no casualties, but none was mentioned.

A month later, in August 1872, the southern and northern telegraph lines were joined at Frew's Ponds by the northern contractor, Robert Patterson. From that time the Territory would be divided into two distinct administrative regions – the tropical 'top end' with its characteristic annual wet and dry seasons, and 'central Australia' with a drier climate in which rain could fall in summer or winter but not often in very large quantities. The line dividing the two very different regions ran roughly through today's town of Katherine. From 1870 the 'top end' was governed with the help of a Resident administrator and a police contingent based in Palmerston/Darwin; while 'central Australia' was governed and policed from Adelaide. Both regions were ultimately responsible to the government in Adelaide although local administrative arrangements varied.

The completion of the telegraph line in 1874 offered the government better and more immediate contact with its administrative servants in the Territory but on the whole, better contact with Adelaide produced better ways of subverting any unwanted instructions or restrictions, better ways of covering up acts that might cause condemnation. Regardless of the advantages offered by the new communication channel, distance meant that political control in the Territory was fragile and often irrelevant to those supposedly subject to it.

*****

As the line went through, the country either side of it was put under lease with colonists and their animals appearing in increasing numbers. Along the central Australian sections of the line stock began arriving on the new leases from 1873 with more and more cattle and sheep arriving over the following decade.[19] By 1874 when an anonymous reporter described his travels along the telegraph line he claimed that, 'After leaving Alice Springs (going north) one never sees a lubra [woman]. This, as all old bushmen know, is a sure sign of savageness in the tribe of natives. Barrow Creek', he noted, 'is the prettiest station on the overland line, but it is a perfect hot-bed of hostility ... [he then gives a detailed description of the building, its strengths and loopholes] ... There are six men all told at each of the interior stations, and sometimes the work is warm enough for them. The natives pull the wire down and cut away great quantities of it for the purpose of arming the points of their spears and they also smash the porcelain insulators and use the sharp-edge pieces to scrape their spear blades into shape.'[20] The absence of women suggests that people were angry and that they knew too well that women would be the targets of the invading men. On the whole, neither the Dean of Adelaide's hopeful preaching to the first of the departing line-parties nor Charles Todd's exhortations and contracts had succeeded in preventing either hostility or debauchery as the line was built.[21] The trouble around the Barrow Creek repeater station was about to escalate.

Chapter Thirty-Four

After the Line – Central Australia

In the 1930s one of the senior Arrernte men, Acorar, recorded that he had seen McDouall Stuart travelling through when he was just 9. He told the anthropologist, Olive Pink, how 'they could *smell* the horses – miles off – without knowing what they were – except something unknown! And that they thought Stuart [was] a large spider – in the distance (in his white clothes) & (apparently) riding.' She noted that, 'There are huge spiders & webs in that part of the country, described by Baldwin Spencer in his *Wanderings in Wild Australia*, p. 70, Vol 1. He describes them as the largest ... having a body measuring nearly 2 inches in length – their legs having a total span of 4 inches. The web is often twelve to 15 ft and reaches a height, in the middle, of fully 6 ft.'[1] It was one of these huge creatures that Stuart's arrival brought to their minds.

Colonists had never been particularly welcome in Central Australia but after the telegraph line went through and local waters had to support vast numbers of stock, hostility increased. In 1873 the conversion of Arrernte country to pastoral ownership (often purely for financial speculation) and a more permanent colonial presence gathered pace. The Gilbert brothers' lease covering the waters seen by Stuart as he travelled north became Owen Springs Station, established just south-west of the Telegraph Station.

At about the same time Edward Mead Bagot acquired two blocks on the eastern fringes of the Telegraph Station with access to Jessie

Creek that would become Undoolya Station, although he used it initially to supply beef to the line-parties. Taken together, the two properties occupied about 6000 square kilometres.² But stocking the newly formed pastoral stations was not easy and took time. Undoolya, for example, was not properly stocked until 1876. The other stations in the region came later: Idracowra established from 1876, Love's Creek (Inteyarrkwe) and Henbury in 1877, Bond Springs not until 1881 with Hamilton Downs later in the 1880s.³ Nevertheless, large numbers of cattle and horses were on the track travelling north to stock the first leases by June 1872 as were the herds intended for properties even further north. The numbers of stock grazing and drinking their way along the line were enormous, taxing the natural resources of the country.

In the 1880s Tempe Downs Station alone was carrying 6000 cattle as well as the horses needed for the stockmen.⁴ It was this first denuding of the country that created the conditions that helped the spiny spinifex plants to spread, while at the same time removing stocks of food plants used by local people. Around Alice Springs it was not just the building of the telegraph station nor the provisioning of the small number of men living there that troubled the local Arrernte, but the stocking and over-stocking of the increasing number of pastoral stations, their spread and the inevitable impact on the precious and fragile waters and food stocks of a region in which rainfall was rarely a reliable supplier of water.

By 1880 the over 13,000 cattle, 1,200 horses and 6,500 sheep on the leases around Alice Springs made trouble inevitable. Dick Kimber's research suggests that in the response to an attack on Owen Springs, 'all but a few of a party of 150 to 170 Aborigines ... were shot by a police party consisting of cattlemen, overland telegraph station staff and police.' All in all, he believes, 'on the basis of available evidence probably 500 (and possibly as many as one thousand) Aborigines were shot within a radius of 300 kilometres from Alice Springs in the period 1881–91'.⁵ In the face of such disruption historians have sometimes commented on the way in which the Arrernte custodians of Mparntwe and its surrounds appear to have accepted the colonial order with a remarkable degree of toleration, a toleration that (if it existed) could not last for long.

Two hundred and ninety kilometres further north on country around the telegraph station at Barrow Creek, built on a local well and supplemented by limited surface water supplies, the situation quickly became more volatile. It was there that Mounted Constable Gason, whose time on Diyari country is mentioned in chapter 31, had arrived to deal with trouble there.

At Barrow Creek

Barrow Creek was the most northerly of the repeater stations to be administered and policed from Adelaide. Although each of the repeater stations along the line had been heavily fortified, each was staffed by very few men. They were isolated even while connected, surrounded by local people of uncertain temperament and unknown intention. Barrow Creek repeater station was on Kaytetye country, built on Tyempelkere River. A small waterhole in the nearby hills is a women's place named *Thangkenharenge* for the Bird Women who lived there while *Arelpe*, the Moon Man, was another of the Ancestral Beings who travelled through Barrow Creek. Searching for women, *Arelpe* had left there when he realised that these women were his kin and not available to him.[6]

The telegraph station at Barrow Creek had been built using a good deal of Aboriginal labour. Kaytetye men cut and carted the wood used to stoke the fires needed to burn the limestone that was used to make what they called a kind of cement – a mortar. Kaytetye men also did the back-breaking work involved in quarrying limestone with picks and shovels and then loading the best pieces of stone onto the wagons. It was very hard labour and very cheap. The lack of reciprocity described in Kaytetye narratives of those years show a continuing moral affront. At the time, the Kaytetye men possessed no clothing, they say, a fact that recurs in their narratives of the impact of the building of the telegraph station, an image used to describe their situation that suggests that the consequences of their uncovered bodies quickly became apparent. While some of the labourers received old cast-offs from the linesmen and the men were given some very basic foods they received no money at all.[7] For the women, the lack of clothing had more predictable consequences.

Once completed and the line crews had moved on, the unsettled nature of relations between the small staff of the Barrow Creek repeater station and the local people led to increasingly loud calls for a police presence. With a more permanent population and the flow of travellers along the line, local food and water supplies were threatened. Cattle were speared or stolen, wires cut and insulators removed for use as spear-tips and tools. As early as July 1873 J.C. Watson had already wired a request to Charles Todd for permission to close the Barrow Creek telegraph office for a day so that he could 'disperse the whole tribe'. He and some of his men, he said, had located a Kaytetye camp about fifteen miles west of the station and they wanted them gone. While no reply from Todd has been found, it is clear that the attack took place.[8]

In the language used to report on the violence involved in bringing about peace, 'dispersal' is the word used to mean destroyed or killed. Its widespread use in the colony indicates a crucial break in the connection between a word and its meaning. It is a breakage characteristic of regimes of oppression, an essential element in the way in which political parties and governments speak of the unspeakable to make it sound acceptable. Such breakages of meaning occur within societies that prefer to consider themselves as cultured, civilised and superior. The use of the word 'dispersal' in the context of the situation around Barrow Creek Telegraph Station is a clear signal that all was not well in the heart of government and not at all well, either, in the practices of violence that such linguistic subterfuges were authorising and camouflaging. There is no doubt that by 1873 the telegraph operators at Barrow Creek as well as those travelling and carting goods along the line were facing very angry men. With experience gained while posted to Diyari country, Mounted Police Trooper Samuel Gason was sent north to protect the linesmen from the consequences of their own actions.[9]

Arriving in 1874, Gason was in charge of policing at Barrow Creek. The Kaytetye did not wait for reinforcements to follow. Gason had been there only eight days when, on the evening of 22 February, they made their first attack.[10] At the time there were eight individuals at the station – Mr Stapleton (station master), Mr E Flint (operator), J Maddox (blacksmith), A Murdoch and J Franks (linemen), Samuel Gason (Mounted Constable), Si Jin (Chinese cook), and Jimmy (an Aboriginal man from the Peake Station far to the south). The station-master James Stapleton and the linesman John Franks were killed, while although badly wounded, Ernest (or Ebenezer) Flint survived. On the following morning the Kaytetye attacked again, this time being driven off by the barricaded defenders. An early newspaper report stated that according to Gason, 'it is probable that one or two of the shots took effect, as some of the natives were seen to fall, and he thinks there is no doubt that some of the natives were mortally wounded in the affray of last evening'.[11] Gason went on to say,

> Since my arrival here, on the 14th inst., the natives have been treated kindly, and not interfered with in the slightest manner. The Stationmaster made them several presents, and was endeavouring to make them useful. The attack was made by them, without the slightest provocation, to get possession of the flour and mutton, and to murder all hands was their only object. A great many of the natives who attacked the station can be identified.[12]

It is characteristic that most attacks on colonists and their officials are said to have occurred without provocation but in Gason's account, his statement that the station master was trying to make the local people useful is a reference to the very hard labour the men were carrying out for very little recompense. Gason knew that his readers would approve actions that aimed to teach Indigenous Australians how to work, of efforts to induct them into the lower echelons of a labour force, to make them see how the disciplines of working for others were a basic aspect of the colonial regime and, now, of their own lives.

By the time the report of the Kaytetye attack reached the public,

Charles Todd had telegraphed to Mr Tucker, the station-master of Tennant Creek repeater station to the north, telling him to move south at once 'to render all assistance'.[13] With this instruction Todd set off the wave of punitive killings that lasted for weeks. Regardless of any involvement in the attack on the telegraph station, men, women, children and the elderly – all were killed indiscriminately.

In Kaytetye histories their attack on the repeater station was far from unprovoked. Peter Horsetailer for example has said that 'the white men at the station wanted Aboriginal women'.[14] Demands for women had upset the Kaytetye men, particularly the younger ones, who were worried that the girls who were destined by Law and agreement to become their wives would be taken away from them. They were already aware that the uncovered bodies of young women drew lascivious attention to them that made them vulnerable, a knowledge that made the wearing of clothes a significant issue.[15] In Horsetailer's narrative, colonial lust had set off the attack, a cause confirmed by Tommy Thompson. In their narratives the station staff had looked at the young girls and asked for them to do some work for them. 'Well', he said,

> *she went early to go and do some washing. She worked until about dinner time [at midday]. She had dinner there. They fed her and she worked late because those whitefellas didn't have a nice little lady to do their work for them. They said, 'We should keep her here. We'll camp here with her.' And they took her inside and made her camp overnight with them. The next morning they sent her back to her father and her promised husband. They gave her some salt meat and tobacco, and a little bit of tea and sugar to take back to that old man, her father.*[16]

In this narrative, the young woman was kept inside the men's quarters overnight. How they used her is not mentioned. The Kaytetye men knew very well that young women could be taken away from them at will and it was this that inspired the attack. Indeed the first wife of Peter Horsetailer's father had been taken away from him by George Hayes [snr] while he was working as a guide for camel trains travelling north from Oodnadatta to Alice Springs.[17] In the 1870s the enticements and abductions were taking place in a drought year, at a time when the linesmen's flocks and herds were decimating water supplies and with the Kaytetye men doing a great deal of hard labour.[18]

Because of the shortage of labour, the station-masters on the line were instructed that government rations were to be given only to the old and infirm; everyone else had to work for them. This was in effect a scheme in which the government was creating a wageless labour force, that is to say, a system very close to slavery in which the men drafted into it could no longer help to provide for their relatives. Bush foods gathered by the women had to cover the loss and this in years of drought with water supplies decimated by flocks and herds. No matter how inadequate the rations, the refusal to issue them to all those in need is said also to have been a contributing factor in sparking the attack and later resentments.[19] In the oral narratives handed down through the generations, however, resentment about the treatment of young Kaytetye women remains very strong.

Many commentators draw on census data to explain the sexual relations of the Northern Territory of South Australia. Mulvaney, for example, noted that in 1881 the census indicated that there were three women and seventy-nine non-Indigenous men (probably more) on the country between the South Australian border of the Northern Territory and the telegraph station at Barrow Creek.[20] As late as 1901, he says, there were still only nine non-Indigenous women in Alice Springs. The sexual violence and exploitation of Aboriginal women in central Australia is often put down to this disparity, that is to say, that men's sexual needs were not being met by women of their own kind, the inference being that had more colonial women been available, sexual relations in the Territory would have taken a different form. The presence of more European women, however, has never reduced the interest of colonial men in Aboriginal women. While the census numbers are probably more or less correct, such propositions help to cover over what was involved in a situation in which male colonists held massive power and could treat as they wished such women as survived the various shootings as well as those living near the line and its repeater stations.

More plausible is Peter Forrest's observation that those colonists engaged in establishing the Northern Territory were actively hostile to the presence of colonial women and did everything possible to keep them out.[21] He cites telegrams from Jock MacLennon to the newly appointed manager of Elsey Station, for example, warning him not to bring his new bride to the station.[22] This was in 1902. Forrest understands this statement and others like it as an indication of widespread male fears that the arrival of colonial women would end the old social order put in place as the line was being built with hyper-masculinity at its heart. He argues that the presence of colonial women was seen as a kind of castration. Others have noted the number of assertions that without Aboriginal women, no colonial man would have stayed in the Territory, and Forrest points to the immense power held over Indigenous women by all colonial men there. If that racialised domination were to cease, as they feared it would if wives began to arrive, a different world would come into existence, one mirroring that found in colonial towns in which men had to exercise their powers over a wife and children within a monogamous family. It follows that sexual relations in the Territory were shaped not by an absence of racially appropriate wives and female servants but by the presence of often defenceless Aboriginal women and children combined with the limitless powers of men and their domination over them. These were powers that men would not give up without a struggle. And they did not. They helped shape the sexual relations and spatial separations of a pastoral zone even after colonial women or other critical outsiders arrived. And they shaped a *pastoral zone of exclusion* that survived long after more colonial women arrived in the Territory, as did the particularly violent forms of sexuality that colonisation involved. Indigenous accounts of their attempts to drive off the men staffing the Barrow Creek Telegraph Station provide a glimpse of just such a masculinised, sexualised and racialised colonial world coming into existence.

Writing in his retirement, Mounted Constable Gason described the situation at the time of his arrival in Central Australia: 'During Mr Watson's term of office at Barrow's Creek, the blacks were very troublesome, killing several horses and cutting the telegraph wires. He [Watson] was relieved by Mr Stapleton, who came from the Katherine (NT). About the same time I arrived at and was stationed there, Mr Stapleton received orders to conciliate the blacks as much as possible, which he did or tried to do.'[23] At the time, Gason said, there were about a hundred Aborigines camped close to the station and that they had been well treated. The presence of such a large number of people indicates that women and children were among them and that the women would indeed have been wanted for domestic chores and sex both by the linesmen and passing travellers.

Although a great deal has been written about the massacres that followed the Kaytetye attack, by their nature some of the details remain fuzzy and dependent upon limited information. The attacking party of Kaytetye men seems to have numbered about twenty; they had worked strategically, catching the linesmen off-guard at dusk as they relaxed at the station after their day's work. In the response to the second attack even Gason was prepared to report that it had led to deaths. With trouble also between the Kaytetye and teamsters at Taylor Creek to the north, with newspapers calling loudly for punishment rather than arrest and trial, with Police Commissioner George Hamilton's instructions lifting the need for staying within the law, and with the Chief Secretary in Adelaide calling for the Kaytetye to be taught a lesson, instructions were issued to Gason that made it plain enough that a punitive expedition – reprisals not arrests – was required.

Gason felt free to organise a massive sweep of the country lying between Taylor Creek in the north and Central Mount Stuart in the south. He sought an arrest warrant from Adelaide, naming the offenders as: 'Harry Boy', 'The General', 'Spritely', 'Sunkeyes', Coonarie, Apongita, Tongala, and Umpiganna. The telegraph line facilitated compliance with police procedures as well as the gathering together of men wanting to participate in capturing the attackers. It made possible a rapid call along it asking for volunteers to muster at Barrow Creek.

Gason and at least ten such men were away on horseback for six weeks. As they travelled, Aboriginal camps and possessions were destroyed. No prisoners were taken. Those shot included women and children, the elderly and infirm. Nor were the reprisals limited to the Kaytetye–Warlpiri, Waramungu and Alyawarra people were shot indiscriminately. The people of one entire camp of Anmatyerre were destroyed. The First Nations citizens of the colony who were shot were not named and therefore not those listed on the arrest warrant, but were simply 'said' to have been involved. In the 1900s, Dr Herbert Basedow would write that there had been sharp-shooters among Gason's party, a fact that made the slaughter effective.[24] These killings were still reflected in the genealogies collected by anthropologists much later.

Gason reported eleven Aboriginal deaths.[25] He resigned from the police force in 1876, taking up a hotel in Beltana. From there he moved on to the more remote Gibson's Camp, a coaching inn on the old route to Tarcoola, again taking up a hotel. There he died in his bed, aged fifty-six, most likely a victim of alcohol and possibly disease. Police Commissioner George Hamilton in Adelaide, who had authorised the Barrow Creek 'dispersal', died in 1883. Gason's obituarist noted that 'At the banquet given to the late-Commissioner Hamilton on his retirement that gentleman referred in grateful terms to the conduct of Mr. Gason at Barrow Creek, commenting on his bravery in the brush with the blacks in which Mr. Stapleton lost his life.'[26] Neither 'bravery' nor 'brush with the blacks' seems an adequate description of what Gason and his posse of volunteers was about.

In Police Commissioner Hamilton's life we see again how social class, an educated mind and manner, a trained artist's eye, genial manners and a desire to serve coincide not just with policing and making the mounted contingent more attractive to 'well-bred young men' but with the belief that brutal extra-legal action was justified if it stopped Aboriginal attacks.[27] Like Police Commissioner Hamilton, Charles Todd who had managed the building of the telegraph line was English born, educated, clever and cultivated. His many achievements were recognised and honoured both in South Australia and in England and as has been pointed out, he was a staunch church-going Congregationalist.[28] Yet when he faced a real challenge, his commitment to the civilised and civilising processes of the law seemed to evaporate.

It is important to remember that while it was common to blame poor or criminal people for the violence recorded as the land was taken and for acts committed in apparently lawless districts, the brutal massacres and complete disregard for the law at Barrow Creek were presided over not by outlaw colonists of any kind but by the well-established, wealthy, religious and respectable captains of Adelaide society. Not only were the killings not the actions of people who knew no better, they were disgusting acts by people who knew very much better, those who would be seen as the bearers of the civilising values by which the colony was justified. And in this case, Gason's massacres were co-ordinated and planned and organised by the police, the officers of the law and government who carried the responsibility for preventing precisely such disasters. Gason's shootings and the killings by the 'volunteers' who came to help him are a blot on the historical record of a colony that was, after all, founded on staunch Christian and legal principles from the start. They indicate, however, that the killings and sexual abuses associated with them should not be understood as isolated personal failures of individuals at one or another time but as the result of government intention. Once the lines of influence and control are traced back to the authorisers of the violence, its important place in the making and governing of the colony becomes more evident. The violence arose from the government and the consent of the more prosperous and respected members of society who allowed it to happen. It did not pass unopposed or uncriticised but it happened anyway. It was not violence occurring outside the law but well within its ambit as the government secured its borderlands.

In the graphic nature of the violence we see too well how a new world was being built on the ruination of its predecessor and how the men who created it liked to keep quiet about some of their methods and defer their responsibility onto their victims. We see, too, how necessary words like 'dispersal' and phrases like 'a brush with the natives' become in making language meaningless. The loss of meaning makes possible forms of secrecy as a wider political strategy. The secrets of the violence and predatory sex are not individual secrets hidden with shame, but part of a culture in which violence had come to be seen, sadly, as necessary to the future good of all. It allowed colonial men to collude in keeping an ordinary part of life, something they all knew about and which many practiced – a culture of knowledge and acceptance that formed around a tacit agreement among men *not* to speak unless the circumstances were favourable. Many protested, many sighed in sorrow, and many had no trouble in learning to look away.

Gason's massacres as mentioned in Hamilton's obituary were described as just such a simple 'brush' with the natives – a few spears thrown, a few shots fired. Such was far from the case but all could collude in presenting an image of what could not possibly be true. The new world being created in Central Australia was not a better world and certainly no better than the world they were displacing. For the two men killed and the one man injured, and even when Gason reported that the attackers were recognised and known to them, the Kaytetye and their neighbours paid a very high price. Gason admitted to perhaps eleven dead, others say fifty or even more. The Kaytetye were not, however, deterred. It would be a long time before the fighting stopped. By 1879 it had broken out around the settlement near the telegraph station at Alice Springs.

Chapter Thirty-Five

On Arrernte Country

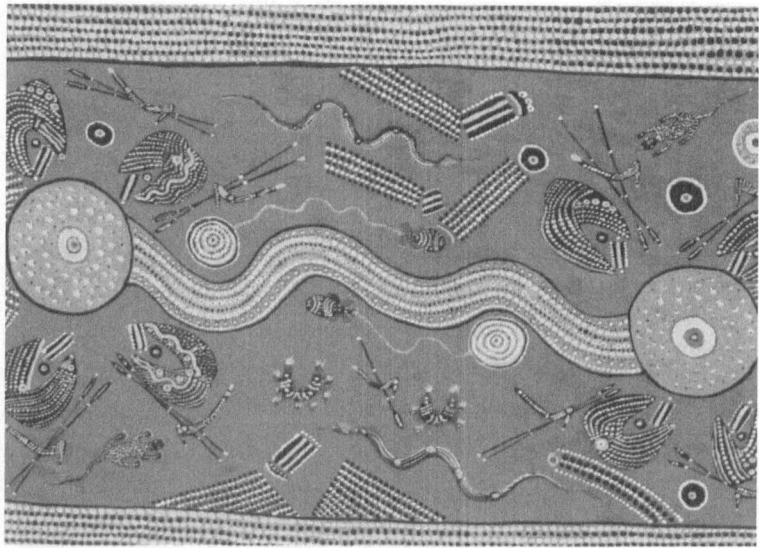

Painting by Wenten Rubuntja, c. 1988, 'Two Women and Mparntwe', Alice Springs, central Australia. Private Collection.

As always, news of the telegraph line and its builders ran ahead of the line parties, arriving well before work began on the station built beside Lhere Mparntwe – the ephemeral Todd River – on a major waterhole named by the colonists as Alice Springs.[1] Mparntwe is the name of the country on which the town of Alice Springs now stands. Mparntwe can be seen in Wenten Rubunja's stained glass windows made for the Araluen Arts Centre, that offer a kind of map showing the intricate travels of the Beings who created, made and sustained Mparntwe.[2]

While an important spiritual centre lies at Tyeretye, near the junction of the Todd with Charles Creek, the country around the town is a centre of great spiritual vitality, cross-cut by the creative activities of a series of important Ancestral figures who live on and who remain important today. The gaps in the MacDonnell Range cut by the beds of the Todd and Emily Rivers are important places of both sacredness and danger.[3] Arrernte histories record that their first sighting of the linesmen was made by Ntyarlkarle Peltharre, a senior custodian of this important place, the living embodiment of one of the three creative Ancestors, Yeperenye, Utnerrengatye and Ntyarlkarle, who live on in Mparntwe and the surrounding ranges. This was good country, densely traversed by the pathways of Ancestral Beings of great creative powers, some of whom interacted while others simply passed by, others of whom were associated with the great trans-continental trade and ceremonial routes running from the far north coast of the Northern Territory south to Port Augusta.

As with the other telegraph stations, that of Alice Springs was built beside a waterhole as a defendable fortress. It was completed and staffed in 1872 just before the Barrow Creek Station. Despite the initial sparse settling of Central Australia around Alice Springs and reasonably good relations between the local Arrernte and the telegraph staff and first pastoralists, by 1875 their country was being leased and stocked with sufficient impact to cause unrest. Inevitably the colonists called for police protection. Most certainly, by 1874, when news arrived of the attack on Barrow Creek Telegraph Station and the punitive massacre carried out under Gason's leadership, levels of fear and anger increased among pastoralists and Arrernte alike. All talk of 'our peaceful natives' was long gone. The people of central Australia made determined efforts to rid themselves of the invaders.

In 1879 calls for protection were renewed when in February, two Aboriginal men were killed while travelling with Alfred Giles' droving party (taking stock up to Dr William James Browne's Springvale Station), probably by Arrernte men, at Temple Bar Gap as the herd was passing through the range.⁴ At the request of Police Inspector Foelsche in Darwin, the two deceased men and one other had been recruited as trackers from Charlotte Waters Telegraph Station by Alfred Giles. Although the request for men to be brought up from so far south was said to be because the northerly people were poor trackers, it is another example of the policy observed in north and south that deliberately brought outsiders into a strange area so that their only loyalties and indeed their safety would lie with their employers. In a similar move, Foelsche had also asked Mounted Trooper Willshire to recruit and take six Indigenous constables from around Alice Springs up to Darwin. These men, it is thought, may have been Arabana people from Country west of Lake Eyre.⁵ If so, they were a very long way from home.

According to newspaper accounts of the deaths, two of Giles' trackers (described as 'two civilised native boys'), had been enticed away from their droving camp at night by local Aboriginal people, then murdered. The killings were assumed to have been the result of a 'tribal grudge' but no real explanation was offered and no grudge identified.⁶ Ernest Flint, who had survived the Barrow Creek attack and transferred to the safety of Alice Springs, claimed that if the murderers were not punished it would encourage others to believe that they, too, could attack colonists with impunity.⁷ This was a specious argument as the law usually ignored killings among Aboriginal people that could be defined as 'tribal'. Generally seen as internal matters that bore no relationship to the safety of the colonists, they were only prosecuted where a demonstration of the reality of British law was felt to be necessary. In this case, Flint seems to have been thinking about the two trackers as being Mr Giles' property, a not uncommon way of thinking about Indigenous people at the time. Flint was not alone in expressing an opinion that was intended to increase pressure on the government for armed reinforcements to be despatched to the frontline. This time the government relented.

In April, Constable John Charles Shirley, a man who appears to have been sympathetic to the situation of the Arrernte, arrived at the Alice Springs Telegraph Station, setting up camp on a waterhole just to its south. In 1882 William Henry Willshire replaced Shirley who had died while leading a search party for a lost pastoralist. At about the same time Erwin Wurmbrand, an Austrian of aristocratic descent, was also appointed, probably in about 1883. By this time, there was considerable unrest in Central Australia with pastoralists complaining bitterly of stock losses, thefts, and destruction of property. In 1884 the South Australian Commissioner of Police in Adelaide, William von Peterswald, authorised the establishment of a Native Police contingent under the control of Mounted Constable Willshire.[8] He chose young men aged from 17 to 26 years old, selecting them from Alice Springs, Charlotte Waters, Undoolya (east of Alice Springs), and Macumba, north-east of Oodnadatta. With this structure in place the policing of central Australia took a very violent turn.

Policing in the Centre

It was not long before Wurmbrand's and Willshire's ruthlessness became apparent to the colonists and welcomed locally. Wurmbrand, for example, is recorded as having shot seventeen people on one occasion rather than the one single man he had reported.[9] The sexual nature of Willshire's activities is expressed in his own words in a book he wrote in an attempt to establish himself as knowledgeable and expert in Aboriginal culture. In his book *The Aborigines of Central Australia with a Vocabulary of the Dialect of the Alice Springs Natives*, Mounted Constable Willshire wrote about how shortly after he arrived in Alice Springs, he rode through Anthwerrke-Emily Gap, a place in the eastern MacDonnell Range that he knew to be of great spiritual power. In March, 1883, he said that,

> when coming from Ooraminna through the Emily Gap [Anthwerrke], three lubras [the word used for Indigenous women] followed close behind my horse, saying that they were going to Alice Springs. Just as I reached the entrance to the Gap, five blackfellows appeared and ordered the lubras to go over the range – as no women were allowed to go through the Gap. The range was 500 feet high, and

> as the lubras had walked 25 miles that day I told the blackfellows that they should follow me through the Gap. At first they assumed defiant and bellicose attitudes, but I cleared them out and passed on, followed by the lubras, who, to my great astonishment, picked up some rags, bushes and grass, and made coverings to their faces, and walked blindfolded, led by the sound of the horses footsteps and my black boy's voice, through the Gap. When they had passed the place in the Gap which is adorned with ... drawings, they told me that no woman or boys were allowed to look at these rude pictures, which are to be seen on the rocks in all gorges and around rocky waters.[10]

As they followed Willshire's horse, the women must have known that despite their elaborate precautions, under their own Law their fate was now sealed. Their forced sacrilege of such an important male spiritual centre led to their deaths.[11] This unfortunate incident does, however, offer a sketch of how Willshire was thinking about himself as an enforcer of colonial law, of his use of his supreme powers to compel women to bend to his will and of how he applied his powers to Indigenous men. Willshire doesn't say how he 'cleared out' the Arrernte men who were trying to keep him away, but it is likely that 'clearing out' is a euphemism for shooting at them. But there are other questions to be asked of his account.

The three women had walked with him, he says, the 25 miles [c. 40 km] from the very reliable Ooraminna rockhole in the south to Anthwerrke-Emily Gap. Gason offers no reason for their presence nor any for his visit to Ooraminna. His wording suggests the women were for some reason on their way to Alice Springs and had attached themselves to him. But why would three Arrernte women choose to do such a thing, especially as Willshire was already known for his violence? It is more likely that Willshire was leading them on a forced march as either a punishment for their husbands or fathers, or that he had simply kidnapped them and forced them to follow him as he rode on; in either case it would be most likely that they were destined for the police camp by the telegraph station that Willshire had established as his own domain. In 1885 or '86, the police camp was moved to a place just outside the southern entrance to Ntaripe-Heavitree Gap, out of the sight of the telegraph staff and any visitors there. These three women were doubly unfortunate – first in their capture or arrest or enticement; and second, in the role they were forced to play in Willshire's display of his superior powers over the Arrernte men of Anthwerreke-Emily Gap who had tried to warn him off.

Anthwerreke-Emily Gap and Ntaripe-Heavitree Gap each have a designated route over the MacDonnell Range for women entering Mparntwe country. For Heavitree Gap the women's path followed the path taken by the Ancestral Two Women who, on a long journey up from the south-west, crossed the range at a small saddle west of the Ntaripe gap, then walked down to where the trees marking where they passed now stand within the courtyard of the Araluen art centre; for Emily Gap, the women crossed a little to the east of the gap containing the paintings that Willshire's women so desperately tried not to see. This is a tragic tale; while it is not the one that Willshire sought to convey it is plain enough. Constable Wurmbrand was a like-minded kind of a man.

Towards the end of 1884 Constable Wurmbrand, two other colonists and three Indigenous trackers, set out from Alice Springs for Glen Helen where there had been an attempt to kill three station-hands who were passing through the Lutheran mission station on the Finke River, Hermannsburg.[12] In a dawn attack, the Aboriginal camps near Hermannsburg mission were encircled by Wurmbrand and his men and then a sweep through them carried out. Three suspects were captured, chained at the neck until, en route to Glen Helen, they were shot, still chained together. Their deaths were reported as having taken place when they escaped and refused to stop when called upon to do so. Wurmbrand and his men continued to search the countryside for other malefactors until at Mt Serle they found a camp and staged a dawn attack. This time the residents heard them coming and fled. Wurmbrand said that four were shot, all huts and belongings burned. No prisoners were taken. Most of Wurmbrand's reports are implausible.

While it is likely that the number of deaths recorded is inaccurate, his report, passed along the chain of command, raised no alarm in Adelaide. On Undoolya Station, Willshire shot three Arrernte and wounded four more. At about the same time, Willshire and his new trackers, all on their way to Darwin, were involved in a shooting around Powells Creek that sounds very much like a training exercise. His eventual report of the killings (described as being in self-defence) also raised no questions in Adelaide.[13]

While the mounted Indigenous police troopers and their officers were now ranging across the central lands without restraint, even their rather ritualised reports of deaths, injuries, the burning and destruction of camps and property, and the rounding up of women and children were accepted either without comment or with praise. Unbelievable as the reports appear, it is telling that Willshire and Wurmbrand felt able to report so much of what they did without fear of questioning or disciplinary action. This was the result of policing by what is often referred to as *policy* rather than by law. Used in this way the word 'policy' sounds official or even neutral, but covers over the fact that police were acting outside the law. Their repetitive claims that men were chased off or shot while resisting or escaping arrest, their claims that while women and children were rounded up, held for a while as a warning of some kind, and then released, also cover up the way that sexual access to such women was one of the rewards for those involved in hunting them down. The Indigenous police rapidly acquired a reputation for brutality and for the sexual abuse of such women as came their way. But of course, their actions were controlled by Willshire and Wurmbrand and could not have taken place had they not wished it. And certainly Wurmbrand and Willshire liked to have their way with Indigenous women.

A photograph of Willshire and Wurmbrand with some of their victims and trackers takes the form of a staged tableau with Willshire having brought Nitranitrinyana and Toobana to Port Augusta to be tried in connection with an attack on Henbury Station. The photograph, Julie Robinson says, 'received glowing praise in the newspaper, being described as transcending any previous images by Taylor ... both in artistic finish and intrinsic interest.'[14] It is one that has been frequently reproduced despite the false claim to be 'in camp'. The stageyness of the scene has something in common with tableaux performed in the nineteenth and early twentieth centuries as entertainments among the more prosperous, or with the moving pictures of cowboys and Indians. Yet the people are real enough, as are the guns and ammunition. Like many photographs of Aboriginal people it can be understood in at least two ways. In one, it is a friendly image with Willshire and Wurmbrand having a benign air, the Aboriginal people supporting and helping the bringers of peace, of the police keeping the sparse population of colonists safe. Alternatively, it offers an image of colonial superiority over semi-naked savages, as well as of the violence on which it is based and the way in which it draws Indigenous people into ambiguous positions within the colonial world. Or it could deliver the possibility of being both at the same time.

In 1884 the concerns of Hermannsburg missionaries about the treatment of Aborigines in Central Australia by police and pastoralists reached the Protector of Aborigines, Edward Hamilton, but with little result.[15] So it was not surprising that in 1885 the station established over the waters at Anna's Reservoir (c. 160 km north of Alice Springs) on Anmatjera Country was attacked and burned down while Mounted Constable Brookes from Barrow Creek police depot was elsewhere with trackers and station hands, looking for those said to have been causing the trouble. Two of the station workers were trapped inside the burning hut and badly injured. In a reprisal, a police party under the control of Willshire and Wurmbrand from the Alice Springs police station was organised. It included the station manager, Billy Benstead (whose diary gives accounts of many actions against Aborigines), one of his station-hands, and a number of Native Constables. Although recording only one death, claiming it as self-defence, they are said to have shot at least fifteen Anmatjera men.[16] Willshire was up around Anna's Reservoir for ten months, hardly likely if it had not been worth his while in bodies. Local accounts say at least fifty died at Italinga on the northern edge of Harts Range. Erhard Eylmann, a German doctor who travelled through there five years later said that in his view the trouble at Anna's Reservoir was sparked by passing drovers. They had had sexual intercourse with a girl who was still a child. After the homestead was burned down Anna's Reservoir was abandoned.

Richard Kimber has set out the escalation of hostilities: troubles at Glen Helen and at Boggy Hole on the Finke River, and then the thefts of property and stock from the struggling Hermannsburg-Ntaria mission station established west of Alice Springs from 1875, and others. By 1888 the pastoralists were demanding more police to deal with the killing of cattle on Tempe Downs. In Adelaide a group of interested parties met with the Chief Secretary, J.G. Ramsay, to tell him why.[17] The manager of Tempe Downs, J.F. Thornton, said he had on one occasion arrived at a camp of alleged transgressors at 9 a.m. one morning to find that the people had fled leaving behind spears, meat and 'other things'. Then, as Thornton and a 'black boy' [tracker] were drinking at a waterhole, rocks and boulders rained down upon them from the cliffs above, forcing them out. As had been the case further south, the argument made again was that if more police were not provided, pastoralists might be tempted to see to the matter themselves or, as the Hon H. Scott put it, 'the country would become lawless' as indeed it was. In fact, as Mr J Bagot, the following witness remarked, 'stock-owners found that the only thing they could do was to arm a large number of men to scour the country with stockwhips and when they came upon a camp to follow it and use the whip very freely.' In supporting the request for more police, Bagot drew on his earlier experience on occupying the country around Peake Station in the north of South Australia or, as Kimber believes, relied on events that took place around the valuable waters of Dalhousie Springs on the edge of the Simpson Desert.[18] There is little doubt that the whip was active in and around Alice Springs as the Arrernte and Luritja felt the impact of the herds and then that of the rifle and the pistol.

One of those at the meeting with the colony's Chief Secretary downplayed the value of arms to the respect generated by police patrolling the country, referring to the aura of 'mystery' surrounding the police in Indigenous eyes and the way in which the police represented the great power standing behind them. The mystery surrounding the policeman was, I fear, an oblique reference to the wave of terror set in motion as they tried to take control of the country and a reference, too, to the impunity of the colonists and their predatory sexual practices. The use of predatory sex as a technique of humiliation to demonstrate the failure of Indigenous masculinity was widespread. It was a practice that created an absolute divide between colonising and colonised males that marked out the boundaries of a hardening racial separation with women occupying a vulnerable position in both. On the one side were men with access to any woman they wanted and to do to them whatever they would; on the other were men with access only to women of their own society and even then, not always.

The possible reversal of these sexualised racial relations, of which there was no possibility in the 1880s, provoked an absolute moral disgust at such a relationship and great anger at even the possibility of a colonial woman living with or having a sexual relationship with an Indigenous man. Such a relationship became unthinkable, forming a bar that remained in place until at least the 1960s. The widespread abuse of Aboriginal women in central Australia, however, had consequences: it created a widespread fear of retribution that took the form of a fear of rape among both colonial women and men. For those wanting to understand the kind of society that eventually grew up in the colony, it is important to understand just how tightly entwined, sex and forms of masculinity are with racial barriers and conventions and how these humiliations and their associated violence actually shaped the social worlds of both perpetrators and victims. In reality, there were very few cases indeed in which Aboriginal men either attacked or raped colonial women.

By 1888 the manager of Tempe Downs was facing constant harassment, theft and cattle killings. On one occasion he and his tracker had been trapped up a gully and had some difficulty in getting out. Although an extra constable was assigned to Alice Springs the troubles on Tempe Downs continued despite the regular patrolling of the property by police. It was at about this point that Willshire moved his police base to Boggy Hole near the Tempe Downs homestead. Gordon Reid has suggested that the police presence there actually contributed to creating the violence – Willshire no longer needed to wait for a transgression to take place but could punish in anticipation of it. He also had a troop of six or so Indigenous men as trackers and armed assistants. Willshire's violent reign on Tempe Downs led eventually to the charges laid against him by Frank Gillen, the stationmaster of the telegraph station at Alice Springs. But the violence on Tempe Downs continued for decades – more sporadically, perhaps – as did the efforts of pastoralists and their supporters to clear the land of its Indigenous custodians.

*****

In the meantime, the tropical zone of the colony known as the 'top end' of the Northern Territory that was administered from Palmerston, the town that later became Darwin, had also been facing an influx of those seeking their fortunes – not just from pastoralism but also from gold. Drovers and their herds were travelling westward from Queensland right across the Top End to the Kimberley region of Western Australia as well as arriving from the south. All were facing intermittent attack. In Adelaide the situation in the Top End had also led to a shift away from attempts to deal with Indigenous attackers through law to what was referred to as 'policy'.[19] By about 1878 the government in Adelaide had effectively handed over control to the police and pastoralists.[20] Already the Resident Administrator's calls for more protection had led to the appointment of German-born Police Inspector Paul Heinrich Matthias Foelsche. Foelsche understood what the government's shift from 'law' to 'policy' implied and felt able to conduct the business of policing as he saw fit. Like Mounted Constable Gason he would play a critical role in the violence that would turn the 1880s into 'the killing times'. He devoted nearly thirty-five years to 'quietening' the Aboriginal people of the Top End, retiring in 1904.

Chapter Thirty-Six

The 'Top End' of the Territory

Once the telegraph line was built the conversion of the lands of the Northern Territory into a pastoral zone was rapid and concentrated. In the years between the line's completion in 1872 and 1885, an area the size of the state of Victoria came to be held by just fourteen pastoralists. Theirs were vast stations intended to run gigantic herds.[1] The urgency of the land grab, opposition from those being displaced, the management problems created by the size of the stations and the amount of capital required to make them profitable, all took place in a country that was already regarded as something of a 'no-man's land'. Despite its suggestive words, a no-man's land is not a place without men, but one which is without civilisation or law and thereby understood as a wild place inhabited by savages or barbarians. The definition provided by the editors of the Oxford dictionaries suggests something embedded in the term lying within it, something submerged in a kind of mystery: 'between Riverside Drive and Central Park West was a no man's land, a zone of welfare tenements'. Their example brings out the connection between a no-man's-land and the dispossessed – in their case, the people living in tenements, but in the Australian use of the term, the seemingly 'uncivilised' Indigenous owners were therefore classed as wild. The man who will enter into this no-man's land will see himself as entering a 'wild' world, a characterisation that was fundamental to the way that colonial men viewed their actions once there.[2]

During the 1880s huge stations like Victoria River Downs and Wave Hill (1882) were being created to the west of the telegraph line, leased and stocked. As in Central Australia, the processes of colonial pastoralism generated great hostility among those standing in its way. Deborah Bird Rose quotes Old Johnson Pitutu on what happened up around the Victoria and Wickam rivers. 'In the 1880s', she says,

> *there was a group of adult clansmen whose country included some of the rough ranges and mesas of the Wickham River catchment. The men were clan brothers but had different mothers and fathers so their ages were widely disparate. I was privileged to meet the youngest of these men, Old Johnson Pitutu. In 1980 he was about eighty years old, and he died not long after I met him.*[3]

She goes on to describe how his words and narratives influenced her own thinking, particularly when, with 'his succinct eloquence he articulated an ethic of fidelity that is shared by most of the Aboriginal people I have ever met'. At the time that she came to know Old Johnson Pitutu he was living on an outstation established on his own country. There, she says,

> Old Pitutu told me that the 'Wickham River is filled with blood of Blackfellas killed in those days. Their bones are all broken up along the bottom ... We are camping now on the blood of Aboriginal people killed in those days.'

The Wickham River referred to by Old Pitutu is one of those feeding Victoria River Downs Station, established over country that McDouall Stuart had dreamed of owning but never could. Relations between the people living around the Wickham and the colonists were not always hostile. But as their mistreatment increased they became so. Victoria River Downs and the other stations built on the desirable country around the rivers did not come easily into existence. The killing that Old Johnson Pitutu spoke of was widespread, carried out on a grand scale. Rose estimates that, 'In the period 1880–1930 the loss of Aboriginal population [from war and disease] was about 93%.'

Similarly, while writing of the fate of the Karangpurru people whose country was traversed by the track leading west from Queensland across the top of the Top End and on to the pastures and gold fields of the Kimberley district in northern Western Australia, Rose noted that by 1894 there was no mention of the Karangpurru people at all. They had almost entirely disappeared, shot indiscriminately, often for sport. Before the track went through, there had been at least 500 of them, she says, perhaps three times as many. The gold-miners and pastoralists using the track labelled the Karangpurru as 'vindictive'.[4] Others labelled their defiance as 'savage' and 'treacherous', all three words designed to make the violence of colonisation appear as necessary and morally justified. *They* were not the savages, it was only the savage, treacherous and vindictive people standing in their way.

To the east of the telegraph line Tony Roberts' detailed research into the violence involved in its colonisation uncovered at least fifty massacre sites with more discovered since his research was published in 2005. But possibly as many as seven or eight hundred died as the land was brought under colonial occupation. In the same period twenty colonists were killed with, he notes, 'not a single white woman or child harmed in any way'.[5] The Indigenous custom of preserving the lives of women and children even in battle continued into their fighting with the colonists, their behaviour standing in stark contrast to the unbridled savagery of the punitive posses.[6]

The estimates of both Rose and Roberts demonstrate the disproportionate nature of the deaths involved in installing a pastoral regime in the Top End of the colony and what the colonial use of the term 'clearing' the land really meant. Their statistics and others like them show that on either side of the telegraph line, right across the north of the Territory, massacres not only of fighting men but of the elderly and crippled, of women, children and babies – often described by posses of colonists as acts of mercy – was typical and routine. Because so much of the killing was indiscriminate and unreported as well as under-estimated, and because much of it was carried out by the police, in general I prefer the higher estimates of both the pre-existing populations as well as the numbers of deaths rather than the lower. Indeed, I expect both numbers to rise as more factual information becomes available. Having read so much of the public and private record and taken into account the growing archive of Indigenous records, I believe the higher estimates give a better picture not only of the violence unleashed across the Territory in the wake of the telegraph line but of the ways in which those events are remembered by colonists and Indigenous Australians alike. The numbers of dead and the manner of their dying introduce matters that challenge important elements of the ways in which the descendants of the colonists like to think about their past and how they came to own the land. That those estimates are telling and uncomfortable today is evidenced by the strenuous efforts of revisionist historians to find ways of diminishing them.

Captain Cook

For a long time most Australian narratives of European colonisation traced the origins of today's Australia back to the claims Captain James Cook made on his visit to the continent's east coast, to his compulsive flag-raising as he went ashore, and the eight days he spent at Botany Bay in 1770. Cook's exalted position as a founding father of the modern nation is repetitively embedded and circulated in popular culture, in his anniversaries, in place-names like Cooktown, in heritage monuments and, as Katrina Schlunke has shown, in children's schoolyard rhymes.[7] Captain James Cook, she says, has to be continuously re-invented, honoured by all and kept alive in order to make Australian history live as truth.

First Nations histories also place Captain Cook as the powerful originator of today's Australia but they recount his coming and his consequences differently. In the powerful voice of Hobbles Danayarri, a Mudburra man born in the Territory in about 1925, Cook's arrival from England and the coming of the colonists heralds the arrival of a terrifying immorality. In a failure to observe the courtesies required of a stranger, the visitors failed to treat properly with the Aboriginal people. They failed entirely to recognise them and their real status as the possessors of the land. Instead Cook and his people were determined to categorise the true owners of the country as 'wild' people, a term of great significance as Cook's followers arrived with their herds. Cook's followers would not recognise them, did not see them as people. The Indigenous people Cook met, says Danayarri, were not wild people but 'the bosses for the land', its legitimate owners, a reversal that makes the colonists into the truly 'wild' men.[8]

The killing started with Captain Cook in Sydney, Danayarri continues. Then Cook went to the Northern Territory, to Darwin Harbour, and the killing started there: 'he didn't give Aboriginal people a fair go – he's the bloke who started to kill my people up in the Northern Territory. This is the biggest country and we own it. He should have asked. Captain Cook started it, not us.'[9] This is most certainly true as even if Cook never went personally to the Northern Territory his numerous replicas, the bearers of the morality and mentality of his first coming, most certainly did so.[10] The picturing of the British colonists as being *all* 'Captain Cooks' invading their country is a powerful image indeed. In it we hear the continuing First Nations challenge to colonial ownership, a challenge that begins with the placing of Cook as a totally immoral Being, the man who brought violence and lawlessness in his wake. In the 1980s an Aboriginal elder would travel to England to stake a claim to that country in 'retaliation' for Captain Cook's claiming of Australia.[11]

Hobbles Danayarri's historical account of colonisation is one among an extensive and varied Australia-wide cycle of narratives describing the genesis of the immoral colonised world in which the true owners of the Country have been forced to live ever since.[12] Captain Cook appears in Indigenous narratives along the east coast of Australia, for example, in the Kimberley region of Western Australia, in Arnhem Land to the east of the telegraph line, and in the western desert among the Martu people who lived adjacent to Western Australia's border with the Northern Territory. There, for example, Billy Gibbs noted that,

> When Captain Cook came to this land he had a look and said it was an empty land. He took the land through the white law. But the land

was there with the Martu law. Captain Cook split the people up. But all the people were still there. Captain Cook made the country a different story.[13]

In many places, Cook has entered everyday language and ways of speaking. The distinguished Arrernte painter and political activist Wenten Rubuntja used the term 'Captain Cook side' when discussing how the successful artist, Albert Namatjira, learned to paint according to the conventions of English landscape painting.[14] Rubuntja himself painted using the visual conventions of both his Arrernte side and Captain Cook's side, sometimes painting a place to tell about it in both styles, side by side.[15]

But as is the case with popular Christian saints like the Virgin Mary, the Indigenous Captain Cook jumps up anywhere and as he does so, appears in many different incarnations – he can be a man of sorrows, a good man, a man to laugh at, an ancestor even; and often, as in the historical narrative of Hobbles Danayari, he can be both a bringer and a transgressor of Law.

The colonists' Captain Cook also appears as a bringer of law, a civilising law that would bring justice to all, a law that was borne inwards from the coasts by the pioneering pastoralists, cattlemen, farmers, civil servants and missionaries, the brave men whose endurance and determination shaped the national character of modern Australia. For after all, South Australia was lawful from the start, was it not? It was distinguished from other colonies in the way that its first colonists were neither the criminals nor the paupers sent to the others as exiles. The colonists of South Australia were hard-working, largely Protestant families who arrived to live, from the very first day, as a colony of equals, all under the rule of civilised English law. They had a court and a judge to make sure that it was so. English law declared that if a criminal act was alleged, a judge would preside over a trial of the culprit, evidence would be heard, witnesses could be called by lawyers for the defence as well as for the prosecution, so that a person acquitted would be set free, the guilty whipped, jailed or hanged. There was no provision in those laws for the killing of sheep to be punished directly by killing the stealer of the sheep, nor for witnesses to be chained or imprisoned in order to get them to court, or supposed thieves to be chained, whipped, starved or shot without trial; nor did English law permit the deaths of several colonists, as occurred at Barrow Creek and elsewhere, to be avenged by the massacre of dozens of men, women and children who had nothing to do with the killings. But as the Top End was put under pastoral leasehold and fortune hunters from China as well as the other colonies flooded into the gold fields first at Pine Creek (from 1872) then thousands more to Hall's Creek (from 1885–86) just over the border in Western Australia, Indigenous resistance and defiance increased. Among the colonists a terrible determination to rid themselves of such troubles once and for all was unleashed, unrestrained by law. This was colonial police 'policy' at work under Police Inspector Foelsche in Darwin.

Occupation in the 'Top End'

The reality of the occupation of country north-west of the line has been described in a remarkable series of publications by Deborah Bird Rose and more recently by the Gurindji people themselves, in *Yijarni, True Stories from Gurindji Country*.[16] It's not just the violence the Gurindji histories set out that is so appalling, it is also the scale of the tragedy. Much of Rose's research took place in the pastoral zones that had been impressed upon the country to the north-west of the telegraph line, country that had lured John McDouall Stuart northwards in hope of finding a way to the country described so favourably by those who had seen it. The country that Stuart coveted would become covered over by Victoria River Downs Station and many others. In *Hidden Histories. Black Stories from Victoria River Downs, Humbert River and Wave Hill Stations* Rose has recorded how that country became a 'deathscape'.[17] On the other side of the line, in *Frontier Justice: A History of the Gulf Country to 1900*, Tony Roberts has carefully mapped out the massacres that took place to its east.[18] When taken together these two very different histories offer a disturbing picture of the way in which from 1872 the far north was taken. When they are added to the more recently published Gurindji stories, not just those of Ronnie Wavehill mentioned above, but those of Dandy Danbayarri, Violet Wadrill, Banjo Ryan, Biddy Wavehill Yamawurr, Topsy Dodd Ngarnjal, Peanut Pontiari, Maurie Ryan, Vincent Lingiari, Jimmy Manngayarri, Blanche Bulngari and Pincher Nyurrmiari, all of whom record, locate and discuss the massacre sites on their countries, the scale of the killings is extraordinary.[19] As all these narratives show, the violence involved was sexualised, endemic, horrific, excessive, and often petty. The drover Sam Croker (1852–1892), one of those immortalised in the Stockman's Hall of Fame in Longreach, is remembered as once shooting a Gurindji man in the back for trying to take a bucket.[20]

Then there is Jimmy Manngayarri's eye-witness account of his uncle's death at the hands of Jack Cusack and Jack Carpenter, a record created in 1975:

> *Cusack and Carpenter meikim im cartim jangilany. 'Alrait yu cartim wud.' Wal imin gedim wud na. Imin gedim wud, stackimap. 'Rait yu stand up deya. Stand up longsaid langa faya.' Jutim deya binij on top of the wood. Gedim kerosin an barnimap rait deya top of the wud jukim kerosine barnim. Puka kartiya brobli. Dat ai bin siim acting langa mairoun eye ai bin siim wen ai was piccininny.*
>
> Translation: *Cusack and Carpenter made my uncle get some firewood. 'Alright, you cart some wood,' they told him. Well, he got some wood then and stacked it up. 'Right you stand up there,' they said. 'Stand lengthways to the pile of firewood.' Then they shot him so he fell on top of the wood. They got some kerosene and burnt him right there. Those whitefellas were rotten to the core. I saw them do these things with my own eyes when I was a child.*[21]

Then there was Jack Beasley. Among the Gurindji and right across the region his name recurs as a monstrous violent man and rapist. Illiterate, Beasley used his cattle brand as his signature. Darrell Lewis, who has researched extensively the droving life of the Victoria River district, found that:

> *Aborigines from one side of the Victoria River district to the other remember Beasley as a very hard [violent] man and one of the main culprits in early massacres. He certainly was in the district early enough to have been involved in such killings, and Aboriginal oral traditions as widespread and consistent as this should be taken seriously. There is only one piece of written corroboration. When Doug Moore became bookkeeper on Ord River in 1900, Jack Beasley was the head stockman there. Years later Moore wrote a short memoir and he remembered Beasley as 'a rough good natured chap who talked about gouging out blackfellows eyes with a blunt pocket knife'. At the time Moore thought it was 'only talk', but he was forced to reconsider when 'some built on it later'. Jimmy Manngayarri, one of the oldest Aboriginal men I interviewed, had known Beasley years ago.[22]*

But men like Beasley were far from unique. Ronnie Wavehill's histories show how the massacres followed a fairly common pattern. A dawn raid on a sleeping camp of men, women and children, their wholesale slaughter and then the burning of the bodies. Treated like dogs, in Ronnie Wavehill's words.

> *The two men heaped up wood until there was a large pyre. Then they dragged them one by one – an old man ... another woman ... another man, dragging them across. They threw them all on the fire. They didn't bury them the decent way. They just threw them on the fire and burnt them like dogs. In those times, they would just burn those ngumpin [Aboriginal people] where they shot them, not put them up in tree platforms ... to protect them and let their spirits finish up properly. There was nothing like that; they just piled them up! Let the fire burn them till they're done! Another body was dragged along.[23]*

Later, Ronnie Wavehill tells of how his forebears speared two of the interlopers in a revenge attack.

Predatory Sex and the Pastoral Zone

Deborah Rose captured something important of the nature of the violence unleashed against the people living west of the line when she described it as 'orgiastic'.²⁴ It is a word that captures the type of acts that lay at the heart of that violence, its sexualised nature: the rapes, kidnappings of women, the sadistic punishments meted out to women, the stealing of children of both sexes for sex and servitude, of women forced to track down members of their own families and kin who were wanted by pastoralists for some reason, of women dragged away from the babies they were still nursing. She refers to a conversation with Hobbles Danayarri in which he set down a record of how Gurindji women who had refused to submit to a gang rape were shot near Daguragu in the 1920s. These were murders that left the survivors shattered.²⁵

Orgiastic is the word that captures events like these: of the dragging along of women to be broken in like horses; the reports that Jack Watson on Lawn Hill had forty pairs of ears nailed on his wall (or doorpost) to mark his 'kills', and that he had got a skull from Constable Willshire to use as a spittoon; the chaining of men and women and the constant opportunities to earn a frightful whipping or kicking or bashing just for looking at the boss in the wrong way.²⁶ Indigenous children had to be taught the techniques essential to surviving in such a terrifying world. Jimmy Manngayarri's account of one of Jack Beasley's murders gives some idea of station life west of the line. He was talking about Daguragu, now a settlement of Gurindji people.

> *He's the proper really bugger that one. Beasley shot a lot of them. He killed one woman too. He was married with that girl. He had a black woman, old Jack Beasley ... And they [Aboriginal men] were messing around with that woman. Some ngumpin [Aboriginal person or people], you know. Well Jack Beasley come up and he said: 'Ah, you knock about longa them boys, eh?'*
>
> *And that woman [said] 'yes'. He gave her a hiding, and that woman ran away and climbed on the big hill. Not too far from Beasley, old homestead, old Beasley house ...*
>
> *[He] saw her there. She got that, you know early days that old turkey red clothes? He saw her, he followed her up, get his horse and get the bloody kerosene, put it in the drum, tie it on to bloody*

saddle ... get his gun. Find her: 'oh, hear her in the fucking cave:. Kiyu-u-u-u [shooting/whistling sound].' Killed her. Shot her. Pulled her down. Pulled her down and carting the wood and burn her up. Put the kerosene on.

They did that a-a-a-all, all over the place.[27]

And of another incident, Jimmy Manngayarri said:

Oh, they've been doing that in my time. I saw it. When I was big one now, I saw that. Same thing, when I was [a] very little boy, he was doing that for my mother. Harry Reid was kicking my mother here on the kidney. He kicked her in the kidney till she dropped dead. I was only a little boy, that big about four years old.

In 1883 Emily Creaghe observed some of this as she and her husband travelled from Normanton in Queensland westwards toward the telegraph line with the explorer Ernest Favenc. She noted in her diary that her host at Carl Creek Station, Frank Shadforth and his son Ernest, had arrived home with a new Aboriginal woman, one speaking no English at all. 'Mr Shadforth put a rope round the gin's [woman's] neck & dragged her along on foot, he was riding. This seems to be the usual method', she said, as indeed it was.[28] On the following day she noted that the woman was given the name of Bella and was 'chained up to a tree a few yards from the house, she is not to be loosed until they think she is tamed'. Two days later, Emily wrote: 'The new gin made Topsey (an older woman) jealous, & the latter threw a fire-stick at her & said she would kill her. The stick flew past Mrs. Shadforth's face so Madame Topsey got a thrashing.' The following night 'Bella' escaped. Fortunately the river had risen to a level that prevented her pursuit.

Creaghe's diary entry offers a rare glimpse of how pastoralists in the northern regions treated Indigenous women as well as an insight into the ambiguous nature of relationships across the colonial divide, of the way that violent actions were either accepted or not commented on. What did Mrs Shadforth with her ten children think about the arrival of a young woman kidnapped and dragged along by her husband

and son to be 'broken'? Why was Topsey 'jealous' of the kidnapped woman? What privileges might have been at stake for her in such an environment? What role did rape play in 'Bella's' 'breaking' and was it unwanted sex with 'Bella' that lay at the heart of the quarrel between the two women? And indeed, who had had sex with 'Bella' to break her in, Shadforth senior or his son?

In Emily Creaghe's brief diary notes we see not only the brutality of colonisation but the ways in which it creates a particular kind of reversed social world, one in which the bringers of a civilisation built upon a monogamous Christian family are no longer paragons of civilisation but have become the savages they despise and intend to tame. Creaghe's diary notes record the practices of violent masculinity that breed brutality in individual fathers, unlimited licentiousness in their sons and the complicit silencing of mothers and wives who must be protected from the savagery. The women who have to live beside such men with knowledge of at least some of their actions live also with the fear that the affections of their legal protector will slip over to the other side, the dark side of the civilised imagination. These are the same practices described so carefully by the American writer Toni Morrison on the effects of slave ownership on slave owners. Inevitably, the reversal of the sustaining fantasies of civilisation and savagery has the potential to inflame the needs of those who would maintain their superiority, injecting a kind of desperation into the violence that intensifies it until one wonders what was it that they were trying to purge or get rid of from themselves? Did they pretend to themselves that their victims incited them, that they 'made them do it'? Were they trying to beat their moral, Christian, guilt out of their victims? To send them to the fires of hell?

*****

It was no accident that when the pastoralists in the Victoria River district found that too much of their time was taken up in protecting their stock and water supplies from Indigenous peoples and called for police protection it was the disgraced Mounted Constable Willshire who was sent to them.

In an unusual move, Frank Gillen, telegraph operator and *de facto* magistrate at Alice Springs, had charged Willshire with shooting two unarmed men, one of whom was asleep at the time, and then with burning the bodies. Willshire was not much worried by the charges but of course they were inconvenient. He had to appear before Justice Bundey and a jury in far-away Port Augusta. In the small courtroom of 1891, when Mounted Constable William Willshire was declared to be not guilty of the murders of two Arrernte/Luritja men on Tempe Downs Station in central Australia, public joy at the verdict was palpable.[29] The not guilty verdict, the result of a shameful abuse of legal process by Sir John Downer and Thomas Gepp, one of the most important lawyers in the colony, left Willshire still employed within a police force grown a little uneasy by public concern about the fate of the people they were civilising.

After a short time of semi-exile to the more settled areas Willshire was posted to the Victoria River district in the Top End where his special skills in 'handling' Indigenous Australians made him, in the eyes of Inspector of Police Paul Foelsche, local pastoralists and the tiny general populace, the right man for the job. There, from a base established on Gordon Downs, Willshire and a band of Native Police under his control were left to rampage at will.[30] He arrived in 1894, setting up his base camp on Gordon Downs, ready to usher in even more violence. We know about it because he wrote about it.

Chapter Thirty-Seven

Willshire, Pornography and a Man's World

Mounted Constable Willshire's world was one from which colonial wives and children were almost entirely absent. In the Territory most colonial women lived in Palmerston, the seat of Top End administration, where a large and important Chinese community as well as traders from the islands around Australia's north far outnumbered the thousand or so colonists. Beyond Palmerston, however, the Northern Territory was a world and society of men fighting for supremacy and land. As noted earlier, in 1881, in the country lying between the Territory's border with South Australia and the Barrow Creek Telegraph Station there were three non-Indigenous women, one of whom was Mrs Alfred Giles on Springvale. Mrs Oakes, the manager's wife, arrived at the Elsey Station in 1891 but such women were few and far between.[1] The 1901 census recorded three such women in the tiny town of Alice Springs. Even after years of violence, the Indigenous population still outnumbered the colonists while the large Chinese presence gave Palmerston a cosmopolitan air.

For the men living and working on the land away from Palmerston it was not just that women and families were absent from their world, they were not wanted there. Excluded and resisted, opposition to their presence was explicit. Pastoralists and their workers, drovers, miners, tradesmen and others lived quite outside the conventions, customs and restrictions of civilised, Christian society – of decent society as it was understood in the late-Victorian era despite the sexual indulgences prevalent among the men of empire. The arrival of wives would bring their rough masculine freedoms to an end. A new morality would be imposed.[2] As noted earlier, they preferred the world of maleness established there with its unlimited access to Aboriginal women and the practices of violent domination that was allowed them. Willshire and the others like him were the founding heroes of their world, a world based on violence of epic proportions.

The male world of the Territory was not one without women, quite the reverse. Indigenous women were there for the taking. In a key and widely quoted paragraph, Mounted Constable Willshire stated clearly his view that men needed sexual intercourse with women.[3] That need, he suggested, was met by a gift from God who 'has placed them [women] wherever the pioneers go'. What he was 'speaking about,' he wrote, 'is only natural, especially for men who are isolated away in the bush at out-stations where women of all ages and sizes are running at large' – a phrasing of his that carries the sense that Aboriginal women are little different from the animals roaming across the land. In characterising Indigenous women in this way Willshire draws his readers' attention to one of those facts of Territory life that are known but little noticed, that the men 'out there' fighting to make the colony safe and civilised much preferred their free access to Aboriginal women to having to deal with wives, domestic life and the mores of the civilisation they claimed to be bringing to the 'savage natives'.

One of the curiosities of this hyper-masculine world of white supremacy was its assumed heterosexuality. In the colonies established directly to the north of Australia by the Dutch or British, it was common to see the men of local populations drafted into aspects of domestic service. This was not the practice in the Territory where Aboriginal men worked and lived outside the house. It was Aboriginal women who worked sometimes as domestic servants. Although it is possible to find examples of the employment of male Chinese cooks they were not prevalent on the stations in these late decades of the nineteenth century. But in the colonies to the north of Australia, in Indo-China, the East Indies, Malaya and Borneo, 'house-boys' were commonplace.[4] In a situation in which predatory sex was the order of the day, the absence of house-boys on the stations when so many young men and boys were there for the taking, is something of an anomaly. As their apparent absence points up the heterosexual manliness of the heroes involved in taking the land, the difficulty of locating male homosexuality is understandable. The carefully posed photograph of Frank Hann and his favourite 'boy', Talbot, suggests that its absence might be something of a mirage.

'Frank Hann, explorer & his 'boy' Talbot, c. 1910. Anonymous photographer.
C.M. Nixon of Fremantle & Northam.
State Library of South Australia

Hann was another of the well-known, educated and respected pastoralists. He was known also for his violence and brutality in dealing with Aboriginal people at Lawn Hill and elsewhere.[5] His entry in the *National Dictionary of Biography* lists no wives or children. Talbot, however, a young man from Normanton, is said to have travelled everywhere with Hann, staying with him even in the best hotels. The donor's inscription on the back of the photograph mentions Hann having married 'Mrs Daisy Bates' after the unidentified writer. In placing the name Daisy Bates in quotation marks, the writer may be referring to the journalist and political activist, Daisy Bates, with whom Hann is said to have corresponded; the use of quotation marks around the name suggests it is a pseudonym or nick-name, a common device of gay men of the time and later. It may be that it referred to a time in which Talbot had worked for a man named Bates (Daisy O'Dwyer married one such man, the drover, Jack Bates). It was unusual, however, that a man of that time would have travelled with an Aboriginal man as his companion and servant, particularly one as handsome and well-dressed as Talbot was, whose nickname was Mrs Daisy Bates. Their photograph suggests a relationship built on more than outdoor labour, one suppressed but not unknown at all.

The Territory's special world of men in the final decades of the nineteenth century was built on foundations of violence and sexual predation that ran along racial lines, creating as it did so, men immersed in a particular kind of masculinity, a violent kind. It was a culture into which newcomers to the Territory needed to be initiated if they wanted to be regarded as real men, a culture of extreme male 'mateship' and semi-secret rituals of death and sex. In it, violence was normal, condoned, and enforced. For newcomers wishing to be recognised as a man who would also become a 'mate', acceptance of the violence was required. Operating within the zone of law that was so precious to the colony's founders, violence corrupted the principles of justice that politicians, police, magistrates, justices of the peace, and juries should have been defending. As always, violence acted as a creative force upon both perpetrators and victims, making this a strange and terrible world of violent men in which Indigenous women were targeted while colonial women were not wanted. They had no place in it at all.

The Land of the Dawning

Of all the elements involved in 'settling' the country, early colonists and their descendants find the treatment of women the most difficult to deal with. It remains the most hidden part of Australian colonial histories although accounts can be found in newspapers, novels or hinted at in memoirs and reminiscences. Because of a very natural reluctance to talk about such unpleasant matters the little booklet published by Constable Willshire is important.

Mounted Constable (Second Class) William Willshire was active in the Territory in the midst of all its violence, first in Central Australia working around Alice Springs and then in the Top End. His desire to justify his activities and his literary pretensions led him to become one of few to have left a published account of the way the Territory was policed in his time. *The Land of the Dawning*, he called his small book, sub-titling it with an eye to the market, *Being Facts Gleaned from Cannibals in the Australian Stone Age*.[6] It was published just after he left the Top End for the last time, in 1896. Much of *Land of the Dawning* appears to have been written while Willshire was based on Gordon Downs, working with his team of Native Police around the Victoria River district. In his account of his time in the Top End, Willshire presents himself as fully engaged in the incidents he describes in his book, incidents in which he appears as the hero bringing peace and order to an unruly world and as a loyal scion of empire.

His book is interesting now, not because it offers a factual account of what policing in the Top End had become, nor because it gives a picture of the type of man he would like respectable society to know him as, nor even because a close study of it might reveal something of the psychology of a man consumed by the pleasures of violence. What it can tell us is something important about the way a Top End colonial society towards the end of the nineteenth society was being built. There is no secret about this. If not all incidents were recorded in police records (and many were not) the reign of violence in the Territory has always been known, sometimes only implicitly perhaps, but often more clearly. Sometimes it has faded from view (as in many early entries published in the *Australian Dictionary of Biography*) only to reappear later to again face denunciation from those who dislike knowing about it. Recent academic scholarship and Indigenous history-writing, however, has made available a vast amount of information about it.

The crucial role of rape, torture, and every other form of predatory sex, sexual enslavement and abuse in the founding of the colony has, however, remained shadowy. In part this is because of efforts by governments and perpetrators to conceal it with platitudes and omissions, in part because Australian studies of colonial politics, history and anthropology were focused on men as bringers of civilisation and their triumphs that needed to have 'wild' Aborigines to conquer and study as curiosities. As elsewhere, women's contributions to the colony's establishment were routinely omitted, but even with the advent of feminist research and Aboriginal scholarship, the lives of the Aboriginal women subjected to the violence have remained shadowy, often undocumented, sometimes dismissed by men who simply do not believe the claims of rape, abductions, killings and savage whippings. Often, the shame felt by Aboriginal women who suffered at the heart of the violence has meant that they have been unwilling to mention it. They have not wished to discuss the dreadful decisions they had to make in order to survive under such terrible conditions, or what they were forced to do in order to protect their families. As a result, the predatory and sexual nature of the violence of colonisation has not been properly recorded or understood. It has generally appeared as an unfortunate by-product of early times or perhaps as limited and isolated instances of personal perversions. Nor have its consequences, then and now, been considered.

Those failures and avoidances have in turn meant that, as elsewhere, general histories of colonisation in South Australia have often left intact the heroics of the pioneering legends of conquest and manliness so dear to the colonial heart. The absence of any real understanding or record of the role of predatory sex in founding the colony means that the important structuring contrasts of the great foundation myths of Australia can go unnoticed and unchallenged. Myths of manliness (pioneering, mateship, and explorers) are the myths that help to maintain the starkness of the colonial contrast between British 'civilisation' and Aboriginal 'savagery': the contrast between Christianity and 'heathenism', and the moral superiority of the pale-skinned over black 'races' that underpin a colonial sense that the colonists were and remain good people. These are myths of entitlement as well as of moral progress, myths that have justified the presence of colonists on lands not theirs, myths that allow them still to think of themselves as innocuous 'settlers' rather than as cruel, immoral invaders. Failure to understand the very remarkable and constant sexual aspect of the violence means that the moral vacuum at colonisation's heart has not been easily recognised. Whether First Australians or colonisers, those who have pointed to it have found themselves disbelieved, criticised and demeaned by some very raucous voices.

This is why Willshire's book requires more consideration. It is not just that he was a continual perpetrator but that his way of writing about his alleged exploits shows how Indigenous women lay at the heart of the violence of colonisation and how they were used as a weapon against Indigenous men as well as a prize of war.

To see how this male world of violence worked, you need to read his book in a particular way. To do that, you need to know how he structured it to speak to two different sets of readers. One set consisted of those with a general sort of commitment to the British empire and the opportunities that dreams of a new colony offered to speculative capitalists as well as to those who in England had nothing to sell but their labour.

The second set of readers were those who knew what turning the Countries of the First Nations of Australia into property and capital really involved. When Willshire published his book at the very end of the nineteenth century when the violence seemed to be over, some felt sufficiently removed from it to be able to look back at the 'early days' and the 'early colonists' with interest rather than fear or shame.[7] Others, depending on age and whether they had a specific if limited direct role in taking the land (newspaper reporters, administrators, missionaries, police, judges, politicians, etc.) had more knowledge. Willshire wrote for both sets of readers by taking on the persona of a cheerful colonial boy with his 'native police' fighting forward in a wild land and casting his exploits as incidents of the manly derring-do of colonial boys-own true-life adventures. As a result, some readers of Willshire's adventures in the wild could see only a jolly romp in brilliant country that left them wondering how he did it. Others may have enjoyed the chases he described but knew very well how he did it. They could develop a quite different understanding of what had engaged Willshire's attention because they understood what Willshire was saying about women and what happened to them.

Willshire's pornographic treatment of women can sometimes be minimised or overlooked. Some have commented upon the way in which 'dusky maidens' flit across his pages but it has remained easy to miss the ways in which sexual domination and violence are not peripheral or accidental side-effects in his story-telling but central to it. If he and his men are out looking for Aboriginal cattle-killers, it is generally women who are found and captured. When he writes of the men 'escaping' up the cliffs or into the scrub it is, as Aboriginal histories and memories record, much more likely that the men escaped into the chasm of death. It can be easy to miss, too, the ways in which his stories of his own cleverness and endurance have been combined to produce the salaciousness and stereotypes so typical of nineteenth century pornography, pornographic conventions with which many of his male readers would have been familiar.[8]

Nineteenth-century pornographic books and pamphlets offered British readers of the Victorian era repetitive sexual fantasies focused on male domination, a conception of male sexuality in which,

Steven Marcus says, 'the aggressive and sadistic components almost exclusively prevail'. It can be seen in books like *The Lustful Turk, or Lascivious Scenes from a Harem*, published in 1828, in which each story begins with a virgin who is beaten, flogged and raped into submission. Such texts express a form of male sexuality that Steven Marcus traced back to earlier eras, but one that pervaded not just nineteenth- and then twentieth-century British pornography but also fed into popular romances, and later, detective stories (in some of those of Agatha Christie, for example). One of the key propositions put forward in these books is that women love a masterful, dominating man – that women actually want to be dominated and, depending on the audience, domination involves some form of violence. These practices are all present in Willshire's book.

Willshire's Pornography

Willshire offers his readers a series of theatrically designed scenarios. To illustrate how he presents scenes of sexual violence and female consent to it, I have selected and abridged just one of them. The language is all his.

He begins by describing the dramatic country he and his Native Police travel through. Their tracking took them first into 'a weird chasm of black boulders and red cliffs; thence into wonderful stalagmitic caverns'. Then:

> *The first discovery inside the caves was of two lubras huddled together in a dark corner. We got them out to the entrance of the caves. They were filled with bashful terror, and were practically inseparable. The next discovery was a phlegmatic looking old male nigger, who was kicking and talking as fast as he could, probably giving us a lecture. As far as we were concerned, his words fell on dull unsympathetic ears and his acting to viewless space. We hawked the Sultan out to where the lubras were, and fastened him to the root of a stunted boxwood-tree; then continued our exploration. ... On returning to the newly discovered aborigines one of my boys informed*

> me that the two lubras were the daughters of the old fellow ... He was chewing at them [his bonds] and kicking sideways like a cow. I thought it prudent to make a refined aboriginal suggestion to the old gentleman, so we assured him that he would imperil his daughters' prospects if he continued to kick out like a cow.
>
> I unfastened him, and left him sitting at the mouth of the cave, watching the far-away skyline of his primeval wastes, while we went on with his daughters, who unerringly pursued a viewless undeviating path through the trackless mimosa scrub and tangled undergrowth. These girls were doing the tracking for my boys.
>
> ... Whilst I was writing up my journal, which was an every-night occurrence, my boys had divided, forming themselves into half-sections with the lubras, and perfecting themselves in the art of love. I judged that they were doing admirably well. They eventually succumbed to the thralldom of sleep, and I was left awake amidst the overwhelming majesty of nature.

In the morning,

> I ascertained that they [the young women] enjoyed themselves immensely, that there was another camp of natives some distance away, and that they would like to accompany my party for the rest of their natural lives ...

When Willshire reached his base-camp at Gordon Creek again, he made the girls return to their 'poor old father', he said, much to the disappointment of his trackers.[9]

Here Willshire has described a stereotyped scene – a hunt and discovery, capture, the restraint and humiliation of the old man, the kidnapping of two young women, the handing of the women over to the Native Police for the night for gang rape, the later use of the girls as informers, and then the long walk back to Willshire's camp at Gordon Creek while the masters rode. This is a scene of violent sexual predation dressed up as a happy bush scene with a happy ending when, as the good policeman, Willshire insists on sending the young women back to their father, who is most unlikely to have been left alive. It is a scene in which the capture and rape of the young women is absolutely central – the same methods in use throughout the Territory that were in one case observed and described by Emily Creaghe (in Chapter 36) during her journey into the Top End. And how cheerful and willing those young women are made to appear. Willshire, as the 'honest' narrator of this story is, of course, portrayed as not indulging in sex with the captive women. Even when they tempt him.

There are many such scenes in Willshire's little book – variations of course, and sometimes more shootings, but essentially the same. In one, Willshire is chasing cattle-killers on Victoria River Downs when after the shooting, in a most improbable way, a young woman runs up to him to lead him out of danger. This beautiful woman refused to leave them, staying in their camp, sitting on their swags ... One of Willshire's trackers said the beautiful young woman wished to travel to the station with them. His consent, he said, led to 'a thrill of delight [going to] her heart and hope once more dawned'. The pornographic theme of mastery and rape could hardly be clearer.

In another, 'When we had finished with the male portion we brought the black gins and their offspring out from their rocky alcoves. There were some nice-looking boys and girls among them. One girl had a face worthy of Aphrodite as she dwelt in a Grecian sculptor's brain.'[10] The mention of the nice looking children could be an expression of the pornographic fixation with virginity (and thus syphilis-free) as well as the British interest in sex with children. This group of women were treated kindly, he said – the sick were assisted by their sisters, the children collected pretty flowers and a healing tea was made. One woman was so kindly treated that she gave birth to a child. On another hunt, Willshire says, a very staunchly resisting young woman 'later became a paragon of gentleness, and her animal passions subsided into tranquillity, becoming head over heels in love with the tracker who had caught her.'

And so he goes on. On, and on, and on. Always the violence, always the hunt and the finding, always the women, always the begging of women who long to go to the men who are now their masters, and the miraculous pacification and love that emerges from violent sexual intercourse. As with other forms of pornography, it is all so repetitive. The reader knows what is going to happen long before reading begins. By turning his violence into happy stories of adventure and triumph he covers up some of the realities of the events he describes in order to create a more acceptable character for himself.

But most men of the colony would have had little difficulty in understanding what they read. It is possible that none of Willshire's stories is true in the sense of referring to a particular incident at a particular place or time although it would not be surprising to find that they refer to his greatest successes or excesses; it is equally possible that each story is wishful thinking or erotic fantasy divorced from reality. Unfortunately a good deal of Willshire's life is public property. His reputation for exceptional violence and sexual predation is uncontradicted by known facts. He was a man who lived with being loathed, despised and hated by many in Adelaide and by some in the Territory, men like Frank Gillen the telegraph operator in Alice Springs, for example. If his stories represent the sexual fantasies of a man seeking love though violence, one must pity him. But I do not think so. His life became fantasy incarnate.

The more 'practical' men of the colony could read Willshire's book using two separate but intertwined contexts. First, they could read from within their knowledge of the real violence taking place, violence in which they may well have participated. They knew that the idyllic scenes of glens, lagoons, mighty red cliffs and beautiful maidens was simply cover for the events taking place there. They understood his language. They knew what 'first we dealt with the men' really meant, what it meant to tell the old father in the excerpt quoted above that his protests would 'imperil' his daughters, and knew also what would have happened to the young woman who 'in her maidenly confusion, exhibited an extravagant affection of modesty.' Then they knew from experience or gossip how Aboriginal women were kidnapped, 'tamed', used by Willshire, and only then handed on to his trackers for further use and abuse. They could ignore tales in which children supposedly beg to accompany the murderers of their parents, children and women who, once 'civilised' by residing in the camps of Willshire and his men, are described as not wishing to return to any of their families who might have survived.

On the other hand, male readers of *The Land of the Dawning* could draw on the erotic charge of nineteenth-century pornography that offered images of masculinity (that is, of how to be a man) that were expressed as domination, violence and rape. As such the theatrically staged scenes of capture and rape found in Willshire's books, as well as in photographs of him showing the same themes, fed on and into the conventions and titillating styles of nineteenth-century Victorian-era pornography.

Part Eight
Zones of Exclusion

Chapter Thirty-Eight

Zones of Exclusion

Forged in violence and sustained through continuous exploitation, colonial Northern Territory became a deeply racialised society in which Aboriginal Australians were governed quite differently from those governed through laws and legal principles imported directly from Britain. In the Territory three distinct but separate zones of exclusion operated to produce a society stratified by the racial fantasies of the colonists. Although most clearly visible in the Territory, the fantasies of entitlement, race-based superiority, and male control of women hammered out there shaped not only the society of the Territory but that of the whole colony. Through them the violence used in converting Indigenous Country to pastoralism, grazing and mining became normal and legitimate. The role of these three zones of exclusion – zones from which inconvenient aspects of law and human and social rights were excluded on the basis of racial and social differences – was to justify the terrifying violence of colonisation that ensured the disappearance of Indigenous opposition, either through death, terror and enslavement or alternatively, the total racial and social absorption of Indigenous Australians through their assimilation into the race of their British masters. Given their important political and social significance, it is not surprising to find that despite good intentions, racially based zones of exclusion originated very early in the life of the colony. Such zones existed throughout colonial South Australia just as they did in the other Australian colonies.

The three zones of exception operating lawfully in the colony were the *mission zone*, the *pastoral zone* and *the zone of Indigenous policing*. Each zone was defined along the lines of race, each dealt in racial violence, and in each women were pivotal and the greatest losers. Each zone originated in the policies and problems of the earliest days of the colony; each was fuelled by the difficulties of taking land and turning it into saleable property, and the parallel 'problems' of turning Indigenous Australians into Christian replicas of the colonists. By the 1870s when the Northern Territory was being 'opened up' for conversion to colonial economic management and government, the methods used in taking over the land and the new way of living on it were well-established, well-known and accepted.

Each zone was created through the legal withdrawal of the legal rights, entitlements and protections provided to non-Indigenous colonial citizens either through birth or naturalisation. It was the withdrawal of human and economic rights that allowed each zone to operate as a separate world of its own, one that differed from the world outside it even though it was encapsulated within it. In each zone, as legal rights and autonomy were withdrawn from Indigenous South Australians, legal powers rightfully held by governments were delegated to pastoralists and their proxies, to missionaries and to police. With those delegated powers in hand, the incoming colonists could do pretty much what they liked. Those governed within the zones of excluded rights found themselves excluded from the new capitalist economy, subject to sometimes unspeakable forms of violence and depraved sexual practices, unable to marry without permission, subject to forced unpaid labour, refused wages let alone pensions, often shifted off their own Country to become strangers on Country to which they did not belong, and subject to regimes of improvement and moral education that were intended to break the family and to destroy Aboriginal religious beliefs and culture. Aboriginal Territorians were largely excluded from any form of access to government although they had to learn to live under its perpetual surveillance. Report after report, investigation after investigation, and policy after policy failed to bring about the improvements so many politicians and philanthropists have always said that they brought to Australia and said that they hoped for.

The three zones of exclusion overlapped in ways that produced the disasters described in earlier chapters. First the pastoralists would arrive. They would call for more police to deal with Aboriginal resistance and sometimes for a 'native police' force to be established to help with guiding and tracking. When police arrived in a district they came specifically to police Indigenous Australians, creating a zone of operations in which they used methods quite different from those authorised for use in policing the colonists. Police and pastoralists would co-operate in the violence of dispossession. If missions were permitted, they arrived to protect and to train those living under a rule filled with ambiguity and contradiction, one focused on an evangelical determination to enforce the new family structures and a new set of religious beliefs. In the efforts to entirely reshape the nature of an Aboriginal person, the mission zone could not avoid becoming a zone in which those living within it experienced missionary powers as a violent assault upon both their minds and bodies, an assault on their sense of themselves as autonomous, self-sufficient, moral persons. Throughout the colony of South Australia and its Northern Territory more and more Indigenous citizens came to live within one or more of these three zones. While each of the zones could be seen as differing from the others, they shared a great deal – perhaps because their purpose and attitudes were similar, perhaps because the face of power does not vary too much. But most importantly, Indigenous women were of great interest to those controlling each of the zones and suffered accordingly. Male attitudes to their sexual and labour rights over women were shaped in these three zones and continue to generate, to shocked public horror and protests, evils that can be found deeply embedded within the political parties and legal privileges that traipse along the corridors of the national Parliament.

Chapter Thirty-Nine

The Pastoral Zone

The colonial pastoral zone was an encapsulated space of racial segregation in which colonists and Aborigines lived side by side but quite separately and in very different ways. Relationships to land, laws and social worlds could not have been further apart. As privatised property, a pastoral station formed a bounded space with permeable borders through which some could pass more easily than others. Police, for example, could pass into the zone and out again if they chose to enforce some element of the law, form a labour brigade, or locate guides and interpreters. At the same time the movement of Aboriginal people across the borders of stations, missions and homesteads could be circumscribed. Most importantly, information about the actions of those living within the boundaries of the zone could be controlled. As noted in earlier chapters, significant government and legal powers could be delegated to station owners and managers by making them Justices of the Peace or distributors of government rations.

Always a male space in which 'real' men lived and worked, it was not until 1902 that 'Aeneas' Gunn would ignore the warnings and pleas of his workers and friends *not* to bring his new wife with him to Elsey Station.[1] In a highly romanticised account of the station life that his wife found at Elsey she provided a description of the station settlement as it was then, mentioning a 'nigger hunt' as well as its essential structures of segregation. Roughly one hundred miles (*c.* 160 km) south of Katherine and covering some of the Country belonging to the Mangarrayi and Yangman peoples, Elsey homestead was 'mostly verandah and promises', she said, but her description of the settlement sprawled around the homestead at Galyag (Warloch Ponds) gives a picture of the scale and racial segregation of the pattern common in the pastoral zone. She listed:

> *The cook's quarters, kitchens, men's quarters, store, meat-house, and wagon house, facing each other on either side of this oblong space [that] formed a short avenue – the main thoroughfare of the homestead – the centre of which was occupied by an immense wood-heap, the favourite gossiping place of some of the old blackfellows, while across the western end of it, and looking down upon it, but a little aloof from the rest of the buildings, stood the House ... As befitted their social positions, the forge and blackboys' 'humpy' kept a respectful distance well round the south-eastern corner of this thoroughfare; but, for some unknown reason, the fowl-roosts had been erected on top of Sam Lee's sleeping quarters.*[2]

Sam Lee was the Chinese cook; by sleeping directly under the precious chickens he was probably protecting them from predators, human and those not. The pattern in which the 'blackboys' humpy' was kept out of sight of the house was a regular structural characteristic of the pastoral zone, as was the 'respectful distance', the term that she used to describe the set of powers held by owners or managers of properties like Elsey. It was a pattern established very early. When Glen Helen, located near a major waterhole about a hundred kilometres west of Alice Springs, was first stocked at the end of 1878 the drovers pegged out a line around their first huts, across which unknown Aboriginal people were forbidden to pass – a usual practice, Dick Kimber noted, when fences and gates were non-existent but also an important part of a regime of control.[3] The highly racialised and divided system described by the drover Matt Savage on his Central Australian property early in the twentieth century was not exceptional. When he first arrived in the northwest, he said, *a white man was not expected to speak to a black at all, unless it was to tell him what to do. If you had a normal conversation with one of them, the other fellows would say you were becoming too familiar and probably you would not last very long in your job. This did not apply so much to the black women who, after all, did have their place in the scheme of things. But the boys were little more than slaves, and other than that they were of no account at all.*[4]

Savage had a reputation as a brutal station manager; when travelling along the Tanami track in 1934 from Wave Hill he had a young child with him. When the anthropologist, Olive Pink, asked about the child she was told it was a boy.[5] A single young child travelling far from home with two drovers was perhaps most likely to be a girl but in any case was one of the many children 'picked up' by such men. Savage also, however, had a long-term Aboriginal partner and later moved into Alice Springs to be closer to his daughter.[6]

Most commonly, Aboriginal people lived down by a creek or waterhole, out of sight of the main house but within easy reach of a whistle, bell, or messenger. Their quarters were usually referred to as 'the blacks' camp'. From there, Aborigines with a reason to approach the house might go to the kitchen door, or, like the old men she describes as lounging comfortably on the woodpile well away from the house, she draws on the imagery of American and Caribbean slave plantations and the established vocabulary used to demean and degrade those who were without civil rights. Here, the phrase 'the nigger in (or on) the woodpile' marks a real boundary, unpassed without a specific reason or invitation. For those on the Aboriginal side of the racial divide theirs was a world of always impending, if not actual, violence, a world in which survival demanded great care. It was a segregated system, however, in which those living just beyond the boundaries of the settlement inevitably knew far more about the activities of the owners and workers than was known about them. Despite this, pastoralists became a major source of (mis)information about the inherent nature of Aboriginal people, their alleged laziness and their resistance to change.

While the distance between the two social worlds granted some respite from surveillance to Aboriginal workers and their families, the boundaries of their camps were open to all seeking women for sex. It was common that a woman's refusal to co-operate would lead to threats to sack her husband, or kill him; or alternatively, to take a younger sister or daughter instead.

As might be expected, the names of the pastoralists and pastoral workers who enjoyed the sexual relations of the pastoral zone are not always recorded and indeed, are usually ignored as respectability beckons. One such beneficiary was Lewis Alexander Bloomfield (1870–1944) who had left home aged fourteen, initially working with his half-brother on Todmorden Station in South Australia and Henbury (from 1887) in the Northern Territory. By 1908 he was able to buy a half-share in Loves Creek Station. His wife from 1911 was Lillian Myrtle Kunoth with whom he had a son and three daughters, all of whom married into the established, respectable, pastoral families.

Baden Bloomfield's mother had been Jessie, a young woman whose father was Walter Parke, one of two brothers who took up Henbury Station. Jessie then had three more children with her husband, Ungwanaka. She also had Johnson Breaden, fathered by Allan Breaden. She kept house for Allan and her son Johnson on Idracowra Station. Jessie was not the only woman with whom Lewis Bloomfield had relations – he had a daughter, Susie, with Leisha. Of the intricacies of these relationships, the linguist T.G.H. Strehlow noted that Jessie, a woman of great natural charm and dignity, 'had always been in a difficult marital position'.

> *Being a half-white woman, she had always been expected to live with any white station man who might take a fancy to her. Generally the man who had the first right to her would have been the station owner or manager himself, or else the white head stockman. None*

> *of these men, who enjoyed supreme authority over the station and its inhabitants, would ever have dreamed of legally marrying her.*[7]

In any case, such marriages were frowned upon, sometimes needed permission from the government, and were often illegal. Fortunately, many Aboriginal men fathered children abandoned by property owners, managers or workers. There was no Indigenous concept of illegitimacy. There are many such stories, often passing unnoticed, their content and consequences softened by scholarly or literary language, or simply omitted in order not to shame the colonial families involved or their descendants.

The presence of a pastoralist's wife in the main house did not stop these practices. Sometimes the children of Aboriginal women were acknowledged by their non-Aboriginal fathers, usually not. These were the 'free and easy' sexual relations that in the Top End the pastoralists fought to maintain by excluding women. The strength of the racial divide in the Territory from the 1870s onwards is illustrated in Mounted Constable Willshire's writings, as is his obsession and hatred of the children of European fathers by Indigenous women. He was one of many who opposed any breach of the racial divide as it would blur the essential differences between the two peoples that justified his violence. The social chasm between colonists and Aborigines and the skin-colour code that so many in the Territory adhered to required separation and segregation. Like many, Willshire saw the children of European men by Aboriginal women as bearers of the worst characteristics of both categories of person.

While tales of Aboriginal laziness circulated widely, with laziness being seen as a racial characteristic, much labour on the big stations was carried out by Aboriginal people, both inside the house and out, both skilled and unskilled. On some of the big stations there could be hundreds of Aboriginal workers. The presence of workers' families in the station camps provided a widely accepted excuse for refusing to pay wages, giving instead meagre quantities of 'rations', usually provided by the government – the tea, flour and sugar supplemented by the unwanted portions (head and feet, perhaps) of any animal slaughtered for the house or the non-Indigenous workers. The women in the Aboriginal camps, whether they worked in the house or not, as well as those associated with drovers (some of whom were women, some children) remained at continual risk of violation.

It was a pattern that suited the big pastoral companies and corporations very well. Vestey Brothers Ltd, the British cattle company, offers a good example of the kind of corporate autonomy within the pastoral zone that became normal. When in 1911, succumbing to the fantasies of great fortunes to be made in the north, the Commonwealth Government took control of the Northern Territory from South Australia, they allowed the secretive family company, Vestey Brothers Ltd, to show how it could be done. They sold vast regions to Vestey Brothers at very low rates. Between 1914 and 1916 the Vesteys were able to lease 36,000 square miles at 5/- per mile. Geoffrey Gray found that: 'Unwitting or not, this policy also placed companies such as Vestey outside the control and sanctions of government agencies concerned with Aboriginal welfare and the upkeep of the land'.[8] This was nothing new and suited the government. Indeed, it is an example of how a government benefits from a façade that appears to prevent them from seeing or knowing the consequences of government actions and policies. Alex Kruger has recorded the difficulty he had when he plucked up the courage to ask the Bloomfields of Loves Creek Station for wages.[9] Most pastoralists staunchly opposed paying wages to Aboriginal workers who, in any case, in 1911, had any money paid to them given to a government Protector or his nominee. What was wanted was a form of slave labour (which Matt Savage had taken for granted) with regulations that prevented people from absconding. It was a system that made sure that the labour that converted Indigenous Country to colonial property did not have the same effect for Aboriginal labourers.

Although seeming to be beyond the control of government, Vestey exercised a good deal of control over their borders, controlling access to their outstations and dependent settlements. Their property was very private. They kept relatively few records, Geoffrey Gray found, and were not good at sharing them; they had absolute power within their boundaries, absolute power over the Aboriginal labour force on which they relied.

the Vesteys never saw the report although Elkin sent a copy to the Territory's Director of Aboriginal Affairs. A version of the report resulting from an investigation into Vestey's labour practices (from August 1944 to March 1946) by the anthropologists Ronald and Catherine Berndt, was eventually published as *End of An Era*, but not until 1987. The precise causes of the delay in publication are, as Gray says, messy. It was due in part to fear of the Vesteys' economic and political power and a belief that accusations against Vestey could lead to court, in part to delays originating through amendments sought by A.P. Elkin (Professor of Anthropology at the University of Sydney).[10]

A detailed analysis of Vestey, anthropology and government policy has had to wait on Geoffrey Gray's *Abrogating Responsibility? Vesteys, Anthropology and the Future of Aboriginal People*, published in 2015. But it shows how important the pastoral zone has been in creating the conditions that produced vast profits for a global company based in England using a largely unpaid and denigrated workforce, while at the same time treating their unpaid labour force and their families with brutal contempt. But it was not just under the Vesteys' rule that the practices of the pastoral zone flourished. Smaller properties display the same patterns of racialised, brutal violence, a brutality that forges a culture that necessarily affects colonists as well as Indigenous Australians. It is inevitable that a regime of brutal violence brutalises its perpetrators, just as predatory sexual violence affects all aspects of the nature of colonial men, perpetuating forms of male sexuality that reverberate across the pastoral zone and into concepts of masculinity practised outside it.

Because careful studies of life in the pastoral zone are few and far between, the lives recorded within those few are generally set within the framework of popular myths of pioneering male heroism and triumph, together with heroic self-defence from 'savage natives'. A recent account prepared by Rick Morton, *100 Years of Dirt*, offers a different story, one that shows how life on huge cattle stations in the north-east of South Australia could make brutal owners and managers into brutal husbands and fathers. From the 1930s George Morton owned the vast Pandie Pandie Station built upon Karanguru country. Eventually they held about 30,000 square kilometres, some of it on the 'channel country' that feeds into the rivers that in turn feed Katithanda-Lake Eyre. In the nineteenth century these were lawless lands. In the time of George Morton, his grandson Rick says, Pandie Pandie Station, held by the Morton family for 70 years, was like a prison inside which George could do as he wished – and what he wished was violence against his family and those working for him. His kingdom, Rick says, was built on terror, his victims were his wife and children.[11] There was no escape and no-one to come to their rescue. It is not clear why George Morton was such a terrible man but his was violence that ruined those within his reach. While not all pastoralists were men like George Morton his actions were enabled by common fantasies of male entitlement to control, absence of retribution, and of course, the racialised social life within the pastoral zone that made violence such a very ordinary part of daily life. As is shown in a case on Eva Downs that came before the court in 1955 (mentioned in the Prologue), such patterns of segregation, violence and sexual abuse have been hard to shift, persisting into the 1950s.

Chapter Forty

A Zone of Indigenous Policing

Two forms of policing operated within the colony – one used the legal codes of British parliamentary law that applied to all equally (more or less), the other operated through a series of understandings, known sometimes as the *policies* that have already been mentioned, policies that applied only to the policing of the Indigenous owners of Country being converted to colonial property.[1] The aims and methods used in each were very different. One was intended to protect colonial life and property through parliamentary laws and regulation; the other was murderous in intent, relying on a partnership of pastoralists, volunteers and police that resembled an irregular militia force.[2] That partnership created the distinct Zone of Indigenous Policing that was separated out from the parliamentary laws governing the rest of the colony along a strictly enforced racial divide. It would be a mistake to imagine that acts carried out within the Zone of Indigenous Policing were unlawful. They were not and their legality could be, on occasion, challenged. But, as attempts to challenge those operating in the police zone through the courts of law show, penalties for police and settler violence *against* Indigenous Australians were almost non-existent.

The failed nineteenth century prosecution of Mounted Constable Willshire for murders committed on Tempe Downs Station illustrates the point; the 1955 case on Eva Downs demonstrates how the extraordinary nineteenth-century sense of impunity that saved vicious colonists from prosecution continued on into the twentieth.

It remains evident today in the readiness of police to shoot unarmed Aboriginal citizens like Kumanjayi Walker, shot in his home at Yuendumu in the Northern Territory.[3] The pastoralists and leaseholders of land in the Territory had been happy to raise funds for Mounted Constable Willshire's bail and to employ the best legal brain possible, Sir John Downer QC, a member of parliament from 1878 until 1901. Under political pressure it was Police Commissioner von Peterswald in Adelaide who had authorised much of the work of Willshire, and Inspector Brian Besley who had put six men as Native Police under Willshire's control in November 1884, despite knowing about Willshire's methods on Undoolya Station and elsewhere. In ordering Inspector Besley to place the Native Police under Willshire, von Peterswald took the precaution of writing to Richard Chaffey Baker, Minister for Justice in the Colton government, to advise him of the steps he had taken.[4] In a farcical trial, Willshire was allowed to question Arrernte witnesses for the prosecution in their own language, translating their answers for the benefit of the court. With such support it is not surprising to find Willshire acquitted and allowed to return to duty. Willshire's trial is just one demonstration of the way in which the details of the 'clearances' in the Territory were far from secret; they came about as a result of a chain of command that began with politicians, then passed along the line. Willshire was an appalling character but his methods were instigated, condoned and unleashed from Adelaide.

Running in tandem with such practices, those First Nations people who actually lived to face the courts of the general zone of law (for killing a colonist or a cow, for example) were given short shrift and treated very harshly. They could find themselves facing evidence fabricated by police or pastoralists, forced confessions, further violence while awaiting trial, flawed and prejudicial court procedures, deeply prejudiced juries, and lazy or improperly acting judges like Judge Wells. And they could be shot while allegedly absconding from their captors.

The methods of policing used against the First Nation people of the colony differed from those authorised under parliamentary laws and regulations. In the Indigenous Zone of Policing a police investigation might be triggered by an offence – a theft, an assault or a murder, for example – but an actual offence was not required. The pursuit of an alleged criminal could be carried out either by a single officer accompanied by his trackers, or by a posse that could include police officers, pastoralists and other station-workers, as well as trackers. Collective guilt was assumed. Information about supposed miscreants could be obtained through force and torture; magistrates, courts and lawyers were avoided wherever possible, but where they became involved they acted in accordance with the interests of pastoralists and other colonists. Often, the police acted as judge and jury and as is plain in the Territory, very often as executioners. In some cases, policing and punishing was carried out by proxy, by station managers and employees acting alone who were able to do so largely free from fear of prosecution. And most importantly, a key plank in the structures of Indigenous policing was the replacement of the crucial 'presumption of innocence' by a 'presumption of guilt'. Perhaps because it is even less visible than violent acts and compromised legal and political processes, the reversal of that common presumption of guilt has been a most difficult aspect of police, legal and public behaviours to undo. It is still to be found in play today, as arrest and jail rates for First Nations Australians are among the highest in the world.

When played across the pastoral zone, the methods used in the zone of Indigenous policing ensured that Indigenous subjects of the Queen in England had no civil rights or personal protection of life or limb and no access to money or the economy of everyday life. When required to work, those fleeing the violence could find themselves hunted and returned to their 'boss'. This led to what might legitimately be compared to the 'lynch laws' of America as practised in the 1870s in the wake of their Civil War. As in Australia, the spectacular killings, tortures, burnings and rapes of African-Americans seen in the United States were intended to terrorise as well as to demonstrate to both to its victims and the perpetrators themselves, the superiority of forms of colonial masculinity and the god-like powers that came with it. In

South Australia the race-based methods of policing interlocked neatly with the pastoral zone that was coming into being at the same time. Its success can be seen in its longevity, sustained by the economic and political interests that brought it into being and the continuing salience of widespread assumptions about race and the superiority of being a white-skinned bearer of a superior, Christian, civilisation.

Because of its transgressive qualities, a distinct Zone of Indigenous Policing dedicated to the destruction of Indigenous resistance to colonisation could not have emerged without the support and consent of the more powerful among the colonists – the most senior officers of the police, elected politicians and their senior public officials, judges and lawyers, wealthy pastoralists and financiers, newspaper owners and, most importantly, a public among whom were many willing to look away from what was happening in front of their eyes. Because they were so directly involved in many different capacities in policing Indigenous Australians (as Protectors, for example) the most important members of that coalition on the ground were the senior officers of the police force who commanded their junior officers and the armed Aboriginal police working as trackers, guides and negotiators.

*****

The colony's Commissioner of Police, responsible for policing the entirety of the colony, was based in Adelaide over 3000 km away from Darwin and 1500 kilometres from Alice Springs.[5] The most senior police officer in the colony's Northern Territory was German-born Inspector Paul Foelsche who answered most directly to the Government Resident in Darwin and only after that to the Commissioner in Adelaide if they felt it to be really required. The two together could act as a kind of filter. While not responsible for policing the whole of the Territory, Foelsche is important because he worked effectively with the government's official Resident Administrators in Darwin, holding his post from 1870 until his retirement in 1904; and also because, helped by the telegraph line, his managerial and political reach was so extensive.[6]

While Foelsche was formally charged with policing the Top End of the colony, the policing of the district of 'Central Australia' was carried out by officers who reported first to an Inspector based in Melrose in the Flinders Ranges and later in Port Augusta. From 1881 until his death in 1894 aged 58 years, that office was held by English-born Inspector Brian Charles Besley (1836–1894).[7] It was on Besley's watch that Mounted Troopers Willshire and Wurmbrand and their helpers were allowed to kill, maim and rape all around Alice Springs without fear of retribution. Both officers had worked directly to Inspector Besley. If Constable Wurmbrand excelled in writing reports full of lies and deception, Willshire took the precaution of refusing to keep any records at all. When Besley asked him to 'reconstruct' the missing journals required by police regulations he refused; complaints against him from Hermannsburg's missionaries he dismissed as lies. Besley's half-hearted efforts to get Willshire to make his reports seemed to sink without trace, little more than efforts to cover his own back in case of need.[8] Although also appointed as a Protector of Aborigines, Besley was always ready to defend his officers from charges of murder and violence, including Constable Wurmbrand's 1884 murder of three Arrernte men while they were chained at the neck in Glen Helen Gorge. Besley joined Stipendiary Magistrate H.C. Swan and the missionary C.E. Taplin sent to the Finke River to find out what the Lutheran missionaries at Hermannsburg were complaining about. They found nothing amiss.[9] In the course of that investigation, Besley sent Wurmbrand's entirely improbable report of the killings to Commissioner Peterswald in Adelaide marked 'for perusal' rather than for investigation.[10] Peterswald noted it and put it away.

Inspector Besley was one of a well-connected colonial Catholic family. His sister Amelia married Frank Gillen who was in charge of the Alice Springs Telegraph Station from 1875, the man who helped with the charges laid against Mounted Corporal Willshire that were heard in Port Augusta. Brian Besley's brother, Jack, worked for Gillen; Amelia Gillen's stepbrother, Patrick Byrne, was on the Charlotte Waters Telegraph Station, while a cousin was in charge at Tennant Creek.[11] When Besley died in Port Augusta the obituaries could not have been kinder, his funeral more lavish. After a mass at the Catholic cathedral in the morning, the funeral procession to the cemetery after lunch was half a mile in length. Led by the Police band playing the 'Dead March' from Handel's *Saul* and a contingent of mounted police, then came fifty-four foot police and two Aboriginal Trackers, with the hearse accompanied by Commissioner of Police W.J. Peterswald and two of his Inspectors. Then came Besley's horse saddled with his boots reversed and led by an Aboriginal Tracker. The 'chief mourners' were followed by three Catholic priests, a procession of a hundred children from the Sisters of Mercy school, a contingent of civil servants, and then members of the general public on foot. They in turn were followed by vehicles carrying representatives of five District Councils, forty traps and buggies carrying local residents, friends, and two members of Parliament representing the government. After the service at the graveside had been read the Police Band played 'Go Bury Thy Sorrow', a hymn not so often heard now but popular at the time.

The public acclamation of press and politicians, Besley's obituaries and his funeral with such a substantial police presence marks the great satisfaction he gave in presiding over some of the worst years of violence in the district of central Australia for which he had been responsible. It also demonstrates the linkage of violence within the Zone of Indigenous Policing with the upper ranks of the Police Force, with politicians of great distinction, and a range of important public officials.

Nevertheless it was Inspector Foelsche who was the most effective of the two Inspectors, he who took over Willshire's management from Besley, sending him out to Gordon Downs. Foelsche was not averse to joining a posse himself if he felt his presence could be camouflaged. A religious man (born into the Lutheran faith but turning to the Wesleyan Methodist church on marriage), a Freemason, and very good at languages, Paul Foelsche is now most remembered for his skill as a photographer of the Indigenous peoples of colonial Darwin and for his odd personality, with his policing practices safely lodged in a remote past.[12] His notes on Aboriginal society were respected but his interest in Aboriginal people was, Gordon Reid noted, 'quite detached and he never showed sympathy for the position of the Aborigines, whose land was being appropriated by strangers'.[13] It was Foelsche also who, while he may not have invented it, put into circulation the infamous phrase 'a picnic with the natives' as a euphemism used to gloss over punitive expeditions or massacres.[14] In 1875 when conflict on the Roper River led to the death of the station-master and the wounding of two others, Foelsche authorised a punitive search and attack party by issuing ambiguous orders that left the party free to act as they pleased.[15] And they did. In 1878, when Police Trooper William Stretton led a revenge party that shot seventeen Aborigines allegedly resisting arrest, Foelsche would tell his close friend, the pastoralist and politician John Lewis, that 'he could not have done better than Stretton during his "nigger hunt"'. He was, he said, satisfied with the outcome 'and so is the public here'.[16]

Foelsche may have spent much of his time in Darwin rather than in field operations but he was the man at the top of the police force in the Northern Territory, the man who presided over the long years of violence and terror unleashed around him, and the man who shifted his officers from policing according to the law to policing according to his own 'policy'. In doing so, Foelsche brought into formal existence the extreme version of the Zone of Indigenous Policing that characterised the last three decades of the nineteenth century in the Territory.

Despite Foelsche's benign public reputation, in investigating his role in the violence unleashed upon the Territory's Indigenous peoples Tony Roberts came to the conclusion that Foelsche was the man who had 'masterminded more massacres in the Territory than anyone else', his willingness to do so bolstered by his 'capture dead or alive' orders and instructions to act 'without waiting to be molested'.[17] Foelsche was a man who was, Roberts concluded,

cunning, devious and merciless with Aboriginals, yet he was supported by every South Australian government from the founding of Darwin in 1870 until his retirement in 1904, when King Edward VII honoured him with the Imperial Service Order. Kaiser Wilhelm

> gave him a gold medal, possibly for the specimens and written material on Aboriginals he sent to museums in Germany. Some considered him an expert on Aboriginals, not knowing the skulls he studied were not merely collected by him.[18]

*****

Regardless of how cunning and devious he was, such a man could not act alone – he had to be permitted to make that shift from legal civilian police practice to that of the anticipatory, punitive, delivery of terror. His actions were not only not secret but were called for and lauded in the press. He received support from the local newspaper, from the Government Resident in Palmerston and, while never receiving any promotion, had tacit support from the government in Adelaide through his friends – men like the politicians John Lewis, Richard Chaffey Baker and Vaiben Solomon.[19] Baker was a long-standing and influential politician, knighted and deeply involved in the federation negotiations, who had extensive pastoral and mining interests in the colony.[20]

Foelsche's response to the Mangarrayi attack of June 1875 in which several telegraph linesman from the Daly Waters Telegraph Station (c. 600 km from Darwin) were wounded and one killed, is an example of how action in the Territory articulated with the institutions of government, the first of these being the structure of the police force itself. Foelsche's orders to his officers followed directly on instructions issued from Adelaide. There, Police Commissioner George Hamilton had authorised what Amanda Nettelbeck has described as 'anticipatory' policing, the effective legalisation not only of punitive forms of policing but also of punishments meted out before any offence had been, or might have been, committed. It was a crucial step in establishing a specific zone of law quite outside of normal legal practice, one specifically governing the policing of Indigenous Australians that was indeed an incubus.

In the Daly Waters case there was no question of anticipating the crime. It had already been committed and what was wanted was vengeance. Predictably, the *Northern Territory Times* was demanding that any of the attackers who could be shot should be, and that any of the culprits who were caught should be hanged from the nearest tree.[21] The newspapers of the Northern Territory have often been active in stirring up public support for harsh treatment of Aborigines as well as in generating government support and public sympathy for the colonists. Although Territory newspapers changed hands many times during those years they usually required or received financial backing from established pastoral and mining interests based in Adelaide. With such a small population it was inevitable that wealth and government overlapped, the one leading to the other. In the South Australian House of Assembly of 1888 the Territory was given two seats. A former Resident of the Territory, J.L. Parsons, held one, while from 1889 Vaiben Louis Solomon, owner and editor of the influential *Northern Territory Times and Government Gazette* from 1885, held the other.[22]

Solomon's political attitudes, expressed in strongly racist terms, are most often connected to his belief that Chinese immigration to the colony should be restricted. His views intensified as the Top End entrepreneurs found they no longer needed Chinese labour on the goldfields nor to help build the railway line from Palmerston out to the Pine Creek diggings. Solomon's anti-Chinese language was often virulent, eventually feeding into the first legislation of the federated Commonwealth states that from the beginning framed the new nation as 'white'. There is less comment concerning Solomon's views on how Aboriginal Territorians should be treated although a published article gives the flavour of them. In referring to the Daly River massacre that followed in the wake of an Aboriginal attack on some miners, he wrote that:

> *Of course it is simple for fireside humanitarians to blacken the fair names of our poor dead settlers, by attributing these murders to retaliation by natives for outrages committed upon their women, but such slurs are utterly false. The natives are not moral – far from it. They trade their womankind without the slightest scruple ... murders [among them] are of monthly occurrence ...*[23]

The *Northern Territory Times* was staunch in supporting the bloody response.

*****

The sadism and brutality of many of the men involved in colonising the Top End of the territory has often posed a problem for historians, particularly as many of those men and many of the clean-handed beneficiaries of the violence are honoured for their achievements and respectability. Foelsche's friend, Richard Baker, for example, personally approved the dispatch of four punitive parties in 1884, arming them with government guns and ammunition that the Government Resident in Darwin issued to them. When Superintendent of Telegraphs the deeply religious Charles Todd, and Ebenezer Ward, the colonial government's Minister for the Northern Territory, both urged the government to send out a punitive expedition against the people living along the Roper River.[24] The role of the rich and politically powerful in the violence of their minions needs to be understood for what it reveals of the great harms done.

A clearer view of the causes of the violence and intentions of the colonists shows how quickly the good intentions of the colony's English backers and the first waves of emigrants vanished when private property and cheap labour are the key to great powers, status and wealth; it reminds us of how time so quickly papers over uncomfortable knowledge of the most terrible of deeds, and it shows what religious people of good education and impeccable social standing were prepared to have done in their name in order to build the new world that was intended to be so much better than the old. The role of the rich and powerful in initiating and condoning the methods of taking land also shows up their assumption and determination that the new world should be their world, not the world of the First Nations peoples forced off their lands.

The coalition of powers in Adelaide allowed the deadly work carried out within the Zone of Indigenous Policing to continue in a systematic alliance that could not be easily undermined. It was a set of institutions that were a part of the colonial government that formed a system that supported, in turn, a racially defined society with a free-wheeling, free market, nineteenth-century form of unregulated capitalism. This was a system that could not be easily undermined by the efforts of the religious, philanthropic and charitable organisations dedicated to trying to protect Indigenous lives and interests. This was the more so because of the religious beliefs and culture of missionary stations that removed or reduced the legal rights of the people they intended to help and protect.

Chapter Forty-One

The Mission Zone

William Cawthorne's moving painting shows girls from the Anglican Native School in Adelaide on their way to Sunday church service in 1846. Any one among them could have been married young to a boy of the Protector's choice and sent to Poonindie mission settlement, or to work as a servant in an Adelaide household.

Cawthorne has illustrated the tragedy of colonisation as he observed it in 1846 – of young women walking in disciplined pairs accompanied by a male guardian in top hat and formal jacket. Dressed in the clothing they would have made themselves to cover their customary nakedness, exhibiting their mission-learned comportment, the girls are watched by men on the sidelines, men remaining outside the zone of colonial law yet within it, their bodies dressed in their customary manner. They do not speak. They watch their children walking away from them. These were the young women on whom missionary evangelising had come to focus, those imagined as being better off under the tutelage of missionaries rather than their parents. The young men, their brothers and cousins, are not there. Where were they on this Sunday in Adelaide? Cawthorne's painting shows how very important the control of the bodies of Indigenous women had become in attempts to civilise, evangelise and create the future envisaged for them in the new colony.

*****

In addition to the reign of colonial law that insisted that all in the colony lived under it with all equally entitled to its protections, missions came to operate as a third space of exclusion within the colony, a *mission zone* that took shape within colonial law and society. The shifts of intention and governance at Poonindie that moved it from a land-owning, wage-labour, relatively open evangelical model to one built on property-less, often unwaged labour, living under high levels of inmate surveillance and punishment' marked the opening up of a distinctive zone of exception. Myra Tonkinson's use of the concept of a mission as a 'closed society' describes an essential element of living there, one that contributed to the abuses that were often reported within it.[1]

Although encapsulated within English colonial law, the mission zone was governed quite differently from it. It is the separate but encapsulated space I refer to as a *zone*, an enclosed social world of its own characterised by a particular way of exercising power through surveillance and missionary control. Although its borders could be porous, borders nevertheless existed and could be enforced. In the mission zone, civil rights enjoyed by the colonists were severely circumscribed for the Indigenous people living there, often almost entirely absent. The evangelical effort in the Australian colonies may have been patchy but it was widespread and, however imperfectly, sustained. Its missionaries could not help but be deeply involved in the processes of colonisation regardless of what they saw of its effects, regardless of whether they saw themselves in providing a haven for a cruelly treated people, regardless of the actual services they provided or did not. Despite the opposition of pastoralists and many smaller landholders, South Australia became an evangelist's paradise for Christian churches as well as for 'faith missionaries' like Annie Lock – the independent individuals who felt called by God to embark upon an independent and personal mission unsupported by regular ecclesiastical funding and interference.[2] As the missionary presence expanded and retreated according to funding, available staff, and attitudes of the times, fundamental characteristics of the mission zone survived and developed.

Within the bounds of mission settlements the man of God was

also the man of mission government. The missionary stood as an all-powerful direct representative of the Christian God, a rather Old Testament incarnation of God the Father with a sacred father's rights and obligations. His was the right to make the laws by which the inmates would live; his was the right to punish or to forgive, to bar miscreants, to send them into permanent exile if he wished and to call for police support. Life on the mission was therefore realised within a theocratic mode of government in which, regardless of age, the Indigenous inhabitants were considered as children rather than as adults, with the powers of the missionary exceeding those available to those governing the rest of the colony.

As seen at Poonindie, the purpose of a colonial mission was always to create Christian individuals with the habits and monogamous families of the Christian civilised world in which the colonists believed they lived. No matter how deeply felt, stated intentions of benevolent protections, education and health care would always be secondary to the saving of souls and conversion and never equalled standards enjoyed outside the zone.

Again, as conversion to Christianity required accepting a new and very different moral code, the mission was a place within which the moral values of Indigenous Australians had to be re-shaped entirely. As a result, new ways of being a man, a woman, a husband, a wife, or a child also had to be learned. At the same time, a new convert's family life required entirely new ways of regulating and understanding hierarchies based on gender and the relationship of sexual intercourse to new social objectives rather than to those of the traditional alliances of male power. The moral reconfiguration sought by the missionaries therefore directed their attention and efforts not just to educating the mind but toward the presentation of the body, to ways of being an adult, to sex and sexual activity and procreation.

Because of its particular godly forms of governance and the scope for conversion, the mission zone became a place of intensive and intrusive surveillance, to which, of course, there was resistance but also a necessary accommodation. But in installing patterns of surveillance to help missionaries control and monitor intimate details of the lives of those living on the mission, a second consequence could emerge. Missionary engagement with the intimate and personal lives of those under their control produced the facts through which knowledge of Aboriginal life could be generated, transmitted and circulated as authentic truths. To some extent, mission administrations therefore controlled what others could know about what took place under their tutelage, they filtered knowledge, they shaped it through their own understandings of supposedly 'savage' life, as well as acting as gate-keepers, able to keep out undesirables, both Indigenous and those among the colonists (including anthropologists) wishing to work in their region. Here the Lutheran missionary focus on Indigenous languages helped.

Within the mission zone, the country on which it stood became property, just as in any other form of settlement and appropriation. It was made over to the mission in one form or another (by leasehold, gift, reservation) but never to the Aboriginal people living on their lands within the mission zone.[3] That exclusion from the wider property market has remained a feature of Indigenous land-holdings, which when finally they came through heritage and native title recognition were anchored onto a new form of communal title that aimed to prevent the sale of the land titles so hardly won.

In summary, the mission zone is a place in which almost unlimited powers are held within the person of the missionary and mission staff so as to create a theocratic space. Those powers are set to work in a project of re-making every aspect of the lives of those living under mission control. Such extreme changes to the fundamental structures of a way of life, its laws and customs, as well as to the sense of what it is to be a person and the presentation of the person through the body, cannot be brought about easily.

It should not come as a surprise to find that with so much focus on instilling new moral values relating to legitimate sexual behaviour and the difficulty of doing so, the authority of the missionary will lead readily into a system of discipline and punishment that at first sight appears alien to the teachings of Jesus, particularly in relation to Mary Magdalene in her medieval character as a repentant prostitute or sinner of some kind. Lisa Curtis-Wendtlandt's account of these forces working themselves out on the nineteenth century Lutheran mission settlement on the Finke River in Central Australia gives a picture of the complexities of life there when options for those living within the zone were in some ways somewhat limited.[4] In practice, when persuasion failed, when mission discipline was breached and when converts failed to conform to the approved sexual and other moral codes, discipline could be and was applied both to women and men. Penalties ranged from withholding food or care, to extra work, to penitential actions, to floggings for men, women and children, and to exile – a tragic punishment when one's family and livelihood remained bound to the mission.

The ways in which each mission wished to implement and manage its programmes varied according to local conditions, funding, the nature of the staff employed and the ways in which local people sought to engage politically with the colonial government in its missionary formation. Whether Catholic-inspired or Protestant, wealthy or poor, whether located in the far north of South Australia or on Ngarrindjeri country around the lakes at the mouth of the Murray River close to Adelaide, there are clear commonalities. As those commonalities emerged most forcefully around children, women, and the disciplining of the body according to the normative codes of the religious, they are critically important.[5] But the commonalities of the project of conversion and re-fashioning of an individual's moral code coupled with the authoritarian exercise of powers within the zone help in understanding why physical violence and sexual predation *within* the mission zone should so often accompany the violence and predatory sexual exploitation outside it that was just as regularly deplored.

The final characteristic of the mission zone, that it was an eroticised zone in which sex, violence and racism circulated in distinctive ways, is essential to reaching an understanding not only of the constant stream of accusations of moral collapse that still drive racialised government policies and practice, but also of the ways in which sex, gender, imagined cultural, moral and racial differences, as well as violence, play out in the colonising non-Indigenous peoples now living in Australia.

If Poonindie mission's drift away from a form of community village living to the authoritarian regime of disempowerment characterising its later administrators is set within the context of the general characteristics of the mission zone, its beginnings seem even more remarkable, while the later shifts appear as less than unexpected. Poonindie differed in some important ways from other missions, but not in others. It was not as if the first missionary there was without enormous power or did not employ a range of disciplinary measures. He did.

Reactions to accounts of any violence and sexual predation within the mission zone are often defensive. Many people like to think, in agreement with L.P. Hartley's constantly cited phrase that 'the past is a foreign country', that things were done differently then.[6] The immediate attraction and continuing resonance of Hartley's phrase comes from the way in which it encourages a sense that history is motivated by a hidden motor driving forward relentlessly, independent of human action. But as anthropologist Gillian Cowlishaw has pointed out, 'to claim that beliefs and activities are merely products of their time is to see human action as some automatic playing-out of an inevitable history that is created elsewhere, and to see our own part in oppressive relations as beyond our recognition.'[7]

Her view that such 'interpretations are an easy and complacent way of dealing with historical vicissitudes,' is a reminder of the ways in which colonial culpability is so easily blocked out of popular understandings of colonisations, particularly when the present so often resembles that past that is supposedly 'different.'[8] There have always been other voices offering other options, other paths to follow, just as there are now. Poonindie's ruin is often explained in terms of the moral failure of those living there rather than as a consequence of authoritarianism, demoralisation, the pillaging of its resources and a lack of concern for the well-being of its people by the Church of England.

Most commonly, missions are defended by pointing immediately to all the good that was intended and done, to lives saved from the horrors of the world outside, to the role of the mission as sanctuary and the missionary as protector, to the mission's essential benevolence, to their important role in recording the customs, beliefs and languages of the people under their charge, and to the benefits to the soul of the gift of Christ. Recent polarising commentary that attempts to weigh up numbers of lives saved, to detail the consequences of cultural destruction, or to estimate whether or not the good outweighs the bad misses the point. Nor do regular assertions like those of the anthropologist, Kenelm Burridge, that at least 'they tried' help.[9] It was *what* they tried to do that lies at the heart of the matter rather than whether they did it well or poorly, or kindly or horribly. The missions were very much a part of the wider colonial society, working in a privileged space excised from colonial law through which they were allowed to impose the drastic projects of transformation intending to bring into existence entirely new persons. Being re-born in Jesus so as to take the path to eternal life, becoming the new person who was to live in the new world, and learning that regular labour is a form of prayer, meant your previous life and world was being torn apart. These are in essence violent processes projected onto the bodies of those within the mission zone that were strongly resisted but which had to be accepted as part of life in it. How people dealt with it varied.

Indigenous engagement with life in the mission zone had to deal both with the physical and sexual violence through which it was constituted and applied to them, as well as with the government and personal practices originating outside the zone. The ways in which those living within the mission zone dealt with these regimes, the politics of moral re-fashioning, their opportunities and attempts to engage strategically with the powers being exercised upon them, and the intellectual, philosophical and theological reckonings made as circumstances within and beyond the mission zone shifted, are not always documented. When they are, they are often extraordinary in their theological and political creativity, pragmatic and tactical in their efforts to survive, and subtle in their deceptions and avoidances.

The creation of colonial mission zones necessarily took place within the spread of the forces of dispossession – the taking of the land, the too common ruination of Country through pastoralism and inappropriate forms of agriculture, and the destruction of the Indigenous economy. The educational practices within the mission zones were generally intended to provide a pathway into the encapsulating capitalist economy. Schooling of a kind (rarely up to the standard of equivalent schooling outside the zone), agricultural labouring skills, household skills, and habits of work and cleanliness were generally provided in some form. The crucial elements required for the new economy – land ownership, the transformative effect of labour and wages on it – were missing. Where lands within a mission zone became productive they also became desirable to colonists. Land made productive through Aboriginal peoples' labour could become a commodity just as did productive land within other domains of the colony. The difference between labour in capitalism and *Indigenous labouring* in a colony was that only within the economy of capitalism could labour perform its task of transforming land into property; only within the economy of capitalism could labourers become independent wage earners (no matter how poorly paid) with a proper stake in it. As was the case with the Anglican mission at Poonindie, the labour applied to making land productive within a mission zone created mission property that could then be transferred back into the general colonial economy.

Many years later, the same discounting of Indigenous labour occurred when the Jesuits at Daly River in the Northern Territory took the same step. In an outline of the disposal of the considerable mission assets involved there when the mission was closed and sold up, Deborah Bird Rose wrote:

> *The mission was brought to an abrupt and unexpected end in mid-1899 by a decision made by the European Superiors of the Australian Jesuits. By 1899 the mission consisted of a large house, a church and school, dormitories, native houses, stables, a printer,*

granary, and steam engine for the irrigation system. There was a sawmill, wells, pipelines, shed stores, and forges. The mission had 2000 goats, 150 cattle, 130 pigs, and 33 horses. And then, over a period of a few days in July 1899, the Aborigines were dismissed, the buildings they had helped to construct were dismantled, and the livestock they had helped herd were sold off. I would guess that the irrigation was cut off to the gardens they had worked as their own. In short, the work of their lives was put out for sale. The former mission was purchased by a well-to-do cattle baron: gardens, irrigation, buildings, livestock – all the product of the labour of Aboriginal people (along with the missionaries) became the property of others'.[10] The Catholic church tried to do the same thing with the cattle station built up with Aboriginal labour and promised to them by the missionaries on their settlement at Bidyadanga (then La Grange) in Western Australia; only spirited opposition from Fr Kevin McKelson prevented it.[11]

These same practices live on in the present, shaping the lives and futures of Indigenous peoples. Dr Maggie Brady gives a very clear picture of the life of mission surveillance and manipulation involved in shifting various Great Victoria Desert peoples from the permanent waters and convenient transport of the passing trains of Ooldea to what was seen as the grey dust of Yalata in order to keep them safe from radiation sickness arising from atomic tests carried out at Maralinga. 'The United Aboriginal Mission Station at Ooldea was closed', she says,

> *a portion of their land was appropriated for atomic test sites at Emu and Maralinga, and the people were excluded from the sites and walking routes of their country. They were relocated further south, where new missionary carers, Lutherans, took them in and monitored their previously free-ranging mobility.*[12]

Brady's account of the ways in which they resisted, adapted and bent an unwelcome way of life to meet their needs is well worth reading.

Within the mission zone the colonial law of the land had severely limited application and those living within its boundaries had very limited rights. While those boundaries existed (as in the sentencing of people to exile or to specifying where individuals could or could not reside) they were not always marked by high fences or walls. They appeared to be open communities, but eventually outsiders came to need a permit to visit there while anyone regarded as undesirable (journalists and anthropologists in particular), could be excluded. Furthermore, the boundaries of the mission zone were never impermeable to the enforcers of the precepts of colonial law that was imagined as covering the colony in its entirety. If a police officer wished to call upon the mission in search of cattle thieves or for any other purpose, no permit to enter was required. Residents of the mission zone could readily find themselves on the way to court, to a leper 'colony', or to a magistrate hundreds of miles away from their own country. So if mission settlements were to be mapped, their boundaries should be imagined and drawn with a dotted line to emphasise the nature of that boundary: that it was open to most colonists but could be closed to the Indigenous inhabitants of the zone. Although individual missions could be run quite differently, in many cases Indigenous residents who left without permission risked being sent back to it and punished for breaking the rules. Whose rules? The missionary rules.

After Poonindie (founded in 1850) mission activity in South Australia moved first to Raukkan (Point McLeay) south of Adelaide on Ngarrindjeri country around Lake Alexandrina, followed by a decade of German Lutheran and Moravian missionary activity in the far north of the colony during the 1860s, first on Diyari country lying to the north of the Flinders Ranges and then more broadly. This was to prove something of a challenge. The country of the Diyari and their neighbours was regarded by the colonists as dry and desolate, known for its great salt lakes relying on occasional flooding rains flowing down the Diamantina River and Cooper's Creek. This was the country known today as the Lake Eyre Basin. Its limited water supplies seen in a good year made it very attractive to those moving north from the Flinders Ranges.

Part Nine

At the End of the Century

Chapter Forty-Two
Adelaide, 1880s–90s

Poltalingada Booboorowie (1830–1901), known to the colonists as
Tommy Walker, with his wife, Niledali, known as Ada Walker.
Painted by Oscar Fristrøm in 1894. Private Collection.
Art Gallery of South Australia.[1]

At the time that the worst of the violence of occupation was taking place in the Top End, public interest in Indigenous Australians in and around Adelaide had to some degree receded. The 'early days' seemed sufficiently distant to be safely in the past, to have become heroic, the financial hardships of the first forty years seemed to have been overcome, while the Kaurna, Ngarrindjeri and other local peoples were thought of as quietly fading away. They were included in the census figures that, difficult as they are to interpret now, show only just over three thousand Indigenous South Australians remaining in 1891, an unworrying number who were no longer troublesome to the colonists of Adelaide. A deep feeling of quiet colonial melancholy hangs over Fristrøm's 1894 painting of Poltalingada Booboorowie with his wife, Niledali. They stand so still as they look towards the painter, their faces finely realised but inscrutable. Around the time that Fristrøm painted this well-known couple, Adelaide's fortunes were rising. Although still small when compared to the towns of the east coast (in 1881 Sydney claimed 237,300 people), the number of colonists living in Adelaide increased from 103,942 in 1880 to 133,252 by 1891.[2]

Despite the prosperity of the 1880s turning into the severe economic downturn of the nineties, two things stand out from these years. One is the cultural diversity of the colonists – a heady mix of new and older emigrants who, apart from those locally born, as the census of 1891 reveals, came from just about everywhere. And second, an equally varied religious life – who else would be recorded as Zoroastrians other than the two people who hailed from the romantic lands of Persia? And what other colony founded so strictly on the basis of its being a province of England would find itself home to a total of fifty-seven different religious congregations, many of whom reflected the remarkable propensity of Protestants to fragment into the myriad churches and chapels that earned Adelaide its later title of 'city of churches'. It was from this nineteenth century diversity that the remarkable 'religious climate' of South Australia could grow.[3] Perhaps other colonies in the era of empire also contained this kind of vibrant mix of belief but in South Australia it stands as a distinctive contrast to the kind of society that by the 1950s it would become – largely monolingual, bland, comfortable with a kind of politically conservative liberalism supported by a political gerrymander, and pervasively 'English' in its attitudes, manners and ways of speaking. At least until the 1960s, many South Australians still called England 'home'. In a sense that has now been lost, England as 'home' had been such a part of the way in which Adelaide's young women were reared that it seemed absolutely natural. Despite being separated from England for five generations, as one of those young women stepping down from the train onto London's Victoria station I can testify to a feeling of homecoming intense enough never to have been forgotten.

By the last two decades of the nineteenth century, however, Adelaide had grown into a surprisingly cosmopolitan township that reflected the widely differing origins of the colonists. As in its beginning, the colony remained almost bilingual with German as well as English still widely spoken. In their own schools, the Lutherans used German as their language of instruction; among a prospering Jewish community both the English of the first emigrant Jews from England, the German of those arriving after the 1850s from the Baltic rim regions of northern Europe could be found; while the French of some of the merchants could all be heard.[4]

Therese Victorsen, early Jewish emigrant to South Australia from what was then part of Russia, now Germany. Photo: Jack Kauffman, private collection.

Many of the German-speaking Jewish emigrants got their start in small rural townships like Clare (the Victorsen family), Yorketown on the Yorke Peninsula (the Marcus family), the Judells in Orroroo and Kauffmanns in Truro. Feodor Heilbronn established himself as a general trader, hotelier and agent in the tiny railway settlement of Oodnadatta. Soon the small Adelaide Synagogue had to be enlarged.

The smaller number of Muslims, mainly connected to the cameleers and the northern transport networks, together with some who had arrived as servants to emigrants from other parts of empire, had a mosque in Gilbert Street that might attract up to a hundred worshipers for the important communal prayers, the Eid al-Fitr linked to the fast of Ramadan, and the Eid al-Adha, the Feast of Sacrifice commemorating Abraham's willingness to sacrifice his only son upon an altar.

There were also a few Chinese families engaged in commerce, the best known of whom became Miss Gladys Sim Choon who dealt in linens and fancy goods imported from China, with fireworks from the same source. Many of the first wave of the colony's Chinese were transient, simply landing at the tiny port of Robe in order to walk overland to the booming goldfields of Victoria using Aboriginal or colonial drovers as guides. Too poor to pay the poll tax demanded by the Victorian government, once the South Australians followed suit, that first wave of Chinese immigrants largely ceased. A second wave entered the colony through one of the northern ports to head to the goldfields at Pine Creek in the Top End in the 1870s. Hostility to them there was fanned by politicians in Adelaide but many stayed, giving Darwin its very different, tropical, Asian atmosphere. But unlike Melbourne, Adelaide never had an established Chinatown.

If a great deal of colonial wealth generated in these decades went back to England in the pockets of those who wished to established themselves there as prosperous gentlemen of leisure, in the good years of the 1880s there was enough money in the colony to create a life and a style for a colonial gentry. It was already customary for property owners to live in Adelaide, employing a manager to run and care for their stock. Many were able to live in large, comfortable houses built for entertaining as well as to house their large families and their visitors. Already built by F.H. Faulding in 1861, 'Wooton Lea' had an indoor swimming pool; later it was large enough to become the home of the Presbyterian Girls' College; Simpson Newland enlarged 'Undelcarra' in 1881 to make it the grand house it is today; Harry Ayers built 'Dimora' on the East Terrace of Adelaide's square mile, making the terrace an address of distinction; while with mining profits from Broken Hill, Charles Rasp was able to buy the substantial 'Willyama House' in the suburb of Medindie and add another twelve rooms to it. In North Adelaide, its characteristic mansions, often showing a mix of architectural styles, were also being built. The town was taking the shape familiar to today's residents – the small busy central shopping precinct that never quite filled the square mile of the city centre, the North, South, East and West Terraces that bounded it, North Adelaide across the river with its wide streets and then Medindie and Walkerville just a fraction further out, all with their share of substantial, gracious, houses, many still standing.

Then there were Adelaide's public buildings – a substantial Town Hall with a fine organ for concerts standing opposite the General Post Office built at the southern end of the overland telegraph line, while the cultural institutions of the town were lining up along North Terrace giving it the shape it retains today. There the National Gallery was opened by Princes Albert and George, there was a public library, a university founded from mining profits given by Walter Watson Hughes, and later a School of Mines (1889). Adelaide also had a Botanic Garden with a palm house built of glass and iron imported from Bremen, a Zoological Garden established on 6.5 hectares just across the river, a small lake created from the uncertain waters of the Torrens by the building of a weir and an elegant rotunda for concerts in the park beside it. In the town centre the new Adelaide Arcade with its shops, tea rooms, fountain and Turkish baths opened in 1885.[5] These institutions speak to the development of a busy cultural life in the town through which people sought to create the future by rebuilding the lives they had left behind in England and Europe, only better. After the hardships of the early years, money was being made from pastoral properties (sheep, cattle and horses), mining, agriculture, commerce and trade. Adelaide prospered in the boom years of the 1880s.

Despite the diversity of the population there were also rising conflicts around the nature of colonial society that were making concepts of race a flashpoint. The Chinese were particular targets, facing allegations of undercutting local businesses by using cheap labour. As noted earlier, much of the fear and hatred unleashed against the Chinese was just as likely to come from politicians and the wealthier members of society as from the poor. So as well as the descendents of the cameleers who had something of a monopoly on inland transport known collectively as Afghans, the colony had two other racial minorities in its midst, neither of whom appeared to be 'white'. By the 1880s, of the two, First Nation Australians appeared as the less alarming. A set of beliefs about their imminent demise, the removal and retraining of children, their segregation, and the savage methods of policing them pushed them out of sight, making it easy to put them out of mind. It was not that they were not seen, but they were seen in ways that made them easy to be overlooked.

All this activity – the building, the creation of personal fortunes and large families, the comfortable social life with its customs, entertainments, style and interest in the arts and education – marked the establishment of a wealthy class of property owners, professionals (lawyers and doctors), manufacturers and merchant traders. They were hard-working, enterprising, and often philanthropic in their commitment to serving the community and assisting those who were struggling or missing out altogether. They were often progressive in their social attitudes but by no means always, and they had a firm grip on the government of the colony.

*****

As the colony's capital city, Adelaide also housed its parliament. Granted self-government in 1857, a two-chamber parliamentary model was introduced, over which stood a governor appointed from England to represent the Queen and her interests. While non-British subjects had to be legally naturalised in order to vote in elections, all men regardless of wealth or education were joined to the franchise, including Aboriginal men. They elected the members of a House of Assembly. For the upper house, the Legislative Council, voters had to be property-holders, thus excluding most working men, a structure intended to protect the interests of the more prosperous. The voting qualification for the Legislative Council was based on the value of land owned freehold – £50 in 1894. Although the limited franchise for the Legislative Council was constantly challenged by members of the lower House of Assembly (forty times without success) South Australia was the last state to get rid of it, agreeing to do so only in 1973–5. The staunch resistance from the propertied and privileged members of colonial society is a good indication of the importance of the upper parliamentary house in maintaining their powers, their cultural interests and their 'Englishness'.

In his major history of the colony's early years, Douglas Pike noted that from its earliest days, 'independence and irresponsibility [among politicians] marched hand in hand'.[6] It was personal interest rather than ideological differences that created the shifting coalitions that bedevilled self-government. But from it emerged the later forms of government in Australia that Judith Brett sees as having grown from the early 'paternalism' of colonial settlement that is visible in South Australia, where originally, in the absence of a tax base, the early colony was funded not so much by private wealth as by governments.[7] The members of the upper house felt it proper that this system should continue. While the mix of religions in the colony was to some extent found among elected parliamentarians it was in the Upper House that members of the Church of England had a firm grip on the numbers. In it, conservative Anglicans, loyalists of England and empire, were strongly represented from the first – for the 1850s there were men like John Baker (whose religious sympathies actually lay with the Unitarians who denied the Trinity), Charles Harvey Bagot, Francis Dutton, John Morphett, John Bentham Neales, and Boyle Travis Finnis, first Premier of the colony in 1856; then Richard Chaffey Baker, Lancelot Stirling and George Hawker for example.[8] The Governors of the colony were Anglicans for over a century, apart from Dominick Daly, Irish and Catholic. While the opening of the first part of the Catholic cathedral in 1858 shows the growing wealth and congregation of Adelaide's Catholic congregation, the grip of Anglicans on political power can be seen in the religious affiliations of the premiers of the colony from 1856 until WW1. Ten were Anglicans (38%) which exceeded their numbers in the population during those years. Of the others, nine were Methodists, Baptist or Congregationalist, three were Unitarian/Anglican, along with one Jewish, one Presbyterian and two unknown.

In addition to the important role of Anglicans in the higher reaches of government, two other features of the colonial electorate stand out. The first is that Aboriginal men and women who were on the electoral roll were able to vote. There were not many of them, but they were there. In the 1890s, for example, Point McLeay-Raukkan mission on Lake Alexandria had a polling booth.[9] Their right to vote would be lost when the colonies federated to become states of the new Commonwealth of Australia in 1901, although those already on the South Australian roll remained there. The second is that after a long struggle, the colony's women were admitted to the electorate in 1894, earlier than elsewhere. They did not, however, receive the right to stand for election. That came much later and was not readily taken up. Here we see the strength of colonial gender roles that made women subordinate to men as well as creating middle class uncertainties about how women should behave in public, what they should be allowed to do and indeed, what powers they should be able to exercise over men, if any. Many assumed that women voting as wives or daughters would follow the lead of the head of the household. That made women voters less of a threat. But their entrance into the male world of public political decision-making was an altogether different matter especially as any change had to pass through the conservative halls of the upper house. It was not until 1959 that candidates for the Liberal and Country League, Joyce Steele in the lower house (member for Burnside) and Jessie Cooper (member for Central No.2) in the upper, would take their seats.[10] In their triumph, we can see the conservatism of Adelaide's culture and society that went hand in hand with elements of social progressiveness. In the 1880s and 1890s the cosmopolitan populace and a degree of wealth allowed votes for women, votes for Aboriginal Australians, a strong commitment to good works, early entry of women to the university and many other social reforms. What it could not do was come to grips with race, its effects and the kind of society that was being built.

Where, after all, did Aboriginal people stand in a cosmopolitan, colonial society with its variety of national origins, languages, religions, and social classes? The answer to this question is a short one. They were not seen as part of colonial society but as being entirely outside it – sometimes they were itinerant workers, sometimes confined within the zones of exclusion established on mission and pastoral stations, but more often they remained something of a curiosity, always on the margins of the imagined world of the colonists. Their position in the colony was organised along a racial border line that pushed them to the margins, onto land that no others wanted. Generally lacking private property of any kind and lacking a place within cosmopolitan Adelaide, the only space they could occupy in town was the street and from time to time, the parklands. Their presence in these spaces was always contested, controlled in part through the laws of vagrancy and public drunkenness. Sometimes there were performances of corroborees at public celebrations, but for most colonists, Aboriginal homes and lives lay out of sight, elsewhere. These consequences of landlessness and social and legal strictures mark a social boundary defined entirely by race. It was quite visible, but went largely unnoticed by those not disadvantaged by it.

*****

The Census of 1891 gives the Aboriginal population of South Australia, including the Northern Territory, as follows:

South Australia Proper	Males 1,661	Females 1,473	Total 3,134
Northern Territory	Males 12,849	Females 7,806	Total 20,655
			Grand Total 23,789

But even if the census figures were roughly correct, where were those people? Some were still to be seen in or around Adelaide, living on Country they continued to regard as their own. And although pushed further out as the town grew and despite high death rates, some of their living places remained in use for generations. The settlement by the Patawalonga River at Glenelg was not finally closed down until 1899 when, in August, the last of its inhabitants were sent off on the morning train to Milang. There, under the charge of Mounted Constable Tromson, they were walked to their own country at Raukkan on Lake Alexandrina, to be placed under the control of the missionary there.[11] Their Patawalonga camp was burnt. The clearance, prompted by 'drinking and begging habits', had made their presence undesirable. From that time there were to be no more camps at or near the city.[12] It became more usual to find Aboriginal people living and working in small settlements either around the city or around the small towns nearby, with large numbers based around Encounter Bay, Wellington and Goolwa.

From 1859 a number of Kaurna, Ngarrindjeri and some of the river peoples had chosen or been forced to live on the mission station at Raukkan, the mission established in response to the concerns of about the impact of colonisation on them. The Aborigines Friends' Association sent the Congregationalist teacher, George Taplin, to govern the mission to be known as Point McLeay. As the land granted to the mission by the government was always going to be too small to support the missionary, his family, mission staff, and the Indigenous people living there, life could become something of a struggle. By 1859 the opportunities to hunt, to seek out native plants, especially the reeds so important for food, housing and medicines had already become unlikely to offer self-sufficiency. The difficulty increased as more and more land was turned over to pastoralism. Raukkan was run along the lines of the other missions, a mix of discipline and teaching, labour and religious instruction. Not everyone wanted to live in that way.

One who did not was Polpalingada Booboorowie, a Ngarrindjeri man born in the 1830s and painted by Oscar Fristrøm. Known to the colonists as Tommy Walker, he visited the mission from time to time but chose to live outside its disciplinary restrictions. He preferred to work independently and to live among those others living and working from the small living-places around the town. It was he and his second wife, Niledali (known as Ada), who were painted by Oscar Fristrøm in 1894. Tommy Walker spoke English well, worked from time to time and may even have gone to the Victorian goldfields in the 1850s.[13] His trademark was a top hat worn at a rakish angle. As he walked around the town 'he assumed an air of conscious dignity'. He and his wife were well-known in Adelaide where he socialised, was sometimes arrested, and sometimes entertained an audience with his skills as a story teller and mimic. He is said to have entertained the crowds in the intervals during cricket and football matches. His mimicry of the magistrates he saw during his court appearances were greatly appreciated. He died in 1901.

Tommy Walker's body fell into the hands of the Coroner, Dr William Ramsay Smith, who removed the skull for scientific study.[14] The discovery of this defiling of his body caused a great storm among those who had known him. Members of Adelaide's Stock Exchange, from whose steps Tommy Walker had entertained members and passers-by, had paid for his headstone in the West Terrace cemetery. Now it seemed that his body was incomplete and had been sent to the University of Edinburgh. The *Adelaide Chronicle* published a long article about the matter titled 'Tommy Walker. He Rests in Pieces'. In it, is the suggestion that more than just the skull was missing and that very few of those Aboriginal people who had the misfortune to have died over the last twenty years had been buried with their bodies intact. The term 'body-snatching' was mentioned. In an era when evolutionary anthropology was in the ascendant, a board of inquiry found that the coroner's actions had been 'indiscreet' and that he had allowed his 'zeal in the cause of science to outrun his judgment'.[15] 'Ada Walker' was photographed for a lantern slide in later life, unclad, showing the facial hair that was commonly worn without shame by elderly women, her head hair cut short, perhaps in mourning or perhaps due to some kind of health condition. I should very much like to know who took the photograph and for what purpose. It is an image of the kind used in documenting racial differences; it may also have been used for display at meetings intended to illustrate the progress of missionisation for fundraising. In either case it is sad to see an elderly woman put on display as a specimen in such an undignified and powerless pose. In one sense, the forcing of this pose can be seen as coming out of the same kind of thinking that led to the collection of the bones and heads taken from Aboriginal bodies. This is an image from which all of Niledali's self has been removed. Dehumanising in its own way despite her strength and endurance.

The trajectory of Ngaiponi, Anglicised to David Unaipon, was very different. He is remembered now for his many accomplishments and writings although he, too, would suffer at the hands of William Ramsay Smith. As his father, James Ngunaitponi (1835–1907) had been one of Taplin's early converts, David, born in 1872, was educated on the Point McLeay-Raukkan mission station from the age of seven, growing to adulthood there. As a young man he found work as a servant, learned the trade of a bootmaking, later becoming the bookkeeper for the mission store. Unaipon is said to have spoken English with a Scottish accent, to have been a great public-speaker, to have dressed in a suit and tie and carried a cane, in other words, to have conducted himself in every way as an educated colonial man. Unaipon grew to be an effective advocate for his people's interests, as well as an inventor. Despite his abilities and qualities, both his writings and his inventions (among them a modification for the handpiece for shearing) were stolen from him. William Ramsay Smith's published account of Aboriginal mythologies, *Myths and Legends of the Australian Aboriginals*, was based on Unaipon's work but never acknowledged.[16] Unaipon's life was one of remarkable achievement despite the real difficulties in working within a political context in which Indigenous opinions about the value of Christianity and the value of their own beliefs were very uncertain. He was a gradualist, Philip Jones suggests, when it came to some aspects of social change although in his own life he seems to have grasped the changes with both hands, moving quite rapidly from

Point McLeay into a colonial world of music, philosophy, writing and preaching. Despite speaking English well, despite dressing impeccably and despite his interests, hard work and achievements, when looking for accommodation Unaipon had to face discrimination on the basis of race. Despite preaching the Christian gospel until he was 87, David Unaipon died in poverty.[17]

David Unaipon (1872–1967) *c.* 1908, State Library of South Australia

In David Unaipon we see a talented man who came up against the realities of race and racial thinking in a society based fundamentally on racial distinctions, one of which was skin colour, another of which were the great mythologies of blood as a carrier and transmitter of race. As a child of two Aboriginal parents, Unaipon could never achieve full whiteness even if he had wanted it; never quite achieve the effortless equality granted to other colonial Australians by birth alone, never achieve the recognition of his achievements that was so well-deserved.

*****

Racial thinking and the organisation of races into a hierarchy governed by skin colour and moral failure provides a convenient way of thinking about one's own superiority. It functions to give all of the superior race, regardless of any divisions created by wealth or poverty, a measure of superiority over those deemed to be members of an inferior race. It is a way of thinking that gives everyone someone to look down upon as a lesser being than yourself. Politically, this kind of thinking is very useful in building people of diverse backgrounds (like those living in and around Adelaide) into a unified nation or state.

Racial thinking has a second effect that is also politically useful. This comes from the way concepts of race obliterate other important social cleavages, like social class or religion. It does so by including working class people into the same group that the wealthy belong to. As the nineteenth century progressed society was imagined as a hierarchy of social classes: the Queen and a landed aristocracy at the top, then the upper gentry, the middle classes, then the working classes and perhaps the 'even lower'. They were all, in the Australian case, imagined as 'white' and all could be 'Australians' by virtue of being born white-skinned with a place within society granted solely on the basis of being born in South Australia. Because being part of the Australian white race included the white working classes, in a hierarchical society imagining itself as topped by a landed aristocracy that sat above a broad middle class who had to earn rather than inherit their wealth, with a largely uneducated working class having only its labour to sell into the market, racial thinking has no way of placing anyone below the working classes other than as slaves. They were those whose bodies as well as their labour could be bought and sold in the market, those who fell outside the structures of society unless admitted in specific roles that ensured they remained the property of their masters. It was a kind of thinking that attempted to remove all autonomy from a group of people through a set of government laws and practices.

This is what happened as the violence by which the colony was taken from Indigenous ownership created the new, white, racially superior, English Province of South Australia. In certain forms of economy, slave labour is the most profitable form of labour (for example on the cotton plantations of the American south) because even if inefficient it offers other benefits: an enslaved workforce reproduces itself by breeding and providing new young slaves for sale as a commodity; it provides slave-owning men with unlimited sexual access to women and children;

it provides domestic services, including child-minding; it provides a space of theatre for the exercise and demonstration of male violence and superiority; and it places the slave-owners in the position of a god who cannot be penalised, no matter what. While it is hard to come to terms with, the taking of South Australia and the treatment and thinking about Aboriginal people has some striking parallels with slave colonies in the nineteenth century. Capitalism has had great difficulty in weaning itself off slavery, and practices it still.

While the violence described in earlier chapters has been in focus most strongly in the Northern Territory, it was not confined to that region. It was found all over South Australia and in the other colonies. No matter how distasteful or disconcerting it is important to reckon with colonial violence because it is not a lamentable side-effect of colonisation but is central to it. The colony was built from it, and by it – the violence was the foundation of the colony, making theories of racial superiority and the 'rights of whites' a matter for continuing discussion whether polite or not. What is harder to acknowledge is that built into those violent foundations was a deep racial divide and the zones of exclusion through which Aboriginal lives were taken, lost and controlled. The new model of society created in South Australia had little place in it for the colony's First Nations citizens. They lived 'outside' it.

In one form or another, South Australia gave its First Nations citizens the choice of absolute assimilation or perpetual outsideness. They could enter into the 'Australia' of the new world by giving up their moral principles and religious beliefs, their independent way of life, language and with the help of suitable white men, by breeding themselves into whiteness – in short they would need to give up being Aboriginal. If you were not prepared to vanish into whiteness there would be no real place for you. In the meantime, we will take your children away and give them their chance to enter the bottom ranks of the colonial society by giving them new names and putting them in 'half-caste' institutions run either by missionaries or the government, or into good 'white' families who would teach them how to be white. It is easy to put these acts down to a kind of pervasive, often puritanical, religious righteousness encapsulated within the phrase, 'saving the children', but it is more helpful to try to think about them as acts of genocide or specific acts of racially inflected thinking that offers nothing to those living outside the supposed whiteness of colonial society, the whiteness that gave them their greatly cherished superiority. Racism can be very hard to see. Even harder to acknowledge. If you look closely though, and think carefully, Unaipon's life is an illustration of it at work in a cosmopolitan, religious and prosperous society. So is Tommy Walker's. Their lives also illustrate the resilience and determination in coming to grips with that often invisible and unnoticed colonial racism.

Chapter Forty-Three

Colonial Holocaust

Holocaust (1) A sacrifice wholly consumed by fire, a whole burnt offering; (2) A complete sacrifice or offering; a sacrifice on a large scale; Complete destruction by fire, or that which is so consumed: complete destruction, especially of a large number of persons; a great slaughter or massacre.[1]
Shorter Oxford English Dictionary

And Abraham rose up early in the morning, and saddled his ass, and took of his young men with him, and Isaac his son and clave the wood for the burnt offering, and rose up, and went to the place of which God had told him ... And Abraham took the wood of the burnt offering, and laid it upon Isaac his son; and he took the fire in his hand, and a knife; and they went both of them together ... Genesis 22: 3, 6 ff[2]

In order to speak about her research on Victoria River Downs Station, Deborah Bird Rose coined the word 'deathscape' to describe the violence of the 1880s and 1890s in the Top End of the Northern Territory. It is a good word to use as it refers directly to the scale and persistence of the killings there. But I have felt that in speaking of the violence and terror in the colonial Northern Territory described in earlier chapters a word focused on the mechanics of the deathscape, like 'holocaust', might be appropriate and helpful.

The word 'holocaust' is useful for example in summing up the totality of the events in the zones of exemption within which First Nations peoples have had to live for generations. The word itself has a Biblical basis (Genesis 22) that carries over to its secular uses and draws attention to the ritualistic aspects of the burning of bodies in colonial South Australia's zones of exclusion. Importantly, the word holocaust also calls to mind the massive twentieth-century European Holocaust.

It is a word heavily freighted with long-established concepts of ritual sacrifice, of the value of the burnt offering to the gods, and the total extinction of the person through both total obedience and the burning of the body into nothingness. It is a word that links together atrocities both ancient and modern, a powerful word of horror, fear and fright.

Like the distinguished Aboriginal anthropologist Marcia Langton, I cannot help but feel that there is indeed something about creating this colony that calls up the word holocaust, the 'something' that she described as 'This insistent falling towards that place that so many Jews write about'. It is worth repeating her words:

> *The disgust at the pornographic and trivialising revisions, the new historiography lauded by the New Right, the accusations of cannibalism, infanticide and the litany of charges made against Jews and the 'Elders of Zion' in medieval pamphlets, repeated in the hateful diatribes against Aborigines; these recent incursions by those who do not want what happened to us and our ancestors remembered into 'history', make me wonder whether we are not shuffling along the same road as Primo Levi and others like him.*[3]

Parallels drawn between the European Holocaust and those of the colonial *deathscape* described by Rose as South Australia's colonists moved to take the Countries of the north are bound to be unsettling but they are there. Recognising them offers at least some protection against repeating them, a protection required now as much as ever. Perhaps it will help to recall that Hitler was also a coloniser. He phrased his claims to settle on the lands of others as the German right to *lebensraum* or 'living space' for his purified Aryan race. Racial thinking was the tool he used to separate out his superior blue-eyed blond-haired population from supposedly inferior others, the natural masters from those born to be their slaves.

In South Australia the impact on those being forced to live daily within the tricky hierarachically organised, racially divided social space that separated colonisers and Indigenous peoples was significant. Under this regime the slightest slip would lead to a severe bashing, the taking of women for sex, tortures (sometimes referred to as 'rough handling'), deadly whippings, shootings and often, death. Those who had to do so under these conditions had to find ways to survive within a field of terror. Children had to learn how to avoid punishment just as adults did. Regardless of whether colonial women were present or not in the Northern Territory during its years as an almost entirely male place and society, the killing, the shooting, and the grotesque punishments were all carried out by men. That women and men of the First Nations were drawn into finding ways of coping with the perpetrators of those dreadful events was essential as well as inevitable.

Sometimes a protective rapprochement could be sought, sometimes by developing ways to placate rather than resist. While some responded by attack and force, some accepted employment of a kind, attracted by the lure of access to rifles and women in an attempt to join the colonial brotherhood of 'mates'; women, forced into accepting concubinage, domestic service, sometimes general labour or droving, and some opting to try to use conversion to Christianity as protection from the worst. Sometimes walls of secrecy were put in place in an effort to create some kind of private space within a world in which there was none; at other times trafficking in information provided a means of finding a small pocket of freedom within a vast field of hostility. Rachel Perkins' recent film *The Australian Wars* (2022) discusses these strategies and their consequences in some detail. Whatever way was found of surviving and engaging with the presence of colonists on their country – even when granted considerable license – Indigenous lives were subservient even when relatively comfortable, always under threat. Their dealings were with the colonists as masters, their opportunity for individual choice severely constrained and at first, their knowledge of the unpredictable habits of the new men offered little guidance as to how best to deal with their situation.

To speak, then, of the arrival of the colonists as unleashing a *holocaust* makes it clear that any suggestion of Indigenous 'complicity' in their own destruction is entirely inappropriate, serving only to reinforce the initial injury. This is the case regardless of what individuals may or may not have done as they found themselves facing such loss, such extremes of violence and eventually, the lives that had to be lived within the racialised structures and conventions of the zones of exclusion operated by missions, pastoralists and police. The sadistic nature of the killings and violence, the sexualisation of the terror, the numbers of people destroyed and the methods used, must bring to mind the Biblical word holocaust.

Fire

First Nation histories of those years record how colonial men out hunting for Aboriginal 'offenders' often carried cans of kerosine with them, just in case they needed to burn the bodies of any they killed.

It is hard to read of the burnings of Aboriginal people's bodies without being struck by their resonance with the Old Testament story of God's demand that Abraham should sacrifice his son to Him as a burnt offering. It remains a popular story that provides a powerful image of absolute obedience to the One God whose law drives all humanity. The story of 'the binding of Isaac' for sacrifice by his own father allows the father to act in God's place, to make patriarchal powers of life, death and punishment within the family appear as both natural and sanctified.[4] It describes, too, the idealised child, obedient to the last, trusting absolutely to the father who is about to slaughter him. Some pictures of the event now show just the pile of wood that would be used to complete the act but earlier European painters like Titian and Tiepolo as well as many church windows, show the child tied and bound, lying upon the sacrificial fire with his father holding a large knife, about to strike.[5]

Aboriginal people who witnessed body-burnings regarded them as 'somehow the epitome of cruelty and barbarousness of the whole sequence of events'.[6] It was a form of cruelty impossible to understand, a reduction to nothingness that bemused Elsie Raymond when she testified to a massacre at Yerrerdbay, Double Rockhole, near Old Delamere Station on Wardaman country. Elsie's father's father, Yiwalidagarl, had found a small baby still living after the massacre, a baby who had grown up to become the old man known to Elsie who, much later, spoke to her of those events.[7]

Despite a stream of comment and criticism from observers in colonial Adelaide, the ritualised burning of Aboriginal bodies was only loosely related to the need for concealment. For a good many years, the remoteness of the locations, and the collaboration of so many of the small number of colonists provided a consensus of fraternal approval that extended far beyond the Territory itself. That the temper of the times rendered concealment largely unnecessary is an example of the ways in which terrible violence and death-dealing can shape the ways in which a society establishes normalcy and norms of male and racial and sexual superiority. As well as being a fiery demonstration of colonial power in which each pyre offered a riveting visual confirmation of the terror intended to subvert resistance and guarantee compliance, it is hard not to see the watching of these ritualised defilements and burnings as containing an element of voyeurism, an eroticised privileged male act of looking without being seen that offered an intense sexual pleasure.

For the men who burned the bodies of those they had killed, the fire and often the crushing and scattering any bones that survived it, had a second aspect that came from the imagery of fire itself – its well-established Biblical connections with sacrifice, the notion of the voice of God speaking through flames or, as in Deuteronomy 4: 24, of God himself as a consuming fire. Biblical fire also appears as a punishment in which cities are razed to the ground and turned to dust; or in the personal punishment of the fires of hell awaiting those who transgress. All these texts are well-known to Christians, Jews and indeed to Muslims, to the degree that they form an almost unnoticed cloud of normalcy that is always there, available and swirling around to be called up when things – actions – need to be made right and righteous.

Biblical imagery forms a kind of backdrop to the theatre of terror and death-dealing they so assiduously promoted.

When thinking of the sadism deployed in the Territory – the brutal flesh-cutting whippings, hobbling chains, the rapes of children as well as adults, and other bodily mortifications – the firing and total destruction of so many bodies seems to fit easily into that brutal list. Considered together, they appear as theatrical exhibitions of extreme forms of colonial masculinity in which the pastoralist, or stockman, or policeman, or any other of the foot-soldiers of the vigilante posses were able to stand in the place of the gods (whether Christian, Jewish, Muslim or pagan), to become for an hour or so, the voice speaking out of the fire, the voice able to become, in the Christian case, the Lord God of Deuteronomy who 'is *a consuming fire,* even a jealous God.' Among the crucial elements here are the fire not simply of death (horrible as such a death may be) but man as god and fire as total annihilation, fire as the creator of absolute nothingness. That was what they wanted.

Chapter Forty-Four

1901 – The Birth of a Racial State

In 1901 South Australia with its northern territory joined the other colonies to become one of the federated states of a new *Commonwealth of Australia*. In the division of political responsibilities negotiated in the lead-up to federation, the government of Aboriginal citizens was left to the states. As in the other new states, in South Australia this arrangement has meant that the fundamental organisational structures of colonial society, government and law remained largely in place in two important ways. First, the *state* of South Australia was built directly onto the political structures of the three zones of Indigenous exclusion laid down as the colonists sought to take control of the land; and, second, the society and culture of the new state was built on the important consequences of colonial myths of whiteness, pioneering male heroism, a cult of male mateship, male superiority to women, and permissible male violence that had developed around the silences and evasions surrounding the realities of colonial occupation. Each has had consequences for both Aboriginal and colonial women. This is because women and children ensure racial boundaries remain intact so that the dominant race itself remains 'pure', untainted by any of their non-white progeny. Male violence against women and their sexual rights to control them are seen in colonial terms, as ways of protecting their race into the future.[1] Whether explicit or subterranean, the colonial era's practices of violent and predatory sex could not but influence the nature of the society of the newly formulated race-based state. Male control of women remained central to legislative agendas with women remaining largely available to male sexual predation and various forms of financial exploitation and exclusion. Similarly, the violence characterising the zone of Indigenous policing could not but influence the policing practices of police more generally. Facing always the very fine line between legitimate violence and its illegal use, the methods and culture of Indigenous policing continued to fuel all policing practices in the federated state era, eventually blowing out into a force little different to a politicised militia. Patriarchalism also remained strong. As a result, the life and society of the new state of South Australia–Northern Territory remained remarkably similar to its colonial predecessor. There was no real break and thus no 'post-colonial' state.

Within a decade of federation the South Australian government found governing the Territory unrewarding. It was handed over to the new Commonwealth government in 1911. Under Commonwealth control the Northern Territory was governed by an Administrator who answered to the federal government in Canberra. It was a weak form of government that allowed for interlocking personal and social relationships across the institutions of administration – the police, the judiciary, public servants – and to small cabals of men with common interests (pastoralists, miners, newspaper proprietors and hoteliers). All exercised influence and a degree of autonomy. It was not until 1978 that the Commonwealth allowed the Territory to govern itself, an arrangement which has had the very mixed results that have led to some current critics labelling it a 'failed state.' Its failures are in the areas of financial management, political probity, and of course in almost everything to do with the interests and lives of Aboriginal Territorians.

In the first years of statehood, however, government of the Territory continued largely unchanged. Apart from powers ceded to the Commonwealth (foreign affairs, for example, customs, a treasury and the right to tax income to fill it, and a few other areas held to be of national importance), the new *state* of South Australia was administered directly through a state government in Adelaide aided by a well-established threat: the threat posed by supposedly yellow hordes at the gates who were seen as only too willing to sweep in and destroy the white nation that was only just coming into being. By 1901 and federation, anti-Chinese sentiment had reached a blazing level of hostility in South Australia, just as it had in the other colonies. The new Commonwealth of Australia's first piece of legislation was the *Immigration Restriction Act, 1901*. It provided a legal basis for what became known as the 'White Australia policy' that was used initially to exclude Chinese and other Asian or Pacific Islander peoples but later extended. The tests by which entry was to be decided required facility with the English language. Despite being defined as Asian or 'coloured,' exceptions were made for a small number of Christian families from Lebanon, Syria and other Middle Eastern countries. Here we see the new nation being defined and brought into being as white, English-speaking, and Christian, a triumvirate of hopes that has changed in its language and methods but sustained it ever since. In 1901 race was doing its work of unifying the disparate colonies of the new Australia into a nation in which the supposed racial superiority of the white-skinned races was used to minimise class divisions based on economic and financial disparities, particularly those between the wealthy and the labouring classes and their hated trades unions. Australia as a whole was whitening and becoming less tolerant of cultural differences rather than more. In South Australia, German remained widely spoken until the enmities of two world wars made it unpopular. In its commitment to being an explicitly white nation, federation created a foundation of racial exclusion that included not only non-Australians wanting to enter but also the First Nations peoples who were still under attack as the former colonies attempted to complete their project, the taking of the land, making it empty and making sure it was white.

The pairing of violence and sex in the Nothern Territory was bound to have consequences for all those engaged within its field of force. While the Territory's holocaust caused great harm to those subjected to it, its perpetrators were forced into a position of having to reconcile their actions against the social, religious and moral standards of the new world they were seeking to bring into being. Deborah Rose came to wonder whether the massive drunken sprees characterising the male society of the colonial pastoral zone were in part a consequence of the effects on them of the horrors of their own actions – the horror of what they had done, of what they saw, and what they had heard – a reaction to their own form of violent, predatory manliness. In so far as there can be said to be a local origin point for the excesses and ecstatic consumption of a drug of oblivion and forgetfulness that legitimates male violence against women, it was a practice that spread far beyond the Territory and is thoroughly integrated into the era of the federated Australian states of today. The relationship of alcohol to Australian forms of masculinity is one that ensures that the consumption of alcohol in the Territory today remains far, far higher than average. People from all over Australia go to the Territory to indulge in alcohol in vast quantities and to take part in the ecstasy of out-of-control masculinity, violence and sex.

It was certainly a practice that was easily mimicked by young Aboriginal men seeking a place as real men within the new colonial world they faced. How could it not? Indeed, alcohol abuse and the male violence associated with it have come to be used as reliable markers of chaos and moral disarray in Aboriginal society in the Territory today – a diagnosis that ignores notable levels of Indigenous abstinence in the Territory, and very high levels of alcohol and drug consumption among the non-Indigenous populace, and the widespread legal, religious and social tolerance for predatory and violent male sex. In 2007 alcohol abuse and sexual violence were used by the extremist neo-liberal Howard government to justify sending in the army in to restore 'order' to Aboriginal communities in the Territory. This they tried to do by removing human rights and taking control of their monies from them, a practice that, as predicted by scholars like Andrew Lattas, would soon move out of its Indigenous framework to be used more widely. As I write, the consequences of the Howard government's removal of civil rights, increased surveillance and creation of powerlessness can be seen in the Northern Territory today.

1901 – THE BIRTH OF A RACIAL STATE

The consequences of years of violence, government control and zones of exclusion for the Aboriginal people of South Australia and the Northern Territory have been many. Many have been forced to live side by side with their tormentors, for example, stuck on pastoral properties, corralled into missions and government run 'reserves' and subjected to further abuse, and never allowed access to the capitalist economy available to others. In Alice Springs, as elsewhere, they have watched their sacred places built over, eradicated and defiled, watched their streets being named after the men who had terrorised their parents, massacred their grandparents – the 'hard men' who worked on, undisciplined.

Remarkably, new Indigenous ways of living, loving and earning evolved. Distinctive forms of Christianity that were compatible with Aboriginal beliefs emerged, offering dignity and respect that were rarely understood beyond their bounds. And education was seized on where it was possible so that those not ruined by discrimination and abuse could demand their civil rights and the return of their country. But so often what little was given or allowed was kept provisional, ready for removal or revocation at will. Attitudes changed in all the ex-colonies of Australia but still there was that wish for 'the problem' to go away, while the power of those glorious pioneer histories led many people of goodwill towards thinking that things would be better if only 'they' would give up being Aboriginal and just be like one of 'us'.

This is destructive, racial, genocidal thinking. By encasing fantasies of superiority in the language of apparently neutral regulations and the bureaucratic conventions of governing, the nature and appearance of violence changes but not the exercise of violence itself. The new wave of colonisation implemented by men like John Howard and his acolytes is a shape-shifter dripping from the tip of a government pen. It is very hard to track and catch hold of but it does keep the racial dreams of a 'white' Australia' intact and secure. But it is sad to have to map the path to apocalypse that took those first colonists from, as Maggie Brady has noted, 'a colony, established by free-settlers as a cradle of experimentation and communalism, with no one religion dominant and dissenting sects open to radical ideas'.[2]

Chapter Forty-Five

The Mission Zone in the 'Post-Colony'

When thinking about Australia today, some like to refer to it as being a 'post-colony'. They mean this hyphenated word to indicate a decisive break in history that is imagined as having taken place at federation. It is a word that imagines the death of the colony in order to allow for the birth of a modern nation of a 'common wealth'. This is hopeful, perhaps, but wrong. Colonial society did not die but lived on and lives still. The important structures of colonial government, its three zones of exclusion (sometimes boosted with the good ideas of other colonies), were simply incorporated into the new nation in ways that ensured that Australia, like so many other modern nation-states, emerged from its first incarnation as a colony of England to become a race-based state – a state governed through racial distinctions and hierarchical and discriminatory racial practices identical to those of the pre-federation colonies.

The presence of the interlocking workings of the three colonial zones of exclusion within the new state of South Australia–Northern Territory is clearly visible in the post-federation mission zone. Its role has been of great importance because of the way in which the children of families in which only the mother was Aboriginal (the 'fatherless' children of the imagination) came to be a particular focus of missionary rescue efforts in the twentieth century that with good reason Regina Gantner has labelled 'the mission century'; I would describe it as the time during which the mission zone expanded dramatically because of its role in maintaining the foundational racial division of a society that promoted itself as white, English-speaking and Christian.

Along the racial divide sexual relationships were strictly regulated in ways that, as described in earlier chapters, gave colonial men unlimited access to Aboriginal women and established their sexual access as a demonstration of racial superiority and white male power. They were powerful enough to ensure that the women on their own side of the racial divide remained there, in part by creating in colonial women a largely unjustified fear of rape by Indigenous men. But their children by Aboriginal women stayed on their mother's side of the divide, defined as Aboriginal children of 'mixed race'. In a society strictly built on racial differences they were seen as a major problem, about which something needed to be done as otherwise the crucial whiteness of the superior race might be lost. The removal of children from their families was authorised first by colonial laws and customs and then by the new laws of the state of South Australia.

In the mission zone the removal of children from their families was framed as a rescue mission. The rescues were government policy carried out through a wide range of individuals, police, patrol officers or mission staff; some were destined for adoption or fostering, others for one of a network of mission-based, mission-staffed orphanages and 'homes'. The explicit aim was to prevent the children from slipping back into the heathen savagery and licentiousness that was imagined as characterising life 'in the camps'. Regardless of missionary motivation and their other charitable activities, for generation after generation their focus on getting children away from their families in order to ensure they were Christianised and reprogrammed socially and mentally has been a terrible disaster. It is the scale of that disaster that makes arguments over the righteousness of missionary activity irrelevant or at least peripheral. Two examples illustrate the ways that the mission zone and its relations with the new *state* of South Australia and its Territory in the north actually worked.

*****

The Bungalow in Alice Springs

In 1934 the superintendent of the Bungalow home in Alice Springs, Keith Freeman, was charged with having had 'immoral relations with a half-caste girl of 16 years of age, from the ['Half-caste'] institution.'[1] At his trial, five girls gave evidence that Freeman had come to the door of the girls' dormitory in his pyjamas and asked for a young girl to come out to him. He took her into the school room and sexually assaulted her there.[2] Freeman was fined £100 or three months jail time, with one month to pay. As a result, he was dismissed. Mrs Freeman stayed on for a short time after his trial. Alec Kruger's description of Mrs Freeman, the matron at the Bungalow, 'as something of a shadow round her husband,' hints at her subordinate status or even at a loss of self or personhood. Mr Freeman was, Kruger recorded,

> *a bully who enjoyed flogging us. God knows why he became a missionary ... But that was the trouble. It was bad enough being snatched away from your family, but then no one cared enough to protect us from the sick sad people that often enough ended up taking these types of jobs.*

Freeman, he said,

> *would sometimes come over to the dormitory half-charged and wake us all up. We would be ordered out of the room and sent away out of his sight for the night. This was perhaps a way for him to spend time with his girl interest of the time ... In the morning he would sober up and get nervous about what he had done.*

'Mrs Freeman,' said Alec Kruger as a mature man, 'must have known of his behaviour without being able to do anything about it. Perhaps she was part of getting him exposed, charged and convicted'.[3] Perhaps she was, but the wives of such men were often in very difficult situations in which they had to deal with shame as well as violence or economic dependency keeping them quiet, unable to do much to change their own situation or anyone else's.

Given Kruger's recollections it seems likely that she knew her husband drank excessively, knew he beat the children badly and knew that he was not always in her bed at night. The Freemans had come to the Bungalow via the settlement at Jay Creek associated with Hermannsburg mission; before the first World War, they had worked with the Anglican Forrest River Mission in Western Australia.[4] Kruger is correct to point to the way that children's institutions of all kinds were deliberately targeted by men with a lust for illicit sex and violence. That is why the answer to Alec Kruger's questioning of the reasons behind such a man being a missionary is simply that overt religiosity has always provided a cloak for abusers. Children's homes and schools are a magnet for such people, delivering them their targets with religiosity providing a cloak for even the most bestial of behaviours. Not so hard to understand, really. This was certainly a factor at the Retta Dixon Home in Darwin.

Retta Dixon

We know what happened to children in the Retta Dixon Home because of Prime Minister Julia Gillard's *Royal Commission into Institutional Responses to Child Sexual Abuse* (2013) and the first-hand Aboriginal evidence given to it. Named for Margaret (Retta) Long, née Dixon, Dixon was the instigator and motivating force of the Baptist-run Australian Inland Mission's Darwin establishment she founded in 1947.[5] The Royal Commission's investigation revealed the details of decades of sexual abuse of children at Retta Dixon – a regime of rape and exploitation of both boys and girls from a very early age, that was sustained by massive violence and the incorporation of older boys into the system by giving them free rein, by corrupting them with the rewards of perpetration and immunity. The evidence presented by six survivors of Retta Dixon Home to the Royal Commission was summarised:

> *The levels of abuse and horror which those children experienced as a consequence of being 'cared for' at the Retta Dixon home beggars belief. It cannot and will not be understated in this Submission.*

Despite everything our clients were subjected to they were still able to step forward and tell their stories detailing the horrendous experiences they underwent as vulnerable young aboriginal children in the care of Retta Dixon Home [from 1946 to 1980].

They have given evidence which talks about physical, emotional and sexual abuse of the highest order. They described tales of horrific cruelty committed upon them as young, vulnerable Aboriginal children, by grown adults who had responsibility for their guardianship and care. This included cruel physical beatings with canes and belts [the buckle-end] upon children which at times drew blood. We have heard of emotional and psychological torture which included instances of punishment by forced cleaning of skirt boards with a toothbrush to force feeding a child her own vomit. We have heard of children being humiliated because of their bed-wetting by having them wear, as twelve year olds, nappies in front of other Retta Dixon children. We have heard about children having faeces wiped on their faces and chained to their beds for punishment.

We have heard the typical concomitant of this physical and psychological cruelty, namely, gross sexual abuse. Anal rapes of children, constant sexual fondling combined with a blanket inability of said children to do anything about their predicament. The level of abuse committed upon the children was gross, cruel, inhumane and had the inevitable devastating effect upon them.[6]

Evidence was given to the Royal Commission by one of the housemothers of her attempts to report the violence to the superintendent and to the police, and of how the eventual but reluctant prosecution of those concerned just seemed to dribble away into nothingness. Newly appointed Harry Giese, Director of Welfare in the Northern Territory Administration from 1954, had tried to stop the violent punishments but a missionary at Retta Dixon, E.R. Stretton, appealed against Giese's ruling and succeeded. Eventually reports of the wicked violence at Retta Dixon reached Sir Paul Hasluck (born 1905). Hasluck, whose parents had run Number 1 Boy's Home for the Salvation Army in Collie,

Western Australia, dismissed the reports of constant violence on the basis that corporal punishment was needed to maintain discipline.[7] And finally, the evidence given also records the way in which the taking of the children from their mothers led to generation after generation of Christian and government abuse.

The submissions from various institutions show, too, how a willingness to look away is common in mission and government stations for orphans and stolen children. Looking away generally underpins an established culture of not-knowing about what is not only in plain sight but that has also been reported to them. In her evidence to the Royal Commission one witness, for example, then aged 66, told of how she was taken from Kahlin Compound in Darwin, a miserable place for Aboriginal Australians run by the Australian government. Before her, her mother had been taken from her family while they were living on the Daly River and had been sent to live in the Kahlin Compound where by 1923 conditions were so bad that they eventually led to it being closed. Her child, conceived at a very young age, was in turn taken from her. Which is how this witness entered Retta Dixon. Kahlin Compound was replaced by an institution not just based on race but one divided according to how much 'white' blood ran in the children's veins. The Bagot Reserve took in the children with two Aboriginal parents while the Retta Dixon home set beside it and run by Baptist missionaries was for the specifically designated children of a non-Aboriginal male parent. The two were kept apart even if the children in one category shared a parent with a child in the other. *Pure blood* and *contamination* were key concepts of government policy and religious thinking.

The great harm inflicted by missions and governments through child-stealing policies, violent institutions, and today's refusal of government and church compensation stands in stark contrast to the ways in which Aboriginal people, victims of these policies, have reacted. One young man who was interned at Retta Dixon and later on Croker Island has recorded his meeting with Ted Evans who had worked as a Welfare Officer in the Northern Territory:

> *I was in time later to meet the person who removed me from my family and Wave Hill [Station]. Ironically, he was the president of my football club, the Wanderers ... Ted Evans used to cry ... and I thought he was crying because of the scores ... I was sitting down there one night ... and I said to Ted, 'Look Ted, don't worry, you know. It's only a game.' ... And he looked at me and he said ... I've got to tell you something ... I was the person that removed you from your family.' I looked at him and he was still crying, and I just hugged him. I said, 'It's alright Ted. What you did is what public servants do today, you had to do a job.' He said, 'After I'd taken you and Bonnie, I'd never ever removed another person.'*[8]

Ted Evans worked in the Northern Territory for many years. As a Welfare Officer he was important in corroborating the evidence given to Constable R.F.H. Corbin by those who had been so badly beaten by the owners and men on Eva Downs Station that was described in the Prologue. Sir Paul Hasluck's views on the Eva Downs prosecution fit in with his views on the necessity for corporal punishments in institutions like Retta Dixon. Katherine Booth and Lisa Ford have pointed out that:

> *In* Shades of Darkness, *an account of Aboriginal affairs between 1925 and 1965, [Sir Paul] Hasluck complained of the 'gross distortion' of the situation of Aboriginal people employed on cattle stations by several organisations who were 'active in spreading stories overseas to the discredit of Australia', to the London office of the Aborigines Protection Society, within United Nations circles and in several African countries. He referred specifically to an incident (likely the one at Eva Downs) where an Aboriginal worker was struck with a stockwhip by a white cattleman. Though the cattleman was subsequently arrested, tried and sentenced, Hasluck lamented that: 'This was not told as a story that it was against the law to strike an Aboriginal and that a strong penalty had been imposed on a white man for breaking the law. It was passed around as a story*

that black 'slaves' on Australian cattle stations were flogged when they displeased their slave-driving masters.[9]

The Royal Commissioners also received a submission from the solicitors acting for the Reverend Trevor Leggott, the General Director of the Australian Inland Missions (now renamed as Australian Indigenous Ministries) during the Royal Commission's hearings. In it Reverend Leggott appears as a person able to simultaneously admit and deny the culpability of his organisation and staff. The submission shows, too, how such a violent and predatory system could be permitted under the rule of a strict Baptist branch of the Christian church that also said to the Commission that they could not afford to compensate any of their victims still living as it would mean their missionary work would be curtailed. They were trying, they said, to move away from the past. It is not hard to understand why. Their refusal to consider compensation to the victims of their mission 'home' shows no remorse or recognition of harm inflicted but rather the continuing strength of the belief that their missionary evangelism is their first and only priority and that the needs of their victims have none at all.

*****

Over past decades, Christian missions and their personnel have been criticised for their harshness, for the sustained attempts to evangelise by destroying Indigenous religious beliefs and way of life, and for the ways in which Aboriginal children were often taught by missionaries to think about Aboriginal people as inferior or dirty. In the eyes of missionary evangelists their missions have been guided by a desire to protect Aboriginal people from the dangers they faced in the new world around them, as well as to teach them of Christian love and all it offers. Within the mission zone the discipline and punishment that so many of its inmates recalled were cloaked in doctrines of Christian love that allowed many missionaries to believe that they were acting for the best, acting in the best interests of those whom they wished to tutor and convert.

I can understand the pain that criticism of missionary work and institutions has caused and also why it has been defended by some of those who lived and grew up under mission rule. John Strehlow's response to criticism of colonial Hermannsburg missionaries in claiming that it was fuelled by a hatred of Christianity is defensive and misses the mark, but it gives a sense of how beleaguered mission supporters have come to feel. For there is no doubt that most of the nineteenth-century missionaries endured considerable hardship and privation in establishing and maintaining their missions. One of the benefits of the missionary years that is important to recognise has been their documentation of Aboriginal culture and language, sometimes in great detail. It has been of value to those now involved in land claims and the native title negotiations of recent years. John Strehlow does not mention here another of the common justifications of missionary work, that the missions offered a safe haven, saving many Aboriginal people from the violence they faced outside its boundaries. His comment about the difficulties involved in maintaining law and order on a mission station like Hermannsburg, however, points directly to an aspect mission life that is indeed a key to understanding the set of powers in play, resistance to them and manipulation within them, and their implementation within the zone. Yet even if correct, neither the proposition that criticism of missions stemmed from a deep hatred of Christianity (rather from horror at what critics saw there), nor the defences that missionaries documented what would otherwise have been lost (languages, social customs) nor that they created protective safe havens within a world of violence offer any insight into the how the mission zone was integrated into the colonial forms of governance in South Australia. The common stories of heroic mission battles to protect, develop and create viable citizens who could live comfortably in the new world around them are wrong.

So we need to look at the missions from a slightly different angle in order to see better where they stood in the broader world they inhabited. For they occupied a crucial space, a zone of exclusion that was locked into the project of colonisation, the preservation of whiteness, and government. Missionaries lived and worked along a racial division in society that was seen as very important. It proved the superiority of the colonists and confirmed their rights. Indeed, what has not been well understood is the way that from the years of colonial government through to the federated states of the Commonwealth government of Australia, missions played a very particular role in the race-based politics on which the nation-state of 1901 was built. For the missions formed an entirely race-based aspect of both the Protestant and Catholic churches. Those in their care were selected on the basis of their race and the elaborate distinctions of degree of whiteness or Aboriginality it required. And with the focus so strongly on children and the need to get them away from the 'savagery' of their parents and cultural practices, it is not surprising to find that a good many missions were founded in order to provide 'homes' for those taken away from their families. Orphanages and children's homes proliferated in the mission zone in both South Australia and its Northern Territory regardless of religious denomination. And with their focus on race and as the number of children without Aboriginal fathers steadily increased, the missions to children came to be situated along the border between an Aboriginal race and a conglomerate of supposedly 'Aryan' peoples with paler skins. Missions flourished along a racial divide that their inmates illustrated and challenged. They made race visible and significant.

The evidence given to the Commission revealed the culpability of the highest levels of the Retta Dixon Home's management under successive superintendents. The Commission noted that a history of denying knowledge of violent sexual and physical assaults was continued by the Reverend Leggott in the evidence he gave. The evidence showed that concern for the Australian Inland Mission's evangelical aims and reputation came first, and that difficulties in staffing Retta Dixon were solved by hiring anyone at all who said they would like to go there. As a result they employed the life-long, never-prosecuted pedophile Donald Henderson, along with a Mr Powell and a Mr Pounder who engaged in the same behaviour, as well as violent men like E Richard Stretton. The evidence shows an almost complete absence of concern for the real welfare of the children in the mission's care, often by the lawyers and police who played a large role in bringing in children, making things look legal and refusing to allow people to leave or to go to court. And it revealed the ways in which a culture could be established into which staff could be drawn if they wished to keep their jobs, so that violence and rape became something they could not effectively stop nor mention. More disturbingly, they record how other staff have to find a way of working within such cultures. The Royal Commission evidence gives some idea of how some of the wives of the 'house parents' in charge of each cottage, could become passive bystanders or facilitators. Whether they were also subject to violence and abuse has not been recorded but the young Alex Kruger, who was in the Bungalow at the time of the arrest of its superintendent, Gordon Freeman, has also reflected on these matters. It is interesting to read about the Freemans because they were liked and respected in Alice Springs. Even the anthropologist Olive Muriel Pink, who had a reputation for keeping an eagle eye on such matters and knew the Freemans well, was utterly shocked and surprised.[10] No wonder the government was keen to keep Olive Pink away from reserves and institutions housing Aboriginal people.

*****

I have documented some of the processes of colonisation that the colonists and their descendants prefer neither to notice nor to dwell upon. It has been harrowing to write this way, to create this story, a story that focuses on issues that are important in reaching a better understanding of why things today are the way they are. It shows where governments and the beneficiaries of colonial dispossession need to look when they start to think about how the disastrous statistics that measure the scale of Indigenous disadvantage can be remedied. It shows where individuals and non-government agencies (churches and charities) need to look, what to see and what they need to do to force a change in public and political minds that will bring about the restoration of full civil and human rights for Indigenous Australians, to stop the ways police forces build up the very high rates of Indigenous incarceration rates of adults and children and to release people from the hyper-surveillance and vicious policing practices that create so much damage and harm. Nothing is really hidden – it is in plain sight. The regulation and control of so many of the First Australians remains mired in practices of colonialism that form the basis of non-Indigenous governance. Social policies like 'income control' are often trialled on Indigenous peoples. From there they move out into the methods of controlling or policing more broadly, creating social and moral insensitivities and the acceptance of punitive and often violent forms of policing. Australia's colonial origins continue to have terrible consequences, whether they are noticed or ignored. But whatever they are, they are neither unknown nor unseen. It is important to learn to look, see, notice and accept reality rather than myths about its nature. Allow knowledge to lift the guilt that comes from pretence and lies. No more apologies – that time has long gone. Abandon the sense of moral and social superiority; grasp the need, the chance, to undo the harms of race. Let go of fear. It is not so hard once you are willing to notice, to see race at work. Get an Aboriginal Voice to Parliament and get rid of slogans like 'un-Australian' that mask the workings of race and exclusion which in reality shape the present just as much as in the past. There is *no* post-colony yet. Colonial occupation remains a potent political force, one that produces great harm and distortions. The failure of the Voice Referendum illustrates its living, shameful presence.

Notes

Prologue
1. Robert Foster, Rick Hosking and Amanda Nettelbeck 2001, *Fatal Collisions* pp. 74–93.
2. Matthew Moorhouse, 'Quarterly Report – Aborigines Department', *South Australian Register* 5 May 1849.
3. Billy Griffiths and Lynette Russell 2018, 'What We Were Told', *Aboriginal History* 42: 31–53.
4. Maurie Ryan 2016, *Yijarni. True Stories from Gurindji Country*, ed. Erika Charola and Felicity Meakins, pp. 129–132.
5. Mary Anderson 2015, *Every Hill Got a Story*, ed. Marg Bowman, p. 85.
6. *Yijarni. True Stories from Gurindji Country*, ed. Erika Charola and Felicity Meakins, Canberra: pp. 60–62.
7. Tony Roberts 2005, *Frontier Justice*, pp. 227–229.

Chapter One ~ Utopian Dreams and a *Good* Colony
1. Michel Foucault 1984 (1967), 'Of Other Spaces', Diacritics, Spring, pp. 22-27.
2. Richard J. Evans 2016, *The Pursuit of Power*.
3. 'Some Social Aspects of Early Colonial Life', *South Australian Register*, 26 October 1878.
4. Deborah Bird Rose 2017, 'Reflections on the Zone of the Incomplete', in *Cryopolitics: Frozen Life in a Melting World*, ed. Joanna Radin and Emma Kowal, Cambridge: MIT Press. For the ways in which utopian dreams fed British beliefs in their racial superiority and moral righteousness, see Rudyard Kipling and C.R.L. Fletcher's *History of England*, last published in 1954.

Chapter Two ~ The Pre-Colony
1. Sylvia Hallam 1983, 'A View from the Other Side of the Western Frontier', *Aboriginal History* 7(2): 134–156; Isobel White 1980, 'The Birth and Death of a Ceremony', *Aboriginal History* 4(1): 33–41.
2. Philip A. Clarke 1998, 'The Aboriginal Presence on Kangaroo Island, South Australia', in *History in Portraits*, p. 14; J.C.H. Gill 1966, 'Genesis of the Australian Whaling Industry, paper read originally to the Royal Australian History Society, 1850
3. Ronald M. Berndt and Catherine H. Berndt with John Stanton 1993, *A World that Was*, p. 292.

NOTES

4   Mrs James Smith 1880 (1965), *The Booandik Tribe of South Australian Aborigines*, pp. 41, 25–26; Amanda Nettelbeck 2001, 'Seeking to Spread the Truth', *Australian Feminist Studies* 16 (34): 83–90.
5   Ronald M. Berndt and Catherine H. Berndt with John Stanton 1993, *A World that Was* p. 292.
6   Cf. demeaning remarks on chastity among Aboriginal women attributed to Alfred Giles in 1899; Ronald and Catherine Berndt 1951, *From Black to White*, pp. 54–55.
7   Schürmann 1987: 49. The constant raising of these issues indicates the centrality of the answers to troubling questions about whether the European presence has visited more good than harm upon Indigenous Australians.
8   Amery, Rob, 'Sally and Harry', in Simpson and Hercus, *History in Portraits*, p. 86.
9   Rob Linn 1993, *Frail Flesh & Blood*, pp. 16–18; Hilary M. Carey and David Roberts 2002, 'Smallpox and the Baiame Waganna of Wellington Valley' *Ethnohistory* 49(4): 821–869.
10 C.G. Teichelmann and C.W. Schürmann 1840 (1962), *Outline of a Grammar*.
11 Carey and Roberts, 'Smallpox and the Baiame Waganna of Wellington Valley'.
12 Cf. Cawthorne 1927, writing in 1844 and referring to observations made 1841–1844.
13 Berndt and Berndt 1951, *From Black to White*, p. 83.

Chapter Three ~ The Righteousness of Colonisation

1   Mary P. Mack 1962, *Jeremy Bentham*, pp. 396, 413, 419.
2   Elizabeth Elbourne 2003, 'The Sin of the Settler', *Journal of Colonialism and Colonial History* 4(3)
3   John Beecham 1838, *Colonization. Being Remarks on Colonization in General*.
4   Beecham, *Colonization*, pp. 4–5.
5   Beecham, *Colonization*.
6   He energetically pursued a mission to sailors, providing facilities for them in port cities. Douglas Pike 1957, *Paradise of Dissent*.
7   Paul Daley in *The Guardian* online edition, 21 September 2018.
8   Pike 1957, *Paradise of Dissent*, p. 129 & 119 for Edwin Hodder's biography Angas.
9   'Robert Gouger', http://adb.anu.edu.au/biography/gouger-robert-2109.
10 Edwin Hodder 1891, *George Fife Angas*, pp. 419–420. George Fife Angas did not arrive in South Australia until 1851.
11 W.H. Leigh 1839 (1982), *Reconnoitering Voyages and Travels with Adventures in the New Colonies of South Australia*, p. 152.

Chapter Four ~ Empty Lands

1   Jones 1994, 'Obituary for Norman Barnett ("Tinny") Tindale', *Aboriginal History* 18(1): 5–8.
2   Written by Friedrich Wilhelm-Møller in the 1940s.
3   Jane Simpson and Luise Hercus, eds 1998, *History in Portraits*, n15.
4   Ronald M. Berndt and Catherine H. Berndt (with John E. Stanton) 1993, *A World that Was*, p. 330, map 10.
5   The Australia-wide map, drawn up by Catherine and Ronald Berndt, consolidates and adds to earlier material provided by McCarthy. Ronald Berndt and Catherine H. Berndt 1964, *The World of the First Australians*, Sydney, p. 19.
6   Berndt and Berndt, *A World that Was*, p. 117.
7   Teichelmann & Schurmann 1840, *Outline of a Grammar*, give *yerbanna* as the name of this powerful ochre from the north.
8   Ronald Berndt 1941, 'The Bark-Canoe of the Lower River Murray', p. 24.

9   R.M. Berndt and T. Harvey Johnston 1942, 'Death, Burial, and Associated Ritual at Ooldea, South Australia', 89–208; Ronald M. Berndt 1941, 'Tribal Migrations and Myths Centring on Ooldea, *Oceania* 12(1): 1–20; Ronald and Catherine Berndt 1942, 'A Preliminary Report of Field Work in the Ooldea Region', *Oceania* 12(4): 305–330.
10 Berndt 1941, 'Tribal Migrations and Myths Centring on Ooldea, South Australia'.
11 For flint mines and Ooldea see M. Brady 1987, 'Leaving the Spinifext: pp. 35–46; Norman B. Tindale 1976, 'Some Ecological Bases for Australian Tribal Boundaries'; T. Harvey Johnston 1941, 'Some Aboriginal Routes', pp. 33–65.
12 For more detail cf. Deborah Bird Rose 1996, *Australian Aboriginal Views of Landscape and Wilderness*, Canberra: Australian Heritage Commission, 1996, chapter 1.
13 Catherine H. Berndt 1989, 'Retrospect, and Prospect. Looking Back Over 50 Years', pp. 1–20; Catherine J. Ellis and Linda Barwick 1989, 'Antakirinja Women's Song Knowledge 1963-72', pp. 21–40.
14 Ellis and Barwick, 'Antakirinja Women's Song Knowledge 1963-72', p. 22.
15 In an important discussion of music and dance and ecology, the words of Mussolini Harvey have been translated by John Bradley and cited by Deborah Bird Rose (2008: 118) in 'Dreaming Ecology: Beyond the Between'. Also, Rose, *Australian Aboriginal Views of Landscape*.
16 Veronica Strang 2000, 'Showing and Telling: ', *Journal of Material Culture* 5: 275–299 (see p. 277).
17 Udo Will and Catherine Ellis 1996, 'A Re-Analyzed Australian Western Desert Song: Frequency and Interval Structure', *Ethnomusicology* 40(2): 188–222.
18 Catherine J. Ellis 1979, 'Functions and Features of Central and South Australian Aboriginal Music', p. 22; Catherine J. Ellis 1984, 'The Nature of Australian Aboriginal Music', pp. 47–50. Mussolini Harvey is a Yarralin man, from the Victoria River district that is referred to again later. The term 'performative map' has come from work among people living at Kowanyama on Western Cape York Peninsula.
19 Ronald and Catherine Berndt 1952, 'A Selection of Children's Songs from Ooldea, Western South Australia'.
20 Ellis, 'The Nature of Australian Aboriginal Music', 49.
21 Steve Hemming 1994, 'In the Tracks of Ngurunderi', *Australian Aboriginal Studies* 2: 38–46.
22 John Mulvaney n.d., '"... these Aboriginal lines of travel"', *Historic Environment* 16(2): 47.
23 For the quote from Charles Sturt see Mona Stuart Webster 1958, *John McDouall Stuart*; 'South Australia', *Australian*, 27 March 1838; D.J. Mulvaney, 'The Chain of Connection: The Material Evidence', in Peterson, *Tribes and Boundaries in Australia*.
24 Erich Kolig 1980, 'Noah's Ark Revisited', *Oceania* 51(2): 118–132; *No Roads Go By* was the title of Myrtle Rose White's popular book about the years from 1915 to 1922 spent living on a station, 'Lake Elder', in the north of South Australia.

Chapter Five ~ Land into Landscape

1   W.J.T. Mitchell (ed.) 1994/2002, *Landscape and Power*, Chicago: University of Chicago Press.
2   For Carlyle see Nicholas Mirzoeff 2006, 'On Visuality', *Journal of Visual Culture* 5(1): 53–79.
3   http://nla.gov.au/nla.obj-135761989/view.
4   John Michael Skipper was born in 1815 at Norwich; the nephew of 'James Stark, a member of the Norwich School of landscape painting'. Early in the nineteenth century, Norwich was a centre of intellectual ferment and cultural activity.
5   Beth Duncan 1998, 'Mary Thomas. South Australian Pioneer, 1787–1875'. Unpublished manuscript, State Library of South Australia.

NOTES

6   Evan Kyffin Thomas (ed.) 1925 [1983], *The Diary and Letters of Mary Thomas (1836–1866)*.
7   David Elder 1984, *William Light's Brief Journal and Australian Diaries*, pp. 63 and 64.
8   Theresa S.E. Snell Chauncy 1836–37, 'Journal of a Residence of Three Months in the British Province of South Australia', unpublished transcript, State Library of South Australia.
9   David Wheeler 2010, 'The Personal and Political Economy of Alexander Pope's "Windsor-Forest"', *South Atlantic Review* 75(4): 1–20.
10 W.H. Leigh 1839 [1982], *Reconnoitering Voyages and Travels with Adventures in the New Colonies of South Australia* p. 138. Malvern Hills border Worcestershire. The calls of Australian birds are noted for their clatter or noisiness rather than the songs of European birds like the blackbird or lark.
11 Mary Hindmarsh was the youngest daughter of Sir John Hindmarsh, first Governor of South Australia. She arrived with her family in 1836.
12 Jeffrey Auerbach characterises a picturesque landscape as having three distinct sections: the foreground is dark and detailed, the middle ground (or screen) is strongly lit, while the background, often the sky, is hazy. Jeffrey Auerbach 2004.
13 Francis Pryor 2010, p. 402.
14 *First Enclosure Act* was in 1604 but in the first half of the eighteenth century over 200 individual Acts were passed. In 1836 the *General Enclosure Act* was passed. It benefitted large landholders by allowing them to enclose land even if smaller land-holders objected. Properties were required to be fenced, making smaller fields expensive (Francis Pryor 2010: 466).
15 John Dixon Hunt 1992, *Gardens and the Picturesque*, p. 45. For a broader history of Castle Howard see Lance M. Neckar 2000, 'Castle Howard: An Original Landscape Architecture', *Landscape Journal* (19)1–2: 20–45. For 'emparkation' and the shifting of villages see Francis Pryor 2010: 471.
16 Mary P. Mack 1962, *Jeremy Bentham*.
17 Information provided by Kaurna elder Lewis O'Brien to Tracey Lock-Weir 2005, p. 66. See also Lewis O'Brien 1990, 'My Education', *Journal of the Anthropological Society of South Australia* 28(1 & 2): 106–126.
18 Bill Gammage 2011, *The Biggest Estate on Earth*, p. 41. For Green Hill see Valmai Hankel 2013.
19 Jane Hylton, 2012, p. 57.
20 Evan Kyffin Thomas (ed.) 1925 [facsimile 1983], *The Diary and Letters of Mary Thomas (1836–1866)*, p. 53.

Chapter Six ~ The Kaurna See the Colonists

1   Edwin Hodder 1893, *The History of South Australia*, pp. 51–52. About forty tents and huts in 1836 (Evan Kyffin Thomas (ed.) 1925 [facsimile 1983], *The Diary and Letters of Mary Thomas (1836–1866)*, p. 53).
2   John Adams 'My Early Days in the Colony', *Journal of the Anthropological Society of South Australia* 26 (6): 3–11.
3   The name Mikawomma is given in Tracey Lock-Weir 2005: 12. She cites work carried out by Steve Hemming and Rhonda Harris for an Adelaide Parklands Management Strategy in 1998. Jane Simpson 1998, 'Introduction', in Simpson and Hercus, *History in Portraits*, p. 4. The name Kaurna for the Adelaide Plains People was approved of by Ivaritj, the 'Princess Amelia' of the colonists. Tom Gara also accepts the name Kaurna; see his 'Mullawirraburka (1811–1845)', *Australian Dictionary of Biography*, National Centre of Biography, Australian National University, http://adb.anu.edu.au/biography/mullawirraburka-13119/text23739, accessed 22 October 2012. Philip A. Clarke (1991) sees Kaurna as a probable version of Coma or Kona, most likely a word meaning 'man', and very much a late nineteenth century name; but he accepts that it

4   Pike 1957: 180. Pike's figures are divided into emigrants brought out by the Colonisation Commission who travelled free of charge, and superior persons who paid for their own passage. In total, he gives: 1836 941; 1837 1279; 1838 3154; 1839 5320; 1840 3148; giving a total of 13,842 over the first 4 years of the colony (bearing in mind that the 1836 figures applied only from December of that year).

5   Valmai Hankel regards Skipper's paintings as accurate. See Valmai Hankel and Colin Harris, 'The pre-European environment of the Adelaide Plains', Unpublished lecture delivered to the Royal Geographical Society, South Australia, 7 May 2013.

6   Letter 4, 17 February 1839, in Evan Kyffin Thomas (ed.) 1925 [facsimile 1983], *The Diary and Letters of Mary Thomas (1836–1866)*. The first people arrived 31 December 1836, she records.

7   Sylvia Hallam 1983.

8   W.A. Cawthorne 1927, 'Rough Notes on the Manners and Customs of the Natives', *Proceedings of the Royal Geographical Society of Australia, South Australian Branch*, 27: 47–77, pp. 67–68.

9   For a detailed discussion of the conventions governing encounters between groups of people see Hallam (1983).

10 Theresa S.E. Snell Chauncy, 1836–37, 'Journal of a Residence of Three Months in the British Province of South Australia', Unpublished transcript, State Library of South Australia, entry for10 January 1837.

11 This first visit took place on 31 December 1836. Evan Kyffin Thomas (ed.) 1925 [facsimile 1983], *The Diary and Letters of Mary Thomas (1836–1866)*, p. 53.

12 Tom Gara 1990, 'The Life of Ivaritji ("Princess Amelia") of the Adelaide Tribe', *Journal of the Anthropological Society of South Australia* 28 (1 & 2): 91.

13 Gara 1990, 92.

14 Sally White notes that early colonial records show Aboriginal people taking an intense interest in the military ceremonials of the colonists. She documents the incorporation of a military drill staged by Matthew Flinders near Albany, WA, in 1801, and mentions a 'Tiwi dance derived from observations of the Marines at the Port Dundas settlement in 1824–1829.' Isobel White 1980:39.

15 Gara says 'Rodney' was one of the first men encountered by the settlers. This man's name was recorded as 'Ootinai' which, he thinks, might be heard as 'Rodney'.

16 Theresa S.E. Snell Chauncy, 1836–37, 'Journal of a Residence of Three Months in the British Province of South Australia', 10 January 1837. Unpublished transcript.

17 Non-Conformist usually refers to those who could not accept the Thirty-Nine Articles of Faith of the established Church of England.

18 Douglas Pike 1957, pp. 106–107.

19 Beth Duncan 2007: 19, citing Brown's diaries.

20 A canny and enterprising young man of twenty-six, as a servant of the South Australia Company James Cronk had travelled steerage on the *Africaine*.

21 Letter from James Cronk to his mother, 2 November 1837. Downloaded from the website of the Tea Tree Gully & District Historical Society, Inc, July 2013. As one of very few letters written by a steerage passenger, the letter is important. Cronk later married and he and his wife, Jane Storer, had 10 children. From very modest beginnings he was able to speculate in land. In his letter he says that he bought ¾ acre at £10/acre and quickly sold it for £23.

22 Theresa S.E. Snell Chauncy, 1836–37, 'Journal of a Residence of Three Months in the British Province of South Australia', Unpublished transcript. Entry of 10 January 1837.

23 W.A. Cawthorne 1927, p. 68.

24 John Blackett 1911, p. 52.

(Note: item above the list begins) is now current among local Aboriginal people and as such, acceptable. So I have used it, despite its ambiguities, at least until a more convincing term emerges.

25 This incident is recorded in Theresa Chauncy's Journal; it seems to have taken place in about April of 1837.
26 Thomas, Evan Kyffin 1925: 76.
27 Their description as 'outstanding, clever personalities' is from the missionary Clamor Schürmann, who met them in November 1838. Edwin A. Schürmann 1987, *I'd Rather Dig Potatoes.*
28 Mullawirraburka, (also known as Kertamero, 'King John' and 'Onkaparinga Jack') Kadlitpinna (given the name, Captain Jack) and Ityamaitpinna (given the name, King Rodney of Willunga).
29 Tom Gara, 'Mullawirraburka (1811–1845)', *Australian Dictionary of Biography*, National Centre of Biography, Australian National University,
30 Jane Hylton (1994: 57) notes that Theresa (née Chauncy) Walker's wax portraits were regarded as excellent likenesses. Figures modelled in wax became popular in England early in the nineteenth century. Billie Melman 2011, 'Horror and Pleasure', pp. 26–46.
31 Tom Gara 1990, pp. 64–105.
32 For a short biographical note for Gilbert see Blackett's *History of South Australia*, p. 412.
33 John Adams 1988, 'My Early Days in the Colony', p. 5.
34 William Cawthorne has left many important pictures and sketches of colonial South Australia. Tracy Lock-Weir (2005:76) discusses his work and quotes from his diaries.
35 This description is taken from the note on the inside cover of Robert Edwards (n.d.).

Chapter Seven ~ Locke's Blessing

1 I have drawn extensively on the careful and thoughtful analysis of John Locke's writings on land and labour carried out by Professor Eva Mackey (2016) in *Unsettled Expectations. Uncertainty, Land and Settler Decolonization.* See particularly chapter 2, 'Fantasizing and Legitimating Possession'.
2 Cf. Christopher Hill 1980 [1997], *Some Intellectual Consequences of the English Revolution.*
3 Eva Mackey (2016) in *Unsettled Expectations.*
4 John Locke 2005 [1689], *Two Treatises of Government and a Letter Concerning Toleration*, Digireads.com Publishing: Stillwell: KS
5 Lisa Ford (2010) p.15 – 'John Locke … combined the North American empire and the Hobbesian state with the new English ideology of improvement to create a uniquely Protestant and English synthesis …'
6 Keith Thomas (1971), *Religion and the Decline of Magic*, p. ix.
7 John Locke, *Second Treatise of Civil Government*, Chapter 5, 'Of Property'. For the Biblical foundations of English society see Alister McGrath (2001) *In the Beginning. The Story of the King James Bible'.*
8 Jacques Le Goff refers to mediaeval debates over 'the significance of labour, both from a theoretical and a practical point of view', Jacques Le Goff 2015, *Must We Divide History Into Periods?* New York: Columbia University Press, p. 60.
9 For discussions by Karl Marx see, 'On the Jewish Question', reprinted in Robert C. Tucker 1972, pp. 24–51.
10 Lisa Ford (2010) p. 15 – 'Between 1680 and 1690, he [Locke] combined the North American empire and the Hobbesian state with the new English ideology of improvement to create a uniquely Protestant and English synthesis, independent of the legal archive of Crusade.'
11 Gerber says that the refugee/exiles were from the varied ranks of peasantry, from small-holders to landless, from an area badly affected by the land reforms of the Prussian government that 'abolished personal serfdom (while preserving the

obligation of service to landlords), granted hereditary land tenures to peasants, and encouraged the enclosure of small holdings', David A. Gerber, 1984, p. 503.
12   David A. Gerber, 1984, 498–522; Christopher Hill 199i, p. 99.
13   Mary P. Mack, 1962, *Jeremy Bentham.* p. 394.
14   D. Pike 1965, p. 79.
15   The strength of Locke's ideas is revealed when it is realised that when he wrote his Second Treatise during years described as being the 'golden age' of equity, 'a discretionary system of jurisprudence which supplemented and corrected the common law'. Report prepared for the Economic Union, 'Report from England and Wales by Professor Peter Sparkes, Professor of Property Law, University of Southampton, Subject Sections Secretary of the Society of Legal Scholars' (nd). http://www.eui.eu/Documents/DepartmentsCentres/Law/ResearchTeaching/ResearchThemes/EuropeanPrivateLaw/RealPropertyProject/England%20and%20Wales.
16   For dissent from Locke's view see John Beecham 1838, *Colonization.*
17   From John Brown's diary, 1835, cited by Beth Duncan, in *Mary Thomas, Founding Mother.* pp. 19 & 269.
18   Letter to Sir George Grey, Parliamentary Under-Secretary, from Robert Thomas, 16 January 1836, cited in Beth Duncan 2007, *Mary Thomas, Founding Mother,* pp. 20 & 269. SLSA PRG1160/4.
19   Locke's understanding of the basis of private property and the category of waste land.
20   Downloaded 3 December 2013, from: http://www.austlii.edu.au/au/legis/qld/consol_act/awla1855235/s3.html.
21   In the struggle to legitimate landownership Locke's understanding of the basis of private property and the category of waste land remains valuable in law. In 1988, the year of Australia's bicentenary celebrations, the High Court found that the Queensland Act contravened the *Racial Discrimination Act of 1975* and disallowed it. The *Racial Discrimination Act* has been in the sights of radical conservatives ever since.
22   Edwin Hodder volume 1, p. 31.

Chapter Eight ~ The First Degree of Separation

1   Edwin A. Schürmann, 1987, *I'd Rather Dig Potatoes.*
2   Robert Amery, 2018, 'Koeler and the Dresdeners', p. 162.
3   'The Queen's Birthday', *South Australian Register,* 30 May 1840, pages 6–7. 'Lower Kaurna (Walpara branch): also Kona, Korna and Nganawara. Wyatt wrote of an Aboriginal named Encounter Bay Bob, Parroo Paicha, as being a Kaurna man. The term usually referred to the Adelaide tribe. All the evidence we obtained suggested close association of Lower Kaurna with the main body of Kukabrak.' Berndt and Berndt 1993, page 303. The Berndts use the name Kukabrak as an alternative for the Narrindjeri living along the southern coast of the Fleurieu peninsula to the far end of the Coorong.
4   'Aboriginal Customs. Tribal Laws', *Advertiser,* 10 March 1893). Simpson Newland, who grew up at Encounter Bay lamented this failure in 1893. The original suggestion seems to have come from his father, the Reverend Ridgeway Newland.
5   Edwin Hodder, vol. 2, 'Summary of Events', pp. 148, 153.
6   Schürmann, 1987, *I'd Rather Dig Potatoes.*
7   Kathleen Hassell, 1921 (1966), *The Relations Between the Settlers and Aborigines in South Australia 1836–1860,* p. 19. Edwin Hodder (1893: 83–4) says that Bromley's main aim was to form the new community of Adelaide on a moral and religious basis. Bromley arrived on the mainland in May 1837 where he was appointed Acting/Protector of Aborigines; by May the following year he was dead – drowned in the Torrens, probably drunk, *Southern Australian,* 2 June 1838.

NOTES

8. John Adams. 1988.
9. Letter to the Editor, *South Australian Gazette and Colonial Register*, 23 June 1838. Kathleen Hassell 1921, pp. 20–24; 26.
10. Parsons, citing McNeil 1989, *Common Law Aboriginal Title*, says that 'The common law rights of indigenous inhabitants were clearly understood at the time, as shown by McNeil 1989. Despite the attempt in South Australian settlement to declare all land as Crown land, the right of the Aborigines to the fruits of the land, including timber, was accepted.' Michael Parsons 1997, pp. 46–69.
11. For rock art in Peramangk country see, R.B. Coles 1992, pp. 33–56.
12. W.H. Leigh, 1839 [1982].
13. Simpson Newland, 1895, 'Some Aborigines I Have Known', part 1, *South Australian Register*, 13 December 1894, p. 7
14. *South Australian Gazette and Colonial Register*, Adelaide, June 3, 1937. 'On 5th April, 1837 His Excellency in Council this day appointed Captain Bromley, ad liberim, Protector of Aborigines. Robert Gouger, Colonial Secretary.' For an updated location map of Piltawodli see Christine J Lockwood, 2007, 'A Vision Frustrated: Lutheran Missionaries to the Aborigines of South Australia 1838–1853', Unpublished Doctoral Thesis, University of Adelaide, p. 103.
15. Anne Scrimgeour, 2007, 'Colonizers as Civilizers: Aboriginal Schools and the Mission to "civilize" in South Australia, 1839–18445', Unpublished Doctoral Thesis, Darwin University, pp. 43–44.
16. SPES, 'The Aborigines. To the Editor of the *Southern Australian*', Southern Australian, 22 December 1838.
17. Kingston's map of 1842 shows the 'Aborigines Location'; available from the website of the State Library of South Australia. William Wyatt was appointed as the third Protector of Aborigines by Hindmarsh in 1837 but was without proper funds and had little authority. See: Alan Rendell, 'Wyatt, William (1804–1886)', *Australian Dictionary of Biography*.
18. For a succinct and useful account of the colony's earliest years see Tom Gara's 2006, 'Adelaide at the time of Hermann Koeler's visit', pp. 7–24.

Chapter Nine ~ Intimations of Unrest

1. Adams, John 1988, pp. 3–11.
2. 'Mr Teichelman's Report Upon the Natives. At the Wesleyan Missionary Meeting', *Southern Australian*, 26 January 1841.
3. George Taplin, 1879, 'The Narrinyeri', p. 65.
4. John Adams, 1988; Adams' stories about his early life in the colony were told to his grand-daughter, who recorded them.
5. Tom Gara, 2006, p. 20.
6. The Kaurna used reeds as well as paper-bark sheeting in building their dwellings, just as the reeds of Lake Alexandrina were used by the the Narrindjeri to build substantial huts that were wind and rain-proof. In Steve Hemming's (1985a) account of the reminiscences of Thomas Martin there is mention of the people camped at Port Willunga (south of Adelaide) using rushes from the creek in making string and rope for fishing nets and freshwater from a spring close to the reef..
7. A 'Dead Men's Bones. Burial Ground Uncovered. Fox Hunt at Fulham', *The Mail*, 5 November 1927. Karl Winda Telfer and Gavin Malone 2012, *Kaurna Meyunna Cultural Mapping*.
8. John Adams, 1988.
9. *The Official Civic Record of South Australia. Centenary Year, 1936*, facsimile edition, p. 44.
10. Edwin Hodder, 1893, vol. 1: p. 109.

11 'Dinner to Gouger', *Australian Gazette and Colonial Register*, 26 January 1839, p. 3;
12 David Elder.
13 Henry W. Breaker's reminiscences recorded in 'One of the First', *The Register*, 29 December 1915. Also, Rhondda Harris 2017, *Ashton's Hotel*, p. 32.
14 Karl Winda Telfer and Gavin Malone 2012, *Kaurna Meyunna Cultural Mapping. A People's Living Cultural Landscape*, Adelaide: City of Charles Sturt. In 'Funeral of a Native', the unnamed writer describes the death and funeral rites of Wariato, the second wife of Munaitja. Munaitja may have been Schürmann's informant, Wattewattipinna Munnitya, referred to extensively in Clamor Schürmann's diary. 'She was one of the stoutest and most robust of her countrywomen; her age was about thirty.' There is no cause of death given for one dying so young. *South Australian Gazette and Colonial Register*, 9 March 1839, p. 8.
15 John Adams, 1988, pp. 3–11.
16 Alan Pope, 2011, *One Law for All?* & Edwin Hodder 1893, volume 2, p. 144.
17 Isobel White, 1972, 'Hunting dogs at Yalata', *Mankind* 8: 201–205.
18 'Coroner's Inquest', *South Australian Gazette and Colonial Register* 17 March 1838, p. 3.
19 Keryn Walshe, 2008, 'Pointing Bones and Bone Points' pp. 167–203.
20 Tom Gara, 'Mullawirraburka (1811–1845)', *Australian Dictionary of Biography*, Australian National University, http://adb.anu.edu.au/biography/mullawirraburka-13119/text23739, accessed 22 October 2012; Robert Clyne 1987, *Colonial Blue*, p. 120.
21 'Coroner's Inquest', *South Australian Gazette and Colonial Register*, 17 March 1838, p. 3.

Chapter Ten ~ The Coming of Colonial Law

1 Alex C. Castles and Michael C. Harris 1987, pp. 55–73.
2 'Session of Gaol Delivery, 13 May 1837', *South Australian Gazette and Colonial Register*, 3 June 1837.
3 'Session of Gaol Delivery, 13 May, 1837', *South Australian Gazette and Colonial Register*, 3 June 1837.
4 'Session of Gaol Delivery', 13 May, 1837, *South Australian Gazette and Colonial Register*, Saturday 3 June 1837.
5 *South Australian Gazette and Colonial Register*, 'Session of Gaol Delivery, 13 May 1837'; 8 July 1837; Kathleen Hassell 1921 (1966), p. 18; J. Blackett, *History of South Australia*, p. 46.
6 The interim judge, Henry Jickling, presided over the trial of Michael Magee.
7 James Horton 1838, 'First Execution in the New Colony of South Australia', *Launceston Advertiser*, 31 May 1838, p. 3.
8 Alex C. Castles and Michael C. Harris 1987, *Lawmakers and Wayward Whigs*, pp. 55–73.
9 Alan Pope, 2011, *One Law for All?*, p. 14.
10 Report on 'South Australia', *The Sydney Herald*, 27 May 1839.
11 'Apprehension of the Native Murderers', *South Australian Gazette and Colonial Register*, 11 May 1839, p. 2; 'South Australian News (From the South Australian Gazette, May 25)', *Launceston Advertiser*, 20 June 1839, p. 4. For the names of convicted men, see Tracey Lock-Weir 2005, p. 70.
12 'South Australian News. (From the *South Australian Gazette*, May 25)', *Launceston Advertiser*, 20 June 1839. The third was released.
13 'South Australian News. (From the *South Australian Gazette*, May 25)', *Launceston Advertiser*, 20 June 1839.
14 Schürmann, 1987, *I'd Rather Dig Potatoes*, p. 49.

NOTES

15 Schürmann, 1987, *I'd Rather Dig Potatoes*, p. 95.
16 30 March 1840.
17 Lloyd Blunden, 1951, 'Bushrangers and Blacks Worried Police', *News*, 28 July 1951, p. 5.

Chapter Eleven ~ Governor Gawler's Time in the Colony Begins

1. Letter of Mary Thomas, 14 October 1838, in *The Diary and Letters of Mary Thomas (1836–1866)*, ed. Evan Kyffin Thomas 1925, p. 112.
2. R. Hetherington, 'Gawler, George (1795–1869), *Australian Dictionary of Biography*, Australian National University; Brian Dickey n.d., *Holy Trinity. Adelaide's Pioneer Church. A Brief History*.
3. Maria Gawler to her sister, Jane, 1 November 1838, State Library of South Australia PRG 50, series 1–44, Gawler Family Papers.
4. Maria Gawler to her sister, Jane, 1 November 1838, State Library of South Australia PRG 50, series 1–44, Gawler Family Papers.
5. Mary Thomas described her 1836 feast in the very new colony as made of ham and parrot pie with a rather makeshift pudding to follow. By 1837 things were a little more settled.
6. State Library of South Australia PRG 50, series 1–44, Gawler Family Papers.
7. Schürmann, 1987, *I'd Rather Dig Potatoes*, p. 35. Maria Gawler also described the day, see Robert Foster, 1989: 65.
8. Tracey Lock-Weir 2005, p. 70. For Stephen's biography see: http://adb.anu.edu.au/biography/stephen-george-milner-1294.
9. *Chronicle*, 3 August 1933.
10. Tom Griffiths, 1988 (ed.), *The Life and Adventures of Edward Snell*, p. 102, fn 30.
11. Griffiths, *The Life and Adventures of Edward Snell*, p. 111 & p. 102, fn 30.
12. R. Hetherington, 'Gawler, George (1795–1869)', *Australian Dictionary of Biography*. Gawler was interested in using Indigenous place names on the new maps being created, replacing the name 'Thames' with Patawalonga and 'Field's River' with Onkaparinga.

Chapter Twelve ~ The Massacre of the Survivors of the Wreck of the *Maria* 1840

1. The *Fanny* was wrecked near Cape Jaffa on the colony's south coast in June 1838.
2. Schürmann 1987: 74. Berndt & Berndt give his name as Paroo Paitcha.
3. 'Official Communication. To the Editor of the Southern Australian. Police Commissioner's Office; July 27th, 1840', *Southern Australian*, 28 July 1840.
4. Simpson Newland, 'Some Aboriginals I Have Known', *South Australian Register*, 1 January 1895.
5. The map shows the overland track to Port Phillip Bay running close by Lake Hawdon and it shows the land as the colonists saw it before 1846, the date of its publication.
6. In later newspaper reports, the skeleton would be presented as an act of cannibalism, the detail of the intact ankles perhaps suggesting such an interpretation. It was not reported in this way at the time.
7. Pullen's report to Governor Gawler, *The Southern Australian*, 14 August 1840.
8. George Hall, for the Governor, 'Supposed Wreck and Murder at Encounter Bay', *The Southern Australian*, 14 August 1840.
9. Robert Foster, Rick Hosking and Amanda Nettelbeck 2001, *Fatal Collisions*.
10. John Mayo, 'Tolmer, Alexander (1815–1890), *Australian Dictionary of Biography*,
11. 'Summary Execution of Four Natives. – Reports of Major O'Halloran', *South Australian Register*, 12 September 1840. The published reports were those written by O'Halloran to Gawler.

12 'Summary Execution of Four Natives. – Reports of Major O'Halloran', *South Australian Register*, 12 September 1840.
13 'Summary Execution of Four Natives. – Reports of Major O'Halloran', *South Australian Register*, 12 September 1840.
14 'Summary Execution of Four Natives. – Reports of Major O'Halloran. Second Report of the Commissioner of Police to His Excellency the Governor', *The Australian*, 13 October 1840.
15 Jane Hylton, 2012, *South Australia Illustrated. Colonial painting*, p. 92.
16 Blackstone's influential *Commentaries on the Laws of England* were published 1765–1769.
17 'Judge Cooper's Charge to the Grand Jury – Summary Execution of the Natives', *South Australian Register*, 7 November 1840.
18 'Proceedings of Council, Adelaide, Sept. 15, 1840', *Southern Australian*, 18 September 1840.
19 S.D. Lendrum, 1977–78, 'The "Coorong Massacre", *Adelaide Law Review* 26 – 43
20 Foster, Hosking and Nettelbeck, *Fatal Collisions*, p. 14, have this picture attributed to Skipper while the AGSA website has it as 'Unknown'.
21 Julie Evans, 2009, p. 17.

Chapter Thirteen ~ The First Missionaries – The Dresden Lutherans

1 Christine J. Lockwood, 2007, 'A Vision Frustrated', p. 9.
2 Lockwood, 'A Vision Frustrated', p. 6; Gerhard Ruediger 2011, pp. 25–40.
3 Cf. the 'Postscript' written by William v Blandowski in 1862: '… one has to reject categorically the assumptions that they should be relegated to the level of animals.' Harry Allen (ed.) 2010, *Australia. William Blandowski's Illustrated Encyclopedia*, p. 163.
4 Lockwood, 2007, 'A Vision Frustrated', p. 9.
5 Robert Amery, 2018, 'Koeler and the Dresdeners', p. 160.
6 Amery and Williams 2002: 273.
7 Cf. Robert Foster, 1990, 'The Aborigines Location in Adelaide: South Australia's First "Mission" to the Aborigines'.
8 Schürmann, 1987, p. 36.
9 Schürmann, 1987: 63–67.
10 Schürmann, p. 72.
11 'The Natives', *South Australian Gazette and Colonial Register*, 3 November 1838. Governor Gawler's 1838 address was given by him in English and then repeated in Kaurna by Protector Wyatt (presumably translated by James Cronk).
12 'The Queen's Birthday', *Sydney Monitor and Commercial Advertiser*, 28 June 1839.
13 *South Australian Register*, 'The Queen's Birthday', 30 May 1840. The translation was carried out by Schürmann.
14 Lockwood, 'A Vision Frustrated', p. 73, citing Schürmann's diary entry of April 1841.

Chapter Fourteen ~ Eyre's Children

1 Valentin Groebner, 2009, 'The Carnal Knowing of a Coloured Body', pp. 220–221.
2 David Dabydeen ,1987, *Hogarth's Blacks*. For Darwin, see his autobiography as edited by his son.
3 Miles Kemp in *The Advertiser* 20 April 2019, utilising the database being established for colonial compensation records at University College-London.
4 Shirleene Robinson 2013, 'Regulating the Race:', pp. 302–315.
5 Julie Evans, 2002, 'Re-reading Edward Eyre', p. 181 footnote 21.
6 Edward John Eyre, 1845, *Manners and Customs* … p. 214.

NOTES

7 Yelbourne is given as Yalbone in Eyre's Autobiogaphical Narrative, 1832–1839; the editor, Jill Waterhouse, gives as correct, the name of William Henry Yaldwyn, later a Queensland member of the Legislative Council whose overseer, John Coppock, was in charge of the advance party.
8 Edward John Eyre, 1984, *Autobiographical Narrative of Residence and Exploration in Australia, 1832–1839*, edited by Jill Waterhouse, p. 105.
9 Eyre, *Autobiographical Narrative*, p. 106.
10 Roslyn Poignant, 2004, *Professional Savages: Captive Lives and Western Spectacle*.
11 Eyre, *Autobiographical Narrative*, p. 115.
12 Eyre, *Autobiographical Narrative*, p. 124.
13 Cf. Jill Waterhouse, 1984, 'Introduction', in Eyre, *Autobiographical Narrative*.
14 Eyre, *Autobiographical Narrative*, p. xxv.
15 Brenda Niall, 2012, *True North*. pp. 157–158; Niall is quoting from Mary Durack's *Kings in Grass Castles*, 1959.
16 Paintings of adult slaves often show a carefully drawn leg-ring to which a chain is attached; among images of child pages, however, the leg ring and chain is less common. Sometimes the chain alone is shown masquerading as a jewel.
17 Cf. David Dabydeen, 1987, *Hogarth's Blacks*. pp. 21–23.

Chapter Fifteen ~ Becoming a Man

1 Billie Melman, 1993, pp. 5–41.
2 Catherine Hall 2009, 'Macaulay's Nation', pp. 505–523.
3 Catherine Hall, 'Competing Masculinities'; 'Imperial Man: Edward Eyre in Australasia and the West Indies, 1833–66', in *The Expansion of England: Race, Ethnicity and Cultural History*, ed. Bill Schwartz, London: Routledge, pp. 130–170; and 'Histories, Empires and the Post-Colonial Moment', in *The Post-Colonial Question*, ed. Iain Chambers and Lidia Curti, 1996, London: Routledge, pp. 65–77.
4 Eyre, *Autobiographical Narrative*, p. 122.
5 Geoffrey Dutton, 1982, p. viii.
6 Edwin Hodder, 1893, *The History of South Australia*, volume 1, p. 121.
7 Clamor W. Schürman, 1879 [1997], 'The Port Lincoln Tribe'.
8 Geoffrey Dutton, 1966, 'Eyre, Edward John (1815–1901)', *Australian Dictionary of Biography*, Australian National University.
9 'Eyre's Journey to Albany', 1891, Initials engraved in image l.l.: J.M. Samuel Calvert engraver. Samuel Calvert arrived Adelaide on *Symmetry*, 1848, after Eyre had left. Went to Melbourne, retired to England in 1888.
10 The names of the two other Aboriginal men with Eyre are given as: Neramberein (Joey) and Cootacha (Yarry) by Mitchell Rolls and Murray Johnson 2011, p. 179.
11 Geoffrey Dutton 1982, *In Search of Edward John Eyre*, pp. 23–24.

Chapter Sixteen ~ Heroes & Myths

1 Richard J. Evans, 2019, *The Pursuit of Power: Europe, 1815–1914*; Anne O'Brien 2008, 'Missionary Masculinities' pp. 68–85.
2 'The Public Dinner to Edward John Eyre, Esq.', *South Australian*, 27 August 1841.
3 Thomas Carlyle, [1840] 1993, *On Heroes, Hero-Worship*, p. 102.
4 A.W. Howitt, 1901, *An Episode in the History of Australian Exploration*.
5 'Dinner to Mr. McKinlay', *Adelaide Observer* 15 November 1862.
6 'Dinner to Mr. McKinlay', *South Australian Register* 13 November 1862. Strangways was Commissioner of Crown Lands and Immigration.
7 'The Great Stuart Demonstration', *South Australian Register* 22 January 1863.
8 Thomas Carlyle, 1993, *On Heroes, Hero-Worship*, pp. 3–4.

9   Michael K. Goldberg, 1993, 'Introduction', in Carlyle, *On Heroes, Hero-Worship*.
10 Michael K. Goldberg, 1993, 'Introduction', in Carlyle, *On Heroes, Hero-Worship*, p. xxxiii.
11 Other Australian explorers fit this model too. For reconsiderations of the explorer Ludwig Leichhardt, see Andrew Hurley and Katrina Schlunke 2013, 'Leichhardt After Leichhardt', pp. 537–543.
12 Michel Foucault, 1976 [1981] *The History of Sexuality. Volume One: An Introduction*,.
13 Purity was prominent in Thomas Carlyle's thinking about manliness. See Trev Lynn Broughton 1997, 'Impotence, Biography', *Journal of the History of Sexuality* 7 (4): 501–536.
14 Dutton, 1982, p. 44.
15 Charles Sturt on his first journey down the Murray had to row upstream all the way in order to return to NSW; John McDouall Stuart, was born in the same year as Eyre, 1815, but his major journeys and physical disciplining of the body began some seventeen years later, in 1858.
16 Daisy Bates, 1938, *The Passing of the Aborigines*. chapter 15.
17 His published account of the journey from Port Lincoln to King George Sound in Western Australia expresses gratitude to those accompanying him from Port Lincoln, leading him to water supplies and pointing to food sources like the hidden eggs of the bush turkey. Nor was the country uninhabited.

Chapter Seventeen ~ Fear Rising

1   Moorhouse letter to Governor Gray, 13 September 1841, in G. Taplin 1879 [1967], *The Folklore, Manners, Customs, and Languages of the South Australian Aborigines*; This letter expands on the first letter, written from Lake Bonney.
2   Letter from Henry Inman for publication: 'The Late Attack of the Natives', *Southern Australian*, 7 May 1841. According to one website, Grey is said to have sent 68 men to the Rufus River under O'Halloran – a huge number.
3   Amanda Nettelbeck n.d., in 'Mythologising Frontier:'; also Robert Foster & Amanda Nettelbeck 2012, *Out of the Silence*, p. 35.
4   Henry Inman, 'The Late Native Affray on the Murray', *South Australian Register*, 1 May 1841.
5   Inman, 'The Late Native Affray On the Murray', *South Australian Register*, 1 May 1841..
6   Robert Foster & Amanda Nettelbeck 2012, *Out of the Silence*, p. 35.
7   Robert Foster, Rick Hosking and Amanda Nettelbeck 2001, *Fatal Collisions*. pp. 30–31.
8   'Expedition to the Murray', *Southern Australian*, 28 May 1841.
9   Foster Robert & Amanda Nettelbeck 2012, *Out of the Silence*, p. 35.
10 Edwin Hodder 1893, *The History of South Australia*.
11 'Departure of Major O'Halloran and Party for the Murray', *Southern Australian*, 1 June 1841. The donors were: the South Australian Company, V. & E. Solomon, J. Hopkins, August, Cooke & Co, J. Snooks, H. & F. Jones, Jas. Frew & Co, W.H. Neale, J.W. DeHorne, E.W. Andrews, C.B. Rodwell, Wicksteed & Gratwick, T. Hornsby, G. Hamilton, C. Beck & Co, N. Bentham, J. Newman, A.H. Davis, W. Bernard, N. Hailes, C. Darke, W. Pearce, A. Young & Co, W. Green, Mr Samuel, W. Turner, W.S. Whitington, J. Ellis, Captain Allen, W.B. Edmonds, Messrs Hayward, Allen, Emmett and White, A. Fordham, F.H. Dutton, Captain Buckland, W. Blyth.
12 'Departure of Major O'Halloran and Party for the Murray', *Southern Australian*, 1 June 1841.
13 Tolmer had arrived in Adelaide in January of 1840. O'Halloran's report to the Governor, written from the fortified camp 'The Hornet's Nest', 240 miles from

Adelaide, 27th June 1841, published as: 'The Murray Expedition', *Southern Australian*, 6 July 1841.

14 O'Halloran's report to the Governor, written from the fortified camp 'The Hornet's Nest', 240 miles from Adelaide, 27th June 1841, published as: 'The Murray Expedition', *Southern Australian*, 6 July 1841.

15 O'Halloran's report to the Governor, written from the fortified camp 'The Hornet's Nest', 240 miles from Adelaide, 27th June 1841, published as: 'The Murray Expedition', *Southern Australian*, 6 July 1841.

16 O'Halloran's report to the Governor, written from the fortified camp 'The Hornet's Nest', 240 miles from Adelaide, 27th June 1841, published as: 'The Murray Expedition', *Southern Australian*, 6 July 1841.

17 For example: *South Australian Register*, May 29, 1841. 'HER MAJESTY'S NATIVE SUBJECTS.'

18 Mount Dispersion was taken up first by Finniss; Frederick Dutton used the run for the 5000 sheep overlanded for him by Alexander Buchanan in about 1839. Dutton renamed it Anlaby. Francis Dutton was his first overseer. Anlaby became famous for its flocks and gardens. Both brothers played a role in politics.

19 'Further Outrage of the Natives', *Southern Australian*, 22 June 1841.

Chapter Eighteen ~ Lake Victoria and the Rufus River – Prelude

1 'News of Captain Sturt and His Party', *South Australian Gazette and Colonial Register*, 25 August 1838; R.M. Berndt 1941, 'The Bark Canoe of the Lower River Murray, South Australia'; Robert Edwards 1972, *Aboriginal Bark Canoes of the Murray Valley*..

2 Report of Imlay and Hill's journey in January of 1838, *The Australian*, 27 March 1838.

3 'Overland Communication with New South Wales – Official Report of Captain Sturt', *South Australian Gazette and Colonial Register*, 12 January 1839. So that in all, there were 17 or 18 men under Sturt's leadership.

4 Edward John Eyre 1985, *Reports and Letters to Governor Grey from E.J. Eyre at Moorunde*, Adelaide: Sullivan's Cove; Edward John Eyre 1845 (2010), *Manners and Customs of the Aborigines and the State of Their Relations with Europeans*, p. 225.

5 'News of Captain Sturt and His Party', *South Australian Gazette and Colonial Register*, 25 August 1838.

6 Steven Hemming 'Conflict Between Aborigines and Europeans ', pp. 3–21.

7 Colin Pardoe 1993, pp. 77–84; Judith Littleton & Harry Allen 2007, 'Hunter-Gatherer Burials', p. 283.

8 Hawdon named Lake Victoria in honour of the Queen of England. Gwenneth Williams 1919, pp. 44–45.

9 Gwenneth Williams 1919, p. 47. H.J. Gibbney, 'Sturt, Charles (1795–1869)', *Australian Dictionary of Biography*.

10 Eyre said that west of the Darling river, Aborigines were numerous but 'for the most part tractable and friendly'. He had given small gifts and used tomahawks to barter for fishing nets and other local objects, *South Australian Gazette and Colonial Register*, 12 July 1838.

11 Robert Foster 2009, 'Don't mention the War', p. 4; Robert Foster and Amanda Nettelbeck 2012, *Out of the Silence*, p. 34.

12 Evan McHugh 2010, *The Drovers*. McHugh notes that not all drovers were men, 'among them "Red Jack" and Edna Zigenbine'. There were more women involved in droving than these two. McHugh's argument that women's presence means that droving was not an exclusively male domain confuses exceptions with the rule and ignores the ways in which the great myths of droving exploits express a male space in which women, particularly Indigenous women, have very sexualised and subordinate roles.

13 Geoffrey Dutton 1982, p. 12.

14 'Overland Communication with New South Wales – Official Report of Captain Sturt', *South Australian Gazette and Colonial Register*, 12 January 1839.

Chapter Nineteen ~ Massacre on the Rufus

1 Evidence given, 22 September 1841 published as, 'Conclusion of the Inquiry into the Circumstances Attending the Deaths of a Number of Natives on the Murray', *Australasian Chronicle*, 9 November 1841. Teichelmann interpreted for Pangke Pangke. Moorhouse's report to Grey of 4 September 1841 in G. Taplin 1879 [1967], *The Folklore, Manners, Customs, and Languages of the South Australian Aborigines*.
2 'Philip Levi', in R. Cockburn 1925 (1975), *Pastoral Pioneers of South Australia*, 2 vols, pp. 28–29; and obituary 'The Late Mr Philip Levi', *South Australian Register*, 16 May 1898, p. 6. For A.T. Saunders see: https://en.wikipedia.org/wiki/A._T._Saunders
3 'Statement of Mr Robinson', *Inquirer*, 24 August 1842; Dorothy Roysland 1977, p. 13.
4 'Statement of Mr Robinson', *Inquirer*, 24 August 1842.
5 'Inquiry into the Circumstances Attending the Death of a Number of Natives on the Murray', *South Australian Register*, 25 September 1841.
6 'Statement of Mr Robinson', *Inquirer* Perth, 24 August 1842.
7 Moorhouse's report to Grey of 18 August 1841, in G. Taplin 1879 [1967], *The Folklore, Manners, Customs, and Languages of the South Australian Aborigines*, Printer; Foster, Hosking and Nettelbeck 2001, p. 34.
8 Phillipson's evidence, 'Inquiry into the Circumstances Attending the Death of a Number of Natives on the Murray', *South Australian Register*, 25 September 1841.
9 Christobel Mattingley and Ken Hampton (eds) 1988, *Survival in Our Own Land*.
10 Moorhouse's report to Grey of 13 September 1841, in G. Taplin 1879 [1967], *The Folklore, Manners, Customs, and Languages of the South Australian Aborigines*, Adelaide: Government Printer.
11 Cf. information available to the distinguished scholar Isabel McBryde that promises to provide 'certain goods in return for the services of Aboriginal women' had not been honoured. McBryde 1984, p. 147.
12 Tom Gara, personal communication, December 2020.
13 Robert Foster 2009, 'Don't mention the War', p. 4.

Chapter Twenty ~ After the Rufus

1 Dorothy Roysland recorded that the grandmother of one of her friends, Mrs Gamble of Cal Lal near the river, spoke about the massacre, and of the terrible shock it gave them. Dorothy Roysland 1977, p. 22.
2 Daniel George Brock 1975, entry for 10 September 1844.
3 William Robinson who went ashore at Oyster Bay in search of water in Oct 1843 had been involved in Rufus River massacre. Skye Krichauff 2008, 'The Narungga and Europeans: Cross-Cultural Relations on Yorke Peninsula in the Nineteenth Century', Unpublished MA Thesis, University of Adelaide, p. 54.
4 For Eyre as remarkable bringer of peace both on the Rufus and on the Eyre Peninsula see: http://www.southaustralianhistory.com.au/johneyre.html.
5 Foster & Nettelbeck, *Out of the Silence*, p. 38. Rigney mentions Moorundie in his 'Foreword' to, Anne Chittelborough, Gillian Dooley, Brenda Glover & Rick Hosking (eds) 2002, *Alas, for the Pelicans. Flinders Baudin and Beyond*. The 'infamous' is from him. Raised in Manchester, this regiment served mainly to control convicts in NSW and South Australia. The regiment rioted in Launceston in 1845. For the 96th in Port Lincoln where they arrived in April 1842, see, Foster & Nettelbeck, *Out of the Silence*, pp. 45–48.
6 Geoffrey Dutton 1982, p. 47.
7 Ronald Berndt 1941, 'Bark Canoes ...', pp. 24, 25–27.

NOTES

8 For a stereoscopic picture of bark canoes on the Murray at Overland Corner near the lakes at Barmera, a staging post for drovers travelling to Adelaide, see Julie Robinson and Maria Zagala 2007, *A Century in Focus. South Australian Photography 1840s–1940s*, Adelaide, Art Gallery of South Australia, p. 69; and a similar image by Charles Bayliss taken in 1886 at Chowilla near Lake Victoria shows 'Kulkyne Tommy' with a net, King Billy seated at the left on the canoe, while standing is George Monoman (on p. 123). These are the domestic canoes, not the large ones that carried the River people out of reach of the colonists' guns.

9 John Blackett 1911, *History of South Australia,* p. 355. Eyre's words come from the 'Preliminary Remarks' he prepared for the summation of his views on Indigenous culture and society written up on board the ship returning him to England and published as *The Manners and Customs of the Aborigines and the State of their Relations with Europeans,* 1845.

10 Geoffrey Dutton 1982, pp. 48–49.

11 Quoting Melville: 'I am satisfied that the terror that the whites inspired amongst the tribes east of the Murray and the terrible lesson given them on the upper Murray was the means and I believe the only means of making the overland routes safe to travel', in, Robert Foster and Amanda Nettelbeck 2012, pp. 38–39.

12 Sari Braithwaite, Tom Gara & Jane Lydon 2011, 'From Moorundie to Buckingham Palace: Images of "King" Tenberry and his son Warulan, 1845–55', *Journal of Australian Studies,* 35 (2): 165–184; Jane Lydon & Sari Braithwaite, 'Photographing South Australian Indigenous People: far more gentlemanly than many', draft manuscript 2014.

13 Captain Cadell, 'Journal Kept on Board the "Lady Augusta" Steamer, During Captain Cadell's Voyage up the Murray', *South Australian Register,* 12 September 1853.

14 Captain Cadell, 'Journal Kept on Board the "Lady Augusta" Steamer, During Captain Cadell's Voyage up the Murray', *South Australian Register,* 12 September 1853.

15 Sari Braithwaite, Tom Gara & Jane Lydon 2011, 'From Moorundie to Buckingham Palace: Images of "King" Tenberry and his son Warulan, 1845–55', *Journal of Australian Studies* 35 (2): 165–184; Jane Lydon & Sari Braithwaite, 'Photographing South Australian Indigenous People: 'far more gentlemanly than many', draft manuscript 2014.

16 Edward John Eyre 1985, *Reports and Letters to Governor Grey from E.J. Eyre at Moorunde,* Adelaide: Sullivan's Cove.

17 Under the heading 'Corporal Punishment', the website of the Adelaide Gaol gives the following information: 'There were 24 listed offences which could warrant a flogging. The cane or birch would be used on offenders under the age of 18 and whips of very light whipcord soaked in water were used on adult offenders. Up to the end of the 1890s, a prisoner could be sentenced to receive up to 150 strokes. In the 1930s this was reduced to 25–30 strokes and in the final years an average of 8–12 strokes. Whippings were abolished in the Adelaide Gaol in 1976 although the last whipping was performed in July of 1964.' South Australia was one of the last states to abolish corporal punishments. Downloaded 6 November 2014 from: http://www.adelaidegaol.org.au/Adelaide_Gaol_Life.htm

18 Henry Dudley Melville 1887, Transcript of unpublished manuscript, 'Compensation for a Life's Service Under Civil Service Regulations of South Australia', State Library of South Australia, D6976/1.

19 Edward John Eyre 1845 (2010), *Manners and Customs of the Aborigines and the State of Their Relations with Europeans,* p. 371.

20 18 April 1851, *South Australian Register;* sub-Protector Scott's report on Moorundie.

21 Douglas Pike 1957, p. 291. Pike cites O'Halloran's report of 8 April 1843.

22 Edward John Eyre 1845 (2010), *Manners and Customs of the Aborigines and the State of Their Relations with Europeans,* p. 215. For a brief reference to a 'shooting star' see Carey & Roberts 2002, p. 836.

23 Cawthorne arrived in Adelaide on 15 May 1841 on the day that Gawler's position was terminated.
24 Archer Russell 1933, 'Riverina Tracks. The Murray–Darling Country', *Sydney Morning Herald*, 15 April 1933.
25 Amanda Nettelbeck, Rick Hosking, Robert Foster among others e.g. Cf. Foster, Robert, Rick Hosking and Amanda Nettelbeck 2001, *Fatal Collisions. The South Australian Frontier and the Violence of Memory*.
26 Kay Shaffer 2001, 'Handkerchief Diplomacy', in Lynette Russell ed, *Colonial Frontiers: Indigenous–European Encounters in Settler Societies*, pp. 134–150.
27 'At least four Jamaican authors have created works in which the Rebellion figures prominently.

Chapter Twenty-One ~ Wellington

1 Ronald M. Berndt and Catherine H. Berndt (with John E. Stanton) 1993, *A World that Was*.
2 Moorhouse's report to Grey of 13 September 1841, in G. Taplin 1879 [1967], *The Folklore, Manners, Customs, and Languages of the South Australian Aborigines*, Adelaide: Government Printer.

Chapter Twenty-Two ~ 1842, Murder of George McGrath

1 'Police Commisioner's Court', *South Australian Register*, 16 January 1845; *South Australian Register*, 21 January 1845. *South Australian*, 21 January 1845, 'Wira Maldira (or Muldira), the Lake native, was again brought up on the charge of murdering George McGrath, on 2nd June, 1842.'
2 Alan Pope 2011, *One Law for All?* 'Appendix', Tables 1 & 2.
3 For example, in cases like that of Tatty Wamboureen who was charged over the death of Richard Carney discussed in chapter 23.

Chapter Twenty-Three ~ Cannibals at the Margins of Society

1 *South Australian Register*, 25 September 1841, 'Inquiry into the circumstances attending the death of a number of natives on the Murray.'
2 Shirley Lindenbaum 2004, 'Thinking About Cannibalism', *Annual Review of Anthropology*, 33: 475–498.
3 See particularly, Liz Conor 2016, *Skin Deep. Settler Impressions of Aboriginal Women*.
4 Under the direction of Hugh Morgan, Western Mining Corporation funded a series of allegedly independent pressure groups (like the Samuel Griffith Society) to pursue free trade and anti-landrights agendas. Hugh Morgan's claims about Aboriginal life and customs became extreme and he has now retired. Further information on this group can be found in my essay 'What's At Stake? History Wars, the NMA and Good Government', *Cultural Studies Review*, March 2004; and Andrew Clark, 'In their own image', *Australian Financial Review*, March 2001.
5 Herbert Basedow, 1935, *Knights of the Boomerang. Episodes from a Life Spent among the Native Tribes of Australia*, first published in 1935, republished in Heidi Zogbaum 2010, *Changing Skin Colour in Australia. Herbert Basedow and the Black Caucasian*, Melbourne: Australian Scholarly Publishing.
6 *Adelaide Observer*, December 1865.
7 Daisy Bates 1985, *The Native Tribes of Western Australia*, Edited by Isobel White, Canberra: National Library of Australia.
8 Isobel White 1990, 'The Lives of Aboriginal Girls and Women According to Daisy Bates', *Olive Pink Society Bulletin*, 2 (2): 26–28.
9 Daisy M. Bates 1928, 'Cannibal Aborigines', *Australasian* 26 May 1928.

NOTES

10   Cf. Andrew Lattas 1987, 'Savagery and Civilization: Towards a Genealogy of racism', pp. 39–58.
11   See, Andrew Lattas, 1987, 'Savagery and Civilization: Towards a Genealogy of racism', *Social Analysis: The International Journal of Social and Cultural Practice*, 21: 39–58; Andrew Lattas, 1986, 'The Aesthetics of Terror and the Personification of Power: Public Executions and the Cultural Construction of Class Relations in Colonial New South Wales, 1788–1830', *Social Analysis*, 19: 3–21.
12   Robert Foster, & Amanda Nettelbeck 2012, *Out of the Silence*, p. 81.
13   See Leith Macgillivray 1989 for a clear account of the struggle for colonial control in the south-eastern segment of the colony, mainly on Buganditj country, pp. 25–38.
14   *South Australian Register*, 9 December 1846. For Cameron see, Leith Macgillivray undated, We Have Found Our Paradise: the South-East squattocracy, 1840–1870, downloaded from: www.sahistorians.org.au/.../we-have-found-our-paradise – -the-south-east.; V. Feehan, 'Alexander Cameron: A Biographical Sketch', (unpublished dissertation), 1979; Cockburn, Vol. I, p.170; Border Watch, 2 Nov 1935; GRG24/6/1851/2844; C130 and C21, SRSA.
15   *South Australian Register*, 30 Dec 1846.
16   *Maitland Mercury and Hunter River General Advertiser*, 16 January 1847, 'The Murder by the Blacks'.
17   'Cannibalism in South Australia', *South Australian Register*, 4 September 1847.
18   Leith Macgillivray, 1989, 'We have Found Our Paradise: the South-East Squattocracy, 1840–1870', *Journal of the Historical Society of South Australia* 17: 25–38.
19   Alan Pope 2011, *One Law for All?* Chapter 5 and p. 90.
20   Alan Pope, 2011, *One Law for All?*, p. 63ff.
21   Tracey Banivanua-Mar, 2010, pp. 255–281.
22   Roslyn Poignant, 2004, Professional Savages, pp. 10–11.
23   For the legal defence of necessity in the case of 'survival cannibalism' see, Katherine Biber 2005, 'Cannibals and Colonialism', *Sydney Law Review* 27: 623–637.
24   Cf. https://www.law.cornell.edu/wex/cannibalism for an outline of US laws.

Chapter Twenty-Four ~ Port Lincoln

1   Robert Foster, & Amanda Nettelbeck 2012, *Out of the Silence*, p. 40.
2   Clamor A. Schürmann 1879 [1967], 'The Aboriginal Tribes of Port Lincoln in South Australia. Their Mode of Life, Manners, Customs, Etc', in *The Folklore, Manners, Customs, and Languages of the South Australian Aborigines*, ed. George Taplin, Adelaide: E.S. Wigg & Son, p. 209. Australians might not have met the height standards for British Guardsmen of the day, but enlistment records show a common height of around 5 feet and six inches.
3   Robert Foster, & Amanda Nettelbeck 2012, *Out of the Silence*, p. 53. I have relied on their account, given in chapter 3, of the colonisation of the country around Port Lincoln. In his 1879 introduction to the volume of essays, *The Native Tribes of South Australia*, George Taplin felt able to state that, 'In South Australia there have been no wars against the Aborigines'.
4   Steven Anderson, 2015, 'Punishment As Pacification: p. 6.
5   http://adb.anu.edu.au/biography/schurmann-clamor-wilhelm-13284.

Chapter Twenty-Five ~ 'Dead or Alive Without Discrimination'

1   Schürmann, Edwin A 1987, *I'd Rather Dig Potatoes* pp. 113–117.
2   Schürmann, Edwin A 1987, *I'd Rather Dig Potatoes*, page 139; 'cheeky' meaning in OED saucy or impudent to seniors, but in Aboriginal English often meaning dangerous.
3   Schürmann, Edwin A 1987, I'd Rather Dig Potatoes, p. 141.

4   James McLean's 'Police Experiences with the Natives. Reminiscences of the Early Days of the Colony', pp. 66–92, Digital version.
5   Foster, Robert & Amanda Nettelbeck 2012, *Out of the Silence*.
6   Pope, Alan 2011, *One Law for All?*, p. 88.
7   Foster, Robert & Amanda Nettelbeck 2012, *Out of the Silence*, p. 40.
8   Anderson, Steven 2015, 'Punishment As Pacification', p. 6.
9   Schürmann, Edwin A 1987, *I'd Rather Dig Potatoes*, pp. 149–150.
10 Hugonin and the 96th arrived in Port Lincoln 17 April 1842. Foster, Robert & Amanda Nettelbeck 2012, *Out of the Silence*, p. 45.
11 *South Australian Register*, 4 June 1842.
12 Foster, Robert & Amanda Nettelbeck 2012, *Out of the Silence*, p. 45. They cite a letter from Schürmann to Matthew Moorhouse, Protector of Aborigines, held in the Lutheran Archives, Correspondence file, 18 May 1842.
13 Schürmann, Edwin A 1987, *I'd Rather Dig Potatoes*. Clamor Schurmann, pp. 149.
14 Schürmann, Edwin A 1987, *I'd Rather Dig Potatoes*, p. 152.
15 For a comprehensive account of these atrocities see, Foster, Robert & Amanda Nettelbeck 2012, *Out of the Silence*. The History and Memory of South Australia's Frontier Wars, Adelaide: Wakefield Press.
16 Anderson, Steven 2015, 'Punishment As Pacification', p. 26.
17 *Southern Australian*, 12 July 1842.
18 Steven Anderson 2015, 'Punishment As Pacification', p. 3–26.
19 Foster, Robert & Amanda Nettelbeck 2012, *Out of the Silence*; For Pinkerton's station see: Foster, Robert, Rick Hosking and Amanda Nettelbeck 2001, *Fatal Collisions*, p. 46.
20 Foster, Robert, Rick Hosking and Amanda Nettelbeck 2001, *Fatal Collisions*, p. 47.
21 Published extracts from the report of Matthew Moorhouse, *South Australian, Government Gazette*, Thursday, Nov. 1 —Aboriginal Department', 6 November 1849.
22 This incident and the diary entry of Nathaniel Hayles comes from the discussion in, Christobel Mattingley and Ken Hampton (eds) 1988, *Survival in Our Own Land*, p. 41.

Chapter Twenty-Six ~ Poonindie

1   Brock, Peggy 1993, *Outback Ghettos*.
2   A. De Q. Robin, 'Hale, Mathew Blagden (1811–1895)', *Australian Dictionary of Biography*, Australian National University.
3   See, Claudia Nelson 1989, 'Sex and the Single Boy: Ideals of Manliness and Sexuality in Victorian Literature for Boys', *Victorian Studies* 32 (4): 525–550. Quote is from p. 21 of online edition, https://archive.org/details/manlinessofchris00hughrich/page/n11.
4   M.J. Alroe 1988, 'A Pygmalion Complex Among Missionaries.', in, Swain, Tony and Deborah Bird Rose 1988, (eds) *Aboriginal Australians and Christian Missions*.
5   Hale, Mathew 1889, *The Aborigines of Australia, Being an Account of the Institution for their Education at Poonindie*. Short, Augustus 1853, *The Poomindie Mission, Described in a Letter from the Lord Bishop of Adelaide to the Society for the Propagation of the Gospel*, London: Society for the Propagation of the Gospel.
6   'List of Inmates', *South Australian Gazette and Mining Journal*, 19 February 1852.
7   Christobel Mattingley and Ken Hampton (eds) 1988, *Survival in Our Own Land*, page 180.
8   For the effects and pain of imposing European patterns of time and season onto those of colonised peoples see, Giordano Nanni 2011.
9   Brock, Peggy 1993, *Outback Ghettos*. Cambridge: Cambridge University Press, p. 34.
10 'List of Inmatest', *South Australian Gazette and Mining Journal*, 19 February 1852.

NOTES

11 A. De Q. Robin, 'Hale, Mathew Blagden (1811–1895)', *Australian Dictionary of Biography*, National Centre of Biography, Australian National University.
12 William Blackstone 1765, *The Commentaries on the Laws of England*; Mary Wollstonecraft 1792, *A Vindication of the Rights of Woman*.
13 Larry Wolff 1996, 'The Boys Are Pickpockets, and the Girl Is a Prostitute'; Deborah Gorham 1978, 'The "Maiden Tribute of Modern Babylon" Re-Examined: Child Prostitution and the Idea of Childhood in Late-Victorian England'.
14 Hale, Mathew 1889, *The Aborigines of Australia*. Short, Augustus 1853, *The Poonindie Mission, Described in a Letter from the Lord Bishop of Adelaide to the Society for the Propagation of the Gospel*, London.
15 Brock, Peggy 1993, *Outback Ghettos*.; Neville Green 1988, 'The Cry for Justice and Equality', in, Swain, Tony and Deborah Bird Rose 1988, (eds) *Aboriginal Australians and Christian Missions. Studies*, Adelaide, p. 160.
16 I rely entirely on Brock for information about the Poonindie marriages and Kandwillan's fall from grace. Brock, Peggy 1993, *Outback Ghettos. Aborigines*, pp. 28–29.
17 Brock, Peggy 1993, *Outback Ghettos. Aborigines*, p. 29.
18 Brock, Peggy 1993, *Outback Ghettos. Aborigines*, p. 29.
19 Kempe, H., 'Mortlock, William Ranson (1821–1884)', *Australian Dictionary of Biography*, Australian National University.
20 Sir Samuel Davenport died 1906, aged 89. For an account of his life see, 'Death of Sir Samuel Davenport. A Long and Honorable Career', *The Advertiser* 4 September 1906.
21 See the Act of Parliament No. 631 of 1895, 'An Act to complete the Exchange of Certain Poonindie Lands'. Assented to, 20 December 1895.
22 Heather Goodall 1996, 'Land in Our Own Country' pp. 1–24; Richard Waterhouse, 'The Yeoman Ideal and Australian Experience 1860–1960'.
23 'Death of Sir Samuel Davenport.', *The Advertiser* 4 September 1906.
24 Joan Kyffin Willington (ed.) 1992, *Maisie: Her Life, Her Loves, Her Letters*, p. 429.
25 Brock, Peggy 1993, *Outback Ghettos. Aborigines, Institutionalisation and Survival*, Cambridge: Cambridge University Press, p. 26.

Chapter Twenty-Seven ~ In and Around the Flinders

1 Parachilna red ochre was traded up as far as Boulia if not further, Jones, Philip 1984, 'Red Ochre Expeditions', pp. 1–10.
2 McCarthy, Frederick D. 1939, '"Trade" in Aboriginal Australia' pp. 405–438.
3 Hans Mincham 1964, *The Story of the Flinders Ranges*, pp. 45–6, 86.
4 Tony Hull n.d. 'The Interactions of Whites and Blacks in the Flinders Ranges in the 1840s and 1850s', 12–23.
5 *Adelaide Observer* 18 April 1846.
6 See Mincham (1964) for an account of these years. For Horrocks, see: Jon Chittleborough 2005, 'Horrocks, John Ainsworth (1818–1846)', *Australian Dictionary of Biography*, National For the White brothers and the deaths at Crysta.l Brook see, Tony Hull n.d. 'The Interactions of Whites and Blacks in the Flinders Ranges'.
7 Mincham, Hans 1964, *The Story of the Flinders Ranges*, p. 65; Jodi Frawley and Heather Goodall 2013, 'Transforming Saltbush: Science, Mobility and Metaphor in the Remaking of Intercolonial Worlds'.
8 'The Natives – Suggestions of Captain Grey', *South Australian Register* 18 April 1840.
9 For an account of the way Hayward's violence has been ignored in local histories see, 'Fatal Collisions in the Flinders Ranges', in, Foster, Robert, Rick Hosking and Amanda Nettelbeck 2001.

Chapter Twenty-Eight ~ Hayward and McKinlay

1. Mattingley, Christobel and Ken Hampton (eds) 1988, *Survival in Our Own Land*, p. 35; Hans Mincham 1964, *The Story of the Flinders Ranges*, p. 86.
2. Foster, Hosking & Nettelbeck 2001, p. 103. 'John McKinlay (1819–1872)', *Australian Dictionary of Biography*.
3. http://www.freshford.com/hayward.htm.
4. Mattingley, Christobel and Ken Hampton (eds) 1988, *Survival in Our Own Land*, p. 42.
5. Tony Hull n.d. 'The Interactions of Whites and Blacks in the Flinders Ranges', pp. 12–23.
6. Mincham 1964, p. 86 & 89.
7. Foster, Robert & Amanda Nettelbeck 2012, *Out of the Silence*, p. 110.
8. King James Version.
9. Randall McGowen 2003, 'History, Culture and the Death Penalty'.
10. Foster, Robert, Rick Hosking and Amanda Nettelbeck 2001, *Fatal Collisions*, p. 102.
11. Mincham 1964, p. 90; for McKinlay's career see *National Dictionary of Biography*: http://adb.anu.edu.au/biography/mckinlay-john-4113.
12. Bailey, John 2006, *Mr Stuart's Track*, p. 229.
13. *Catholic Press* (Sydney), 19 September 1918.
14. McKinlay's diary notes, written at Lake Massacre.
15. Blackett, John 1911, p. 364.
16. Blackett, John 1911, p. 364.
17. Mattingley, Christobel and Ken Hampton (eds) 1988, *Survival in Our Own Land*, p. 115.
18. Harry Allen 2013, 'Burke and Wills and the Aboriginal People of the Corner Country'.
19. R. Cockburn 1925 (1975) *Pastoral Pioneers of South Australia*, p. 109.
20. Charles Wiltens Andrée Hayward (1866–1950), journalist and writer, was born on 21 July 1866 at Court Huntington, Herefordshire, England, second son of Johnson Frederick Hayward (1822–1912), gentleman, and his wife Ellen Margaret, née Litchfield.
21. Foster, Robert, Rick Hosking and Amanda Nettelbeck 2001, *Fatal Collisions*, pp. 94–114.

Chapter Twenty-Nine ~ Women and Children

1. Foster, Robert & Amanda Nettelbeck 2012, *Out of the Silence*, p. 69; also, https://veryphotographic.com.au/early-pioneers-of-yorke-peninsula.
2. Foster, Robert & Amanda Nettelbeck 2012, *Out of the Silence*, p. 69.
3. Agnes Newberry (Peg) Orchard 1899–1984, b. Ashby-de-la-Zouche, Leicestershire; married George Bradley Maltby 1922, emigrated 1924 to live in Melbourne.
4. 'Forster arrived at Glenelg in the *Siam* on 25 April 1841. His main task was to take possession of the Barossa estate for Angas. Forster helped to lay out the town of Angaston and was an efficient manager but was disliked for his pomposity and self-importance. N.S. Lynravn, 'Forster, Anthony (1813–1897)'. 'The Natives – Mr Forster – Methodist New Connexion Mission Premises, Walkerville', *South Australian Register* 14 December 1844, p. 3.
5. Adrian Desmond and James Moore 2009 [1991], *Darwin*, p. 106.
6. 'Tea Meeting to the Friends of the Aborigines', *South Australian*, 17 December 1844.
7. 'Sailing of the Symmetry', *South Australian*, 17 December 1844.
8. Stevenson, Charles 1987, *The Millionth Snowflake*.
9. Edward John Eyre 1845 (2010), *Manners and Customs of the Aborigines*, p. 156. Zoe Laidlaw 2007, 'Heathens, Slaves and Aborigines', pp. 133–161.

NOTES

10 On 26 June 1849 the *South Australian* reported that Robert Hall was to take a group of Aborigines with him on his trip to England: *We hear that Mr Hall (the Naturalist), intends taking Denbry [Tenberry], the Murray chieftain, and several other natives, to England, where they will no doubt become objects of passing curiosity. We believe it was Denbry's son who was presented to the Queen by Mr Eyre. The old fellow is a fine specimen of the former lords of South Australia, and is said to be the only real chief among the natives. His authority seems to have been derived entirely from his personal prowess, and is acknowledged by submission to his judgement and the rendering of tribute. What may become of these illustrious strangers in England after the exhibition, it is difficult to say. The British government sometimes requires persons landing savages to give security for their due return to their native land, but we opine it could not do so in this instance, inasmuch as the 'gentlemen in black' are by law no aliens but British subjects.* This quote is taken from *Dictionary of South Australian Photography 1845–1915* by R.J. Noye.

11 Amalie M. Kaus and Edward H. Kaus 1988, *Perfecting the World*, pp. 398–400; Julie Evans 2005, *Edward Eyre, Race and Colonial Governance*; Dutton, Geoffrey 1982, *In Search of Edward John Eyre*. For venereal diseases and their devastating effects over the three years of Eyre's term at Moorundie see, Edward John Eyre 1845 (2010), *Manners and Customs of the Aborigines*, p. 371.

Chapter Thirty ~ Into the Dry Lands

1 G.M. Mudd 2000, 'Mound Springs of the Great Artesian Basin in South Australia'.
2 Jones, Philip 1984, 'Red Ochre Expeditions', pp. 1–10.
3 McCarthy, Frederick D. 1939, '"Trade" in Aboriginal Australia, pp. 405–438.
4 J.T. Allen took up *Mt Enniskillen* on the Barcoo and stocked it in 1861. The first cattle reached *Bowen Downs* in 1862 under the care of R. Kerr leading four colonists, one 'black boy' and three 'gins'. *Aramac* was stocked in 1863; Lacey and a shepherd were speared on *Aramac*. Many other properties were stocked between 1861 and 1865 e.g. *Tambo*. A.C. Towner 1962, 'An Outline of the History of Western Queensland'.
5 Jack Cross 2011, *Great Central State*.
6 First stocked with cattle, Baker later put ten thousand sheep onto *Blanchewater* and *Pernunna*, his head-station.
7 'Incursions and Outrages in the Distant North', *South Australian Register*, 26 July 1865.
8 Ronald M. Berndt 1953, 'A Day in the Life of a Diyari Man'.
9 'An important feature of the "Corner Country" is the mura which corresponds to what is elsewhere in Australia called the 'dreaming track' but can be distinguished from the beliefs found further north. Jeremy Beckett and Luise Hercus 2009, *The Two Rainbow Serpents Travelling: Mura Track Narratives from the "Corner Country"*, p. 2.
10 Some idea of the richness of the fishery can be gained from the scale of the fishing license issued to the owners of *Mulka* Station which covers Lake Hope and Red Lake. Once the lakes are closed off from the Cooper Creek, they are entitled to take 350 tonnes of Golden Perch, Welch's Grunters and the Barcoo Grunter.
11 Ronald M. Berndt 1953, 'A Day in the Life of a Diyari Man'. 'Nardoo' is the prolific and widely distributed *Marsilia* sp.
12 There were three devastating years of drought from 1864–1866 – the 'Great Drought' (Litchfield 1983: 2). The difficulty of the country for pastoralists is illustrated by the way that once the huge flood that came down the Cooper in 1919 receded, the creek and its lagoons remained dry for 30 years.
13 Samuel Gason 1874, *The Dieyerie Tribe of Australian Aborigines: Their Manners and Their Customs*. Having joined the South Australian Police force in 1865, Gason was posted to *Lake Hope* in 1866. Chris Nobbs 2008, 'Talking into the Wind: Collectors on the Cooper Creek, 1890–1910',

14 Samuel Gason 1874, *The Dieyerie Tribe of Australian Aborigines: Their Manners and Their Customs*, pp. 11–12; Samuel Gason 1879, 'The Manners and Customs of the Dieyerie Tribe of Australian Aborigines'.
15 Gason's information about the customary life and language of the Diyari is well-respected. It was used by Alfred William Howitt (1830–1908), regarded as 'an authority on Aboriginal culture and social organisation', who wrote to Gason seeking information on the social organisation, beliefs and customs of the Diyari to supplement observations made while he was searching the Cooper for any survivors of the Burke and Wills expedition in 1861 and 1862. W.E.H. Stanner 1972, 'Howitt, Alfred William (1830–1908)', *Australian Dictionary of Biography*. Howitt located King, the only survivor of the ill-fated Burke and Wills attempt to cross Australia from south to north.
16 Cf. Foster, Robert 2009, 'Don't mention the War'.

Chapter Thirty-One ~ War in the North-East
1   'Night Attack of the Natives near Lake Hope'.
2   *Anna Creek* station is currently 26,000 sqare kilometres.
3   For information on *Mundowdna* see: http://www.southaustralianhistory.com.au/mundowdna.htm; also, Foster, Robert & Amanda Nettelbeck 2012, *Out of the Silence*, p. 110.
4   John Jacob lived on the property to manage it, while his brother lived in town or on one of their other holdings. In early newspaper reports the spelling of Paralana varies. Paralana contains the radioactive springs as well as a creek of water flowing from them. It has since been incorporated into Wooltana, famous for its huge wool clip.
5   Jones, Philip 2007, *Ochre and Rust*, pp. 363–4; 'Inquest on the Natives', *South Australian Register*, 7 January 1864.
6   'Law and Criminal Court, Police Court, Adelaide,' *Adelaide Express* 12 March 1864; *South Australian Register* 4 May 1864; *South Australian Advertiser*, 'Police Court', 4 May 1864. Gason gave evidence at Stuckey's trial. Stuckey was acquitted and wrote about the incident in his Reminiscences; see, Amanda Nettelbeck 2001, 'South Australian Settler Memoirs', p. 101.
7   'Native Outrages in the Far North', Parliamentary Papers (SA), laid on the table of the Legislative Council, 25 July 1865, included a letter from John Jacob to the Chief Secretary, written from *Paralana*, 16 April 1865. At this stage, Jarrold was missing, feared dead.
8   In 1868 Dean and Hack illegally used the *Kopperamanna* lease for cattle belonging either to Elder or to the Jacob brothers when the Moravians left early in 1868. See, Mattingley & Hampton, 1988: 191.
9   This information comes from: http://www.southaustralianhistory.com.au/blanchewater.htm. John Baker and Finke were involved in a shady mining transaction with James Chambers; some details given in: Margaret Goyder Kerr 1980, *Colonial Dynasty. The Chambers Family of South Australia*, Adelaide: Rigby, pp. 124–128.
10 The attack took place in the last days of 1865.
11 A description of the events of that night and the names of those present was supplemented by information from Mounted Trooper Gason and sent on in a letter from John Jacob in December 1865.
12 Jones, Philip 2007, *Ochre and Rust*, pp. 363–4.
13 'Outrages in the Far North', *South Australian Weekly Chronicle* 30 December 1865.
14 At *Blanchewater* the stock losses were massive due to over-stocking – thousands of cattle and sheep and 950 horses. The drought broke in January 1866, the station restocked in 1868.
15 'Outrages in the Far North', *South Australian Weekly Chronicle* 30 December 1865.

NOTES

16   'Outrages in the Far North', *South Australian Weekly Chronicle* 30 December 1865.
17   'Outrages in the Far North', *South Australian Weekly Chronicle* 30 December 1865.
18   'Outrages in the Far North', *South Australian Weekly Chronicle* 30 December 1865.
19   'Henry Dean', in, Cockburn, R. 1925 (1975), *Pastoral Pioneers of South Australia*, 2 vols, pages174–75.
20   Samuel Gason 1874, *The Dieyerie Tribe of Australian*; Otto Siebert. Chris Nobbs 2008, 'Talking into the Wind. 1910'.
21   For a very detailed and scholarly account see, Christine Stevens 1994, *White Man's Dreaming. Killalpaninna Mission 1866–1915*, Melbourne: Oxford University Press.

Chapter Thirty-Two ~ The Silence of the Lands, 1870

1   *South Australian Register* 29 August 1870. 'St Paul's Anglican Church was built on the corner of Flinders Street and Pulteney Street in 1863. Adelaidia, History SA, http://adelaidia.sa.gov.au/places/st-pauls-anglican-church, accessed 20 November 2016. Alexander Russell died 1886, photo of his funeral at SLSA, http://collections.slsa.sa.gov.au/resource/B+43149.
2   For a thorough, scholarly account of anti-semitism in nineteenth-century Germany see, Favret–Saada, Jeanne and Josée Contreras 2004, *Le Christianism and Ses Juifs, 1800–2000*.
3   *South Australian Register* 29 August 1870.
4   Examples of stained glass windows showing Jesus as shepherd can be found in the Bethlehem Lutheran Church on Flinders Street in Adelaide; the Anglican Church of St Michael in Mitcham; the Scots Church on North Terrace; and in the Uniting Church in Gawler. Victorian preachers and commentators frequently referred to the figure of the Good Shepherd, which provided consolation to young and old *and became the subject of thousands of stained glass windows throughout the Empire* [my emphasis]. Many Victorian charitable institutions, such as hospices and 'magdalens', were named after the Good Shepherd, a figure who also became a focus for devotional literature and art. Abstract from: Michael Wheeler 2012, ' "That they might have life".
5   *South Australian Register* 29 August 1870. Different newspapers give slightly different versions of the Dean's homily, adding or subtracting from it to suit their view of what was important. One version published by the *Register* in September, gives slightly more detail.
6   *South Australian Register* 10 September 1870.
7   Van Reyk, William 2009, 'Christian Ideals of Manliness'. For the views of Thomas Arnold on the turning of boys into Christian, manly men at Rugby school, see, Heather Ellis 2014, 'Thomas Arnold, Christian Manliness and the Problem of Boyhood'.
8   The name of the Congregational church reflects the independence of each congregation to govern itself rather than being under the authority of a ranked order of bishops and in the case of the Church of England, the monarch.
9   The men working in the Northern Territory sections of the line 'have entered into an engagement under which the strictest discipline is to be maintained. ... we believe that specific instructions have been issued to those in charge to prevent collision with the natives, to ensure the health of the men and to promote the speedy execution of the work'. *South Australian Register*, 10 September 1870. Charles Todd was 'one of the founders in 1859 of the Brougham Place Congregational Church, North Adelaide, and of the Stow Memorial Congregational Church, Adelaide, in 1865. W. Symes 1976, 'Todd, Sir Charles (1826–1910)', *Australian Dictionary of Biography*.
10   Moyal, Ann 1984, *Clear Across Australia*.
11   *South Australian Register*, 6 September 1870.

12. Goyder was a Swedenborgian. See, David Hilliard 2005, 'Unorthodox Christianity in South Australia. For the history of the Swedenborgian New Church in Adelaide see: http://newchurch.net.au/locations/adelaide/adelaide-about-us. The New Church teaches that life after death, heaven and angels are all real.
13. Pike, Glenville 'The Northern Territory Overland Telegraph.'

Chapter Thirty-Three ~ Building the Line

1. Crowder, W.A. 1871–73, unpublished diary, transcribed and researched by volunteers at the State Library of South Australia in 2007. Captain Sweet, already known as a photographer, was on board with Crowder.
2. Moyal, Ann 1984, *Clear Across Australia*.
3. When Crowder was at the Bar in 1872, some forty linesmen camped nearby were in desperate need of food. Crowder, W.A. 1871–73, unpublished diary, transcribed and researched by volunteers at the State Library of South Australia in 2007.
4. Roberts, Tony 2005, *Frontier Justice*., p. 111.
5. Melville arrived at Port Essington on the *Fly*. See Harden S. Melville, *Aboriginal Australians at Port Essington*, c. 1849. National Library of Australia, Rex Nan Kivell Collection NK942
6. Cf. Wells, Samantha 1995, *Town Camp or Homeland?*
7. Wells, Samantha 1995, *Town Camp or Homeland?*, p. 11.
8. This incident occurred just after Foelsche's arrival, during the period that Millner was standing in as Resident until Douglas arrived. Reid, Gordon 1990, *A Picnic with the Natives*, p. 38.
9. Wells, Samantha 1995, *Town Camp or Homeland?* p. 11. See also reminiscences of Mrs Dominc Daly. She published 'Digging, squatting and pioneering life in the Northern Territory of South Australia' in 1887. Upon returning to England she became the London correspondent for the *Sydney Morning Herald*, dying there on 25th August 1927.
10. For more information see, Merlan, Francesca 1978, 'Making People Quiet'.
11. Crowder, W.A. 1871–73, unpublished diary.
12. Crowder, W.A. 1871–73, unpublished diary.
13. Macfarlane, Ingereth A.S. 2010, 'Entangled Places.
14. Macfarlane, Ingereth A.S. 2010, 'Entangled Places', pp. 172–175.
15. Roberts, Tony 2009, 'The Brutal Truth'.
16. In this chapter I have drawn on Ingereth Macfarlane's research into the building and working of the telegraph station there. Her important research was carried out with Indigenous collaboration and permissions. It is the most recent and most detailed discussion of the impact of the line on Indigenous lives. See, Macfarlane, Ingereth A.S. 2010 'Entangled Places'.
17. Macfarlane citing Herbert Basedow, pp. 186–187.
18. Glenville Pike, 'The Northern Territory Overland Telegraph. An Epic of Courage.'
19. Kimber, Richard G. 1991, *The End of the Bad Old Days*, p. 8.
20. 'Seventeen hundred miles along the overland telegraph', *Adelaide Observer* 24 January 1874. This article had been published previously under the name of 'Central Australian'.
21. For details of trouble on the Roper river for country around *Elsey* station, see Merlan, Francesca 1978, 'Making People Quiet'.

Chapter Thirty-Four ~ After the Line – Central Australia

1. Quotation from field notes of Olive Muriel Pink, courtesy Lisa Watts.
2. Suzanne Jipp 1990, 'Edward Mead Bagot', *Northern Territory Dictionary of Biography*, vol. 1.

NOTES

3 David Carment 1991, *History and the Landscape in Central Australia*, Darwin.
4 Stuart Traynor 2016, *Alice Springs. From Singing Wire to Iconic Outback Town*, p. 86. Mulvaney, D.J. 1989, *Encounters in Place. Outsiders and Aboriginal Australians 1606–1985*, p. 126. Tempe Downs was established in 1889 by the seven partners who made up the Tempe Downs Passtoral Company: John Lewis, Charles Chewings, S. Drew, J. Drew, D.W.H. Patterson, W. Liston & J. Shakes.
5 R.G. Kimber 2008, 'Willshire, William Henry (1852–1925)', in, *Northern Territory Dictionary of Biography*, Volume 1.
6 Grace Koch and Harold Koch 1993, *Kaytetye Country*. p. ix.
7 Tommy Thompson Kngwarreye 1993, 'Cutting Limestone', in, Grace Koch and Harold Koch 1993, *Kaytetye Country*, pp. 51–53.
8 Vallee, Peter 2008, *Gods, Guns and Government*, p. 117.
9 In addition to Gason's posting to Barrow Creek, a policeman was stationed at the *Peak* station with another at *Charlotte Waters*. A chronology of the attack is available from the State Library of South Australia's website: 'Notes on steps taken to capture the natives concerned in the attack on Barrow Creek Telegraph Station (February 22, 1874) and the murder of Stapleton and Frank. Item 174.
10 'The Barrow's Creek Tragedy. Attack on a Telegraph Station', *Register*, 18 December 1905.
11 'Murderous Attack of Natives on the Barrow Creek Telegraph Station', *Express and Telegraph*, 23 February 1874.
12 'Murderous Attack of Natives on the Barrow Creek Telegraph Station', *Express and Telegraph*, 23 February 1874.
13 'Murderous Attack of Natives on the Barrow Creek Telegraph Station', *Express and Telegraph*, 23 February 1874.
14 The first wife of Peter Horsetailer's father was taken by George Hayes [snr] [who bought Neutral Junction station c. 1915] while Peter's father was working as a guide for camel trains travelling north from Oodnadatta to Alice Springs. Grace Koch and Harold Koch 1993, *Kaytetye Country. An Aboriginal History of the Barrow Creek Area*, Alice Springs: Institute for Aboriginal Development, fn 4, p. 32.
15 Peter Horsetailer speaking to Grace and Harold Koch at Tara Community, 17 April 1990, in, Grace Koch and Harold Koch 1993, *Kaytetye Country. Area*, pp. 11–12.
16 Tommy Thompson speaking to Grace and Harold Koch at Tara Community, 17 April 1990, in, Grace Koch and Harold Koch 1993, *Kaytetye Country*, pp. 14–16.
17 Peter Horsetailer speaking to Grace and Harold Koch at Tara Community, 17 April 1990, published in, Grace Koch and Harold Koch 1993, *Kaytetye Country*.
18 'A Brief History of Barrow Creek Since 1860', based on work carried out for a land claim by Petronella Vaarzon-Morel, in, Grace Koch and Harold Koch 1993, *Kaytetye Country*, pp. xiii–xx.
19 'A Brief History of Barrow Creek Since 1860', based on work carried out for a land claim by Petronella Vaarzon-Morel, in, Grace Koch and Harold Koch 1993, *Kaytetye Country*, xiii–xx.
20 Mulvaney, D.J. 1989, *Encounters in Place*.
21 Peter Forrest 1990, *They of the Never Never*.
22 Peter Forrest 1990 also notes that in the oral traditions in the area, it was Jock MacLennon who led a number of the killing parties on the *Elsey*. For a summary of Elsey station and the way of life presented in *We of the Never Never* by Jeanie Gunn see: http://www.southaustralianhistory.com.au/elseystation.htm.
23 'The Barrow's Creek Tragedy. Attack on a Telegraph Station', *Register*, 18 December 1905.
24 Roberts, Tony 2005, *Frontier Justice*, p. 113.
25 Foster, Robert 2009, 'Don't mention the War'. p. 4.

26 'A Trooper of the Sixties. The Late Mr S. Gason', *South Australian Register* 16 April 1897.
27 J.H. Love, 'Hamilton, George (1812–1883)', *Australian Dictionary of Biography*, see also: Love, John 2005, 'George Hamilton (1812–1883): Midshipman, Overlander, Police Commissioner, Lithographer, Artist, Poet, Author', *Journal of the Historical Society of South Australia* 33: 102–112.
28 G.W. Symes, 'Todd, Sir Charles (1826–1910)', *Australian Dictionary of Biography*.

Chapter Thirty-Five ~ On Arrernte Country

1 The waterhole had no spring to feed it but relied on a stone reservoir that was replenished from the river and local rains. Stuart Traynor 2016, *Alice Springs*.
2 For details see the information sheet prepared by the distinguished linguist, Jenny Green; it is available from the Araluen Arts Centre, Alice Springs: 'Stained Glass Window. The Painting by Wenten Rubuntja. Interpreted by Jenny Green.'
3 For a clear description of some of the major creation sites visible around Alice Springs see, David Brooks 1991, *The Arrernte Landscape of Alice Springs*, Alice Springs: Institute for Aboriginal Development.
4 *South Australian Chronicle and Weekly Mail*, 1 March 1879.
5 Gordon Reid 1990, *A Picnic with the Natives*, p. 117.
6 Gordon Reid 1990, *A Picnic with the Natives*. p. 116. Reid says that Alfred Giles was a man with undisguised contempt for Aborigines.
7 'The Barrow's Creek Tragedy. Attack on a Telegraph Station', *Register*, 18 December 1905; *South Australian Chronicle and Weekly Mail*, 1 March 1879.
8 Gordon Reid 1990, *A Picnic with the Natives*, p. 114.
9 Foster, Robert & Amanda Nettelbeck 2012, *Out of the Silence*, p. 140.
10 W.H. Willshire 1891, *The Aborigines of Central Australia with a Vocabulary of the Dialect of the Alice Springs Natives*, Adelaide: Government Printer.
11 R.G. (Dick) Kimber 1996, 'The Dynamic Century before the Horn Expedition: A Speculative History', 91–102.
12 Those accompanying Wurmbrand were William Craigie and James Norman, in, Nettelbeck, Amanda & Robert Foster 2007, *In the Name of the Law*, p. 28.
13 Nettelbeck, Amanda & Robert Foster 2007, *In the Name of the Law*, pp. 29–30.
14 Julie Robinson and Maria Zagala 2007, *A Century in Focus.*, pp. 124 & 126.
15 Nettelbeck, Amanda & Robert Foster 2007, *In the Name of the Law*, p. 27.
16 R.G. Kimber 2003, 'Real True History: the Coniston Massacre', Part 1, *Alice Springs News*, 10 September 2003.
17 'Deputations. Police Protection for Northern Runs', *South Australian Register* 32 August 1888. Those named as meeting with the Chief Secretary were: Hon H. Scott, Hon J. Warren, Messrs. F. Krichauff, MP, W.A. Horn MP, C. Giles MP, W.H. Phillips (President of the Chamber of Commerce and Agent for Mesrs Paterson, Chewings & Company), R.A. Tarlton, J. Bagot, Magarey, Rischbeith, Shakes, Drew, and Sella.
18 *The Register* 31 August 1888.
19 Reid, Gordon 1990, *A Picnic with the Natives*, p. 70; Reid, Gordon 1990, 'Foelsche, Paul Heinrich Matthias (1831–1914)', in, *Northern Territory Dictionary of Biography*, 1990, Volume 1
20 Reid, Gordon 1990, *A Picnic with the Natives*, p. 70.

Chapter Thirty-Six ~ The 'Top End' of the Territory

1 Tony Roberts 2009, 'The Brutal Truth', *The Monthly*, November.
2 Lewis, Darrell 2012, *A Wild History*, p. xiii.

NOTES

3   From the website of Deborah Bird Rose, http://deborahbirdrose.com/tag/victoria-river-downs/.
4   Rose, Deborah Bird 1991, *Hidden Histories,* pp. 76–77.
5   Tony Roberts 2009, 'The Brutal Truth', *The Monthly,* November 2009.
6   The Berndts say that in western Arnhem Land the fighting between Aborigines had no discernible impact on the numbers of women and children because women and children were nearly always preserved. Berndt, Ronald M. and Catherine H. Berndt [1951] 1963, *Sexual Behaviour in Western Arnhem Land,* p. 43.
7   Katrina Schlunke 2008, 'Captain Cook Chased a Chook'.
8   Deborah Bird Rose 2007, 'Danayarri, Hobbles (1925–1988)', *Australian Dictionary of Biography,* Canberra: Australian National University; Rose, Deborah Bird 1991, *Hidden Histories,* p. 15 ff.
9   Rose, Deborah Bird 1991, *Hidden* Histories, p. 17.
10 Cf. Fleur Ramsay 2008, 'The Mimetic Life of Captain Cook', 107–168.
11 Erich Kolig 1994, 'Rationality, Ideological Transfer, Cultural Resistance, and the Dreaming', 111–124.
12 Cf. Anthony Redmond 2008, 'Captain Cook Meets General Macarthur in the Northern Kimberley', pp. 255–270; Alan Tucker 1995, *Too Many Captain Cooks*; Fleur Ramsay 2008, 'The Mimetic Life of Captain Cook', pp. 107–168; Katrina Schlunke 2006, 'Historicising Whiteness: Captain Cook Possesses Australia', Paper presented at the 'Historicising Whiteness' Conference, Melbourne University, 22–24 November 2006.
13 Billy Gibbs, deceased, Chairperson, Western Desert Puntu Kurnuparna, writing in a preface to, Sue Devonport, Peter Johnson & Yuwali 2005, *Cleared Out. First Contact in the Western Desert,* p. ii.
14 Rubuntja, Wenten with Jenny Green 2002, *The Town Grew up Dancing. The Life and Art of Wenten Rubuntja,* Alice Springs: Jukurrpa Books, p. 162.
15 Green, Jenny 2002, *The Town Grew Up Dancing. The Life and Art of Wenten Rubuntja,* Alice Springs.
16 Charola, Erika and Felicity Meakins (eds) 2016, *Yijarni. Stories from the Gurindji Country.*
17 Rose, Deborah Bird 1991, *Hidden Histories. Black Stories from Victoria River Downs, Humbert River and Wave Hill Stations..*
18 Roberts, Tony 2005, *Frontier Justice. A History of the Gulf Country to 1900.*
19 Charola, Erika and Felicity Meakins (eds) 2016, *Yijarni. Stories from the Gurindji Country.*
20 Sam Croker worked at one time with Nat Buchanan when Mudbarra men guided them to Muranji waterhole and onwards, 'opening up' the infamous Muranji Track from Queensland across northern Australia to the west and Kimberley region
21 From *Yijarni,* pp. 60–62.
22 Lewis, Daryl 2018, *The Victoria River District Doomsday Book.*
23 Charola, Erika and Felicity Meakins (eds) 2016, *Yijarni. Stories from the Gurindji Country,* p. 37.
24 Jimmy Manngayarri in, Rose, Deborah Bird 1991, *Hidden Histories,* p. 20; photograph of Jimmy with his son, p. 42.
25 Rose, Deborah Bird 1991, *Hidden Histories,* p. 167.
26 For more on Willshire's connections with Jack Watson and on Rose's description of Watson as 'one of the most violent men' in the 1880s and 1890s see Rose 2001. Watson managed Victoria River Downs in 1894 and 1895. The artist Judy Watson refers to the way in which her great-great grandmother, Rosie, survived a massacre at *Lawn Hill Station.* She was found when hiding with another young girl and stabbed with a bayonet. The other girl seems to have died at that time (*Weekend Australian,* Review 31 March–1 April 2012.

27 Jimmy Manngayarri in, Rose, Deborah Bird 1991, *Hidden Histories*, p. 40.
28 Monteath, Peter 1961, *The Diary of Emily Caroline Creaghe, Explorer*. Today there are fourth generation Aboriginal Shadworths. Frank Shadworth is now running a station and tourism business in the Gulf country. They are Garawa people. http://sevenemustation.com.au/about-seven-emu-station/.
29 The men who were killed were known only as 'Donkey' and 'Roger', 'MC Willshire Acquitted', *Express and Telegraph* 24 July 1891. The cost of the defence was paid for by a very large sum raised by subscription, mainly from pastoralists and some other interested parties. John Strehlow 2010, *The Tale of Frieda Keysser*, pp. 431–33.
30 Nettelbeck, Amanda & Robert Foster 2007, *In the Name of the Law*.

Chapter Thirty-Seven ~ Willshire, Pornography and a Man's World

1   Forrest, Peter 1990, *They of the Never Never*, Northern Territory Library Service, p. 6.
2   Mulvaney, D.J. 1989, *Encounters in Place. Outsiders and Aboriginal Australians*, p. 126.
3   Nettelbeck, Amanda & Robert Foster 2007, *In the Name of the Law*.
4   Frank Proscham 2002, 'Eunuch Mandarins, Soldat Mamzelles, Effeminate Boys and Graceless Women. Genders', pp. 435–467.
5   '"I Shoot to Kill". Frank Hann and the Blacks', 20 April 1909 *Daily Telegraph*.
6   W.H. Willshire 1896, *The Land of the Dawning. Being Facts Gleaned from Cannibals in the Australian Stone Age*.
7   Amanda Nettelbeck 2009, 'South Australian Settler Memoirs', 97–104.
8   Cf. D.J. Mulvaney 1989, *Encounters in Place*, p. 124.
9   Willshire, W.H. 1896, *The Land of the Dawning*, chapter 5.
10 Willshire, W.H. 1896, *The Land of the Dawning*, p. 44.

Chapter Thirty-Nine ~ The Pastoral Zone

1   Forrest, Peter 1990, *They of the Never Never*; Merlan, Francesca 1978, 'Making People Quiet' in the Pastoral North: Reminiscences of Elsey Station'; Ellinghaus, Katherine 1997, 'Racism in the Never-Never: Disparate Readings of Jeannie Gunn'.
2   The fowl-roosts might have been intended to keep the precious poultry safe from marauding animals. Mrs Aneas (Jeanie) Gunn 1908, *We of the Never-Never*, chapter 6. Forrest, Peter 1990, *They of the Never Never*.
3   Kimber, Richard G. 1991, *The End of the Bad Old Days: European Settlement in Central Australia, 1871–1894*, pp. 8–9.
4   Tonkinson, Myra 1988, 'Sisterhood or Aboriginal Servitude? Black Women and White Women on the Australian Frontier', p. 30. Mathew James Savage born *c*. 1890 or 1892; worked around the Kimberley in WA for the Duracks and later for Vesteys; Lewis, Daryl 2018, *The Victoria River District Doomsday Book*..
5   Ann McGrath 1987, *Born in the Cattle*, p. 111.
6   Tonkinson, Myra 1988, 'Sisterhood or Aboriginal Servitude? Black Women and White Women on the Australian Frontier'.
7   T.G.H. Strehlow 1969, *Journey to Horseshoe Bend*, pp. 109–111.
8   Geoffrey Gray 2015, *Abrogating Responsibility. Vesteys, Anthropology and the Future of Anthropological People*, pp. 24–5; and 2014, '"He has not followed the usual sequence": Ronald M. Berndt's Secrets', *Journal of Historical Biography* 16: 61–92, downloaded from www.ufv.ca/jhb.
9   Kruger, Alec & Gerard Waterford 2007, *Alone on the Soaks. The Life and Times of Alec Kruger*.
10 See Geoffrey Gray, 2015, *Abrogating Responsibility*, for detailed analysis
11 Rick Morton 2018, *100 Years of Dirt*.

NOTES

Chapter Forty ~ A Zone of Indigenous Policing

1. Julie Evans 2009, 'Where Lawlessness is Law', p. 5.
2. W.R. Wilson 2000, 'A History of the Northern Territory Police Force 1870–1926', Unpublished PhD Thesis.
3. Melinda Hinkson and Thalia Anthony 2019, 'Three Shots. The death of Kumanjayi Walker – the Northern Territory as a Police State', *Arena*, 3 December 2019.
4. Wilson, W.R. 2000, *A History of the Northern Territory Police Force 1870–1926*, p. 313.
5. *Border Watch*, 12 May 1894, 'Besley, Brian Charles (1836–1894)'.
6. 'Paul Heinrich Matthias Foelsche (1831–1914), *Australian Dictionary of Biography*.
7. Vallee, Peter 2008, *Gods, Guns and Government.*, pp. 97–99. Obituary: http://oa.anu.edu.au/obituary/besley-brian-charles-18297; magnificent funeral: https://trove.nla.gov.au/newspaper/article/77542090.
8. Vallee, Peter 2008, *Gods, Guns and Government*.
9. 'The Alleged Ill-Treatment of Aborigines. Charges Without Foundation', *South Australian Register* 24 September 1890.
10. Vallee, Peter 2008, *Gods, Guns and Government on the Central Australian Frontier*, Canberra: Restoration Books, pp. 100–101.
11. D.J. Mulvaney, 'Francis James Gillen', *Northern Territory Dictionary of Biography*, volume 1.
12. Philip Jones 2005, *The Policeman's Eye*, p. 5.
13. Gordon Reid 'Foelsche, Paul Heinrich Matthias (1831–1914)', in, *Northern Territory Dictionary of Biography*, Volume 1.
14. Reid takes this phrase from Foelsche's letter of 1875 to the respected pastoralist and mining entrepreneur, John Lewis where it was used in connection with men mustered to deal with the killing of a telegraph employee on the Roper river in 1875. *Fought and Won*, published in 1922, is his autobiography.
15. Nettelbeck, Amanda 2004, 'Writing and Remembering Frontier Conflict: The Rule of Law in 1880s Central Australia'.
16. Gordon Reid 'Foelsche, Paul Heinrich Matthias (1831–1914)', in, *Northern Territory Dictionary of Biography*, Volume 1.
17. See: Roberts, Tony 2005, *Frontier Justice. A History of the Gulf Country to 1900*, Brisbane: UQP; Roberts, Tony 2009, 'The Brutal Truth. What Happened in the Gulf Country', *The Monthly*, November.
18. Roberts, Tony 2009, 'The Brutal Truth. What Happened in the Gulf Country'.
19. Downloaded and abridged from: https://dtc.nt.gov.au/__data/assets/pdf_file/0008/248732/History-of-Newspapers-NT.pdf.
20. John Playford 1979, 'Baker, Sir Richard Chaffey (1841–1911), *Australian Dictionary of Biography*.
21. Roberts, Tony 2009, 'The Brutal Truth. What Happened in the Gulf Country'.
22. Suzanne Saunders, 'Solomon, Vaiben Louis (1853–1908), *Northern Territory Dictionary of Biography*.
23. Vaiben Louis Solomon, 'The Northern Territory', *The Express and Telegraph* 30 May 1888.
24. Roberts, Tony 2009, 'The Brutal Truth. What Happened in the Gulf Country'.

Chapter Forty-One ~ The Mission Zone

1. Myra Tonkinson 1988, 'Sisterhood or Aboriginal Servitude?.
2. Catherine Bishop 2021, *Too Much Cabbage and Jesus Christ*.
3. Peggy Brock 1988, 'The Missionary Factor in Adnyamathanha History', p. 282.
4. Curtis-Wendlandt, Lisa 2010, 'Corporal Punishment and Moral Reform at Hermannsburg,

5   Alroe, M.J. 1988, 'A Pygmalion Complex Among Missionaries.
6   'The past is a foreign country: they do things differently there', is the first line of Leslie Hartley's novel *The Go-Between* (1953).
7   Cowlishaw, Gillian 1990, 'Helping Anthropologists.
8   Gillian Cowlishaw 1990, 'Helping Anthropologists.
9   Kenelm Burridge 1988, 'Aborigines and Christianity'.
10 Deborah Bird Rose 1998, 'Signs of Life on a Barbarous Frontier'.
11 Alroe, M.J. 1988, 'A Pygmalion Complex Among Missionaries..
12 Brady, Maggie 1999, The Politics of Space and Mobility.

Chapter Forty-Two ~ Adelaide, 1880s–90s
1   For Tommy Walker, see http://adb.anu.edu.au/biography/poltpalingada-booboorowie-13154.
2   Statistics based on the 1891 South Australian Census.
3   Hilliard, David 2006, 'Anglicans in South Australian Public Life'.
4   Among the earliest Jewish colonists, the merchant Emanuel Solomon and family arrived from New South Wales in 1838. He was in business with his brother, Vaiben. Emanuel Solomon's letter book and other documents are held in the State Library of South Australia.
5   Fischer, Peter & Kay Hannaford Seamark 2005, *Vintage Adelaide. Beautiful Buildings from the Adelaide Square Mile.*
6   Pike 2007 p. 95.
7   Judith Brett 2019, *From Secret Ballot to Democracy Sausage.*
8   Hilliard, David 2006, 'Anglicans in South Australian Public Life', *Journal of the Historical Society of South Australia*, 34, p. 6.
9   See, https://guides.slsa.sa.gov.au/c.php?g=410301&p=2794853.
10 For details of women's struggles and the incredible work required before women could enter parliament see, Jones, Helen 1986, *In Her Own Name. A History of Women in South Australia from 1836*; for Steele and Cooper see, Stock, Jenny Tilby, 'Steele, Joyce (1909–1991)' 2014, *Australian Dictionary of Biography*, http://adb.anu.edu.au/biography/steele-joyce-15719; Stock, Jenny Tilby, 'Cooper, Jessie (1914–1993)' 2017, *Australian Dictionary of Biography*.
11 The Aborigines Friends Association established the mission in 1859.
12 'Aboriginal Camps', *South Australian Register* 26 August, p. 5.
13 Robert Foster 2001, 'Tommy Walker'; p. 576; Robert Foster 2005, 'Poltpalingada Booboorowie (1830–1901)', *Australian Dictionary of Biography*.
14 Ronald Elmslie and Susan Nance 1988, 'Smith, William Ramsay (1859–1937)'.
15 http://adb.anu.edu.au/biography/poltpalingada-booboorowie-13154.
16 Susan Hosking 'David Unaipon'.
17 Philip Jones 1990, 'Unaipon, David (1872–1967), *Australian Dictionary of Biography*.

Chapter Forty-Three ~ Colonial Holocaust
1   *The Shorter Oxford English Dictionary. On Historical Principles*, Oxford: Clarendon Press.
2   The Christian Bible, all references to the King James translation.
3   *Australian Humanities Review* 1999, Issue 13.
4   Carol Delaney, 1998, *Abraham on Trial. The Social Legacy of Biblical Myth.*
5   'And he said, Take now thy son, thine only son Isaac, whom thou lovest, and get thee into the land of Moriah; and offer him there for a burnt offering upon one of the mountains which I will tell thee of.' Genesis 22:2.
6   Merlan, Francesca 1994, 'Narratives of Survival.'

NOTES

7   Merlan, Francesca 1994, 'Narratives of Survival'.

Chapter Forty-Four ~ 1901 – The Birth of a Racial State

1   Billie Melman, 1996, 'Under Western Historian's Eyes. Deborah Bird Rose (2001) wrote of the significance of death as a marker of the transfer of power from Indigenous Australians to the colonists.

2   Maggie Brady, 2021, 'The Reinvention of Sweden's "Gothenburg System"' & *Guardian Australia* 31 December 2021.

Chapter Forty-Five ~ The Mission Zone in the 'Post-Colony'

1   'Superintendent Charged', *West Australian* 3 March 1934.

2   'Alice Springs Notes', *Northern Standard NT*, 20 March 1934.

3   Alec Kruger & Gerard Waterford 2007, *Alone on the Soaks. The Life and Times of Alec Kruger*.

4   For newspaper comment on Forrest River Mission see, https://www.theguardian.com/australia-news/2019/mar/08/a-very-tragic-history-how-the-trauma-of-a-1926-massacre-echoes-through-the-years.

5   http://adb.anu.edu.au/biography/long-margaret-jane-retta-10857. Cf. the very interesting first four chapters of, Catherine Bishop 2021, *Too Much Cabbage and Jesus Christ*.

6   Royal Commission into Institutional Responses to Child Sexual Abuse At Darwin, 'Retta Dixon Home – Case Study 17: Submission on Behalf of Lorna Cubillo, Sandra Kitching, AJW, AJA, AKV, AKU.'

7   Greg Pemberton 2014, 'The Price Aboriginal Children Paid at Retta Dixon', *Sydney Morning Herald* 29 September 2014. Hasluck became a civil servant and then a Liberal Party politician.

8   Charola, Erika & Felicity Meakins (eds) 2016, *Yijarni*.

9   Booth, Katherine and Lisa Ford, 2016, 'Ross v Chambers: Assimilation Law and Policy in the Northern Territory', p. 12. For more detail on Hasluck and assimilation, see p. 6 ff.

10   I am drawing on material I gathered in preparing a biography of Olive Pink, *The Indomitable Miss Pink. A Life in Anthropology*, (2001) 2017, Sydney: Lhr Press.

References

— 1990 (1841), 'Two Early Reports on the Aborigines of South Australia (Introduction by Robert Foster)', *Journal of the Anthropological Society of South Australia*, 28 (1-2): 38–63.

Abbott, Agnes 2015, in, Men and Women of Central Australia and the Central Land Council 2015, *Every Hill Got a Story. We Grew Up in Country*, Compiled and Edited by Marg Bowman, Melbourne: Hardie Grant.

Adams, John 1988, 'My Early Days in the Colony', *Journal of the Anthropological Society of South Australia*, 26 (6): 3–11.

Allen, Harry 2013, 'Burke and Wills and the Aboriginal People of the Corner Country', in, Ian D. Clark and Fred Cahir (eds) 2013, *The Aboriginal Story of Burke and Wills. Forgotten Narratives*, Melbourne: CSIRO Publishing.

Alroe, M.J. 1988, 'A Pygmalion Complex Among Missionaries. The Catholic Case in the Kimberley', in, Swain, Tony and Deborah Bird Rose 1988, (eds) *Aboriginal Australians and Christian Missions. Ethnographic and Historical Studies*, Adelaide: Australian Association for the Study of Religions.

Amery, Robert and Lester-Irabinna Rigney 2006, 'Recognition of Kaurna Cultural Heritage in the Adelaide Parklands: A Linguist's and Kaurna Academic's Perspective. Progress to Date and Future Initiatives', Paper prepared for the Adelaide Parklands Symposium, Adelaide.

Amery, Robert, 'Sally and Harry: Insights into Early Kaurna Contact History', in Simpson and Hercus, *History in Portraits*, p. 86.

Amery, Rob and Georgina Yambo Williams 2002, 'Reclaiming Through Renaming: the Reinstatement of Kaurna Toponyms in Adelaide and the Adelaide Plains', in, L. Hercus, L. Hodges and J. Simpson (eds) *The Land is a Map: Placenanes of Indigenous Origin in Australia*, Canberra: Pandanus Books, pp. 255–276.

Amery, Robert 2018, 'Koeler and the Dresdeners: Contrasting Views of Five Early Germans Towards Indigenous Peoples in South Australia', in, *Journal of the Anthropological Society of South Australia* 42: 162.

REFERENCES

Anderson, Mary 2015, 'Unfortunately I wasn't one of those', in, Marg Bowman (ed.) *Every Hill Got a Story*, Alice Springs: Men and Women of Central Australia & the Central Land Council, p. 85.

Anderson, Steven 2015, 'Punishment As Pacification: The Role of Indigenous Executions On the South Australian Frontier, 1836-1862', *Aboriginal History* 39: 3–26.

Anonymous, 'Some Social Aspects of Early Colonial Life. By A Colonist of 1839', *South Australian Register*, 26 October 1878.

Angas, George French 1847, *Savage Life and Scenes in Australia and New Zealand: Being an Artist's Impressions of Countries and People at the Antipodes*, (2 vols) London: Smith, Elder, and Co.

Attwood, Bain and S.G. Foster (eds) 2003, *Frontier Conflict. The Australian Experience*, Canberra: National Museum of Australia.

Auerbach, Jeffrey 2004, 'The picturesque and the homogenisation of Empire', *British Art Journal* 5 (1): 47–54.

Bailey, John 2006, *Mr Stuart's Track. The Forgotten Life of Australia's Greatest Explorer*, Sydney: Macmillan.

Banivanua-Mar, Tracey 2010, 'Cannibalism and Colonialism: Charting Colonies and Frontiers in Nineteenth-Century Fiji', *Comparative Studies in Society and History* 52 (2): 255–281.

Barry, Amanda, Joanna Cruickshank, Andrew Brown-May and Patricia Grimshaw (eds) 2008, *Evangelists of Empire?: Missionaries in Colonial History*, Melbourne: University of Melbourne eScholarship Research Centre, available at: http://msp.esrc.unimelb.edu.au/shs/missions.

Basedow, Herbert 1935, *Knights of the Boomerang*, reprinted in, Heidi Zogbaum 2010, *Changing Skin Colour in Australia. Herbert Basedow and the Black Caucasian*, Melbourne: Australian Scholarly Publishing.

Bates, Daisy 1938, *The Passing of the Aborigines. A Lifetime Spent Among the Natives of Australia*, London: John Murray.

Bates, Daisy 1985, *The Native Tribes of Western Australia*, Edited by Isobel White, Canberra: National Library of South Australia.

Beckett, Jeremy and Luise Hercus 2009, *The Two Rainbow Serpents Travelling: Mura Track Narratives from the "Corner Country"*, Canberra: ANU E Press.

Beckett, Jeremy, Luise Hercus, Sarah Martin 2008, *Mutawintji: Aboriginal Cultural Association with Mutawintji National Park*, Sydney: Office of the Registrar, Aboriginal Land Rights Act 1983. Downloaded from, http://www.oralra.nsw.gov.au/pdf/annualreports/ReportsMutawintji.pdf.

Beecham, John 1838, *Colonization. Being Remarks on Colonization in General, With an Examination Of the Proposals Of the Association Which Has Been Formed For Colonizing New Zealand*, London: Hatchards & Hamilton, Adams & Co.

Bell, Diane 1998, *Ngarrindjeri Wurruwarrin: A World That Is, Was, and Will Be,* Melbourne: Spinifex Press.

Bell, James 2011, *Private Journal of A Voyage to Australia 1838–1839,* Edited by Richard Walsh, Sydney: Allen & Unwin.

Bennett, Bruce 1983, 'Hayward, Charles Wiltens Andrée (1866–1950)', *Australian Dictionary of Biography,* Canberra: Australian National University, http://adb.anu.edu.au/biography/hayward-charles-wiltens-andree-6617/text11393, published first in hardcopy 1983, accessed online 9 June 2015.

Berndt, Catherine H. 1989, 'Retrospect, and Prospect. Looking Back Over 50 Years, in, Brock, Peggy (ed.) 1989, *Women, Rites and Sites. Aboriginal Women's Cultural Knowledge,* Sydney: Allen & Unwin, pp. 1–20.

Berndt, Catherine H, 'Albert Karloan', Australian Dictionary of Biography: http://adb.anu.edu.au/biography/karloan-albert-10656, accessed 1 February 2013.

Berndt, Ronald M. 1941, 'Tribal Migrations and Myths Centring on Ooldea, South Australia', *Oceania* 12 (1): 1–20.

Berndt, Ronald M. 1941, 'The Bark Canoe of the Lower River Murray, South Australia', *Mankind* 3 (1): 17–28.

Berndt, Ronald 1953, 'A Day in the Life of a Dieri Man Before Alien Contact', *Anthropos* 48 (1/2) 171–201.

Berndt, Ronald & Catherine Berndt 1942, 'A Preliminary Report of Field Work in the Ooldea Region, Western South Australia', *Oceania* 12 (4): 305–330.

Berndt, Ronald & Catherine Berndt 1951, *From Black to White in South Australia,* Melbourne: F.W. Cheshire.

Berndt Ronald and Catherine Berndt 1952, 'A Selection of Children's Songs from Ooldea, Western South Australia', *Mankind* 4 (9): 364–376.

Berndt, Ronald M. and Catherine H. Berndt 1964, *The World of the First Australians,* Sydney: Ure Smith.

Berndt, Ronald M. and Catherine H. Berndt (with John E. Stanton) 1993, *A World that Was. The Yaraldi of the Murray River and the Lakes, South Australia,* Vancouver: UBC Press.

Berndt, Ronald M. & T. Harvey Johnston 1942, 'Death, Burial, and Associated Ritual at Ooldea, South Australia', *Oceania* 12 (3);189–208.

Bickford, Katerina 1999, 'An Examination of the Station At Moorundie After Eyre and an Assessment of the Work of E.B. Scott, 1847-1856', *Journal of the Anthropological Society of South Australia,* 32 (1): no page numbers cited.

Birman, Wendy 1967, 'Wylie (?–?)', *Australian Dictionary of Biography,* National Centre of Biography, Australian National University, http://adb.anu.edu.au/biography/wylie-2823/text4047, published in hardcopy 1967, accessed online 16 September 2014.

REFERENCES

Bishop, Catherine 2008, '"She Has the Native Interests Too Much at Heart". Annie Lock's Experiences as a Single, White, Female Missionary to Aborigines, 1903-1937', in, Amanda Barry, Joanna Cruickshank, Andrew Brown-May and Patricia Grimshaw (eds) 2008, *Evangelists of Empire?: Missionaries in Colonial History*, Melbourne: University of Melbourne eScholarship Research Centre, available at: http://msp.esrc.unimelb.edu.au/shs/missions.

Bishop, Catherine 2021, *Too Much Cabbage and Jesus Christ. Australia's Mission Girl, Annie Lock*, Adelaide: Wakefield Press.

Blackett, John 1911, *History of South Australia: A Romantic and Successful Experiment in Colonization*, Adelaide: Hussey & Gillingham Ltd.

Blackstone, William 1765, *The Commentaries on the Laws of England*, Oxford: Clarendon Press.

Bolton, Geoffrey C. 1972, 'Hann, Frank Hugh (1846–1921)', *Australian Dictionary of Biography*, Australian National University, accessed 19 July 2019 from http://adb.anu.edu.au/biography/hann-frank-hugh-3906.

Booth, Katherine and Lisa Ford 2016, 'Ross v Chambers: Assimilation Law and Policy in the Northern Territory', *Aboriginal History* 40: 3–25.

Brady, Maggie 1987, 'Leaving the Spinifext: the Impact of Rations, Missions and the Atomic Tests on the Southern Pitjanthatjara', *Records of the South Australian Museum*, 20: 35–46.

Brady, Maggie 1999, The Politics of Space and Mobility: Controlling the Ooldea a/Yalata Aborigines, 1952–1982,' *Aboriginal History* 23: 1–14.

Brady, Maggie 2021,'The Reinvention of Sweden's "Gothenburg System" in Rural Australia: The Community Hotels Movement', *Journal of Australian Studies*,45 (1): 108–124, DOI: 10.1080/14443058.2021.1871934; & *Guardian Australia* 31 December 2021.

Braithwaite, Sari, Tom Gara & Jane Lydon 2011, 'From Moorundie to Buckingham Palace: Images of "King" Tenberry and his son Warulan, 1845–55, *Journal of Australian Studies*, 35 (2): 165–184.

Brock, Peggy 1985, 'A History of the Adnyamathanha of the North Flinders Ranges – Methodological Considerations', *Journal of the Oral History Society of Australia* 7: 68–77.

Brock, Peggy 1988, 'The Missionary Factor in Adnyamathanha History', in, Swain, Tony and Deborah Bird Rose 1988, (eds) *Aboriginal Australians and Christian Missions. Ethnographic and Historical Studies*, Adelaide: Australian Association for the Study of Religions.

Brock, Peggy (ed.) 1989, *Women, Rites and Sites. Aboriginal Women's Cultural Knowledge*, Sydney: Allen & Unwin.

Brock, Peggy 1993, *Outback Ghettos. Aborigines, Institutionalisation and Survival*, Cambridge: Cambridge University Press.

Brooks, David 1991, *The Arrernte Landscape of Alice Springs*, Alice Springs: Institute for Aboriginal Development.

Broughton, Trev Lynn 1997, 'Impotence, Biography, and the Froude-Carlyle Controversy: "Revelations on Ticklish Topics"', *Journal of the History of Sexuality* 7 (4): 501–536.

Brown, Judith & Barbara Mullins 1980, *Town Life in Pioneer South Australia*, Adelaide: Rigby.

Bucknall, Graeme 1990, 'Pioneers of the Old Track. Oodnadatta – Alice Springs, 1870–1929, Occasional Paper 11, Darwin: Northern Territory Library Service.

Burleigh, Michael and Wolfgang Wipperman 1991, *The Racial State: Germany 1933–1945*, Cambridge University Press, Cambridge.

Burr, Thomas and George Grey 1845, 'Account of Governor G. Grey's Exploratory Journey Along the South-Eastern Sea-Bord of South Australia', *Journal of the Royal Geographical Society of London* 15: 160–184.

Burridge, Kenelm 1988, 'Aborigines and Christianity. An Overview', in, Swain, Tony and Deborah Bird Rose 1988, (eds) *Aboriginal Australians and Christian Missions. Ethnographic and Historical Studies*, Adelaide: Australian Association for the Study of Religions.

Burnstein, Miriam Elizabeth 2010 'Reinventing the Marian Persecutions in Victorian England', *Partial Answers: Journal of Literature and the History of Ideas*, 8 (2): 341–364.

Carey, Hilary M. 2009, 'Death, God and Linguistics: Conversations with Missionaries on the Australian Frontier, 1824–1845.

Carey, Hilary M. and David Roberts 2002, 'Smallpox and the BaiameWaganna of Wellington Valley, New South Wales. The Earliest Nativist Movement in Aboriginal Australia, *Ethnohistory* 49 (4): 821–869.

Carey, Hilary M. 2011, *God's Empire. Religion and Colonialism in the British World, c. 1801–1908*, Cambridge & New York: Cambridge University Press.

Carlyle, Thomas [1840] 1993, *On Heroes, Hero-Worship and the Heroic in History*, Edited with an Introduction by Michael K. Goldberg, University of California Press.

Carment, David 1991, *History and the Landscape in Central Australia*, Darwin: ANU North Australian Research Unit.

Carment, David 2011, 'Stuart's Triumph: Planting the Flag on the Shores of the Indian Ocean', *Journal of Northern Territory History* 22: 97–103.

Carrington, Kerry, Alison McIntosh & John Scott 2010, 'Globalization, Frontier Masculinities and Violence', *British Journal of Criminology* 50: 393–413.

Castles, Alex C. and Michael C. Harris 1987, *Lawmakers and Wayward Whigs: Government and Law in South Australia, 1836–1986*, Adelaide: Wakefield Press.

REFERENCES

Cawthorne, W.A. 1927, 'Rough Notes on the Manners and Customs of the Natives', *Proceedings of the Royal Geographical Society of Australia, South Australian Branch*, 27: 47–77.

Charola, Erika and Felicity Meakins (eds) 2016, *Yijarni. Stories from the Gurindji Country*, Canberra: Aboriginal Studies Press.

Chauncy, Theresa S.E. Snell, 1836–37, *Journal of a Residence of Three Months in the British Province of South Australia*, Unpublished transcript, State Library of South Australia.

Cheater, Christine 2012, 'The Girl in the Red Dress: Imagining Mathinna', Unpublished paper.

Clarke, Philip A, 1991(a), 'Adelaide as an Aboriginal Landscape', *Aboriginal History* 15 (1): 54–72.

Clarke, Philip A. 1998, 'The Aboriginal Presence on Kangaroo Island, South Australia', in, Jane Simpson and Luise Hercus, (eds) *History in Portraits Biographies of Nineteenth Century South Australian People*, Sydney: Southwood Press.

Cleland, J.B. 1966, 'Preface', in, B.C. Cotton (ed.) *Aboriginal Man in South and Central Australia*, Adelaide: Board for Anthropological Research, University of Adelaide.

Clyne, Robert 1987, *Colonial Blue. A History of the South Australian Police Force*, Adelaide: Wakefield Press.

Clytus, Radiclani 2005, 'At Home in England: Black Imagery Across the Atlantic', in, Jan Marsh 2005 (ed.) *Black Victorians. Black People in British Art 1800–1900*, Lund Humphries: Aldershot & Birmingham.

Cockburn, R. 1925 (1975), *Pastoral Pioneers of South Australia*, 2 vols, Adelaide: Publishers Limited.

Coleman, Deirdre 2003, 'Janet Schaw and the Complexions of Empire', *Eighteenth Century Studies*, 36 (2): 169–193.

Commonwealth of Australia 1997, *Bringing Them Home. Report of the National Inquiry into the Separation of Aboriginal and Torres Strait Islander Children from their Families*, Canberra: Human Rights Commission.

Condello, Annette 2011, 'Sybaris is the land where it wishes to take us': Luxurious insertions in Picturesque gardens', *Architectural Research Quarterly (arq)* 15 (3): 261–269.

Conor, Liz 2012, 'The "Piccaninny": Racialized Childhood, Disinheritance, Acquisition and Child Beauty', *Postcolonial Studies* 15 (1): 45–68.

Conor, Liz 2016, *Skin Deep. Settler Impressions of Aboriginal Women*, Perth: University of Western Australia Publishing.

Cooper, Frederick and Ann Laura Stoler, *Tensions of Empire. Colonial Cultures in a Bourgeois World*, Berkeley & London: University of California Press.

Cossins, Annie 2015, *Female Criminality. Infanticide, Moral Panics and The Female Body*, United Kingdom: Palgrave Macmillan.

Cowlishaw, Gillian 1990, 'Helping Anthropologists: cultural continuity in the constructions of Aboriginalists', *Canberra Anthropology* 13 (2): 10.

Cross, Jack 2011, *Great Central State. The Foundation of the Northern Territory*, Adelaide: Wakefield Press.

Crowder, W.A. 1871–73, unpublished diary, transcribed and researched by volunteers at the State Library of South Australia in 2007. Downloaded from: http://www.slsa.sa.gov.au/archivaldocs/d/D8065_CrowderDiary_transcript.pdf

Crowley, Vicki 2001, 'Acts of Memory and Imagination: Reflections on Women's Suffrage and the Centenary Celebrations of Suffrage in South Australia in 1994', *Australian Feminist Studies* 16 (35): 225–240.

Curtis-Wendlandt, Lisa 2010, 'Corporal Punishment and Moral Reform at Hermannsburg Mission', *History Australia* 7: 1.

Davidoff, Leonore and Catherine Hall 2002, *Family Fortunes. Men and Women of the English Middle Class 1789–1850*, (Revised edition) London: Routledge.

Delaney, Carol 1998, *Abraham on Trial. The Social Legacy of Biblical Myth*, Princeton: Princeton University Press.

Dissel, Dirk Van 1976, 'Short, Augustus (1802–1883)', *Australian Dictionary of Biography*, National Centre of Biography, Australian National University, http://adb.anu.edu.au/biography/short-augustus-4577/text7515, published first in hardcopy 1976, accessed online 1 June 2015.

Donovan, Peter 1988, *Alice Springs. Its History & the People Who Made It*, Alice Springs: Alice Springs Town Council.

duBois, P. 2001, *Trojan Horses. Saving the Classics from the Conservatives*, New York: New York University Press.

Duffield, D.W, J.C. Duffield, W.R. Giles and D.F. Jones 1989, *Shady Grove. Tadmor in the Wilderness*, Adelaide

Duncan, Beth 1998, 'Mary Thomas. South Australian Pioneer, 1787–1875'. Unpublished manuscript, State Library of South Australia.

Duncan, Beth 2007, *Mary Thomas, Founding Mother. The Life and Times of a South Australian Pioneer*, Adelaide: Wakefield Press.

Dutton, Geoffrey 1966, 'Eyre, Edward John (1815–1901)', *Australian Dictionary of Biography*, National Centre of Biography, Australian National University, http://adb.anu.edu.au/biography/eyre-edward-john-2032/text2507, published in hardcopy 1966, accessed online 3 September 2014.

Dutton, Geoffrey 1982, *In Search of Edward John Eyre*, Melbourne: Macmillan.

Edwards, Robert (n.d.) *The Kaurna People of the Adelaide Plains*, Adelaide: South Australian Museum.

REFERENCES

Edwards, Robert 1972, *Aboriginal Bark Canoes of the Murray Valley*, Adelaide: Rigby.

Edwards, Bill 2011, 'The Moravian Church in South Australia' in, Peter Monteath (ed.) *Germans. Travellers, Settlers and Their Descendants in South Australia*, Adelaide: Wakefield Press.

Elbourne, Elizabeth 2003 (b), 'The Sin of the Settler: The 1835–36 Select Committee on Aborigines and Debates Over Virtue and Conquest in the Early Nineteenth-Century British White Settler Empire', *Journal of Colonialism and Colonial History* 4 (3), downloaded 6 July 6, 2013: http://muse.jhu.edu.ezlibproxy.unisa.edu.au/journals/journal_of_colonialism_and_colonial_history/v004/4.3elbourne.html. No page numbers available.

Elder, David 1984, *William Light's Brief Journal and Australian Diaries*, Adelaide: Wakefield Press.

Elder, David 1987, *Art of William Light*, Adelaide: Corporation of the City of Adelaide and Wakefield Press.

Ellinghaus, Katherine 1997, 'Racism in the Never-Never: Disparate Readings of Jeannie Gunn', *Hecate* 23 (2) 76–94.

Ellis, Catherine J. 1979, 'Functions and Features of Central and South Australian Aboriginal Music', in, Jennifer Isaacs (ed.) 1979, *Australian Aboriginal Music*, Sydney: Aboriginal Artists Agency Ltd.

Ellis, Catherine J. 1984, 'The Nature of Australian Aboriginal Music', *International Journal of Music Education* 4: 47–50.

Ellis, Catherine J. and Linda Barwick 1989, 'Antakirinja Women's Song Knowledge 1963–72', in, Brock, Peggy (ed.) 1989, *Women, Rites and Sites. Aboriginal Women's Cultural Knowledge*, Sydney: Allen & Unwin, pp. 21–40.

Ellis, Elizabeth Marrkilyi, Jennifer Green, Inge Kral and Lauren Reed 2019, 'Mara yurriku: Western Desert Sign Languages", *Australian Aboriginal Studies* 2: 89–111.

Ellis, Heather (2014) 'Thomas Arnold, Christian Manliness and the Problem of Boyhood', *Journal of Victorian Culture*, 19 (4): 425–441, DOI: 10.1080/13555502.2014.969975.

Elmslie, Ronald & Susan Nance 1988, 'Smith, William Ramsay (1859–1937)', *Australian Dictionary of Biography*, Canberra: Australian National University.

Ernst, Thomas 1990, 'Mates, Wives and Children: An Exploration of Concepts of Relatedness in Australian Culture', *Social Analysis. Journal of Cultural and Social Practice*, 27: 110–118.

Evans, Julie 2002, 'Re-reading Edward Eyre. Race, Resistance and Repression in Australia and the Caribbean', *Australian Historical Studies* 33: 174–198.

Evans, Julie 2005, *Edward Eyre, Race and Colonial Governance*, Dunedin NZ: University of Otago Press.

Evans, Julie 2009, 'Where Lawlessness is Law: The Settler-Colonial Frontier as a Legal Space of Violence, *The Australian Feminist Law Journal* 30: 3–22.

Evans, Richard J. 2019, *The Pursuit of Power: Europe, 1815–1914*, Penguin Books, electronic edition.

Eickelkamp, Ute 2004, 'Egos and Ogres. Aspects of Psychosexual Development and Cannibalistic Demons in Central Australia', *Oceania* 74 (3): 161–189.

Eyre, Edward John 2011, *Journals of Expeditions of Discovery into Central Australia, in the Years 1840-1*, Cambridge: Cambridge University Press.

Eyre, Edward John 1845 (2010), *Manners and Customs of the Aborigines and the State of Their Relations with Europeans*, London: T. & W. Boone.

Eyre, Edward John 1984, *Autobiographical Narrative of Residence and Exploration in Australia 1832-1839*, edited by Jill Waterhouse, London: Caliban Books.

Eyre, Edward John 1985, *Reports and Letters to Governor Grey from E.J. Eyre at Moorunde*, Adelaide: Sullivan's Cove.

Fahy, Norah 2001, 'Prostitution', in, Wilfred Prest (ed.), *The Wakefield Companion to South Australian History*, Adelaide: Wakefield Press.

Favret-Saada, Jeanne and Josée Contreras 2004, *Le Christianism and Ses Juifs, 1800-2000*, Paris: Editions du Seuil.

Favret-Saada, Jeanne 2014 (b), 'A fuzzy distinction. Anti-Judaism and anti-Semitism. (An excerpt from *Le Judaisme et ses Juifs*)', *Hau: Journal of Ethnographic Theory* 4 (3): 335–340.

Feldman, David 2007, 'Jews and the British Empire c. 1900', *History Workshop Journal* 63: 70–89.

Finnane, Mark 2001, 'Crime', in, Prest, Wilfrid 2001, *The Wakefield Companion to South Australian History*, Adelaide: Wakefield Press.

Finnane, Mark & Fiona Paisley 2010, 'Police Violence and the Limits of Law on a Late Colonial Frontier: The "Borroloola Case" in 1930s Australia', *Law and History Review*, 28 (1): 141–171.

Fischer, Peter & Kay Hannaford Seamark 2005, *Vintage Adelaide. Beautiful Buildings from the Adelaide Square Mile*, Adelaide: East Street Publications.

Ford, Lisa 2010, *Settler Sovereignty. Jurisdiction and Indigenous People in America and Australia, 1788–1836*, Cambridge, Mass & London: Harvard University Press.

Forrest, Peter 1990, *They of the Never Never*, Darwin: Northern Territory Library Service.

Foster, Robert 1990 (a), 'The Aborigines Location in Adelaide: South Australia's First "Mission" to the Aborigines', *Journal of the Anthropological Society of South Australia* 28 (1 & 2): 11–37.

REFERENCES

Foster, Robert 1990 (b), 'Two Early Reports on the Aborigines of South Australia', *Journal of the Anthropological Society of South Australia* 28 (1 & 2): 38–63.

Foster, Robert 2001, 'Tommy Walker', in, Wilfred Prest (ed.), *The Wakefield Companion to South Australian History*, Adelaide: Wakefield Press.

Foster, Robert 2005, 'Poltpalingada Booboorowie (1830–1901)', *Australian Dictionary of Biography*, Canberra: Australian National University.

Foster, Robert 2009, '"Don't mention the War". Frontier Violence and the Language of Concealment', *History Australia* 6 (3): 4.

Foster, Robert, Paul Monaghan and Peter Mühlhausler 2000, *Early Forms of Aboriginal English in South Australia, 1840s–1920s*, Canberra: Pacific Linguistics.

Foster, Robert, Rick Hosking and Amanda Nettelbeck 2001, *Fatal Collisions. The South Australian Frontier and the Violence of Memory*, Adelaide: Wakefield Press.

Foster, Robert & Amanda Nettelbeck 2012, *Out of the Silence. The History and Memory of South Australia's Frontier Wars*, Adelaide: Wakefield Press.

Foucault, Michel 1986, 'Of Other Spaces: Utopias and Heterotopias', *Diacritics*, Spring, 22–27.

Gammage, Bill 2011, *The Biggest Estate on Earth. How Aborigines Made Australia*, Sydney: Allen & Unwin.

Ganter, Regina 2018, *The Contest for Aboriginal Souls. European Missionary Agendas in Australia*, Canberra: ANU Press.

Gara, Tom 1990, 'The Life of Ivaritji ("Princess Amelia") of the Adelaide Tribe', *Journal of the Anthropological Society of South Australia* 28 (1 & 2): 64–105.

Gara, Tom 2001, 'Aboriginal-European Frontier Conflict', in, Wilfred Prest (ed.), *The Wakefield Companion to South Australian History*, Adelaide: Wakefield Press.

Gara, Tom 2005, 'Mullawirraburka (1811–1845)', *Australian Dictionary of Biography*, Canberra: Australian National University. http://adb.anu.edu.au/biography/mullawirraburka-13119/text23739, accessed 22 October 2012.

Gara, Tom 2006, 'Adelaide at the time of Hermann Koeler's visit', in, Peter Mühlhausler 2006 (ed.), *Herman Koeler's Adelaide. Observations on the Language and Culture of South Australia by the First German Visitor*, Adelaide: Australian Humanities Press, pp. 7–24.

Gason, Samuel 1874, *The Dieyerie Tribe of Australian Aborigines: Their Manners and Their Customs*, Adelaide: Government Printer.

Gason, Samuel 1879, 'The Manners and Customs of the Dieyerie Tribe of Australian Aborigines', in, James Dominick Woods (ed.) *The Folklore, Manners, Customs, and Languages of the South Australian Aborigines*, Adelaide: E.S. Wigg & Son.

George, Henry 1881, *The Land Question. What it Involves and How Alone It Can Be Settled*, Miami: HardPress Publishing.

Gerber, David A. 1984, 'The Pathos of Exile: Old Lutheran Refugees in the United States and South Australia', *Comparative Studies in Society and History*, 26 (3): 498–522.

Gibbney, H.J. 1969, 'Bonney, Charles (1813–1897)', *Australian Dictionary of Biography*, National Centre of Biography, Australian National University, http://adb.anu.edu.au/biography/bonney-charles-3020/text4425, published in hardcopy 1969, accessed online 28 June 2014.

Gibbs, R.M. 2013, *Under the Burning Sun. A History of Colonial South Australia, 1836–1900*, Adelaide: Southern Heritage.

Gill, J.C.H. 1966, 'Genesis of the Australian Whaling Industry. Its Development Up to 1850', Paper read to the Royal Australian History Society 24 March 1850. Downloaded 26 July 2013 from: http://espace.library.uq.edu.au/eserv/UQ:212779/s00855804_1965_1966_8_1_111.pdf.

Gillen, Robert S. 1995, *F.J. Gillen's First Diary 1875*, Adelaide: Wakefield Press.

Godard, R.H. 1932, 'An Aboriginal Rain-Maker', *Mankind*, 1 (4): 84.

Goldberg, Michael K. 1993, 'Introduction', in, Thomas Carlyle 1993, *On Heroes, Hero-Worship and the Heroic in History*, University of California Press.

Gould, Rosemary 1997, 'The History of an Unnatural Act: infanticide and "Adam Bede"', *Victorian Literature and Culture* 25 (2): 263–277.

Gray, Geoffrey 2015, *Abrogating Responsibility. Vesteys, Anthropology and the Future of Anthropological People*, Melbourne: Australian Scholarly Publishing.

Green, Abigail 2010, *Moses Montefiore: Jewish Liberator, Imperial Hero*, Cambridge, Mass. & London: Belknap Press.

Green, Jenny 2002, *The Tow n Grew Up Dancing*: The Life and Art of Wenten Rubuntja, Alice Springs, NT: Jukurrpa Books.

Griffin, Trevor and Murray McCaskill 1986 (eds), *Atlas of South Australia*, Adelaide: South Australian Government.

Griffiths, Billy and Lynette Russell 2018, 'What We Were Told; Responses to 65,000 years of Aboriginal History', *Aboriginal History* 42: 31–53.

Griffiths, Tom 2003, 'The Language of Conflict', in, Bain Attwood and S.G. Foster (eds) *Frontier Conflict. The Australian Experience*, Canberra: National Museum of Australia.

Griffiths, Tom 1988 (ed.), *The Life and Adventures of Edward Snell. The Illustrated Diary of an Artist, Engineer and Adventurer in the Australian Colonies 1849 to 1859*, Sydney: Angus and Robertson Publishers.

Gunn, Mrs Aneas (Jeanie) 1908, *We of the Never-Never*, London: Angus & Robertson

REFERENCES

Haebich, Anna 2008, 'Marked Bodies: A Corporeal History of Colonial Australia', *borderlands* 7 (2): 1–18.

Hale, Mathew B. 1889, *The Aborigines of Australia, Being an Account of the Institution for their Education at Poonindie, in South Australia*, London: Society for Promoting Christian Knowledge.

Hall, Catherine 1992, *White, Male and Middle Class. Explorations in Feminism and History*, New York: Routledge.

Hall, Catherine 1996 (a), 'Competing Masculinities'; 'Imperial Man: Edward Eyre in Australasia and the West Indies, 1833–66', in, Bill Schwarz (ed.) *The Expansion of England: Race, Ethnicity and Cultural History*, London: Routledge, pp. 130–70.

Hall, Catherine 2009, 'Macaulay's Nation', *Victorian Studies* 51 (3): 505–523.

Hallam, Sylvia 1983, 'A View from the Other Side of the Western Frontier: or 'I Met a Man Who Wasn't There …', *Aboriginal History* 7 (2): 134–156.

Hannaford, Kay Seamark 2005, *Vintage Adelaide. Beautiful Buildings from the Adelaide Square Mile*, (2nd edition), Adelaide: East Street Publications.

Hankel, Valmai 2010, 'Introduction', Edward John Eyre 1845 (2010), *Manners and Customs of the Aborigines and the State of Their Relations with Europeans*, London: T. & W. Boone.

Hankel, Valmai and Colin Harris 2013, 'The pre-European environment of the Adelaide Plains', Unpublished lecture delivered to the Royal Geographical Society, South Australia, 7 May 2013.

Hardman, William 1865, 'Preface by the Editor', for, John McDouall Stuart *The Journals of John McDouall Stuart During the Years 1858, 1859, 1860, 1861 & 1862, when he fixed the centre of the Continent*, 2nd Edition, London: Saunders, Otley, and Co, University of Adelaide: online edition, downloaded from, file:///Users/juliemarcus/Desktop/_s_stuart_john_mcdouall_journals/preface1.html.

Harmstorf, Ian 1979, 'Basedow, Herbert (1881–1933)', *Australian Dictionary of Biography*, National Centre of Biography, Australian National University, http://adb.anu.edu.au/biography/basedow-herbert-5151/text8633, published first in hardcopy 1979, accessed online 20 April 2016.

Haskins, Victoria 1998, 'Skeletons in Our Closet. Family Histories, Personal Narratives and Race Relations History in Australia', *Bulletin of the Olive Pink Society* 10 (2): 15–23.

Hasluck, Paul 1942 [1970], *Black Australians. A Survey of Native Policy in Western Australia, 1829–1897*, Melbourne: Melbourne University Press.

Hassell, Kathleen 1966, *The Relations Between the Settlers and Aborigines in South Australia, 1836–1860*, Adelaide: Libraries Board of South Australia.

Havrelock, Rachel 2007, 'Two Maps of Israel's Land', *Journal of Biblical Literature*, 126 (4): 649–667.

Hemming, Steven 1984 'Conflict Between Aborigines and Europeans Along the Murray River and the Darling to the Great South Bend (1830–1841)', *Journal of the Anthropological Society of South Australia* 22 (1): 3–21.

Hemming, Steve 1985, 'Aborigines at Port Willunga. Reminiscences of Thomas Martin', *Journal of the Anthropological Society of South Australia*, 23 (9): 24–28.

Hemming, Steve 1994, 'In the Tracks of Ngurunderi: the South Australian Museum's Ngurunderi Exhibition and Cultural Tourism', *Australian Aboriginal Studies* 2: 38–46.

Hercus, Luise 1977, 'Tales of Nadu-Dagali (Rib-Bone Billy)', *Aboriginal History* 1 (1): 53–75.

Hercus, Luise A. 1980, 'How We Danced the Mudlunga': Memories of 1901 and 1902', *Aboriginal History* 4 (1): 5–31.

Hercus, Luise and Grace Koch 1996, 'A Native Died Sudden at Lake Allallina', *Aboriginal History* 20: 133–150.

Hetherington, R. 1966, 'Gawler, George (1795–1869)', *Australian Dictionary of Biography*, National Centre of Biography, Australian National University, http://adb.anu.edu.au/biography/gawler-george-2085/text2615, accessed 6 January 2014

Hewitt, Rachel 2010, *Map of a Nation. A Biography of the Ordnance Survey*, London: Granta.

Hilliard, David 2005, 'Unorthodox Christianity in South Australia. Was South Australia Really a Paradise of Dissent?', *History Australia* 2 (2): 1–10.

Hilliard, David 2006, 'Anglicans in South Australian Public Life', *Journal of the Historical Society of South Australia*, 34: 5–16.

Higonnet, Anne 1998, *Pictures of Innocence. The History and Crisis of Ideal Childhood*, London: Thames and Hudson.

Hill, Christopher 1980 [1997], *Some Intellectual Consequences of the English Revolution*, London: Phoenix.

Hill, Christopher 1991, 'The Bible in Seventeenth-Century English Politics', *The Tanner Lectures on Human Values*. From web. File gives no proper reference.

Hill, Rosamond and Florence 1875, *What We Saw in Australia*, London: Macmillan.

Hilliard, David 2005, 'Unorthodox Christianity in South Australia. Was South Australia Really a Paradise of Dissent?', *History Australia* 2 (2): 1-10.

Hinkson, Melinda & Thalia Anthony 2019, 'Three Shots. The death of Kumanjayi Walker – the Northern Territory as a Police State', *Arena*, 3 December 2019. Downloaded from: https://arena.org.au/three-shots-by-melinda-hinkson-and-thalia-anthony/.

Hinkson, Melinda 2014, *Remembering the Future. Warlpiri Life Through the Prism of Drawing*, Canberra: Aboriginal Studies Press.

REFERENCES

Hodder, Edwin 1891, *Angas. Father and Founder of South Australia*, London: Hodder & Stoughton.

Hodder, Edwin 1893, *The History of South Australia. From Its Foundation to the Year of Its Jubilee,* (2 vols), London: Sampson, Low, Marston & Company.

Horsetailer, Peter 1990, in, Grace Koch and Harold Koch 1993, *Kaytetye Country. An Aboriginal History of the Barrow Creek Area*, Alice Springs: Institute for Aboriginal Development, pp. 14–16.

Horton, David (ed.) 1994, *Encyclopaedia of Aboriginal Australia*, Canberra: Aboriginal Studies Press.

Hosking, Rick 2012, 'When Is It Time for "Writing with an Untrammelled Pen"? Reconciling the South Australian Settler Colony with Its Violent Past in Simpson Newland's Historical Novel, *Paving the Way: A Romance of the Australian Bush*', in, Tony Gibbons and Emily Sutherland (eds) 2012, *Integrity and Historical Research*, New York: Routledge, pp. 86–107.

Hosking, Susan 2001, 'David Unaipon', Prest, Wilfrid, *The Wakefield Companion to South Australian History*, Adelaide: Wakefield Press.

Howe, Adrian 2008, *Sex, Violence and Crime. Foucault and the 'Man' Question*, Abingdon: Routledge-Cavendish.

Howitt, A.W. 1891, 'The Dieri and Other Kindred Tribes of Central Australia', *The Journal of the Anthropological Institute of Great Britain and Ireland*, 20: 30–104.

Huggins, Jackie 1998, *Sista Girl. The Writings of Aboriginal Activist and Historian, Jackie Huggins*, Brisbane: University of Queensland Press.

Hull, Tony n.d. 'The Interactions of Whites and Blacks in the Flinders Ranges in the 1840s and 1850s', in, *Cabbages and Kings. Selected Essays in History and Australian Studies*, 12: 12–23.

Humphries, Jane 2010 (b) 'Childhood and Violence in Working-Class England 1800-1870', in, Laurence Brockliss & Heather Montgomery (eds) *Childhood and Violence in the Western Tradition*, Oxford: Oxbow Books, pp. 135–140.

Hunt, John Dixon 1992, *Gardens and the Picturesque. Studies in the History of Landscape Architecture*, Cambridge Massachusetts & London: MIT Press

Hurley, Andrew and Katrina Schlunke 2013, 'Leichhardt After Leichhardt', *Journal of Australian Studies* 37 (4): 537–543.

Hylton, Jane 1994, *Colonial Sisters. Martha Berkeley & Theresa Walker. South Australia's first professional artists*, Adelaide: Art Gallery Board of South Australia.

Hylton, Jane 2012, *South Australia Illustrated. Colonial painting in the Land of Promise*, Adelaide: Art Gallery of South Australia.

Jacobs, Jane M. 1983, 'Aboriginal Land Rights in Port Augusta', unpublished thesis, University of Adelaide, Adelaide. http://digital.library.adelaide.edu.au/dspace/handle/2440/37925.

Jacobs, Jane M. 1986, 'Understanding the Limitations and Cultural Implications of Aboriginal Tribal Boundary Maps', *The Globe* 25: 1–11.

Jacobs, Jane M. 1989, '"Women Talking up Big." Aboriginal Women as Cultural Custodians, a South Australian Example', in, Peggy Brock (ed.) 1989, *Women, Rites and Sites. Aboriginal Women's Cultural Knowledge*, Sydney: Allen & Unwin, pp. 76–99.

Jacobs, Margaret D. 2009, *White Mother to a Dark Race. Settler Colonialism, Maternalism, and the Removal of Indigenous Children in the American West and Australia, 1880-1940*, Lincoln & London: University of Nebraska Press.

Jenkyns, Richard 1980, *The Victorians and Ancient Greece*, Cambridge, Mass: Harvard University Press, p. 1.

Jensz, Felicity 2008, 'Imperial Critics: Moravian Missionaries in the British Colonial World', in, Amanda Barry, Joanna Cruickshank, Andrew Brown-May and Patricia Grimshaw (eds) 2008, *Evangelists of Empire?: Missionaries in Colonial History*, Melbourne: University of Melbourne eScholarship Research Centre, available at: http://msp.esrc.unimelb.edu.au/shs/missions.

Jipp, Suzanne 1990, 'Edward Mead Bagot', David Carment, Robyn Maynard & Alan Powell (eds), *Northern Territory Dictionary of Biography*, vol. 1, Darwin: NTU Press.

Johnston, T. Harvey 1941, 'Some Aboriginal Routes in the Western Portion of South Australia', *Royal Geographical Society of South Australia. Branch Proceedings*, 42: 33–65.

Jones, Helen 1986, *In Her Own Name. A History of Women in South Australia from 1836*, Adelaide: Wakefield Press.

Jones, Philip 1984, 'Red Ochre Expeditions: An Ethnographic and Historical Analysis of Aboriginal Trade in the Lake Eyre Basin', *Journal of the Anthropological Society of South Australia* 22 (7): 1–10.

Jones, Philip 1990, 'Unaipon, David (1872–1967), *Australian Dictionary of Biography*, Canberra: Australian National University.

Jones, Philip 1994, 'Obituary for Norman Barnett ("Tinny") Tindale', *Aboriginal History* 18 (1): 5–8.

Jones, Philip 2005, *The Policeman's Eye. The Frontier Photography of Paul Foelsche*, Adelaide: South Australian Museum.

Jones, Philip 2007, *Ochre and Rust. Artefacts and Encounters on Australian Frontiers*, Adelaide: Wakefield Press.

Judd, Catherine Nealy 2017, 'Charles Kingsley's *The Water-Babies*: Industrial England, The Irish Famine, and the American Civil War', *Victorian Literature and Culture* 45 (1): 179–204.

REFERENCES

Judell, Leopold 1870, 'Diary of His Voyage from Hamburg to Adelaide. May 17th, 1870–August 18th, 1870', D8257(L). Transcript downloaded from State Library of South Australia available online at: http://www.slsa.sa.gov.au/archivaldocs/d/D8257_Judell_diary_GermanEnglish.pdf.

Kaus, Amalie M. & Edward H. Kaus 1988, *Perfecting the World. The Life and Times of Dr Thomas Hodgkin, 1788–1866*, Harcourt Brace Jovanovich Publishers: Boston.

Kaus, David 2008, *A Different Time. The Expedition Photographs of Herbert Basedow 1903–1928*, Canberra: National Museum of Australia.

Kempe, H. 1974, 'Mortlock, William Ranson (1821–1884)', *Australian Dictionary of Biography*, Canberra: Australian National University.

Kerwin, Dale 2010, *Aboriginal Dreaming Paths and Trading Routes. The Colonisation of the Australian Economic Landscape*, Brighton: Sussex Academic Press.

Kimber, Richard G. 1991, *The End of the Bad Old Days: European Settlement in Central Australia, 1871–1894*, Darwin: State Library of the Northern Territory.

Kimber, Richard G. 2003, 'Real True History: the Coniston Massacre', Part 1, *Alice Springs News*, 10 September 2003.

Kimber, Richard G. 2008, 'Willshire, William Henry (1852–1925)', in, David Carment, Christine Edward, Barbara James, Robyn Maynard, Alan Powell and Helen J. Wilson (eds) 2008, *Northern Territory Dictionary of Biography*, Revised Edition,Volume 1, Darwin: Charles Darwin University Press.

Kimber, Richard G. 2012, '(T)jalkalyirri, 'Tiger' (1906–1985)', *Australian Dictionary of Biography*, National Centre of Biography, Australian National University, http://adb.anu.edu.au/biography/tjalkalyirri-tiger-15659/text26855, published first in hardcopy 2012, accessed online 1 February 2015.

Kneebone, Heidi 2000, '"Why Do You Work?" Indigenous Perceptions of Lutheran Mission Work in the Encounter Bay area, 1840–47', Paper presented to the Australian Historical Association Conference, Adelaide University, 6 July 2000.

Kneebone, Heidi 2005, 'Schürmann, Clamor Wilhelm (1815–1893)', *Australian Dictionary of Biography*, National Centre of Biography, Australian National University, http://adb.anu.edu.au/biography/schurmann-clamor-wilhelm-13284/text23925, accessed 22 October 2012.

Koch, Grace and Harold Koch 1993, *Kaytetye Country. An Aboriginal History of the Barrow Creek Area*, Alice Springs: Institute for Aboriginal Development.

Kolig, Erich 1980, 'Noah's Ark Revisited: On the Myth-Land Connection in Traditional Aboriginal Thought', *Oceania* 51 (2): 118–132.

Kolig, Erich 1994, 'Rationality, Ideological Transfer, Cultural Resistance, and the Dreaming. The Development of Political Thought in Australian Aboriginal Society', *Anthropos*, 89: 1/3: 111–124.

Konishi, Shino 2008, '"Wanton With Plenty". Questioning Ethno-historical Constructions of Sexual Savagery in Aboriginal Societies, 1788–1803', *Australian Historical Studies* 39 (3): 356–372.

Krichauff, F.H.H.W. 1890, 'The Customs, Religious Ceremonies, etc., of the "Aldolinga" or "Mbenderinga" Tribe of Aborigines in Krichauff Ranges, South Australia', *Proceedings of the Royal Geographical Society of Australasia, South Australian Branch*, 2: 33–38.

Krichauff, Skye 2011, *Nharangga Wargunni Bugi-Buggillu. A Journey Through Narungga History*, Adelaide: Wakefield Press.

Kruger, Alec & Gerard Waterford 2007, *Alone on the Soaks. The Life and Times of Alec Kruger*, Alice Springs: IAD Press.

Langton, Marcia 1999, *Australian Humanities Review*, Issue 13, http://australianhumanitiesreview.org/category/issue/issue-13-april-1999/.

Larbalestier, Jan 1990, 'Amity and Kindness in the Never-Never: Aboriginal Relations in the Northern Territory', *Social Analysis* 70–82

Lattas, Andrew 1987, 'Savagery and Civilization: Towards a Genealogy of racism', *Social Analysis: The International Journal of Social and Cultural Practice*, 21: 39–58.

Lattas, Andrew 1986, 'The Aesthetics of Terror and the Personification of Power:Public Executions and the Cultural Construction of Class Relations in Colonial New South Wales, 1788-1830', *Social Analysis*, 19: 3–21.

Lattas, Andrew 2006, 'The Utopian Promise of Government', *Journal of the Royal Anthropological Institute* 12 (1): 129–150.

Lattas, Andrew and Barry Morris 2010, 'The Politics of Suffering and the Politics of Anthropology', in, Jon Altman and Melinda Hinkson (eds) 2010, *Culture Crisis. Anthropology and Politics in Aboriginal Australia*, Sydney: UNSW Press,pp. 61–89.

Leigh, W.H. 1839 [1982], *Reconnoitering Voyages and Travels with Adventures in the New Colonies of South Australia; A Particular Description of the Town of Adelaide, and Kangaroo Island; and an Account of the Present State of Sydney and Parts Adjacent During the Years 1836, 1837, 1838*, London: Smith, Elder and Co. (Facsimile edition, Sydney: Currawong Press).

Lendrum, S.D. 1977-78, 'The "Coorong Massacre": Martial Law and the Aborigines at First Settlement', *The Adelaide Law Review* 26–43.

Levinson, James 1993, 'The Trial of Thomas Donelly', *Journal of the Anthropological Society of South Australia*, 30 (2): 54–66.

Lewis, Darell 2007, *The Murranji Track: Ghost Road of the Drovers*, Rockhampton: Central Queensland University Press.

Lewis, Darrell 2012, *A Wild History: Life and Death on the Victoria River Frontier*, Victoria: Monash University Publishing.

Lewis, Daryl 2018, *The Victoria River District Doomsday Book*, Canberra: National Centre for Biography, Australian National University.

Lewis, John 1922 [1985], *Fought and Won*, Adelaide: W.K. Thomas & Co.

Lindenbaum, Shirley 2004, 'Thinking About Cannibalism', *Annual Review of Anthropology*, 33: 475–498.

Linn, Rob 1993, *Frail Flesh & Blood. The Health of South Australians Since Earliest Times*, Adelaide: Queen Elizabeth Hospital Research Foundation Inc.

Litchfield, Lois 1983, *Marree and the Tracks Beyond in Black and White*, Adelaide: Privately Published.

Locke, John 1689, *Two Treatises of Government In the Former, The False Principles, and Foundation of Sir Robert Filmer, and His Followers, Are Detected and Overthrown. The Latter Is an Essay Concerning The True Original, Extent, and End of Civil Government*, Digireads.com Publishing: Stillwell, KS.

Locke-Weir, Tracey 2005, *Visions of Adelaide 1836–1886*, Adelaide: Art Gallery of South Australia.

Lockwood, Christine J. 2007, 'A Vision Frustrated: Lutheran Missionaries to the Aborigines of South Australia 1838–1853', Unpublished Doctoral Thesis, University of Adelaide.

Love, John 2005, 'Hamilton, George (1812–1883)', *Australian Dictionary of Biography*, Australian National University, http://adb.anu.edu.au/biography/hamilton-george-12961/text23427.

Love, John 2005, 'George Hamilton (1812–1883): Midshipman, Overlander, Police Commissioner, Lithographer, Artist, Poet, Author', *Journal of the Historical Society of South Australia* 33: 102–112.

Lydon, Jane 2005, *Eye Contact. Photographing Indigenous Australians*, Durham & London: Duke University Press.

Lydon, Jane and Sari Braithwaite 2014, 'Photographing South Australian Indigenous People: 'far more gentlemanly than many,' in, Lydon, Jane (ed.) 2014, *Calling the Shots. Aboriginal Photographies*, Canberra: Aboriginal Studies Press.

Lydon, Jane (ed.) 2014, *Calling the Shots. Aboriginal Photographies*, Canberra: Aboriginal Studies Press.

Lydon, Jane and Sari Braithwaite 2013, '"Cheque Shirts and Plaid Trowsers": Photographing Poonindie Mission, South Australia', *Journal of the Anthropological Society of South Australia*, 37: 1–30.

Macfarlane, Ingereth A.S. 2010, 'Entangled Places: Interactive Histories in the Western Simpson Desert', Unpublished Doctoral Thesis, Canberra: Australian National University.

Mack, Mary P. 1962, *Jeremy Bentham. An Odyssey of Ideas 1748–1792*, London: Heinemann.

Mackey, Eva 2016, *Unsettled Expectations. Uncertainty, Land and Settler Decolonization*, Halifax & Winnipeg: Fernwood Publishing.

Macgillivray, Leith 1989, 'We have Found Our Paradise: the South-East Squattocracy, 1840–1870', *Journal of the Historical Society of South Australia* 17: 25–38.

MacKinlay, John n.d., *McKinlay's Journal of Exploration in the Interior of Australia. (Burke Relief Expedition*, (facsimile edition) Melbourne: F.F. Bailliere.

Mattingley, Christobel and Ken Hampton (eds) 1988, *Survival in Our Own Land. 'Aboriginal' Experiences in 'South Australia' Since 1836*, Adelaide: Wakefield Press.

McBryde, Isabel 1976, 'The Distribution of Greenstone Axes in Southeastern Australia: A Preliminary Report', *Mankind* 10 (3): 163–174.

McBryde, Isabel 1978, '*Wil-im-ee Moor-ring*: Or, Where do Axes Come From?, in, Jim Specht and J. Peter White (eds) 1978, *Trade and Exchange in Oceania and Australia*, 354–382. Published as *Mankind* 11 (3): 354–382.

McBryde, Isabel 1984, 'Exchange in South-Eastern Australia: An Ethnohistorical Perspective', *Aboriginal History* 8 (2): 147.

McBryde, Isabel 2000, 'Travellers in Storied Landscapes. A Case Study in Exchanges and Heritage, '*Aboriginal History* 24: 152–174.

McCarthy, Frederick D. 1939, '"Trade" in Aboriginal Australia, and "Trade" relationships with Torres Strait, New Guinea and Malaya', *Oceania*, 9 (4): 405–438.

McCarthy, Frederick D. 1939, '"Trade" in Aboriginal Australia, and "Trade" relationships with Torres Strait, New Guinea and Malaya', *Oceania*, 10 (1): 80–104.

McCarthy, Frederick D. 1952, 'A *Werpoo*, or Bone Dagger, from South Australia', *The Australian Museum Magazine* 10 (9): 290–292.

McCauley, Barbara A. 1993, 'Hero Cults and Politics in Fifth Century Greece', Unpublished PhD Thesis, Graduate College of the University of Iowa.

McGrath, Ann 1987, *Born in the Cattle,* Sydney: Allen & Unwin.

McGrew, W.C. 1987, 'Tools to Get Food: the Subsistents of Tasmanian Aborigines and Tanzanian Chimpanzees Compared', *Journal of Anthropological Research* 43 (3): 247–258.

McKinlay, John n.d., *Journal of Exploration in the Interior of Australia. (Burke Relief Expedition*, (facsimile edition) Melbourne: F.F. Bailliere.

Marcus, Julie 1989, 'The Death of the Family. Pierre Rivière, Foucault and Gender', *Criticism, Heresy and Interpretation* 2: 67–82.

REFERENCES

Marcus, Julie (2001) 2017, *The Indomitable Miss Pink. A Life in Anthropology*, Canada Bay, Sydney: Lhr Press.

Marcus, Sharon 2007, *Between Women. Friendship, Desire and Marriage in Victorian England*, Princeton NJ: Princeton University Press.

Marcus, Steven 1970 [1966], *The Other Victorians. A Study of Sexuality and Pornography in Mid-nineteenth-Century England*, London: Corgi Books.

Massing, Jean Michel 2011, *The Image of the Black in Western Art. From the "Age of Discovery" to the Age of Abolition: Europe and the World Beyond*, Cambridge, Mass: Belknap Press of Harvard University.

Mathews, Iola with Chris Durrant 2014, *Chequered Lives. John Barton Hack and the Early Days of South Australia*, Adelaide: Wakefield Press.

Mattingley, Christobel and Ken Hampton (eds) 1988, *Survival in Our Own Land. 'Aboriginal' Experiences in 'South Australia' Since 1836*, Adelaide: Wakefield Press.

Moorhouse, Matthew (1813–1876)', *Australian Dictionary of Biography*, Canberra: Australian National University, http://adb.anu.edu.au/biography/moorhouse-matthew-4239.

Melman, Billie 1993, 'Gender, History and Memory: The Invention of Women's Past in the Nineteenth and Early Twentieth Centuries', *History and Memory* 5 (1): 5–41.

Melman, Billie 1996, 'Under Western Historian's Eyes: Eileen Power and the Early Feminist Encounter with Colonialism', *History Workshop Journal*, 42: 147–168.

Melman, Billie 2011, 'Horror and Pleasure: Visual Histories, Sensationalism and Modernity in Britain in the Long Nineteenth Century', *Geschichte, Emotionen und visuelle Medien. Geschichte und Gesellschaft*, 37. Jahrg., H. 1: 26–46.

Melville, Henry Dudley 1887, Transcript of unpublished manuscript, 'Compensation for a Life's Service Under Civil Service Regulations of South Australia', State Library of South Australia, D6976/1–5.

Merlan, Francesca 1978, '"Making People Quiet" in the Pastoral North: Reminiscences of Elsey Station', *Aboriginal History* 2 (1): 70–106.

Merlan, Francesca 1994, 'Narratives of Survival in the Post-Colonial North', *Oceania* 65: 151–174.

Mincham, Hans 1964, *The Story of the Flinders Ranges*, Adelaide: Rigby.

Mirzoeff, Nicholas 2006, 'On Visuality', *Journal of Visual Culture* 5 (1): 53–79.

Mitchell, Jessie 2005, 'Flesh, Dreams and Spirit: Life on Aboriginal Mission Stations, 1825–1850. A History of Cross-Cultural Connections', Unpublished Doctoral Thesis, Canberra: Australian National University. Web version, downloaded July 2015.

Mitchell, W.J.T. (ed.) 1994/2002, *Landscape and Power*, Chicago: University of Chicago Press.

Monteath, Peter 1961, *The Diary of Emily Caroline Creaghe, Explorer,* Adelaide: Wakefield Press.

Moore, Rick 2005, 'Cones of Stones (or, In the Vernacular of the Day), Explorations around the Mound Springs, Demonstrating Lesser Known Aspects of the Famous Explorer's Journeys, complete with 87 Illustrations,' *South Australian Geographical Journal,* 104: 64–75.

Moorhouse, Matthew, 'Quarterly Report – Aborigines Department', *South Australian Register* 5 May 1849.

Morton, Rick 2018, *100 Years of Dirt,* Melbourne: Melbourne University Press.

Mountford, C.P. and Alison Harvey 1941, 'Women of the Adnjamatana Tribe of the Northern Flinders Ranges, South Australia', *Oceania* 12 (2): 155–162.

Moyal, Ann 1984, *Clear Across Australia. A History of Telecommunications,* Melbourne: Nelson.

Mudd, G.M. 2000, 'Mound Springs of the Great Artesian Basin in South Australia: A Case Study from Olympic Dam', *Environmental Geology* 39 (5): 463–476.

Mulvaney, D.J. 1976, 'The Chain of Connection: the material evidence', in, Nicolas Peterson (ed.) *Tribes and Boundaries in Australia,* Canberra: Australian Institute of Aboriginal Studies.

Mulvaney, D.J. 1989, *Encounters in Place. Outsiders and Aboriginal Australians 1606-1985,* St Lucia: University of Queensland Press.

Mulvaney, D. John n.d., ' "… these Aboriginal lines of travel".' *Historic Environment* 16 (2): 47, downloaded from web: http://www.aicomos.com/wp-content/uploads/these-Aboriginal-lines-of-travel.pdf.

Munz, Hirsch 1936, *Jews in South Australia 1836–1936. An Historical Outline,* Adelaide: Thornquest Press.

Nelson, Claudia 1989, 'Sex and the Single Boy: Ideals of Manliness and Sexuality in Victorian Literature for Boys', *Victorian Studies* 32 (4): 525–550.

Nettelbeck, Amanda 2001 (a), 'South Australian Settler Memoirs', *Journal of Australian Studies,* 25 (68) 97–104.

Nettelbeck, Amanda 2001 (b), ' "Seeking to Spread the Truth": Christina Smith and the South Australian Frontier', *Australian Feminist Studies,* 16 (34): 83–90, DOI: 10.1080/08164640120038935.

Nettelbeck, Amanda and 'Mythologising Frontier: Narrative Versions of the Rufus River Conflict, 1841–1899', downloaded from web: file:///Users/juliemarcus/Desktop/Time%20WEbook%20v1/Rufus%20River/Nettelbeck-Rufus%20R%20massacre.html.

Nettelbeck, Amanda 2004, 'Writing and Remembering Frontier Conflict: The Rule of Law in 1880s Central Australia', *Aboriginal History* 28: 190–206.

Nettelbeck, Amanda 2009, 'South Australian Settler Memoirs', *Journal of Australian Studies,* 25 (68): 97–104.

REFERENCES

Nettelbeck, Amanda & Robert Foster 2007, *In the Name of the Law. William Willshire and the Policing of the Australian Frontier*, Adelaide: Wakefield Press.

Newland, Simpson 1895, 'Some Aborigines I Have Known', part 3, *South Australian Register* 3 January 1895.

Nobbs, Chris 2008, 'Talking into the Wind: Collectors on the Cooper Creek, 1890–1910', in, Nicolas Peterson, Lindy Allen and Louise Hamby (eds), *The Makers and Making of Indigenous Australian Museum Collections*, Melbourne: Melbourne University Press.

Noye, R.J. 1972, 'Foelsche, Paul Heinrich Matthias (1831–1914)', *Australian Dictionary of Biography*, Canberra: Australian National University, http://adb.anu.edu.au/biography/foelsche-paul-heinrich-matthias-3543/text5467, accessed online 25 November 2016.

Obeysekere, G. 1992, '"British Cannibals": Contemplation of an Event in the Death and Resurrection of James Cook, Explorer', *Critical Inquiry* 18 (4): 630–654.

O'Brien, Anne 2008, 'Missionary Masculinities, the Homoerotic Gaze and the Politics of Race: Gilbert White in Northern Australia, 1855–1915', *Gender & History*, 20 (1): 68–85.

O'Brien, Lewis 1990, 'My Education', *Journal of the Anthropological Society of South Australia*, 28 (1 & 2): 106–126.

Parsons, Vivienne 1966, 'Cunningham, Richard (1793–1835)', *Australian Dictionary of Biography*, http://adb.anu.edu.au/biography/cunningham-richard-1943/text2329, accessed online 4 December 2014.

Peacock, Mabel 1896, 'Executed Criminals and Folk-Medicine', *Folklore* 7 (3): 268–283.

Peterson, Nicolas (ed.) 1976, *Tribes and Boundaries in Australia*, Canberra: Australian Institute of Aboriginal Studies.

Pickard, John 2008, 'Shepherding in Colonial Australia', *Rural History* 19 (1): 55–80.

Pike, Douglas 1957, *Paradise of Dissent. South Australia 1829–1857*, London & Melbourne: Longmans, Green and Co.

Pike, Douglas 1965, 'Wakefield, Waste Land and Empire', *Papers and Proceedings* (Tasmanian Historical Research Association), 12 (3): 75–83.

Pike, Douglas 2007, 'The Coming of Responsible Government to South Australia', *Journal of the Historical Society of South Australia*, 35: 93–97.

Pike, Glenville 'The Northern Territory Overland Telegraph. An Epic of Courage – Just 100 Years Ago', downloaded from, https://espace.library.uq.edu.au/view/UQ:207991/s00855804_1970_1971_9_2_95.pdf.

Pocock, Esther 1884, 'Diary of Esther Pocock', State Library of South Australia, 1884, D 7506(L) transcript).

Poignant, Roslyn 2004, *Professional Savages: Captive Lives and Western Spectacle*, Sydney: UNSW Press.

Pope, Alan 2011, *One Law for All? Aboriginal People and Criminal Law in Early South Australia*, Canberra: Aboriginal Studies Press.

Prest, Wilfrid 2001, *The Wakefield Companion to South Australian History*, Adelaide: Wakefield Press.

Price, A. Grenfell 1924, *The Foundation and Settlement of South Australia 1829–1845*, Adelaide: F.W. Preece.

Pryor, Francis, 2010, *The Making of the British Landscape. How We Have Transformed the Land, From Prehistory to Today,* London: Penguin.

Radford, Ron and Jane Hylton, *Australian Colonial Art 1800–1900*, Adelaide: Art Gallery Board of South Australia.

Ramsay, Fleur 2008, 'The Mimetic Life of Captain Cook and Sovereignty in Australia', *Dilemmata. Jahrbuch der ASFPG* 3: 107–168.

Redmond, Anthony 2008, 'Captain Cook Meets General Macarthur in the Northern Kimberley: Humour and Ritual in an Indigenous Australian Life-World', *Anthropological Forum*, 18 (3): 255–270.

Rendell, Alan 1967, 'Wyatt, William (1804–1886)', *Australian Dictionary of Biography,* National Centre of Biography, Australian National University, http://adb.anu.edu.au/biography/wyatt-william-2821/text4043, accessed 8 November 2013.

Reid, Gordon 1990a, *A Picnic with the Natives. Aboriginal-European Relations in the Northern Territory to 1910*, Melbourne: Melbourne University Press.

Reid, Gordon 1990b, 'Foelsche, Paul Heinrich Matthias (1831–1914)', in, David Carment, Robyn Maynard, and Alan Powell (eds) 1990, *Northern Territory Dictionary of Biography, Volume 1: To 1945*, Darwin: Northern Territory University Press.

Rigney, Lester-Irabinna 2002, 'Preface', in, Anne Chittelborough, Gillian Dooley, Brenda Glover & Rick Hosking (eds), *Alas, for the Pelicans. Flinders Baudin and Beyond*, Adelaide: Wakefield Press.

Roberts, Tony 2005, *Frontier Justice. A History of the Gulf Country to 1900*, Brisbane: UQP.

Roberts, Tony 2009, 'The Brutal Truth. What Happened in the Gulf Country', *The Monthly*, November.

Rose, Deborah Bird 1991, *Hidden Histories. Black Stories from Victoria River Downs, Humbert River and Wave Hill Stations*, Canberra: Aboriginal Studies Press.

Rose, Deborah Bird 1996, *Australian Aboriginal Views of Landscape and Wilderness*, Canberra: Australian Heritage Commission.

Rose, Deborah Bird 1998, 'Signs of Life on a Barbarous Frontier', *Humanities Research* 2: 17–35, p. 26. Downloaded from web: http://press.anu.edu.au/wp-content/uploads/2011/02/6_rose_hr2_1998.pdf.

REFERENCES

Rose, Deborah Bird 2001, 'Aboriginal Life and Death in Australian Settler Nationhood', *Aboriginal History* 25: 148–162.

Rose, Deborah Bird 2001, 'The saga of Captain Cook. Remembrance and Morality', in, Bain Attwood and Fiona Magowan, *Telling Stories: Indigenous history and memory in Australia and New Zealand*, Sydney: Allen & Unwin.

Rose, Deborah Bird 2007, 'Danayarri, Hobbles (1925–1988)', *Australian Dictionary of Biography*, Canberra: Australian National University; downloaded from: http://adb.anu.edu.au/biography/danayarri-hobbles-12397/text22285, accessed online 16 February 2017.

Rose, Deborah Bird 2008, 'Dreaming Ecology: Beyond the Between', *Religion and Literature*, 40 (1): 109–122

Rose, Deborah Bird 2017, 'Reflections on the Zone of the Incomplete', in, Joanna Radin and Emma Kowal 2017, *Cryopolitics: Frozen Life in a Melting World* 2017, Cambridge, Michigan, MIT Press.

Rose, E. Alan 1990, 'The Methodist New Connexion 1797-1907. Portrait of a Church', *Proceedings of the Wesley Historical Society*, xlvii: 241–253.

Rose, Natalie 2005, 'Flogging and Fascination: Dickens and the Fragile Will', *Victorian Studies* 47 (4): 505–533.

Rowley, Charles D. 1970, *The Destruction of Aboriginal Society. Volume 1. Aboriginal Policy and Practice*, Canberra: Australian National University Press.

Rowse, Tim 1998, *White Flour, White Power. From Rations to Citizenship in Central Australia*, Cambridge: Cambridge University Press.

Royal Commission into Institutional Responses to Child Sexual Abuse 2017, Canberra: Government of Australia.

Roysland, Dorothy 1977, *A Pioneer Family on the Murray River*, Adelaide: Rigby.

Rubuntja, Wenten with Jenny Green 2002, *The Town Grew up Dancing. The Life and Art of Wenten Rubuntja*, Alice Springs: Jukurrpa Books.

Ruediger, Gerhard 2011, 'The Dresden Missionaries in South Australia 1838–1846. Tracking Their Trails in Archives and Museums in Germany', *Journal of the Friends of the Lutheran Archives* 21: 25–40.

Ryan, Maurie 2016, 'I was Taken', in, *Yijarni. True Stories from Gurindji Country*, Edited by Erika Charola & Felicity Meakins, Canberra: Aboriginal Studies Press, pp. 129–132.

Saunders, Suzanne 2008, 'Solomon, Vaiben Louis (1853–1908)', *Northern Territory Dictionary of Biography* (Revised Edition), Downloaded and abridged from: https://dtc.nt.gov.au/__data/assets/pdf_file/0008/248732/History-of-Newspapers-NT.pdf.

Seamark, Kay Hannaford 2005, *Vintage Adelaide. Beautiful Buildings from the Adelaide Square Mile*, Adelaide: East Street Publications.

Shaffer, Kay 2001, 'Handkerchief Diplomacy: E.J. Eyre and Sexual Politics on the South Australian Frontier', in, Lynette Russell, (ed.), *Colonial Frontiers: Indigenous-European Encounters in Settler Societies*, Manchester: Manchester University Press, pp. 134–150.

Schlunke, Katrina 2006, 'Historicising Whiteness: Captain Cook Possesses Australia', Paper Presented at the 'Historicising Whiteness Conference, University of Melbourne 22–24 November 2006. Web version.

Schlunke, Katrina 2008, 'Captain Cook Chased a Chook', *Cultural Studies Review* 14 (1): 43–54.

Schürmann, Clamor A. 1879 [1997], 'The Aboriginal Tribes of Port Lincoln in South Australia. Their Mode of Life, Manners, Customs, Etc', in, James Dominick Woods (ed.) *The Folklore, Manners, Customs, and Languages of the South Australian Aborigines*, Adelaide: E.S. Wigg & Son.

Schürmann, Edwin A. 1987, *I'd Rather Dig Potatoes. Clamor Schurmann and the Aborigines of South Australia 1838–1853*, Adelaide: Lutheran Publishing House.

Scrimgeour, Anne 2007, 'Colonizers as Civilizers: Aboriginal Schools and the Mission to "civilize" in South Australia, 1839-18445', Unpublished Doctoral Thesis, Darwin University.

Scrimgeour, Anne 2006, 'Notions of Civilization and the Project to "Civilise" Aborigines in South Australia in the 1840s', *History of Education Review* 35 (1): 35–46.

Shaffer, Kay 2001, 'Handkerchief Diplomacy: E.J. Eyre and Sexual Politics on the South Australian Frontier', in *Colonial Frontiers: Indigenous–European Encounters in Settler Societies*, (ed.) Lynette Russell, Manchester: Manchester University Press

Short, Augustus 1853, *The Poomindie Mission, A Letter from the Lord Bishop of Adelaide to the Society for the Propagation of the Gospel*, London: Society for the Propagation of the Gospel.

Simpson, Jane 1998, 'Introduction', in, Jane Simpson and Luise Hercus (eds) *History in Portraits. Biographies of Nineteenth-Century South Australian People*, Sydney: Southwood Press.

Simpson, Jane and Luise Hercus (eds) 1998, *History in Portraits. Biographies of Nineteenth-Century South Australian People*, Sydney: Southwood Press.

Slater, Eamonn 2007, 'Reconstructing "Nature" as a Picturesque Theme Park', *Early Popular Visual Culture*, 5 (3): 231–245.

Smith, Mrs James (Christina) (1880 [1965]) *The Booandik Tribe of South Australian Aborigines: A Sketch of their Habits, Customs, Legends, and Language*, Adelaide: Government Printer.

Smith, Mike, Isabel McBryde & June Ross 2010, 'The economics of grindstone production at Narcoonowie quarry, Strzlecki Desert', *Australian Aboriginal Studies* (1): 92–99.

REFERENCES

Snell, Edward 1988, *The Life and Adventures of Edward Snell. The Illustrated Diary of an Artist, Engineer and Adventurer in the Australian Colonies 1849–1859*, ed. Tom Griffiths, Sydney: Angus & Robertson Publishers.

Sontag, Susan 1975, 'Fascinating Fascism', *New York Review of Books*, 6 February 1975: 1–14.

Steiner, Marie 2003, 'Matthew Moorhouse: A Controversial Colonist', *Journal of the Historical Society of South Australia*, 31: 55–68.

Stevens, Christine 1994, *White Man's Dreaming. Killalpaninna Mission 1866–1915*, Melbourne: Oxford University Press.

Stevenson, Charles 1987, *The Millionth Snowflake. The History of Quakers in South Australia*, Adelaide: Religious Society of Friends.

Stoler, Ann Laura 2002, *Carnal Knowledge and Imperial Power. Race and the Intimate in Colonial Rule*, Berkeley & London: University of California Press.

Strehlow, John 2011, *The Tale of Frieda Keysser. Frieda Keysser and Carl Strehlow: an Historical Biography*, volume 1, 1875–1910, London: Wild Cat Press.

Strehlow, T.G.H. 1971, *Songs of Central Australia*, Sydney: Angus and Robertson.

Strang, Veronica 2000, 'Showing and Telling: Australian Land Rights and Material Moralities', *Journal of Material Culture* 5: 275–299.

Stuart, John McDouall 1861, *Journal of Australian Exploration*, Journal of the Royal Geographical Society, London, volume 31: 100–145. Downloaded from 130.220.8.238 on Tue, 17 Nov 2015 05:03:14 UTC.

Stuart, John McDouall 1863, 'Diary of Mr. John M'Douall Stuart's (Gold Medallist R.G.S.) Explorations from Adelaide across the Continent of Australia, 1861–2', *Journal of the Royal Geographical Society of London*, 33: 276–321.

Stuart, John McDouall 1865, *The Journals of John McDouall Stuart During the Years 1858, 1859, 1860, 1861 & 1862, when he fixed the centre of the Continent*, 2nd Edition, Edited by Wm Hardman, London: Saunders, Otley, and Co. University of Adelaide: online edition, downloaded from, file:///Users/juliemarcus/Desktop/_s_stuart_john_mcdouall_journals/preface1.html.

Sturt, Charles 1849, *Narrative of an Expedition into Central Australia, Performed Under the Authority of Her Majesty's Government, During the Years, 1844, 5 and 6*, London: Boone.

Sugg, Richard 2013, 'Medicinal Cannibalism in Early Modern Literature and Culture', *Literature Compass* 10/11: 825–835.

Swain, Tony and Deborah Bird Rose 1988, (eds) *Aboriginal Australians and Christian Missions. Ethnographic and Historical Studies*, Adelaide: Australian Association for the Study of Religions.

Symes, G.W. 1976, 'Todd, Sir Charles (1826–1910)', *Australian Dictionary of Biography*, Canberra: Australian National University. Downloaded from: http://adb.anu.edu.au/biography/todd-sir-charles-4727/text7843, accessed online 24 November 2016.

Taplin, G. 1879 [1967] *The Folklore, Manners, Customs, and Languages of the South Australian Aborigines*, Adelaide: Government Printer.

Taplin, George 1879, 'The Narrinyeri', in, James Dominick Woods (ed.), *The Native Tribes of South Australia*, Adelaide: E.S. Wigg & Son.

Taussig, Michael 1984, 'Culture of Terror – Space of Death. Roger Casement's Putumayo Report and the Explanation of Torture', *Comparative Studies in Society and History* 26 (3): 467–497.

Teichelmann, Christian Gottlieb 1841, *Aborigines of South Australia. Illustrative and Explanatory Notes of the Manners, Customs, Habits, and Superstitions of the Natives of South Australia*, Adelaide: Committee of the South Australian Wesleyan Methodist Auxiliary Society.

Teichelmann, C.G. and C.W. Schürmann, 1840 [1962] *Outline of a Grammar, Vocabulary and Phraseology of the Aboriginal Language of South Australia*, Adelaide: Robert Thomas & Co.

Telfer, Karl Winda and Gavin Malone 2012, *Kaurna Meyunna Cultural Mapping. A People's Living Cultural Landscape*', Adelaide: City of Charles Sturt.

Thomas, Evan Kyffin 1925, Editor, *The Diary and Letters of Mary Thomas (1836–1866)*, Adelaide: W.K. Thomas & Co. [Facsimile edition, 1983].

Thomas, Keith 1983, *Man and the Natural World; Changing Attitudes in England, 1500–1800*, London: Allen Lane.

Thompson, Tomy Kngwarreye 1993, 'Cutting Limestone', in, Grace Koch and Harold Koch 1993, *Kaytetye Country. An Aboriginal History of the Barrow Creek Area*, Alice Springs: Institute for Aboriginal Development, pp. 51–53.

Thorpe, W.W. 1931, 'Aboriginal Methods of Assassination', *Mankind* 1 (1): 20–21.

Tonkinson, Myra 1988, 'Sisterhood or Aboriginal Servitude? Black Women and White Women on the Australian Frontier', *Aboriginal History* 12 (1): 27–39.

Traynor, Stuart 2016, *Alice Springs. From Singing Wire to Iconic Outback Town*, Adelaide: Wakefield Press.

Tregenza, John 1980, *George French Angas. Artist, Traveller and Naturalist 1822–1886*, Adelaide: Art Gallery Board of South Australia.

Tunbridge, Dorothy 1988, *Flinders Ranges Dreaming*, Canberra: Aboriginal Studies Press.

Udo, Will and Catherine Ellis 1996, 'A Re-Analyzed Australian Western Desert Song: Frequency and Interval Structure', *Ethnomusicology* 40(2): 188–222.

REFERENCES

Vaazon-Morel, Petronella 2012, 'Camels and the Transformation of Indigenous Economic Landscapes', in, Natasha Fijn et al., (eds), *Indigenous Participation in Australian Economies II: Historical Engagements and Current Enterprises,* Canberra: ANU Press, pp. 73–96.

Vallee, Peter 2008, *Gods, Guns and Government on the Central Australian Frontier,* Canberra: Restoration Books.

Van Reyk, William 2009, 'Christian Ideals of Manliness in the Eighteenth and Early Nineteenth Centuries', *Historical Journal* 52 (4): 1053–1073.

Waller, John O. 1969, 'Doctor Arnold's Sermons and Matthew Arnold's "Rugby Chapel", *Studies in English Literature, 1500-1900,* 9 (4): 633–646.

Walshe, Keryn 2008, 'Pointing Bones and Bone Points in the Australian Aboriginal Collection of the South Australian Museum', *Journal of the Anthropological Society of South Australia,* 33: 167–203.

Ward, Damen 2006, 'Constructing British Authority in Australasia: Charles Cooper and the Legal Status of Aborigines in the South Australian Supreme Court, c. 1840–60', *Journal of Imperial and Commonwealth History,* 34 (4): 483–504.

Waterhouse, Jill 1984, 'Introduction', in, Eyre, Edward John 1984, *Autobiographical Narrative of Residence and Exploration in Australia 1832–1839,* edited by Jill Waterhouse, London: Caliban Books.

Waterhouse, Richard 2004, 'The Yeoman Ideal and Australian Experience 1860–1960', in, Kate Darian-Smith, Patricia Grimshaw, Kiera Lindsey, & Stuart Mcintyre (eds) 2004, *Exploring the British World: Identity, Cultural Production, Institutions,* (online) Melbourne: RMIT Publishing.

Watson, Christine 2003, *Piercing the Ground. Balgo Women's Image Making and Relationship to Country,* Fremantle: Fremantle Arts Press.

Watson, Irene 2002, 'Kaldowinyeri – In the Beginning. Wepulprap, the people of the South East', downloaded 10 January 2015 at: http://p8080130.220.236.155.ezlibproxy1.unisa.edu.au/fedora/get/changeme:1133948/CONTENT.

Webster, Mona Stuart 1958, *John McDouall Stuart,* Melbourne: Melbourne University Press.

Wheeler, David 2010, 'The Personal and Political Economy of Alexander Pope's "Windsor-Forest"', *South Atlantic Review* 75 (4): 1–20.

Wells, Samantha 1995, *Town Camp or Homeland? A History of the Kulaluk Aboriginal Community,* Report to the Australian Heritage Commission, Canberra. Downloaded from: http://www.drbilldayanthropologist.com/resources/Wells%2095%20Intro.pdf.

Wheeler, David 2010, 'The Personal and Political Economy of Alexander Pope's "Windsor-Forest"', *South Atlantic Review* 75 (4): 1–20.

White, Isobel 1972, 'Hunting dogs at Yalata', *Mankind* 8: 201–205.

White, Isobel 1980, 'The Birth and Death of a Ceremony', *Aboriginal History* 4 (1): 33–41.

White, Isobel (ed.) 1985, *Daisy Bates. The Native Tribes of Western Australia*, Canberra: National Library of South Australia.

White, Isobel 1990, 'The Lives of Aboriginal Girls and Women According to Daisy Bates', *Olive Pink Society Bulletin*, 2 (2): 26–28.

White, Myrtle Rose 1962 (1932), *No Roads Go By*, Adelaide: Rigby.

Whitehead, Neil L. 2007, 'Violence and the Cultural Order', *Dædalus*, Winter, 40–50.

Whitelock, Derek 1977, *Adelaide 1836–1976. A History of Difference*, St Lucia: Queensland University Press.

Whitmarsh, Tyler 2013, 'Wellington Courthouse. A History on the River Murray,' Report prepared for Flinders University Archaeology Department & the National Trust, available on: http://www.flinders.edu.au/ehl/fms/archaeology_files/dig_library/directed_studies/Tyler%20Whitmarsh%20-%20Wellington%20Courthouse.pdf; accessed 29 January 2019.

Wild, Rex & Patricia Anderson 2007, *Ampe Akelyernemane Meke Mekarle. Little Children are Sacred: Report of the Northern Territory Board of Inquiry into the Protection of Aboriginal Children from Child Sexual Abuse*, Darwin: NT Government.

Will, Udo & Catherine Ellis 1996, 'A Re-Analyzed Australian Western Desert Song: Frequency and Interval Structure', *Ethnomusicology* 40 (2): 188–222.

Williams, Gwenneth 1919, *South Australian Exploration to 1856*, Adelaide: G. Hassell & Son.

Willington, Joan Kyffin (ed.) 1992, *Maisie: Her Life, Her Loves, Her Letters, 1898 to 1902*, Adelaide: Wakefield Press.

Willshire, W.H. 1888, *The Aborigines of Central Australia with a Vocabulary of the Dialect of the Alice Springs Natives*, Pt Augusta: Drysdale.

Willshire, W.H. 1896, *The Land of the Dawning. Being Facts Gleaned from Cannibals in the Australian Stone Age*, Adelaide: W.K. Thomas & Co.

Wilson, W.R. 2000, 'A History of the Northern Territory Police Force 1870–1926', Unpublished PhD Thesis, Darwin: Northern Territory University.

Wolff, Larry 1996, '"The Boys Are Pickpockets, and the Girl Is a Prostitute": Gender and Juvenile Criminality in Early Victorian England from "Oliver Twist to London Labour"', *New Literary History* 27 (2): 227–249.

Woenne, Susan Tod 1980 '"The True State of Affairs": Commissions of Inquiry Concerning Western Australian Aborigines', in, Ronald M. Berndt and Catherine H. Berndt (eds) 1980, *Aborigines of the West. Their Past and Their Present*, Perth: Western Australia, p. 324–356.

Wollstonecraft, Mary 1792, *A Vindication of the Rights of Woman, With Strictures on Political and Moral Subjects*, Boston.

REFERENCES

Wood, Marcus 2002, *Slavery, Empathy and Pornography*, Oxford: Oxford University Press.

Woods, James Dominick (ed.) 1879 [1997], *The Native Tribes of South Australia*, Adelaide: E.S. Wigg & Son.

Woods, James Dominick 1879 [1997], 'Introduction', in, *The Native Tribes of South Australia*, Adelaide: E.S. Wigg and Son.

Wright, R.V.S. 1979, 'Bates, Daisy May (1863–1951)', *Australian Dictionary of Biography*, National Centre of Biography, Australian National University, http://adb.anu.edu.au/biography/bates-daisy-may-83/text8643, accessed online 13 August 2015.

Young, Diana 2011, 'Mutable Things: Colours as Material Practice in the Northwest of South Australia', *Journal of the Royal Anthropological Institute* (N.S.) 17: 356–376.

Zogbaum, Heidi 2010, *Changing Skin Colour in Australia. Herbert Basedow and the Black Caucasian*, Melbourne: Australian Scholarly Publishing.

Wakefield Press is an independent publishing and
distribution company based in Adelaide, South Australia.
We love good stories and publish beautiful books.
To see our full range of books, please visit our website at
www.wakefieldpress.com.au
where all titles are available for purchase.
To keep up with our latest releases, news and events,
subscribe to our monthly newsletter.

Find us!

Facebook: www.facebook.com/wakefield.press
Instagram: www.instagram.com/wakefieldpress

www.ingramcontent.com/pod-product-compliance
Lightning Source LLC
Chambersburg PA
CBHW031949290426
44108CB00011B/730